INVERSION OF THE SUBJECT IN FRENCH NARRATIVE PROSE FROM 1500 TO THE PRESENT DAY

PUBLICATIONS OF THE PHILOLOGICAL SOCIETY
XXIV

Inversion of the Subject
in
French Narrative Prose
from 1500
to the Present Day

by

Paula M. Clifford

Lecturer in French Language
in the University of Reading

PUBLISHED FOR THE SOCIETY BY
BASIL BLACKWELL, OXFORD
1973

© THE PHILOLOGICAL SOCIETY, 1972

ISBN 0 631 14940 6

Library of Congress Catalog Card Number: 72-94201

To my parents

PRINTED IN ENGLAND BY
STEPHEN AUSTIN AND SONS, LTD., HERTFORD

PREFACE

This book is a slightly revised version of a thesis approved for the degree of D.Phil. by the University of Oxford in 1971. Its aim is the investigation of two key aspects of inversion of the subject in modern French, syntactic and stylistic. The former concerns the changing frequency of inversion since 1500, along with the different grammatical structures in which it is found, and the latter indicates the variety of literary effects to which the device contributes. While the material for this study is drawn from the French novel, the forty-four works chosen ranging from Rabelais to Nathalie Sarraute, it is hoped that it will be of interest to the general linguist as well as to the French specialist. The book is intended as an exploration of stylistic method in that it attempts to proceed from a formal syntactic analysis of the examples in each text to their interpretation in terms of stylistic value and effect.

I am greatly indebted to the Philological Society for undertaking publication and to the Hon. Secretary for Publications, Mr. C. J. E. Ball, for his kind assistance. Then I should especially like to thank Professor S. Ullmann for his invaluable help and encouragement as supervisor of the original thesis and my examiners, Dr. P. Rickard and Dr. R. Sayce, for their many useful comments. I am also grateful to Dr. A. J. Krailsheimer for his suggestions regarding the selection of 16th-century texts for analysis, and to Mr. G. O. Rees for regularly providing me with information on newly published material in the field of French language and style.

PAULA M. CLIFFORD

Reading, 1972

CONTENTS

Chapter I

INTRODUCTION

1. PREVIOUS STUDIES OF INVERSION IN FRENCH

ALTHOUGH inversion of the subject is a feature of French syntax which grammarians have recorded in varying degrees of detail since the 16th century, it is only comparatively recently that the stylistic potential of this aspect of word-order has been generally acknowledged. In spite of the widespread exploitation of the device by writers of the 19th and 20th centuries, and also on a more modest scale in earlier periods, the study of inversion has been largely restricted to the fields of historical or descriptive syntax, and its value as a source of expressiveness has as yet received relatively little consideration. With the exception of the work by Le Bidois mostly, but not exclusively, on Proust, and that by Ullmann on the 19th- and 20th-century French novel, which will be discussed below, there seems to have been few attempts to treat the uses of inversion outside the context of the style of a single author. Similarly little effort has been made to relate the history of inversion since the Renaissance to the development of its stylistic functions in French.

Studies of inversion to date thus fall readily into two categories, depending on whether the primary consideration is one of syntax or of style. Those concerned with syntax alone, which constitute the vast majority, may be subdivided into (i) historical works on the evolution of word-order, (ii) synchronic studies of modern French, (iii) specific types of inversion, and (iv) the word-order of a particular writer considered from a predominantly syntactic point of view.

(a) SYNTACTIC STUDIES OF INVERSION

(i) *Diachronic*

The evolution of French from the synthetic language of early Romance with a more or less free word-order, to the modern analytic idiom with a comparatively fixed structure, has received close attention from many scholars, among them Muller, concerning the early stages,[1] and Foulet on the medieval situation,[2] and such works form an essential background to the present subject. As regards the history of word-order in general, and of inversion in particular, one of the fullest discussions is that presented by Lerch in the third volume of his syntax.[3] Here word-order is treated according to three main influences, psychological, rhythmic and logico-grammatical, the last factor being that which is said to predominate in the case of inversion. The subsequent discussion of inverted order is, however, marked by the generalization commonly found on this subject, where imperatives and interrogatives are grouped with optatives, absolute inversion and inverted order after an object, attribute, adverbial, co-ordinating conjunction or subordinate clause (pp. 379 ff.). Inversion after certain modal adverbs is treated under the heading of interrogatives, since in both cases there is the possibility of compound constructions (' wiederholende Inversion ' p. 400), the similarity here being purely formal. Lerch does note, however, the change in status of inversion after the Old French period when it was obligatory after most preposed elements, and, more important perhaps for this study, the stylistic separation of logically related items since the end of the 19th century. He is also among the first to comment on the ' mania ' on the part of certain authors for the separation of elements in the sentence, referring in this case to Proust's tendency to delay the object (p. 365). It will be seen in chapter X how this device is paralleled by inversion of the subject in the same writer.

Perhaps the only attempt to relate studies of the word-order of individual authors in a wider historical context is that by

---

[1] H. F. Muller, ' The beginnings of French fixed word-order ', *Modern Language Notes*, lvii (1942), pp. 546–52.

[2] L. Foulet, *Petite syntaxe de l'ancien français*, 3rd ed. Paris, 1965, pp. 306–32.

[3] E. Lerch, *Historische Französische Syntax III*, Leipzig, 1934, pp. 249 ff.

Wespy in 1884.[4] His thesis assembles the results obtained by scholars such as Morf on the *Chanson de Roland*, Le Coultre on Chrétien de Troyes, Schlickum on *Aucassin et Nicolette*, and Marx on Joinville, concerning the occurrence of inversion over five centuries beginning with the Strasbourg oaths, and supplements them with examples from La Fontaine. Assuming that the criteria for identifying inversions in the works quoted by Wespy are consistent, which is questionable, one general conclusion which emerges is the gradual decline of the proportion of main clauses with inverted order in the course of the Middle Ages. Similar results are presented by Lewinsky in 1949, incorporating more recent studies of this nature.[5] Although the 15th and 16th centuries are not represented in Wespy's sources he concludes that the subsequent comparison with La Fontaine is of value, ' weil sein Stil ein viel altertümlicheres Gepräge trägt, als man von einem Schriftsteller seiner Zeit erwarten sollte ' (p. 150), and he follows this by a quotation from La Fontaine regretting the loss of the more graceful and flexible French of the pre-Classical period.[6] Thus it seems that Wespy's work represents an interesting advance on the studies of his contemporaries, who will be seen to be wholly occupied by a specific author, and had little concern for relating their results to each other or for co-ordinating their methods. The importance of inversion from the point of view of historical stylistics is also hinted at in Wespy, but this is not developed.

Finally, a valuable contribution to the history of inversion is to be found in the third section of Antoine's book on co-ordination.[7] Here the author is concerned with the use of inversion in various periods, rather than with its frequency,

[4] L. Wespy, ' Die historische Entwicklung der Inversion des Subjekts im Französischen und der Gebrauch derselben bei Lafontaine ', *Zeitschrift für neufranzösische Sprache und Literatur*, vi (1884), pp. 150–209.

[5] B. Lewinsky, *L'ordre des mots dans ' Bérinus '*, Göteborg, 1949.

[6] Inversion in La Fontaine is also discussed briefly from the point of view of stylistic effect by J. D. Biard, *The Style of La Fontaine's Fables*, Oxford, 1966.

[7] G. Antoine, *La coordination en français*, Paris, 1958.

and notes its restriction since the 17th century to structures such as those where an introductory adverb constitutes a thematic link with the previous clause, as opposed to more extensive functions in the 14th, 15th and 16th centuries. A notable conclusion is that adverbs and conjunctions do not automatically entail inversion, which depends instead on their function and value in relation to the sentences they are linking.

(ii) *Synchronic*

Although a number of contemporary grammarians have treated the problem of word-order in some depth, the major work on the topic is undoubtedly the study by Blinkenberg,[8] of which a large part is devoted to fairly comprehensive consideration of the place of the subject. *L'ordre des mots en français moderne*, which first appeared in 1928, is valuable both for the richness and variety of documentation, examples of direct and inverted order being drawn from many literary, journalistic and technical sources, and for the frequent acknowledgement of stylistic variants involving both orders. Besides discussing different forms of the group subject-verb, the author relates constructions with an impersonal introductory pronoun such as *il y a*, *il existe*, considered to be a form of inversion,[9] to structures with verbs such as *rester*, *arriver*, *venir* and *sortir* in initial position, all of which are taken to be examples without a pronominal subject. No distinction is drawn here between the constructions with *rester* (to be classified below as deletion operations), where *X resta* and *resta X* are not semantically equivalent, and those with verbs of motion (to be classified as having a zero *invertissant*) where the two orders *X arriva* and *arriva X* are virtually synonymous.

In listing inversions according to their occurrence in main or subordinate clauses, Blinkenberg includes *incise* constructions,

---

[8] A. Blinkenberg, *L'ordre des mots en français moderne I*, 2nd ed. Copenhagen, 1958, pp. 76–152.

[9] For a more accurate estimate of the predicative value of impersonal pronouns see S. Rosenberg, *Modern French ' ce ' :—the neuter pronoun in adjectival predication*, The Hague–Paris, 1970.

where there is generally no alternative order, among inversions after, for instance, an adverbial phrase, where either form is possible, a tendency which may also be noted in Lerch, and to be seen again in subsequent studies. This is followed by a list of ' grammatical ' or obligatory inversions, constituted by a number of adverbs such as *ainsi, peut-être*, together with interrogative and exclamatory constructions. A useful point is that inversion after an adverbial is only obligatory where the verb is of low semantic value (p. 103), and the note that in the case of relatives the meaning of the verb is frequently implied in the antecedent (p. 117). Thus ' le journal que lit M. Chantal ' and ' le journal de M. Chantal ' are presumably equivalent structures, although Blinkenberg does not state this explicitly. Blinkenberg's work with respect to inversion thus constitutes one of the broadest and most objective studies to date, despite some confusion in the arrangement according to main and subordinate clauses, and in the distinction between optional and obligatory inversion.

(iii) *Specific types of inversion*

Along with general works on word-order and inversion are to be found a number of articles dealing with one particular aspect of it, for, as Rickard has noted, ' in a general study of the word-order of one text, whether prose or verse, there is little room for a detailed discussion on only one type . . .' [10] Much has been written, for instance, on the evolution of interrogative constructions in French, in particular by Foulet, who has traced the origins of various alternatives to simple inversion, including the popular forms with the particle *ti* [11] and the structure ' où que tu vas ? ' [12] His study of the locution *est-ce que* has been supplemented by Fromaigeat, who has examined its occurrence in contemporary writers, only to

---

[10] P. Rickard, ' The Word-Order Object-Verb-Subject ', *Transactions of the Philological Society*, 1962, pp. 1–39.

[11] L. Foulet, ' Comment ont évolué les formes de l'interrogation en français moderne ', *Romania*, xlvii (1921), pp. 243–348.

[12] ' Études de syntaxe française ', *Romania*, xlv (1919), pp. 220–49.

find that in interrogatives using a question word other than *que*, 92% of the examples have inversion rather than this formula.[13]

Another type of inversion which has attracted attention and is of greater interest for present purposes, is the order direct object-verb-subject (OVS). This structure, which is to be found only in the 16th- and early 17th-century novels analysed in this book, has been studied in detail by Rickard with reference to the medieval period [14] and by Nöjgaard as concerns modern French.[15] Rickard's examples from Old French show that an OVS order may have a liaison function in the progression from a known effect to an unknown cause, or alternatively from a familiar object to an unfamiliar subject. The exploitation of inversion as a linking device will also be noted below, the examples involving either a direct object or other preposed items. Further details uncovered by Rickard regarding the co-ordinating and logical functions of this order might also be applicable in general terms to other types of inversion, for instance its use in the repetition of an element from a previous context, or in exclamation. The study also shows that the frequency of OVS is statistically higher in verse than in prose, although in both forms the structure is in opposition to the movement of the language towards direct order at this time.

As regards modern French, however, the conclusion reached by Nöjgaard is that the presence of a preposed direct object prevents inversion at least in a subordinate clause, his examples of OVS in a main clause being confined to interrogatives, or cases of absolute inversion containing an object pronoun. He does note, however, that the order VOS is still to be found with fixed expressions such as *avoir lieu*. It will be seen below that this order is seldom found, even in the 16th century, although

---

[13] E. Fromaigeat, ' Les formes de l'interrogation en français moderne ', *Vox Romanica* iii (1938), pp. 1–47.

[14] *Op. cit.*

[15] M. Nöjgaard, ' L'objet direct et l'ordre des mots en français moderne ', *Le Français Moderne*, xxxvi (1968), pp. 1–18 and 81–89.

occasional examples do occur in experimental writers of the 20th. It may be noted in passing that the stylistic value of the position of the direct object either before or after a subject-verb structure, has been discussed by Le Bidois in an article in *Le Monde* in 1968, where he is able to conclude :

'l'habile ordonnance des mots, tout en respectant les lois du rhythme, peut apporter de la lumière et de la beauté à l'expression linguistique '.[16]

Studies of other types of inversion are fewer in number, although reference should be made firstly to an article by Foulet on modal adverbs,[17] and secondly to one by Le Bidois on absolute inversion.[18] The former examines adverbs such as *peut-être, à peine* and *ainsi*, and concludes that their occurrence in initial position followed by inversion is an archaism which is confined to elevated speech or writing. He suggests that adverbs of this type are more normally found in other positions in the sentence, or else, under certain circumstances, with direct order initially. He nonetheless admits that this inversion construction has some stylistic value which tends to be overlooked :

'Ainsi grâce à un archaïsme de syntaxe, maintenu par hasard, on rachète ingénieusement ce que la position initiale de l'adverbe a de contraire à l'instinct de la langue actuelle ' (p. 151)

and this too will be brought out in the analysis of certain contemporary French texts.

Finally Le Bidois' article on absolute inversion deals with a number of constructions with different semantic and syntactic value since he treats stage directions, definitions and administrative formulae together with five types of absolute structures classified according to the nature of the verb. Some

[16] R. Le Bidois, ' Variations stylistiques sur l'ordre des mots ', *Le Monde*, 20 novembre, 1968.

[17] L. Foulet, ' L'influence de l'ancienne langue sur la langue moderne ', *Romania*, lii (1926), pp. 147–56.

[18] R. Le Bidois, ' L'inversion absolue du substantif sujet ', *Le Français Moderne*, ix (1941), pp. 111–28.

useful stylistic conclusions are related to the notion of the verb as the psychological subject of the sentence, e.g. ' plus le verbe est lourd de sens, et plus l'inversion produit un effet frappant ' (p. 126). Thus the expressive value of the construction is recognised, while its effectiveness in a wider context remains to be explored.

(iv) *Inversion in the works of early French authors*

In the course of the 19th century a number of works on French word-order appeared, mainly of German or Scandinavian origin, the majority of which were based on texts of the Old or Middle French periods. Such studies are almost without exception wholly concerned with syntax and with comparing the frequency of inverted and direct order in certain contexts. The usefulness of these works for the history of word-order is limited in that few of them define inversion and therefore it is not possible to compare their statistics. Not infrequently non-expression of the subject in Old French is equated with inversion, and the arguments put forward to support the contention that if the subject were present it would be inverted, are generally unconvincing.

More recent studies of individual authors are those by Nissen, Lewinsky, Price and Papić. Nissen's monograph [19] presents a mass of statistical information on the occurrence of inversion in certain contexts, and he concludes that the frequency of inverted order in Jean d'Outremeuse is around 40% (p. 49). A somewhat unsatisfactory feature of his work is the division of examples into those which are characteristic of Middle French, and those which are still in use (61·4% to 38·6%), since the criteria on which this distinction is based are never stated. Lewinsky's analysis of *Bérinus* [20] is an attempt to establish the characteristics of 14th-century word-order. The results relating to inversion are classified according to the various elements which precede the verb. This method

---

[19] H. Nissen, *L'ordre des mots dans la Chronique de Jean d'Outremeuse*, Uppsala, 1943.
[20] *Op. cit.*

provides much useful information from the point of view of changing *invertissants*, despite R.-L. Wagner's assertion, in his review of the book, that the study might have been more profitably based on sentence types.[21] Interrogative and *incise* constructions are again treated in much the same way as non-syntactic inversions. The author states in her introduction that syntactic and stylistic considerations cannot be kept rigidly apart, but the occasional references to the style of the writer are introduced somewhat randomly, with no attempt at a systematic classification of the various uses of inversion.

A more explicit study than that by Nissen is Price's work on the *Chroniques* of Froissart.[22] His is again a syntactic survey of the occurrence of direct and inverted order within the larger context of the sequence of accentuated elements in the sentence. As in Lewinsky, each inverting element is listed, so there is no doubt as to what is included. There is also the further distinction between inversion after subordinating conjunctions and examples which occur in subordinate clauses but after non-subordinating elements, a principle which will also be followed below. Finally, a very recent account of word-order in Montaigne by Papić [23] examines and classifies certain inversions according to the different structures in which they occur, concentrating in particular on comparatives. It is a little surprising, perhaps, that the results are not investigated with regard to style, and comparison with the findings of other critics is hindered by the idiosyncratic classification of many of the examples.

(b) STYLISTIC STUDIES OF INVERSION

(i) *Inversion within the style of an author*

The stylistic uses of word-order by a particular writer are discussed in an increasing number of critical works on individual

---

[21] R.-L. Wagner, Review of Lewinsky in *Zeitschrift für romanische Philologie*, lxvi (1950), pp. 373–76.

[22] G. Price, 'Aspects de l'ordre des mots dans les 'Chroniques' de Froissart', *Zeitschrift für romanische Philologie*, lxxvii (1961), pp. 15–48.

[23] M. Papić, *L'expression et la place du sujet dans les Essais de Montaigne*, Paris, 1970.

styles. For instance, detailed reference to certain aspects of inversion is made by three leading critics, Spitzer, Cressot and Riffaterre, in their studies of Proust, Huysmans and Gobineau respectively.

Spitzer's detailed investigation of the style of Proust, first published in 1928,[24] deals with inversion in the context of the presentation of impressionistic descriptions, and in a footnote Spitzer mentions the increasing frequency of the construction in modern French literature (pp. 472–73). The delaying aspect of inversion is also acknowledged and is thus regarded as an integral part of Proust's *style-défilé* (*Festzug-Stil*). Spitzer examines individual examples in this light, and then offers an interpretation which is occasionally subjective and generalized, as, for example, this comment on absolute inversion :

' Il me semble que, d'une façon générale, cet ordre de mots a tendance à exprimer l'irrévocable (manifestement sous l'influence de l'inversion usuelle dans les règles et les lois) ' (p. 463)

He also notes the similarity between inversion and devices such as the impersonal pronouns *il* and *ce*, not from a syntactic point of view, as does Blinkenberg, but with respect to descriptive technique. Thus Spitzer's method of progressing from form to content is fully exemplified in certain comments on inversion, which also reveal the critic's sensitivity to nuances of style, although his interpretations may at times tend towards the speculative.

Cressot, in discussing word-order in Huysmans,[25] is less concerned with specifying the effects of individual examples. Having outlined the place of inversion in conveying expressiveness, he turns to the last quarter of the 19th century and distinguishes firstly ' la conception d'une nouvelle musicalité de la phrase ' (p. 85), in which rhythmic features such as the *cadence mineure* tend to be cultivated rather than avoided,

---

[24] L. Spitzer, *Etudes de style*, trans. Kaufholz-Coulon-Foucault, Paris, 1970, pp. 397–473.

[25] M. Cressot, *La phrase et le vocabulaire de J.-K. Huysmans*, Geneva, 1938, pp. 83–124.

and secondly ' la phrase parlée ' (p. 86), in which the frequency of inversion is considerably reduced. While the latter observation will be fully borne out by the decreasing frequencies in direct speech in the 19th- and 20th-century novels analysed below, it seems that the former fails to take account of the number of constructions in which the order is inverted to avoid this unharmonious form. With these points established, Cressot then concentrates on the structural properties of inversion, and lists instances where inverted order is clearly exploited, for example, in the interests of thematic liaison. Inversions are thus explained in this work with reference to their position or function in a wider context and not their expressive value, although the importance of the latter is fully recognized by Cressot elsewhere.[26]

Finally, the remarks by Riffaterre on the stylistic characteristics of inversion in Gobineau's *Les Pléiades* [27] will be seen below to be applicable to the effects achieved by many French novelists throughout the period studied. Riffaterre perhaps over-simplifies the problem in that he sees all such factors reducible to a surprise effect (p. 94). He qualifies this, however, by a perceptive comment on the suspense created by chiastic constructions, which, he says, is intensified if supplemented by lexical or emphatic devices. His study also includes quantitative considerations which are then examined from the point of view of style. He concludes that the low frequency of inversion in Gobineau, as compared with that in Balzac and Flaubert (cf. chapters VIII and IX below) ensures on the one hand simplicity in a *récit familier*, and on the other that the force of inversion is reserved for passages in a more elevated style, and in general ' chaque fois que la tension affective apparaît ' (p. 103).

Thus it seems that outstanding writers on style such as those discussed above, have between them explored many of the approaches open to the critic whose starting point is French word-order. Recent works devoted entirely to inversion of the

[26] In *Le style et ses techniques*, 6th ed. Paris, 1969, pp. 244–45.
[27] M. Riffaterre, *Le style des ' Pléiades ' de Gobineau*, Geneva–Paris, 1957.

subject are beginning to bring together such observations on the structure of the device, its various stylistic effects and its interpretation in a wider context, while also taking account of diverging frequencies in different authors, periods, or styles.

(ii) *Le Bidois and Proust*

Robert Le Bidois' comprehensive survey of inversion in *À la recherche du temps perdu* [28] might be more accurately classed as a work of descriptive syntax rather than a specifically stylistic study. However, while the author is concerned particularly with the conditions under which inversion occurs, the grammatical material is presented in such a way as to be directly amenable to stylistic analysis beyond that outlined by Le Bidois himself, and in this respect the work goes some way towards bridging the gap between language and style.

The stylistic value of inversion is examined with regard to the contribution of word-order to the harmony and balance of the sentence, and the emphasizing of certain elements. The author does not, however, stress the expressive value of emphatic word-order, and the stylistic analysis thus lacks an interpretative component, perhaps on account of the sheer weight of material provided. Instead, the results are explained with reference to the concepts of psychological or grammatical subject and predicate, an approach already used by him in the article on absolute inversion.[29] Similar procedures have been followed by linguists such as Hjelmslev [30] and Gallichet [31] who have considered the problem in relation to the psychology of grammar, but this is of less interest to the stylistician who is concerned with the effects of inversion.

Le Bidois classifies his examples according to their occur-

---

[28] R. Le Bidois, *L'inversion du sujet dans la prose contemporaine (1900–1950), étudiée plus spécialement dans l'œuvre de Marcel Proust*, Paris, 1952.

[29] ' L'inversion absolue du substantif sujet ', *loc. cit.*

[30] L. Hjelmslev, ' Rôle structural de l'ordre des mots ' in *Grammaire et psychologie* (numéro spécial du Journal de Psychologie), Paris, 1950, pp. 51–60.

[31] G. Gallichet, *Essai de grammaire psychologique du français moderne*, 2nd ed., Paris, 1950.

rence in main or subordinate clauses and adds a category of 'propositions de nature mixte', which includes *incises* and restrictive constructions. There is no distinction between structures in which inversion has a syntactic function, such as interrogatives and exclamations, and those where its role tends to be stylistic. In moving from syntax to style, Le Bidois, unlike Lerch, proceeds from the detailed study of constructions to the factors causing inversion, and he distinguishes three reasons for a change in word-order, syntactic, psychological and stylistic. In some cases, perhaps, the more common examples do not merit emphasis as conscious deviations. Nevertheless, *L'inversion du sujet* represents the most comprehensive survey of the construction in a modern French writer so far, and the documentation extends well beyond the work of Proust. It is important not only as a valuable basis for stylistic analysis, but also for the stress which is laid on the frequency of the construction in French.

(iii) *Ullmann and the French novel* [32]

The most detailed work on the stylistic uses of inversion in a wider context, which complements Le Bidois' study in a limited area, is undoubtedly that of Professor S. Ullmann,[33] to which frequent reference will be made in chapters VIII–X. The value of inversion as an expressive device of style is shown in the analysis of a number of 19th- and 20th-century novels. In each case the frequency of 'optional' inversions is stated, permitting comparisons between novelists ranging from Balzac and Flaubert to Romains and Sartre. Ullmann also offers some general conclusions as to the stylistic functions of word-order,

[32] The importance of word-order in the context of a method of stylistic analysis of French prose has been shown by R. A. Sayce, *Style in French Prose*, Oxford, 1953, pp. 88–89.

[33] See especially: 'Valeurs stylistiques de l'inversion dans l'*Éducation sentimentale*', *Le Français Moderne*, xx (1952), pp. 175–88. 'Inversion as a stylistic device in the contemporary French novel', *Modern Language Review*, xlvii (1952), pp. 165–80. 'L'inversion du sujet dans la prose romantique', *Le Français Moderne*, xxiii (1955), pp. 23–28. *Style in the French Novel*, 2nd ed. Oxford, 1964, pp. 146–88.

listing, for instance, in his article on the *Éducation sentimentale*, the phonic, syntactic and semantic effects of inversion, and gives many examples of specific uses of the device in particular writers, bringing out factors such as the idiosyncratic nature of the speech of Legrandin in Proust.

A similar approach to stylistic analysis is attempted in this book, which, in covering a longer period of time, will examine a still wider range of novels and styles. It is hoped that the results obtained will throw additional light on the evolution of this aspect of French narrative style, as well as contribute to the history of inversion as a syntactic structure.

2. THE OPINIONS OF TRADITIONAL GRAMMARIANS

The research on which this book is based originally included a survey of the treatment of word-order in French grammars from their beginnings in the 16th century to the present day, so that some relation between theory and practice might be established. This material was subsequently omitted for reasons of length, but a summary of it might be appropriate here. It should also be noted that relevant comments on inversion by several of the authors studied will be included in the course of the book.

The general conclusion that emerges from the study of grammatical doctrine in the last 400 years is that theorists have usually underestimated the occurrence of inversion in French. Some grammarians deny the very existence of an alternative word-order, while others attempt to limit inversion to a small number of constructions in which it is thought to be obligatory. A few writers dismiss inversions as stylistic variants, without seeking the reason or explaining the effect, and rare are those whose attitude is more flexible and who refer the reader to actual usage, although such ideas are expressed on occasions throughout the period in question.

The grammarians' view of word-order in the 16th century seems to bear little resemblance to the somewhat chaotic state of literary French with its high frequency of inversion.

Ramus,[34] for example, notes the contrast between the stylistic order of Latin and the syntactic order of French, and suggests that inversion in the latter is necessarily confined to the expression of interrogatives and parentheses. Other writers are even more forthright in condemning the construction, among them the poet Ronsard.[35] Garnier, on the other hand, while recognizing a basic word-order in French, also admits considerable freedom in the use of inversion, and gives instances of a number of variant orders.[36] Particularly relevant, perhaps, are his examples of inverted order after *et* in literary usage.[37] The contribution of the 16th-century grammarians, however, as Rickard has suggested,[38] is chiefly that of establishing the idea of a linguistic norm, and as far as word-order is concerned, this norm seems already somewhat remote from common usage, at least in the written language.

It is not surprising to find that in the 17th century the increasing severity of the grammatical purists is accompanied by a decline in the use of a freer word-order, including inversion (see chapters IV and V below), but even so, the alternative orders never disappear, despite assertions to the contrary on the part of many theorists. Early in the century Maupas,[39] and subsequently Oudin,[40] claim to have studied current usage and list exceptions to direct order, among them constructions with certain adverbs and conjunctions. Later, however, Malherbe's comments on the language of Desportes indicate how unacceptable some inversions have become, in particular the absolute construction and a change of order after certain

[34] P. Ramus, *Gramere*, 2nd ed. Paris, 1572, Bibliothèque Nationale 8° X 12667.

[35] See his prefaces to volumes of the *Franciade*, *Œuvres complètes XVI*, ed. P. Laumonier, Paris, 1950.

[36] J. Garnier, *Institutio gallicae linguae in usum iuventutis germanicae*, Geneva, 1558, B.N.Rés. X 2284, pp. 98–99.

[37] *Ibid.*, p. 100.

[38] P. Rickard, *La langue française au XVIe siècle*, Cambridge, 1968.

[39] C. Maupas, *Grammaire et syntaxe françoise* (1607), 3rd ed. Rouen, 1632, B.N. X 9803.

[40] A. Oudin, *Grammaire françoise rapportée au langage du temps* (1632), 2nd ed. Paris. 1690, B.N. X 9795.

attributive adjectives.[41] Typical of a grammarian's disregard
for usage at this time, even his own, is the following comment
on word-order by Laurent Chiflet :

> ' Vous voyez que le Nominatif va devant : puis le Verbe avec
> son Adverbe ; apres quoy suit le Cas, qui est regi par le
> Verbe, où se trouve le Substantif avec son Adjectif : ensuite
> vient le Genitif. ' [42]

As the obsession with linguistic perfection continues into the
18th century, it is reflected by the lowest frequency of inversion
in the texts analysed (chapters VI and VII below). The doctrine
of many grammarians, including d'Olivet, Restaut and Buffier,
is summed up in Rivarol's famous claim, with its own example
of inversion :

> ' Le français, par un privilège unique, est seul resté fidèle à
> l'ordre direct, comme s'il était toute raison. (...) La syntaxe
> française est l'incorruptible. C'est de là que résulte cette
> admirable clarté, base éternelle de notre langue.' [43]

But at the same time there begins to emerge an appreciation of
the stylistic advantages of inversion, and this is eloquently
expressed by Diderot (see p. 236 below). Also, writers such as
Dumarsais, Condillac and Batteux stress the importance of
linking ideas logically, and recognize that this process may be
facilitated by inversion.

Thus, by the mid-19th century, inversion is welcomed by
many for its expressive potential,[44] although the grammars
barely hint at the renewed frequency and vivacity of the
construction in the literature of the period. As regards
contemporary French, the tradition of listing exceptions to a
' normal ' word-order is still a familiar one, and is to be found
in as eminent a linguist as Gougenheim :

[41] See V. E. Graham's editions of the works of Desportes with Malherbe's
commentary, Geneva, 1958–63.

[42] *Essay d'une parfaicte grammaire de la langue françoise*, Paris, 1668.
B.N. X 9827, p. 148.

[43] A. de Rivarol, *De l'universalité de la langue française* (1784), ed. M.
Hervier, Paris, 1929.

[44] See for example C. P. Girault-Duvivier, *Grammaire des grammaires ou
analyse raisonnée des meilleurs traités*, 13th ed., Paris, 1948.

'La place normale du groupe sujet est devant le verbe (...). Dans certaines catégories de propositions il existe une servitude grammaticale qui oblige à placer le sujet après le verbe (...). L'ordre inverse constitue une variation stylistique avec l'ordre normal.' [45]

A wholly more realistic comment on the present situation would seem to be that by G. and R. Le Bidois, with which this book concludes (p. 438 below).

3. THE UNSUITABILITY OF TRANSFORMATIONAL ANALYSIS

Most major textbooks on the subject of Modern Linguistics have commented on the importance of word-order in syntax, particularly in opposing synthetic and analytic languages. Thus Bloomfield [46] postulates ' taxemes of order ', which generally supplement ' taxemes of selection ', the latter being the more complex in languages with a relatively free word-order. Similarly Robins, in his comprehensive introductory work, notes the progression from a complex morphology and fairly free word-order in Classical Latin to a simpler morphology with ' syntactically determined word-order ' in modern French. [47] The place of word-order in the theory of linguistic universals is demonstrated by Greenberg, [48] who, from a sample of thirty languages, concludes that ' the vast majority of languages have several variant orders, but a single dominant one ' (pp. 60–61).

The treatment of variations in word-order within the framework of a transformational-generative grammar has been outlined by Lyons. [49] According to this theory alternative

[45] G. Gougenheim, *Système grammatical de la langue française*, Paris, 1938, p. 111.

[46] L. Bloomfield, *Language*, London, 1935, pp. 197–98.

[47] R. H. Robins, *General Linguistics, An Introductory Survey*, London, 1964, p. 256.

[48] J. H. Greenberg, ' Some Universals of Grammar with Particular Reference to the Order of Meaningful Elements ' in *Universals of Language*, Cambridge, Mass., 1963, pp. 58–90.

[49] J. Lyons, *An Introduction to Theoretical Linguistics*, Cambridge, 1968, pp. 223–24.

versions of a sentence may be generated by means of a 'set of supplementary rules of permutation operating upon the same terminal string'. Such rules would be simplest for languages with freer word-order, and would be complicated by constraints on the order of certain words in others. It may seem that word-order is one feature of syntax which might lend itself to an analysis in terms of transformational theory rather more readily than others, yet the complexity of a descriptively adequate model, in Chomsky's terms, would nevertheless be considerable. This is already suggested by Langacker's description of interrogative structures alone in French,[50] where transformational rules are formed to account for questions involving inversion, reduplication, pronominalization and ellipsis. He claims to have established the basic unity, on an abstract level, of 'a rather wide array of superficially different question types' (p. 600), but it seems that even a clearly-defined area of word-order such as interrogation requires a large number of rules for its description.

The occurrence of inversion in many languages as a feature of style has also been observed by transformationalists. Chomsky himself suggests that 'in any language, stylistic inversion of "major constituents"... is tolerated up to ambiguity',[51] although he does not expand this point further. In a footnote to the statement of rewriting rules in the base component of the grammar, these are said to fail to illustrate 'the use of order-inversion as a stylistic device' and Chomsky adds that 'the discussion of deviation from grammaticalness... offers no insight into this phenomenon'.[52] Subsequent attempts to relate the theory to the analysis of literary style have served only to demonstrate the unsuitability of transformational-generative grammar to stylistics, at least in its present form. Although not specifically concerned with word-

[50] R. W. Langacker, 'French Interrogatives: A Transformational Description', *Language*, xli (1965), pp. 587–600.

[51] N. Chomsky, *Aspects of the Theory of Syntax*, Cambridge, Mass., 1965, p. 127.

[52] *Ibid.*, pp. 227–28.

order, reference should be made to the articles by Ohmann [53] and Thorne,[54] which have provided little of stylistic interest, and have overlooked much which could have been revealed by an examination of the surface structure in place of a deep structure analysis. The inconclusiveness of such studies may thus be attributed in part to the hypothesis that stylistic choice is made at the level of deep structure, which must then restrict any approach to style through syntax in terms of transformational theory.

Since this book is concerned as much with the stylistic uses of inversion as with its syntactic structure, a transformational approach has been rejected on the grounds of its inevitable complexity as regards syntax, and its unproductiveness in the field of style. It will, however, be noted that certain transformational principles are reflected in the method of grammatical analysis described below, in particular the syntactic operations which explain various constructions using inversion of the subject.

4. THE METHOD OF ANALYSIS

The underlying principle of the study which follows is that the investigation of stylistic uses of inversion in each text should be preceded by, and based on, a formal syntactic analysis of the material. There is thus a progression from form to content, with the style of an author studied through his use of inverted order. Other stylistic factors are considered relevant only where they are shown to be related to this device, for instance when inversion is employed to emphasize a technique such as personification or a specific theme or motif. As a result both diachronic and synchronic comparisons may be made between either the syntactic characteristics or the stylistic uses of inversion in the different works.

[53] R. Ohmann, ' Generative Grammars and the Concept of Literary Style ', *Word*, xx (1964), pp. 423–39. ' Literature as Sentences ' reprinted in *Contemporary Essays on Style*, ed. Love-Payne, Illinois, 1969, pp. 149–57.

[54] J. Thorne, ' Stylistics and Generative Grammars ', *Journal of Linguistics*, i (1965), pp. 49–59. ' Generative Grammars and Stylistic Analysis ' in *New Horizons in Linguistics*, ed. J. Lyons, London, 1970, pp. 185–97.

(i) THE TEXTS

The novels selected for analysis are, with some exceptions in the early period, those which have been thought to be among the most influential from the point of view of both language and literature. The texts have also been chosen to represent where possible the various aspects of the novel and its evolution. For the period 1500–1800 four works have been studied in each half-century, while in the 19th century this is increased to five, in view of the number and diversity of important novels at this time. Similarly in the 20th century, six texts have been selected to represent the first fifty years, and four for the years 1950–60. Five more 20th-century texts have been examined as regards frequency of inversion only, one of which was published after 1950.

The average length of a novel is taken to be around 88,000 words, a figure based on a sample of the books studied, which corresponds to 200 pages of both the modern Pléiade editions and the most closely printed of the Classiques Garnier. In calculating the length of a work, allowance has been made for chapter headings and irregular paragraphing, and all non-prose material such as sonnets and epitaphs in the earlier novels is excluded so that even where the above editions are used, the corpus almost invariably exceeds 200 pages. Ten of the novels chosen were considered sufficiently important to be included, despite the fact that they contained fewer than 88,000 words, and in these cases the total of examples has been weighted in order to obtain a comparable average number of inversions per page.

(ii) DEFINITION OF INVERSION IN THIS STUDY

The inversion construction normally comprises three elements, the *invertissant*,[55] finite verb and subject, inversions in participial phrases being excluded.[56] Several verb-subject structures which are dependent on a single *invertissant* are

---

[55] Term taken from Le Bidois, *L'inversion du sujet*.
[56] Discussed by Blinkenberg, *L'ordre des mots I*, p. 127.

counted as separate inversions, provided that the subject nominals are different in each case, although the verb might be repeated. However, the same subject occurring with different verbs only constitutes a second inversion if the *invertissant* is also repeated. Structures in 16th-century texts where a pronoun subject is omitted are clearly not eligible as inversions, regardless of whether a change in word-order may be supposed to have taken place. On the other hand, compound inversions where the proposed noun subject is repeated in pronominal form after the verb are included in the analysis.[57] The proportion of examples represented by such constructions is stated in table 6 in chapters IV—XI.

Inversions which fulfil a syntactic function in interrogatives, imperatives, optatives and exclamations, are excluded from the analysis, as are inversions forming *incise* constructions. In the 16th-century texts the latter are taken to include inversions preceding direct speech which have an *incise* function, although there may be an element present which is normally regarded as an *invertissant*: ' Et dit Amadis " (...) ".' The study also excludes verbs in absolute position where the subject is a relative clause without an antecedent. Such constructions are generally fixed syntactic formulae, ' Rira bien qui rira le dernier ',[58] but less usual examples have been found occasionally in the novels, and will be regarded as special forms of optatives,[59] e.g. ' Ira voir qui voudra de mauvaises tragédies ' (*Candide*, p. 205).

(iii) THE SYNTACTIC CLASSIFICATION OF THE INVERSIONS

In the analysis of the examples, inversions are classified according to (*a*) the operation performed on a hypothetical base structure, subject-verb-complement, and (*b*) the syntactic nature of the *invertissant*. Changes in the base structure are effected by the transposition of one or more elements, which

---

[57] For further details see L. Priestley, ' Reprise Constructions in French ', *Archivum Linguisticum*, vii (1955), pp. 1–28.

[58] Cf. Blinkenberg, *ibid.*, p. 94.

[59] Cf. Le Bidois, *ibid.*, p. 84.

may be combined with the operations of deletion or addition
described below. The *invertissant* may then be defined as the
element which precedes the subject prior to the operation
which entails its inversion. The classification is as follows:

I IMMOBILE 'INVERTISSANT': TRANSPOSITION OF THE SUBJECT ONLY

The *invertissant* is:

Zero

Co-ordinating conjunction

Subordinating conjunction: relative clauses
                                comparative
                                concessive
                                temporal
                                causal
                                purpose/result
                                substantival
                                hypothetical

Immobilized adverb: correlative constructions [60]

Verb plus subordinating element: indirect constructions

II MOBILE 'INVERTISSANT': TRANSPOSITION OF 'INVERTISSANT' AND SUBJECT

The *invertissant* is:

Attribute

Adverb: manner, quantity, time, place or combinations of
adverbs

Adverbial phrase: time, place, manner

Prepositional phrase [61]

---

[60] I am indebted to Dr. P. Rickard for the suggestion of this category: the
invertissant in a correlative construction is immobilized by virtue of its
repetition at the head of successive clauses (*plus . . . plus . . .*), the first
occurrence of the adverb being taken to immobilize the second. Thus
inversion is generally found in the second clause, although there are one or
two examples in the texts analysed of a change in word-order in each half
of the construction.

[61] The *invertissant* here is an indirect object dependent on a verb and the
preposition which normally accompanies it, e.g. *naître/dépendre de, convenir/
se mêler à.*

Direct object
Infinitival
Participial phrase
Subordinate clause
Negative particle

III OPERATION OF DELETION

IV OPERATION OF DELETION AND TRANSPOSITION

V OPERATION OF ADDITION AND TRANSPOSITION

The majority of inversions are the result of a transposition operation, involving (*a*) the subject alone, the *invertissant* being outside the clause:

    le livre que (mon père m'a donné)

  → le livre que m'a donné mon père

or (*b*) an element from within the sentence which becomes the *invertissant* along with the subject which is transposed in consequence:

    le Général arriva vers midi

  → vers midi le Général arriva

  → vers midi arriva le Général

This division depends, therefore, on the mobility of the *invertissant* and corresponds approximately, but not completely, to the traditional subordinate-main clause distinction, and the figures for both categories will always be given.

The reason for adopting an alternative classification is the misleading nature of the terms ' main ' and ' subordinate ' from both a syntactic and a semantic point of view. For instance, an inversion occurring after a modal adverb, which is in turn preceded by a subordinating conjunction (... *qu'à peine*...), is best classified according to the type of *invertissant*, the mobile *à peine*, while strictly speaking it appears in a subordinate clause. The terms also imply an element of subordination which is frequently absent, the most obvious example being the indirect speech construction, where the so-called subordinate clause, dependent on the question-word, is the chief point of interest, the main clause containing the verb of inquiry being often largely incidental.

The remaining inversions are classified with reference to further operations of deletion and addition. Deletion operations are those in which an inversion in apparently absolute position is considered to derive from a structure containing an impersonal pronoun. Thus ' Restait Jean ' is related not to ' Jean restait ', in which case the construction would be one with zero *invertissant*, but rather ' Il restait Jean '. Transposition of the subject following the deletion of a hypothetical conjunction also involves a change of mood in the verb :

même si ce fut vrai → fût-ce vrai...

For present purposes, however, this change in mood may be disregarded,[62] since the inversion construction will be considered as an alternative to the hypothetical clause with direct order. This category also includes a form of concessive construction containing an adverb of quantity, which is more usually found as a mobile *invertissant* ; in such examples the verb is always in the subjunctive mood and a further change in word-order may also be effected :

tant qu'il soit grand
→ tant soit-il grand
→ tant grand soit-il

Such structures are not found after 1700 in the texts analysed here. Finally, the examples classified under addition and transposition include a third operation, the addition of the emphatic structure *c'est... que* to the mobile *invertissant* prior to the inversion of the subject :

Nos amis se sont perdus là
→ Là nos amis se sont perdus
→ C'est là que nos amis se sont perdus
→ C'est là que se sont perdus nos amis

---

[62] The homophonous forms of the past historic and past subjunctive are discussed by C. Camproux, ' Télescopage morpho-syntaxique ? ', *Le Français Moderne*, xxxv (1967), pp. 161–83.

(iv) THE ARRANGEMENT OF THE MATERIAL

Each chapter covers a period of fifty years, and is divided into two sections. The first part is a syntactic analysis of the inversions found in the texts in question and includes examples from the novels of various constructions with inverted order, and a discussion of their frequency and characteristics. The second part contains a stylistic analysis of the examples from each author.

The syntactic analysis is always preceded by twelve tables which contain statistical information provided by the *dépouillement*. All are percentage tables,[63] with the exception of tables 1 and 8, and are as follows :

Table 1 : The frequency of inversion, showing both the total number of examples in each work, and their average frequency of occurrence per page.

Table 2 : The nature of the clause in which inversion occurs; the classification is according to main and subordinate clauses, and the syntactic operations already described.

Table 3 : The distribution of the inversions according to discourse type, i.e. narrative and direct, indirect and free indirect speech.

Table 4 : The position of the inversions within the corpus examined, showing the proportion of examples found at the beginning or end of a sentence, paragraph, chapter or passage of speech.

Table 5 : The position of the inversion in relation to other types of discourse, revealing any tendency for direct, indirect or free indirect speech to be proceded or followed by a clause with inverted word-order.

Table 6 : The nature of the inverted noun phrase, whether this is pronominal or substantival, showing the occurrence of more than one subject element and of any dependent clauses.

---

[63] In these tables n denotes less than 1%, and N indicates the total number.

Table 7 : The proportion of inversions in sentences comprising three or more clauses.

Table 8 : The ratio of inversions to *invertissants*, giving also the total number of inversions and different *invertissants* found in the texts altogether.

Table 9 : The most frequently occurring inversions, with the distribution of the examples among the commonest constructions such as relative or comparative clauses.

Table 10 : The occurrence of *être, faire* and *avoir* as the verbs followed by an inverted subject.

Table 11 : The distribution of direct speech *invertissants*, that is the examples of inversion found in conversation classified according to the syntactic operation involved.

Table 12 : The occurrence of adverbials and clauses in inversion constructions, showing how many examples have additional elements interposed between *invertissant* and verb or verb and subject.

Chapter II

THE SIXTEENTH CENTURY (1)

1. SYNTACTIC ANALYSIS OF THE TEXTS 1500–1550

The texts :
F. Rabelais, *Pantagruel et Gargantua* [1]
Helisenne de Crenne, *Les angoisses douloureuses qui procedent d'amours* [2]
H. des Essarts, *Le premier livre d'Amadis de Gaule* [3]
Marguerite de Navarre, *L'Heptaméron* [4]

Table 2.01 : Inversion frequencies

RAB/PAN GAR	522 : 2·98	
HC/AD	497 : 2·49	(*mean* 2·64)
ESS/AG	650 : 3·25	
MN/HEP	363 : 1·82	

Table 2.02 : Percentage table to show nature of clause in which inversion occurs

	RAB	HC	ESS	MN
Main clause	55	61	75	71
Subordinate clause	39	29	20	24
Non-subordinating *invertissant* in subordinate clause	6	10	5	5
	100	100	100	100
Immobile *invertissant*	49	40	39	52
Mobile *invertissant*	49	57	60	46
Other operations	2	3	1	2
N :	522	497	650	363

[1] In *Œuvres complètes I*, ed. P. Jourda, Paris (Garnier), 1962. *c.* 77,000 words. (RAB)
[2] Paris (Langlier), 1543. B. N. Rés Z. 2745. (HC)
[3] Paris (Hachette), 1918 (analysis to p. 274). (ESS)
[4] Paris (Garnier), 1960 (analysis to p. 221). (MN)

Table 2.03 : Percentage table to show distribution of inversion
according to discourse type

	RAB	HC	ESS	MN
Narrative	68	60	70	64
Direct speech	26	36	28	32
Indirect speech	6	1	2	4
Free indirect speech	—	—	—	—
Soliloquy	—	3	—	—

Table 2.04 : Percentage table to show position of inversion
within the corpus examined

	RAB	HC	ESS	MN
Sentence initial	14	29	41	37
Paragraph initial	17	2	1	4
Chapter initial	2	1	n	n
Speech initial	2	n	4	5
Total initial	35	32	46	46
Sentence final	11	30	11	15
Paragraph final	9	1	—	1
Chapter final	1	n	n	n
Speech final	2	2	4	1
Total final	23	33	15	17

Table 2.05 : Percentage table to show position of inversion in
relation to other types of discourse

	RAB	HC	ESS	MN
Preceding direct speech	3	n	5	2
Following direct speech	4	2	20	3
Preceding indirect speech	2	n	2	6
Following indirect speech	n	n	1	n

Table 2.06 : Percentage table to show nature of the inverted
noun phrase

	RAB	HC	ESS	MN
Pronoun subject	13	11	21	35
Substantive subject	87	89	79	65
	100	100	100	100
2 or more subjects	9	11	7	4
S and dependent (S)	13	24	19	15

Table 2.07 : The percentage of inversions occurring in sentences of three or more clauses

	RAB	HC	ESS	MN
(8)—3 clauses	11	29	29	24
4 clauses	15	13	19	16
5 clauses	7	4	12	11
6 clauses	4	1	1	5
7 clauses	1	—	1	2
7+ clauses	—	—	—	n
	38	47	62	58

Table 2.08 : The ratio of inversions to *invertissants*

RAB	522 : 160—3·24
HC	497 : 133—3·73
ESS	650 : 131—4·96
MN	363 : 88—4·13
Total	2,032 : 284—7·15 (*mean* 4·02)

Table 2.09 : Percentage table of the most frequently occurring inversions

	RAB	HC	ESS	MN
Co-ordinators	6	12	19	27
Relatives	22	10	13	18
Comparatives	14	11	2	2
Indirect construction	5	7	4	3
Modal adverbs	12	7	11	12

Table 2.10 : Percentage table to show the occurrence of ' être ', ' faire ' and ' avoir '

	RAB	HC	ESS	MN
être	21	26	18	13
faire	9	6	7	6
avoir	2	n	3	2

Table 2.11 : Percentage table showing the distribution of direct speech *invertissants*

		RAB	HC	ESS	MN
Immobile *invertissant*		52	45	27	22
Mobile *invertissant*		43	53	70	75
Other operations		5	2	3	3
N :		132	176	179	117

Table 2.12 : Percentage table to show the occurrence of
adverbials and clauses in inversion constructions

	RAB	HC	ESS	MN
V(adv)S	2	3	2	3
(adv)VS	2	2	1	2
V(S)S	—	—	n	n
(S)VS	n	—	n	1

(i) DISTRIBUTION OF THE INVERSIONS

The texts of this period selected for analysis all show a very
high occurrence of inversion (table 2.01), despite a rapid
decline in the second half of the century, where the texts
chosen have a frequency similar to that of the *Heptaméron*.
The high frequency of inversion is accompanied by a large
number of *invertissants* (table 2.08), although in Rabelais, for
example, more than 50% of the 160 *invertissants* occur only
once in the text.

The analysis of the texts above reveals certain characteristics
of medieval syntax, for instance the tendency for inversion to
occur in main rather than subordinate clauses (table 2.02), and
with substantival rather than pronominal subjects (table 2.06).
Inversions in initial position also far outnumber those in final
position in three of the four texts (table 2.04), although in later
periods the distribution becomes more even.

Table 2.03 reveals a fairly high proportion of inversions
occurring in direct speech, while 3% of the total in the
Angoisses douloureuses are found in soliloquies. The sentence
structure of these works is quite simple, with the majority of
inversions in Rabelais and Helisenne de Crenne occurring in
sentences of one or two clauses only, and there are few instances of inversion in very long sentences (table 2.07).
Similarly there is little separation of the major constituents by
adverbials, and there are few examples where a clause is placed
between *invertissant* and verb, or verb and subject (table 2.12).
The occurrence of *être* and to a lesser extent of *faire* in constructions with inverted order is also high (table 2.10). There is
considerable variety in the types of construction in which
inversion is found, and in the case of Helisenne and des Essarts

the majority of examples are found in constructions other than those listed in table 2.09. The most commonly found *invertissants* in all the texts but Rabelais are co-ordinating conjunctions, in particular *et* and *si* which are discussed below, while other frequent constructions with inverted order are relatives and comparatives.

(ii) EXAMPLES

A. IMMOBILE 'INVERTISSANT'

1. *Zero : RAB : 2 : MN : 1*
   ' *Arriva* la contesse, qui la trova en ce pitieux estat ...' (MN p. 78)

2. *Co-ordinating conjunctions : RAB : 32 inversions, 4 'invertissants' : HC : 58,3 ; ESS : 122,3 ; MN : 99,3*
   ' " Seigneur, voicy ma maistresse. *Or* suis je maintenant quitte de la promesse que je vous avois faite. " ' (ESS p. 141)

3. *Relative conjunctions : RAB : 113,11 ; HC : 50,10 ; ESS : 87,7 ; MN : 67,9*
   ' ... un gentil homme nommé Symontault, lequel, ennuyé de la longue demeure *quel* faisoit la riviere à s'abaisser, s'estoit deliberé de la forcer ... ' (MN p. 5)

4. *Comparatives : RAB : 72,18 ; HC : 57,10 ; ESS : 10,6 ; MN : 7,5*
   ' Floride, qui, par ceste mort, perdoit toute consolation, feyt *tel* deuil *que* peult faire celle qui se sent destitutée de ses parens et amys '. (MN p. 71)

5. *Concessives : ESS : 1,1*
   ' Car *quelque* defense *que* feist Dardan, il fut contrainct de se tirer arriere, et ... ' (ESS p. 160)

6. *Temporal conjunctions : RAB : 2,1 ; ESS : 2,2*
   ' " ... je vous serviray *tant que* durera vostre guerre de Gaule '." (ESS p. 66)

7. *Causal clause : RAB : 1,1*
   ' " Doncques, s'il te plaist à ceste heure me estre en ayde, *comme* en toy seul est ma totale confiance et espoir, je te fais veu que par toutes contrées... " ' (RAB p. 361)

8. *Result clause : RAB : 1,1*
' ... et la joye qui toust succederoit luy tolliroit tout cest ennuy, *en sorte que* seulement ne luy en resteroit la soubvenance '. (RAB p. 29)

9. *Substantival clause : RAB : 6,6*
' " Quand est de vostre ranczon, je vous la donne entierement, et *veulx que* vous soient rendues armes et cheval ".' (RAB p. 220)

10. *Hypothetical clause : RAB : 5,2 ; HC : 1,1 ; MN : 1,1*
' " ... et *si* bien deffailloient les forces de povoir poursuyvre ... jamais la volonté ne se doibt esteindre ... " '
(HC I, 95v) [5]

11. *Correlatives : MN : 2,2*
' " Car *tant plus* je tiens ce feu celé et couvert, *et plus* en moy croist le plaisir de sçavoir que j'ayme parfaictement." '
(MN p. 48)

12. *Indirect construction : RAB : 25,11 ; HC : 34,8 ; ESS : 28,9 ; MN : 12,7*
' Mais je vous veulx exposer *dont* procedoit la fidelisme amytié, qui estoit observée entre nous '. (HC II, 6r)

B. MOBILE ' INVERTISSANT '

1. *Attributes : RAB : 12,4 ; HC : 31,7 ; ESS : 27,8 ; MN : 2,1*
' " *Prodigeuse* fut l'incarnation, tresmalheureuse la nativité, horrible la vie, et *execrable* sera la fin." ' (HC I, 101v)

2. *Adverbs—modal : RAB : 61,18 ; HC : 37,15 ; ESS : 69,18 ; MN : 44,7*
' " Sire, respondit il, *paradventure* ay je entendu choses qu'il n'est besoing manifester à aultre qu'à vous seul. " '
(ESS p. 24)

3. *Adverbs—quantity : RAB : 14,8 ; HC : 14,12 ; ESS : 42,13 ; MN : 1,1*
' *Moult* fut louée la damoyselle de ses paroles tant courtoises et gratieuses '. (HC II, 76r)

---

[5] The 1543 edition of the *Angoisses douloureuses* has no page numbers, and each of the four parts is here numbered separately.

4. *Adverbs—temporal* : *RAB* : *24,11* ; *HC* : *46,22* ; *ESS* : *73,15* ; *MN* : *5,5*

' *Adonc* descendit le Damoysel et fut conduict par Agraies en sa tente où il se desarma, et *tandis* commanda Agraies qu'on luy amenast les chevaliers gisans en my le champ ...' (ESS p. 90)

5. *Adverbs—place* : *RAB* : *14,5* ; *HC* : *9,1* ; *ESS* : *1,1* ; *MN* : *2,1*

' *Au milieu* estoit une pareille montée et porte comme avons dict du cousté de la rivière '. (RAB p. 193)

6. *Adverbs—combinations* : *RAB* : *10,8* ; *HC* : *9,4* : *ESS* : *5,3* ; *MN* : *7,4*

' ... *puis incontinent* fut sceu le contraire, tellement que resplendissoie en renommée de chasteté louable ... ' (HC I, 3r)

7. *Adverbial phrase—time* : *RAB* : *18,8* ; *HC* : *17,6* ; *ESS* : *37,7* ; *MN* : *32,11*

' *Le premier jour de septembre*, ... se trouverent à ceulx (baings) de Cauderes plusieurs personnes tant de France que d'Espaigne '. (MN p. 1)

8. *Adverbial phrase—place* : *RAB* : *25,13* ; *HC* : *9,5* ; *ESS* : *9,6* ; *MN* : *14,7*

' *Jouxte la rivière* estoit le beau jardin de plaisance ; au milieu d'iceluy le beau labirynte. *Entre les deux aultres tours* estoient les jeux de paulme et de grosse balle. *Du cousté de la tour Cryere* estoit le vergier ... ' (RAB p. 198)

9. *Adverbial phrase—manner* : *RAB* : *10,4* ; *HC* : *25,7* ; *ESS* : *25,6* ; *MN* : *12,6*

' " Par dieu, respondit il, *de mon gré* n'entreray je en prison de gens si trahistres. " ' (ESS p. 266)

10. *Prepositional phrase* : *RAB* : *42,8* ; *HC* : *42,5* ; *ESS* : *26,6* ; *MN* : *13,5*

' Mais ainsi comme à tel exercice (Pallas) s'occupoit, *d'elle* s'approcha Venus : laquelle... ' (HC III, 11v)

11. *Direct object* : *RAB* : *7,5* ; *HC* : *16,7* : *ESS* : *34,7* ; *MN* : *4,3*

' " Et *ceste-là* seulle veulx-je aymer, reverer et adorer, non comme femme, mais comme mon Dieu en terre ..." '
(MN p. 196)

12. *Infinitival : RAB : 3,3 ; HC : 2,2 ; ESS : 1,1 ; MN : 3,1*

' " ... tu doibs croire qu'*à ce faire* ne suffiroit tout le cours de ma vie : " ' (HC III, 30v)

13. *Participial phrase : RAB : 7,2 ; HC : 11,2 ; ESS : 17,2 ; MN : 11,2*

' *Laquelle nouvelle entendue*, sortirent au devant de luy tous les habitans de la ville, en bon ordre ... ' (RAB p. 374)
' *Luy disans ces parolles*, entra le moyne tout deliberé ... '
(RAB p. 169)

14. *Subordinate clause : RAB : 6,4 ; HC : 14,2 ; ESS : 15,2 ; MN : 15,2*

' Et *pource que Gandales deffendit à ses gens ne faire bruict de leur rencontre : et que les mariniers ... navigarent ailleurs*, furent ces deux enfans estimez freres par ceulx qui ne sçavoient la fortune '. (ESS p. 21)

15. *Negative particle : RAB : 3,1 ; HC : 3,2 ; ESS : 11,6 ; MN : 1,1*

' *Pas* ne dormait à l'heure celle qui attendoit leur venue ...'
(ESS p. 173)

C. OTHER OPERATIONS

1. *Deletion : HC : 7 ; ESS : 3 ; MN : 2*

' " ... je seroye fort malcontent, *n'estoit* une chose qui me conforte, c'est que je ne suis seul abusé de ce variable sexe feminin ... " ' (HC I, 79v)

2. *Deletion and transposition : RAB : 5 ; HC : 5 ; ESS : 5 ; MN : 5*

' " ... et *fust-il* vostre propre frere, vous vous debvez retirer de parler à luy." ' (MN p. 159)

3. *Addition and transposition : RAB : 2,2 ; MN : 1,1*

' *Ce sont* coups de canon *que* n'a guieres a repceu vestre fils Gargantua passant devant le Boys de Vede ... '
(RAB p. 141)

(iii) DETAILS OF THE INVERSIONS

(a) *Immobile* ' *invertissant* '

The four texts chosen in this period provide examples of every type of immobile *invertissant* construction, although there are only single instances of inversion in concessive, result and causal clauses, and few with zero *invertissant* or after a temporal conjunction. The outstanding feature of this category is the frequency of inversion after the co-ordinating conjunctions *et*, *si*, *or* and, occasionally, *mais*. Examples of the latter occur in Rabelais (1) and Helisenne de Crenne (2), e.g.

> ' " Mais me procedent à l'occasion des innumerables desirs et amoureux aguilbriemens, dont je suis oppressée, et... " ' (HC I, 48v)

while the remainder account for a fairly high proportion of the inversions in each text.

There has been some discussion in recent years as to whether these conjunctions may not be adverbial *invertissants*, a view supported by Foulet,[6] but rejected by Wagner and Baulier[7] and Bergh.[8] The latter dismisses Foulet's suggestion that

> ' *et* peut, sous l'influence de *si*, forcer son sens usuel jusqu'à prendre une valeur adverbiale et déterminer ainsi l'inversion ' (p. 310)

while apparently accepting the adverbial value of *si*, and explains inversion after *et* as being primarily stylistic and dependent on the nature of the verb. In the article by Wagner and Baulier, examples of inversion in *Pantagruel* and *Gargantua* are examined with regard to the subject pronoun, and the construction is explained as a development of the common omission of the pronoun and consequent emphasis of the verb. Despite Baulier's assertion that in certain texts non-occurrence of a pronoun subject is *de règle* after *et*, the analysis of the

---

[6] L. Foulet, *Petit syntaxe de l'ancien français*, pp. 307 ff.

[7] R. Wagner and F. Baulier, ' Contribution à l'étude de l'inversion du sujet après la conjonction *et* ', *Le Français Moderne*, xxiv (1956), pp. 249–57.

[8] L. Bergh, ' Quelques réflexions sur l'inversion après la conjonction *et* en ancien et en moyen français ', in *Mélanges ... Michaëlsson*, Göteborg, 1952, pp. 43–55.

Rabelais texts above reveals that seven of the twenty-nine examples with *et* do in fact have such an inverted subject. It thus seems much more likely that the function of inversion is not one of emphasis after an adverbial, but of co-ordination, reinforcing a conjunction.

All but three of the inversions after a co-ordinating conjunction have the *invertissant et* in Rabelais, and seven out of the twenty-nine occur at the beginning of the sentence. In des Essarts this is the most frequent inversion construction, the fifty-seven examples constituting $8 \cdot 7\%$ of the total inversions, and only five of them occurring initially. In the other two works however, *et* is found much less frequently as an *invertissant* than *si*, with only twenty examples in the *Heptaméron*, of which nine begin the sentence. As indicated by Antoine,[9] a co-ordinating *invertissant* in this position may be seen as comparable to an adverbial construction, but not necessarily constituting one, since in these examples there is no clear semantic link between *invertissant* and verb, e.g.

'Et fut mandée la contesse d'Arande, pour aller à Sarragosae, où le Roy estoit arrivé'. (MN p. 69)

and in any case these examples represent only a small proportion of the total, twenty-five out of the 129 in all four texts.

As regards the *invertissant or*, on the other hand, the examples in the texts analysed, one in Rabelais, forty-two in des Esserts and six in Marguerite de Navarre, all occur in initial position. This construction, according to Antoine,[10] persisted despite the change from a temporal to a logical meaning in the 15th century. There is little doubt as to its co-ordinating function in the texts analysed, as for instance in the locution, 'Or est-il ainsy que' (ESS p. 209), where the conjunction is clearly not equivalent to an adverb such as *ainsi*.

The particle *si* which occurs frequently with inversion in the 16th-century texts, differs from the other co-ordinators in that it mostly links a main clause and a preceding subordinate

---

[9] *La Coordination en français*, pp. 600–33.
[10] *Ibid.*

clause, rather than two similar clauses. In the course of the century its occurrence becomes increasingly limited to the locution *si est-ce que,* possibly indicative of a weakening of the rhythmic and co-ordinating functions of the particle alone, and this in turn tends to be replaced by the adverbial *invertissant encore* in the late 16th and 17th centuries. The subordinate clause which precedes is generally either concessive or temporal, e.g.

> ' Combien que les raisons persuasives du prince fussent merveilleusement penetrantes, si n'eurent elles puissance de faire aucunement varier mon cueur '. (HC II, 128r)

In other, less frequent, examples the particle may introduce a main clause in sentence initial position, and thus have the same function as *et* with inversion :

> ' Si fut mandé le conte de Merlieu, lequel...' (HC II, 76r)

Elsewhere it may itself be preceded by a co-ordinating conjunction *mais* or *et,* and thus have a reinforcing function, e.g.

> ' " Vrayement ... je confesse que le compte est trop plaisant et la finesse grande ; mais si n'est-ce pas une exemple que les filles doyvent ensuivre ".' (MN p. 42)

Si does not appear to assume any adverbial value in these positions, and is perhaps comparable to the modern French ' toujours est-il que ' as an emphatic liaison construction.

Some of the immobile *invertissants* employed in these texts are unusual, although the constructions themselves are regular, for instance the relative conjunction *quel* quoted p. 31 (above). In Rabelais there are twelve examples of the archaic *dont* for *d'où,* and this is also found in Helisenne de Crenne and Marguerite de Navarre. Despite the relative freedom in word-order in this period, inversion in constructions such as temporal, hypothetical, causal and purpose clauses are surprisingly rare. The most common hypothetical clause *invertissant* is *si,* but the following also occurs in *Gargantua* :

> ' ... feut decreté que ja ne seroient là les femmes *au cas que* n'y fussent les hommes, ny les hommes *en cas que* n'y fussent les femmes.' (p. 190)

There are two zero *invertissant* constructions in Rabelais, in addition to the example from the *Heptaméron* quoted p. 31 (above), one of which has the verb *rester* and opens a chapter, and the other is with *s'esveiller*, at the beginning of a paragraph. All six examples of inversion in a substantival clause occur in Rabelais and follow common verbs of perception, such as *regretter*, *dire* and *penser*.

(b) Mobile 'invertissant'

The variety of mobile *invertissant* constructions found in these four texts is notable since archaic structures, such as inversion after an infinitival, participial phrase and negative particle are included. These less usual constructions occur especially in the *Amadis*, and are in keeping with the archaizing style of the *roman d'aventures*.

As regards the other inversions, the outstanding feature is the wide range of *invertissants* found for each construction. Even attributives reflect this variety, with the following example showing the attributive use of the negative *rien* :

' Et en verité puis bien dire que rien ne furent les victoyres obtenues par Hannibal en Ausonye, au respect de ceste icy.'
(HC II, 119r)

Except for the *Heptaméron*, the texts provide many cases of inversion after unusual adverbs, some now obsolete. The following, for instance, are found in *Amadis* : *quantesfois*, *assez à temps*, *cherement*, *entandis* and *grandement*, while in Helisenne de Crenne there are the modal adverb *invertissants pareillement*, *au contraire* and *merveilleusement*, the adverbs of quantity *non moins*, *gueres moins* and *plus oultre*, and temporal adverbs such as *perpetuellement*, *journellement* and *presentement*. Adverbial phrase *invertissants* on the other hand are much less common, and of these certain phrases tend to recur, such as the twelve examples of *à ceste parole* followed by inversion and six of *sur ces entrefaictes* in *Amadis*.

Participial phrase *invertissants* are found in all four texts, present and past tense constructions occurring with approximately equal frequency. The subordinate clause *invertissants* in all texts but Rabelais are almost exclusively temporal clauses, the rare exceptions being causal clauses, while Rabelais, by contrast, inverts after comparative, hypothetical and indirect clauses. With the exception of des Essarts the negative particle *invertissants* are restricted to *jamais, point* and *guère.*

Finally, the infrequency of inversion as a result of other syntactic operations may be noted, in particular that of addition and transposition, a device which becomes more common after the disappearance of direct object *invertissants.* As may be seen above, the order OVS is still fairly common in this period, the object taking various forms, including demonstrative pronouns.

2. STYLISTIC ANALYSIS OF THE TEXTS
1500–1550

(i) F. RABELAIS, 'PANTAGRUEL ET GARGANTUA'

The frequency of inversion in Rabelais, 2.98, is the second highest of the four works analysed, and the text contains inversions of every type except in a concessive clause. There are more *invertissants* than in any other text, 160, representing well over half the total of different *invertissants* yielded by the four texts (table 2.08), with consequently the lowest ratio of inversions to *invertissants.* As in the other texts, the disparity between the number of inversions in main and subordinate clauses is reduced when they are reclassified according to the type of *invertissant*, which results in an exactly equal distribution in Rabelais (table 1.02). Table 2.07 shows that only 38% of the examples occur in sentences longer than two clauses, and of these the largest proportion are found in four-clause sentences. Similarly table 2.06 reveals fewer inverted subjects with a dependent clause in Rabelais than in the other texts, although the proportion of examples where there is more than one subject, 9%, is above average.

The most common types of *invertissant* in this text are relatives and comparatives, with 8% of all the examples occurring with forms of *lequel*, and slightly fewer with the comparative *comme*. Unusual *invertissants* include the attributive *quel* for *tel*,

'quel fut Silene, maistre du bon Bacchus' (GAR p. 5)

and a variety of modal adverbs, many of which express some idea of ease or difficulty, for instance *aisement, volontiers, à difficulté* and others having an association of truth value, e.g. *voire, visiblement*. Among various archaic constructions in Rabelais may be noted the inversions after a preposition and the pronoun *iceluy*, used perhaps to give an illusion of antiquity :

'D'iceulx sont descendues les couilles de Lorraine...' (PAN p. 223)

'Et d'iceulx est perdue la race...' (PAN p. 223)

and also the occasional examples of the order VOS :

'Ainsi passa la nuict Panurge à chopiner avecques les paiges...' (PAN p. 317)

The constructions involving other inversion operations are unexceptional, apart from one unusual use of the imperfect subjunctive, normally confined to the verb *être* in such contexts :

'"... et alissiez-vous à tous les diables..."' (PAN p. 270)

The frequency and variety of inversion in Rabelais suggest both the continuing tradition of a comparatively free word-order, and the influence of Classical idioms. According to Huguet, 'la principale originalité de la syntaxe de Rabelais consiste ... dans la hardiesse et la haute fantaisie des inversions',[11] but this originality might be said to lie more specifically in the expressive use of word-order and the concern for harmony and variation. The examples below indicate the various effects achieved by inversion, in particular in the speech of the characters, often involving an extended use of certain rhetorical devices, and the place of inverted order in constructions characteristic of the author.

(a) *Inversion in the speech of Rabelais' characters*

Many of the examples of inversion which are found in direct speech in *Pantagruel* and *Gargantua* illustrate the rhetorical

[11] E. Huguet, *Étude sur la syntaxe de Rabelais, comparée à celle des autres prosateurs de 1450 à 1550*, Paris, 1894, p. 422.

nature of much of the dialogue. Devices of rhetoric are used for
satirical purposes, for emphasis, often somewhat incongruously,
and to characterize the *grand style* of lengthy speeches and
harangues. Inversion thus contributes not only to the linguistic
variety of the text as a whole, but also to the difference in
styles used by the characters in certain situations.

Chiastic and repetitive structures with word-order have clear
differences in their application. The example below opens a
paragraph in the harangue of Gallet to Picrochole (*Gargantua*
ch. XXI) with a series of hypothetical clauses :

> ' " Si quelque tort eust esté par nous faict en tes subjectz et
> dommaines, si par nous eust esté porté faveur à tes mal
> vouluz, si en tes affaires... " ' (GAR p. 120)

Here the inverted order of the second clause serves to relieve the
monotony, and emphasizes the repeated *par nous*, reversing the
original order of the three main elements. By contrast the following chiasmus in the speech of a minor character in *Pantagruel*
reveals a striking incongruity between style and content :

> ' " Je croy ... que les Gothz parloient ainsi, et, si Dieu
> vouloit, ainsi parlerions nous du cul." ' (PAN p. 268)

Similar variation may be noted in the speech of Panurge according to the circumstances, as exemplified in the following
uses of inversion and repetition :

> ' " Je ay employé, ..., une partie de ce que en met Messere
> Francesco di Nianto ... et ce que escript Zoroaster, ..., mais
> je n'y voy rien... " ' (PAN p. 339)

> ' " Vous avez ... plus de force aux dentz, et plus de sens au
> cul, que n'eut jamais Hercule en tout son corps et ame.
> Autant vault l'homme comme il s'estime." ' (PAN p. 359)

In the first instance Panurge uses inverted order several times
in discussing learned references with Pantagruel, while in the
second a similar device occurs in a much less elevated form of
conversation. Nevertheless the emphatic value of inversion in
this example is quite apparent.

The complexity of several such constructions in direct
speech may also be noted, as in a further example from the
harangue mentioned above :

' " ... en tant que par toy et les tiens ont esté ces griefz et tords faictz, qui de toute memoire et ancienneté aviez, toy et tes peres, une amitié avecques luy et tous ses ancestres conceu... " ' (GAR p. 118)

In addition to the opposition between inverted and direct order in the two clauses, with a concluding past participle in each case, there are five examples of couplets constituting epic repetitions, with the emphatic *invertissant toy et les tiens* restated in the second clause.

Inversion in shorter sentences often occurs finally to form an emphatic rhetorical cadence. The first example below concludes a paragraph, and the second a chapter :

' " Quand est de vostre ranczon, je vous la donne entierement, et veulx que vous soient rendues armes et cheval." ' (GAR p. 171)

' " Bouvez donc un bon coup sans eaue. Car, si ne le croiez, non foys je, fist elle." ' (PAN p. 228)

The following inversion forming a hypothetical clause increases the dramatic value of Pantagruel's speech :

' " Voyez cy de noz ennemis qui accourent, mais je vous les tueray icy comme bestes, et feussent ilz dix foys autant." ' (PAN p. 343)

Constructions with the *invertissant si* may also be employed with emphatic effect, since the particle is generally used in refuting preceding statements. Thus the following concludes a speech by Hastiveau :

' " ... aussi meschanceté est tost cogneue et suspecte, et, posé que d'icelle les ennemys se servent à leur profit, si ont ils tousjours les meschans et traistres en abhomination." ' (GAR p. 176)

Alternatively the inversion may come at the beginning of a speech, to contradict the previous speaker, thus :

' " Voire mais, dist Panurge, si faict il bon avoir quelque visaige de pierre quand on est envahy... " ' (PAN p. 295)

The dialogues in which inversion occurs with notable frequency in the two books are often concerned with scholastic or theological topics. Furthermore certain passages seem to

have a particularly high proportion of inversions, such as
the legal debates in chapters X–XIII of *Pantagruel*, and
the speech of the Limousin student in chapter VI. In
certain theological statements inversion not only has an
emphatic function, but the order is reminiscent of Biblical
style, e.g.

> ' " Ce n'est de maintenant que les gens reduictz à la creance
> Evangelicque sont persecutez ; mais bien heureux est
> celluy qui ne sera scandalizé et qui... ' " (GAR p. 209)

In this example spoken by Gargantua, as in the following by
Grandgousier, the device has further significance, since both
extracts are taken to refer to contemporary humanist preoccupations :

> ' " Entretenez voz familles, travaillez, ..., instruez voz
> enfans, et vivez comme vous enseigne le bon apostre sainct
> Paoul." ' (GAR p. 169)

Pantagruel's prayer is in similar vein :

> ' " Doncques ... comme en toy seul est ma totale confiance
> et espoir, je te fais veu que... " ' (PAN p. 361)

This style is continued by an inversion in the narrative which
immediately follows :

> ' Alors fut ouye une voix du ciel, disant... '

Other examples in which the subject contains some Biblical or
learned reference are frequently found in final position, as in
the following by Panurge which concludes a chapter :

> ' " Et, à ce propos, je vous veux dire ... un bel exemple que
> met *Frater Lubinus, libro De compotationibus mendican-*
> *tium.*" ' (PAN p. 296)

The two contexts mentioned above show the importance of
inversion in the course of satire. The following examples occur
in longer than average sentences and represent a parody of legal
language :

> ' " Car je suis sœur que vous et tous ceulx par les mains
> desquelz a passé le proces y avez machiné ce que avez peu
> *Pro et Contra...* " ' (PAN p. 273)

> ' " Car—combien que tout ce que a dit partie adverse soit de
> dumet bien vray... " ' (PAN p. 280)

' " ... comme bien l'a debastu ledict defendeur, la court le
condemne en troys verrassées de caillebottes assimen-
tées... " ' (PAN pp. 286–87)

The inversions in the speech of the Limousin emphasize the
parody of the latinized speech of students of the time. In the
first instance the subject is strongly stressed, both by inversion
and by the cumbersome preposed adjective, while in the second
the latinized verb also receives emphasis :

' " ... mon genie n'est poinct apte nate à ce que dict ce
flagitiose nebulon pour escornier la cuticule de nostre
vernacule Gallicque mais... " ' (PAN p. 246)

' " L'origine primeves de mes aves et ataves fut indigene des
regions Lemoricques, où requiesce le corpore de l'agiotate
sainct Martial." ' (PAN p. 246)

Finally there are of course instances of inversion which are not
necessarily rhetorical, but which occur in simple constructions
to highlight the effect of certain light-hearted remarks, as for
example in the popular saying which is quoted with its terms
reversed :

' " Si n'estoient messieurs les bestes, nous vivrions comme
clercs." ' (GAR p. 66)

Elsewhere there is an ironic reference to a particularly tortuous
hill-path :

' " ilz s'en vont en paradis, aussy droict comme une faucille
et comme est le chemin de Faye." ' (GAR p. 112)

(b) Sentence structure

Much of the grotesque element in Rabelais' prose, and in
consequence much of his satire, derives from the use of the
devices of accumulation and enumeration, where inverted
word-order is frequently employed either for emphasis, or to
ensure clarity and preserve the balance of the sentence.
Among the examples of inversion in these first two books are
instances of enumeration of inverted noun subjects, the
accumulation of adjectives before or after the subject, the
listing of complements and the repetition of verbs or nouns.
The extent to which these traditional rhetorical structures are

exploited is exemplified in the following accumulation of preposed adjectives:

'... la vine, dont nous vient celle nectarique, delicieuse, precieuse, celeste, joyeuse et deïficque liqueur qu'on nomme le piot.' (PAN p. 222)

The accumulation together with inversion increases anticipation, which is followed by a humorous anti-climax in the dependent clause, the popular *piot*, and this also emphasizes the light-hearted extravagance of Rabelais' style. Preposed adjectives are less frequent than postposed ones in inverted nominal groups, but there are seldom more than two or three following the noun, the enumeration of complements in description being more common, e.g.

' au dedans desquels estoient belles gualeries, longues et amples, aornées de pinctures, de cornes de cerfs, licornes, rhinoceros, hippopotames, dens de elephans et aultres choses spectables. ' (GAR p. 198)

The subject is frequently inverted when it is very long, or itself constitutes an enumeration:

' tant ... que passerent xxxvi moys, troys sepmaines, quatres jours, treze heures et quelque peu dadvantaige, sans pluye... ' (PAN p. 228)

a construction in which unexpected emphasis falls on the adverbial *sans pluye*, delayed by the lengthy subject. In the following the *invertissant* is a preceding subordinate clause:

' Ainsi que je regardoys ... ce beau feu ... sortirent plus de six, voire plus de treze cens et unze chiens, gros et menutz, tous ensemble de la ville, fuyant le feu.' (PAN p. 293)

In this example the emphatic position of the subject underlines the whimsical choice of a precise numeral. Where subjects are enumerated and each is expanded, inversion is essential for clarity:

'... apres lesquelz sortirent neuf dromadaires chargés de jambons, et langues de bœuf fumées, sept chameaulx chargez d'anguillettes puis xxv charretées de porreaulx, d'aulx, d'oignons, et de cibotz: ce qui espovanta bien lesdictes saiges femmes...' (PAN p. 231)

A construction containing enumerated epithets may be emphasized by the repetition of the whole structure, as in the following, where the verbs in each case are also stressed, and the contrast between the two sets of adjectives underlined :

‘ Jamais ne feurent veuz chevaliers tant preux, tant gualans, tant dextres à pied et à cheval ... que là estoient, jamais ne feurent veues dames tant propres, tant mignonnes, moins fascheuses ... que là estoient.’ (GAR p. 204)

Verbs may be stressed in inversion constructions by the familiar classical device of two near synonyms or by the use of contrasting tenses :

‘ Par ce moyen feurent tous rompuz et mis en pieces ceulx qui estoient en icelluy.’ (GAR p. 138)

‘ (le lieu) ... feut Nesle, où lors estoit, maintenant n’est plus l’oracle de Lucece.’ (GAR p. 70)

The inversion in the first instance also permits the expansion of the subject by a relative clause, and in the second example the delayed subject receives increased emphasis. The following also illustrates the rhythm and balance of Rabelais’ sentences :

‘ Un jour le seigneur de Painensac visita son pere en gros train et apparat, auquel jour l’estoient semblablement venuz veoir le duc de Francrepas et le comte de Mouillevent.’ (GAR p. 51)

Here the long verb phrase is augmented by an adverb, but is balanced by the two subjects, with inversion giving equal stress to both verb and subject groups.

The examples of inversion quoted above seem to fulfil two major functions. On the one hand the rhetorical aspect of this form of word-order is preserved and extended, so that it is both characteristic of a certain style of speech, which may then be parodied, and is also a humorous device when the content is incongruous. Then on the other hand, inversion is exploited as an important factor in the use of enumeration and accumulation, both for maintaining clarity and for adding emphasis to certain elements. Although the latter function of inversion will be found in most texts in this study, there are few authors, at least in the earlier periods, who develop the expressive possibilities of inverted order to such an extent as Rabelais.

(ii) HELISENNE DE CRENNE, 'LES ANGOISSES DOULOUREUSES'

As will be seen below, the *Angoisses douloureuses*, composed in 1538, comprise four sections which differ in both syntax and style. The overall analysis of the inversions reveals a frequency of $2 \cdot 49$, which is closest of the four texts to the average of $2 \cdot 64$. Table 2.08 shows that the text contains more different *invertissants* than the *Amadis* despite the much higher frequency in the latter, although sixty-six of the 133 occur only once. The text contains the highest proportion of examples in direct speech, 36% (table 2.03), in addition to the 3% already mentioned which are found in soliloquies. As in Rabelais, inverted order here occurs predominantly in sentences of one or two clauses (table 2.07), although the preceding table indicates the highest proportion of inverted subjects with a dependent clause, 24%, as well as the highest frequency of more than one inverted subject, 11%. The sentence structure however, appears simpler than that of the other three texts in that there are no examples of an additional clause separating *invertissant* and verb or verb and subject, although adverbials are found in this position in 5% of the inversions (table 2.12). Table 2.11 shows that the distribution of direct speech inversions differs by only 5% in the case of mobile and immobile *invertissants* from the total distribution.

As in des Essarts and Marguerite de Navarre, inversion occurs most commonly in Helisenne in co-ordinating constructions, although, as in Rabelais, the proportion of inversions in comparative constructions is also high (table 2.10). Apart from the hypothetical construction already quoted (p. 32 above), there are no other examples of inversion in less usual immobile *invertissant* constructions in this text. There are however an average number of inversions after a direct object, participial phrase, subordinate clause and negative particle. Direct object *invertissants* are most usually nouns preceded by the adjectives *tel* or *ce* (nine examples), and there are three instances where the *invertissant* is *ce* alone, e.g.

' Et ce feit il, affin qu'ilz ne fussent apperceuz...' (IV, 3v)

As before there are occasional examples of the order VOS, e.g.

' Et leur feit un grand support Quezinstra ' (II, 96v)

' Aussi endure tresgriefve peine Yxyon ' (IV, 6r)

In the analysis which follows, the occurrence of inversion is examined in relation to the style of the three different narrators in the novel.

Inversion and the different narrative styles

The composition of the *Angoisses* is unusual in that there are three different narrators relating the story of two lovers. Book I is a first person account of the love affair by Helisenne herself, and is characterized by the narrator's analysis of her own feelings, her laments and soliloquies. Books II and III are narrated by the lover Guenelic (' Dame Helisenne parlant en la personne de son amy '), and tell of his sufferings and adventures. The style undergoes a radical change and resembles that of a *roman d'aventures*, while complicated by frequent Classical allusions. The conclusion, Book IV, is narrated by a third party, the lover's friend and companion on his travels, and describes the death of the couple ' avec decoration du stille poetique '.

The inversion frequency of 2.49 for the whole text varies considerably within the novel according to the different narrators thus :

	Narrator	% of text	Inversions	Frequency
I	Helisenne	36	98	1·36
II	Guenelic	42	264	3·14
III	Guenelic	20	99	2·50
IV	Quezinstra	2	36	(9·00)

This clearly indicates the change in style as well as content in Book II where the frequency of inversion is similar to that of the *Amadis*. The final part is clearly too small a sample for adequate comparison with the preceding sections, but the accumulation of inversions in a few pages may nevertheless serve as an indication of the further change in style. It may also be noted that nineteen inversions in Book I occur in soliloquy, and sixty in Book III are in direct speech.

Book I

In the first section Helisenne traces the development in her own feelings and changes in her personality, introducing the ideas of predestination and the fatality of love. The style in Book I is relatively simple, and reminiscent of the analytic approach of Madame de la Fayette. Few of the inversions occur in sentences of more than four clauses, and the sentences are not generally complex. Besides the inversions in soliloquy, twenty-seven of the ninety-eight occur in conversation. Inverted order in Helisenne's soliloquies tends to add a dramatic quality to the style, as in the attributive structures quoted on p. 32 above, and the same theme is stressed in the following exclamation :

> ' " O que j'eusse esté heureuse si le laict maternel m'eust esté venin, ou que du berceau m'eust esté faict sepulture ! " '
> (I, 100r)

Inversion here effectively opposes *berceau* and *sepulture*, while final position underlines the latter. In the next example the repeated idea of finality reaches an emphatic climax in the inverted subject :

> ' " Et pour finale resolution je ne desire que la mort, en laquelle est reservée ma derniere peine, qui autrement me seroit intollerable." ' (I, 55v)

Initial inversion may also form part of a dramatic opposition :

> ' " Bien peult on doubter, mais point determiner..." ' (I, 94v)

The use of inversion in conversation in this section often reflects the intensity of the feelings of the characters involved. In the following, the *invertissant presentement* increases the note of foreboding underlying the speech of Helisenne's husband :

> ' " O meschante femme, presentement est venue l'heure que tu ne pourrois aucunement nyer ta lubricité et non moderée affection." ' (I, 34v)

Another stressed *invertissant* later in the section suggests the disdainful note in the speech of the lover who has heard false reports of her :

> ' " Ma dame, diserte et accommodée est vostre narration, et de telle efficace, que je me persuade de la croire." ' (I, 81r)

An example in which Helisenne declares her feelings is heavily
dramatic by virtue of the three subjects and preposed adjectives, with the emphasis on the final element :

> ' " car en vostre vouloir consiste toute ma presente et future
> beatitude et felicité, ou ma perpetuelle calamité." '   (I, 72r)

The majority of the remaining inversions in the narrative are
immobile *invertissant* constructions. In Helisenne's description
of her emotions, inverted order frequently emphasizes the
change in state as in these examples with the verbs *croître* and
entrer :

> '... et croissoit l'amour si puissant en mon cœur, que le
> reciter seroit incredible à ceulx qui n'ont experimenté
> amours.' (I, 29v)
> '... je commencay à trembler, et entra une si extreme
> froideur dedans mes os, que ... la parolle me fut for (*sic*)
> close...' (I, 47v)

Where the inverted subject is in final position the new state is
strongly stressed :

> ' A la prononciation de mes parolles, je deveins palle, et me
> print un tremblement de tous mes membres.' (I, 28v)

Eleven of the inversions in this section occur in comparative
structures and nearly all of them relate to the author's feelings.
The Classical allusions are simpler and more discrete than in
the later books, and contribute to the somewhat poetic style,
e.g.

> '... tout subit defaillit la vigueur de mon cœur, et ... enclinay
> mon chef en terre, comme faict une violette sa couleur
> purpurine, quand elle est abbatue du fort vent Boreas.'
> (I, 17r)
> '... et la tremeur et crainte non autrement mon cœur
> esmeurent, que faict Zephire, quand dedans les ondes
> aspire : ' (I, 98r)

Although the inversions here are unexceptional with an unstressed verb, it emphasizes in the first example an unusual
metonymic relation between subject and object.   Other
comparatives may stress an element in Helisenne's general
observations :

' ... et feis fermer les fenestres, ne desirant que d'estre
solitaire, et en lieux taciturnes, comme font gens contritz
inconsolablement.' (I, 22r)

' ... nostre condition femenine n'est tant scientifique que
naturellement sont les hommes.' (I, 113r)

Books II–III

With the change of narrator in Book II, the main theme is
that of conventional heroic adventures, with the romantic
interest restricted to references to ill-fated lovers of mythology.
In Book III the element of chivalry still predominates, but
with increasing stress on communication with Helisenne by
letter and finally in dialogue. The style in these sections is
similar to that of the 17th-century *grands romans*, with the
story constantly interspersed with learned quotations and
mythological parallels. The Classical similes account for many
of the comparative *invertissant* structures, which represent
approximately 15% of all the examples in Book II, e.g.

' ... m'exposeroye à plus grand peril que ne feit Theseus
d'Athene, en domptant le monstre Minotaurus, ou que ne
feit Jason à la conqueste de la riche toyson.' (II, 11r)

Classical references also occur in a number of other inversion
constructions, particularly when names are enumerated,
inversion here facilitating their expression and emphasis :

' " Atropos ne sçauroit empescher que perpetuellement ne
dure le noble Scipion, le chevalereux Camille, le victorieux
Cesar, le triumphateur Auguste : desquels les noms sont
encore florissans." ' (II, 69v)

In this section there is a marked tendency to use several
subjects or verbs in inversion constructions, as well as a
number of epithets qualifying the inverted subject. Where
there is more than one verb, there is frequently an epic use of
near synonyms :

' ... en moy estoit decretée et affermée ceste mienne irre-
vocable sentence...' (II, 130v)

' ... et ainsi se consomma et passa ce jour.' (II, 78r)

the latter forming a strong conclusion to a chapter. There are

frequent instances of accumulation of inverted subjects, a
feature virtually absent from Book I, e.g.

   ' " l'on obtient facilement pardon de son peché : ce que
   n'empesche le crime ou enormité d'iceluy, ne la briefveté du
   temps qu'on auroit à vivre, ou l'extremité de l'heure, ou la
   dissolution de la vie...' " (III, 50r)

Elsewhere more than one verb may be paralleled by more than
one subject :

   ' " car presentement à juste cause se doibt blasmer et
   detester nostre rude conception et debile sçavoir...' " (III,
   19r)

Where a subject has several qualifying adjectives these are
generally preposed when the nominal group concludes a
sentence, e.g.

   ' " ... à chascune de vous appartiendroit quelque illustre et
   magnanime Prince.' (II, 74v)

The accumulation of adjectives before or after the noun is
often reminiscent of Rabelais :

   ' Premierement arriva en tressumptueux, tresmagnifique et
   tresriche arroy, Alarians roy de Boetie.' (II, 38r)
   ' ... à ceulx ne s'apparoissent que fantosmes transformez,
   discorrectez et inordonnez...' (II, 37r)

Although most types of inversion are already found in
Book I, many more different *invertissants* occur in the adventure narrative of Book II, in particular adverbs of time, used
to indicate the progression of events, with twenty different
invertissants as opposed to six in Book I. As before the word-
order may reflect the movement expressed in the sentence, e.g.

   ' et lors s'esmeurent furieusement tant d'une part que
   d'autre les chevaliers, et mesmement le Duc de Locres.'
   (II, 44r)

This idea may also be stressed by the repetition of inversions
along with verbs of movement :

   ' Apres venoit en moult noble et pompeuse compaignie
   Silperis Roy d'Athenes ... Apres suyvoit Librius conte de
   Phocides ... Apres venoit innumerable compaignie de
   chevaliers...' (II, 38r–v)

Such adverbial *invertissants* usually begin the sentence and thus contribute to the development of the narrative. On the other hand the example below emphasizes other ideas in a manner bordering on *préciosité* :

' Tousesfoys entre la tierce et quarte vigille, furent les yeulx contrainctz de dormir.' (II, 39v)

The reduced frequency of inversion in Book III is indicative of yet another change in style, since the account of the lovers' eventual reunion contains elements of style already noted in Book I. The soliloquy, for instance, is reintroduced as a means of expressing feelings and analysing emotions, and exclamations are again reinforced by inversion. The first example below is from a monologue by Guenelic, and the second a soliloquy by Helisenne :

' " Par quoy bien heure sera le travail et tresfelice le martyre, qui à telle suavité te conduira." ' (III, 3v)

' " O Guenelic voyla le lieu où est ton supreme contentement : là est ta vray joye que le ciel t'a appareillée ! " ' (III, 27r–v)

Book IV : The ' Ample narration '

In this concluding section, the third narrator Quezinstra, is guided through the Underworld by Mercury to witness the judgement of Helisenne and Guenelic who proceed to the Elysian fields, after which Jupiter orders the publication of the book. The elevated subject matter is treated in a more grandiose style, as indicated to some extent by the number of inversions, thirty-six in only a few pages. In addition it is noted by Sturel that these chapters are characterized by :

' le rejet voulu et systématique du verbe à la fin de la proposition ' [12]

a feature which occurs only sporadically elsewhere in the text. Sturel sees here an example of French Ciceronian prose, reflected in the preoccupation with the choice and order of words.

The apparent predilection for Classical sentence structure is

[12] R. Sturel, ' La prose poëtique au XVIe siècle ', *Mélanges ... offerts à G. Lanson*, Paris, 1922, p. 52.

borne out by examples of a logical sequence of clauses, with inversion preserving the relations between relatives and antecedents where necessary :

> ' là peult on ouyr diversité d'oyseaux, lesquelz chantent en grande armonye et moduleuse resonnance, et les escoutent grande multitude de gens ... qui ... se reposent sur la belle herbe verdoyante.' (IV, 7r–v)

Here the object of the first clause becomes the subject of the second and in turn the object of the third, whose new subject is preserved in the fourth clause. The *rejet* of the verb mentioned above may also be combined with inversion, thus :

> ' disant en moy mesme, que de castigation est digne celuy qui es choses transitoires, sa pensée forme et arreste.' (IV, 9v)

Thus the novel ends in Classical vein, having clearly illustrated three different types of narrative technique. The fluctuation in the frequency of inversion and the different types of constructions used in the three sections underline the change from an analytic style, to that of an adventure narrative and again to an elevated, oratorical form, which echoes that of works of Antiquity. Thus in style as well as content it seems that while Part I anticipates works in centuries to come, Part II reflects the popular form of 16th- and 17th-century France and Part III looks back to Classical tradition.

(iii) H. DES ESSARTS, ' LE PREMIER LIVRE D'AMADIS DE GAULE '

This text is a translation of the Spanish *Amadís de Gaula*, begun by des Essarts in 1540, but the freedom of the translation allows the work to take its place in French literature, to the extent that the style of des Essarts was apparently celebrated for its purity and elegance.[13] As a *roman d'aventures* the work has a strong element of an earlier tradition which the author perhaps seeks to imitate. This is reflected in the high frequency of inversions, 3.25, many of which are accounted for by the repetition of a few constructions such as

---

[13] See H. Coulet, *Le roman jusqu'à la Révolution I*, Paris, 1967, p. 104.

the *invertissants à l'heure, à ceste parole* and temporal adverbs, since, as indicated in table 2.08, the total of *invertissants* is lower than in the two earlier texts which nevertheless had fewer inversions. Among the examples of inversion there are many which parallel constructions in the Spanish, but it is difficult to determine how far these may be attributed to a common narrative style, with the author attempting to reproduce either the style of the original or an earlier French prose form.

Tables 2.02 and 2.03 show that of the four texts analysed, the *Amadis* has the highest proportion of examples with mobile *invertissant* and also the most inversions in the narrative. The proportion of mobile *invertissant* constructions is even higher, 70%, in the examples occurring in direct speech (table 2.11), a tendency also revealed in the *Heptaméron*. The frequency of this construction explains the number of inversions in initial position, 46% (table 2.04), as compared with the very low proportion of final inversions, 15%. Table 2.05 shows that 5% of the examples in this text precede direct speech, while 20% follow it. Most of the *invertissants* in this position are time adverbials, together with some direct objects, and inversion thus seems a characteristic of the return to narrative style. Table 2.07 reveals the occurrence of inversion in longer sentences in the *Amadis* than in the other texts, although it is still rare in sentences of more than five clauses.

While every type of mobile *invertissant* is to be found in the *Amadis*, there are no examples of immobile *invertissants* of hypothetical, result, causal and substantival clauses, of zero *invertissant* or of the addition and transposition operation. The frequency of the *invertissant or* has already been discussed (p. 36 above), and the more outstanding examples in this text are otherwise those with a mobile *invertissant*. There are more examples in this text of inversion after a direct object, participial phrase and negative particle, all reminiscent of an earlier, freer order. In addition there may be noted the frequency of temporal adverbs and adverbial phrases which occur more often than any other adverbial *invertissant* in this text. The examples below show the place of inversion in the narrative style of des Essarts and also various similarities in this respect to the original Spanish.

(a) Inversion and the narrative style

Although the cycle of the *Amadis* evokes an earlier period, there is no reason to suppose, as Huizinga has pointed out, that the ' belated fruits of chivalrous romance ' were anachronistic in their own day.[14] While the form and style of this work exploit the resources of 16th-century French, it is in a fashion different from that of the other writers studied. Whereas in Rabelais, and to a lesser extent in Helisenne de Crenne, it is the expressive and emphatic properties of word-order which are explored, inversion in the *Amadis* is employed for purposes of co-ordination and economy in a style whose outstanding characteristic is its simplicity. Thus the sequence of adventures is not interrupted by inessential detail, unnecessary linkwords and complex sentence structures. Each clause tends to evolve in turn from the one before, e.g.

' Ce qu'il feit, et entra la damoyselle qui luy dit...' (p. 47)
' ... la nuict se passa et s'apparut le jour. Lors Amadis advisa...' (p. 232)
and co-ordination is achieved by means of relatives, repetition, participial constructions and inversion of the subject.

In the use of inversion to co-ordinate events in the narrative, the *invertissant* usually refers to a previous incident, thus :

' Ainsi fut conduict Gandalin chez la Royne, où estoit la princesse Oriane, à laquelle vint la demoyselle...' (p. 166)
In this example the action continues with further inversions linking relatives to antecedents. The frequency of inversion after a great variety of adverbs in this text results in many structures with a co-ordinating function in which the adverbial *invertissant* qualifies the consequences of preceding events :

' Tresvolontiers accepterent ceste guarde le Roy Languines et la Royne.' (p. 43)

---

[14] J. Huizinga, *The Waning of the Middle Ages*, 1924, trans. Hopman, Penguin Books, 1968, p. 77.

' Trop fut esbahy le Damoysel de telle meschanceté, et...'
(p. 55)

The same is true of attributive adjective *invertissants* which are also more diverse than in the modern period. In addition to many examples with *tel* qualifying the subject, e.g.

' Telz furent les propos du bon Roy Lisuart.' (p. 164)

there are various adjectives which relate to the direct object thus :

' Tresagreables eut le Roy Languines ces offres, et...' (p. 84)

' Tresadvisée et prudente l'estima lors Amadis, lequel...' (p. 268)

In both these examples the object refers back to the preceding sentences and the attributive *invertissants* thus constitute an effective co-ordinator.

A further form of co-ordination is that in which inversion is coupled with repetition, as for instance in this conversation :

' " Seigneur, nous ne sçavons si ceste bataille a esté com-. mencée *à tort ou à droict.*" " *A droict* ne pourroit elle estre, respondit le Damoysel, si..." ' (p. 57)

The repetition may be literal, as above, or simply a reiteration of ideas, or both :

' " ... car si vous avez ceste vertu, vous estes le plus accomply, et *le plus heureux* chevalier du monde." *De grand joye* le rembrassa Amadis et luy demanda qu'il avoit fait, *veu, et ouy.* " J'ay, dit Gandalin, *veu et ouy* les felicitez de paradis, et..." ' (p. 171)

In linking conversational remarks as in the first example, the key element may undergo a change of grammatical function, e.g.

' " Est-il possible ... que cette *meschante* ... vous ayt tant laissé vivre ? " " *Meschante* n'est elle pas, respondit Gandales, mais..." ' (p. 31)

Here the repeated adjective is transformed from substantival into attributive in its *invertissant* form.

Inversions after direct speech frequently have an *invertissant* relating to what has preceded, which may be a direct object,

' Ceste parole disoit elle de telle affection que...' (p. 11)

or a participial phrase :

c

'Ces choses dites et accordées, s'en partit Galaor...' (p. 134) and such examples account for the high proportion of inversions in this position (cf. table 2.05). The construction with the direct object *invertissant ce* has a certain emphatic value as well as a co-ordinating function :

'" Si Dieu m'ayde, respondit il, ce ne feray je pas." ' (p. 121) which constitutes a stronger denial than, for instance, the use of a pronoun and direct order.

Finally there are examples of inversion in non-finite clauses, which, although not included in the statistical analysis, have a parallel function :

'De ceste parole se trouvant estonné le Damoysel luy respondit...' 'Estant le roy Perion en chemin...' (p. 21) the latter example ensuring continuity at the start of a new chapter.

In the course of the narrative there are occasional interventions by the author, either to present his own comments, or to advance the action through references to the author of the Spanish *Amadís*. Inversions are found in both contexts with a co-ordinating function, the most common *invertissant* being *or*, e.g.

'Or avons nous longuement continué le propos d'Amadis ; maintenant nous retournons à Galaor...' (p. 256)

'Or se taist l'Aucteur pour le present d'Amadis, voulant ... reprendre le propos de Galaor, lequel...' (p. 185)

In the first instance the sentence containing the inversion concludes a chapter, whereas in the second the *invertissant* opens a paragraph. Occasionally the author's comments are marked by a change to a more discursive style, with longer, more complex sentences. At the end of one such passage, the return to the action narrative is prefaced by an inversion :

'Non sans cause ay je faict ce petit discours, c'est affin que...' (p. 13)

This construction not only links two themes, but indicates the resumption of the concise style of the main narrative.

(b) *Spanish and Classical influences on word-order*

Imitation of Latin syntax was as much a part of 15th-century

Spanish as of 16th-century French, and it is not easy to separate the two undercurrents in des Essarts' translation. Among
the features of word-order imitated in both languages is the
use of inversion in non-finite constructions, which, as noted
above, has a marked co-ordinating function.

A comparison between des Essarts and the first part of the
Spanish text [15] reveals firstly that inversion is generally
retained where the two texts have parallel syntactic structures,
and secondly that inversion may be preserved in French but
with a completely different *invertissant*. An inversion is
sometimes inserted in French where it does not occur in
Spanish, but a Spanish one is rarely omitted. An important
feature of the French text is the separation of an adverb of
quantity from the noun or adjective it modifies, an expressive
usage in medieval Spanish,[16] thus:

' *Mucho* fueron *alegres* estos dos reyes... '

' *Grandement* furent ces deux Roys *esjouis* pour...' (p. 3)

As in the modern languages, Middle French seems to make less
use of the participial constructions, in spite of their popularity
at the time:

' *Esto hecho*, recogida toda la compaña hizo en dos palafrenes '

' Et *sur ces entrefaictes* se rassembla la compagnie ' (p. 4)

The French sentences tend to be shorter and clearer, thus
' Parquoy se leva Elisene ' replaces the co-ordinated '... y
levantándose Elisena '. Des Essarts' tendency to replace
Spanish pronouns by French nouns may also be attributed to
the desire for clarity, as in the substitution of ' et disoit le roy '
for ' y él decía '.

An example of a direct equivalent, where the inverted
subject is retained in its strong position in the following:

'... porque en aquello consistía todo el fin de sus deseos '

'... car en cela seul consistoit le comble de ses affections ' (p. 3)

---

[15] *Amadís de Gaula* in *Libros de Caballerias españoles*, ed. Buendia, Madrid,
1954.
[16] See R. Lapesa, *Historia de la lengua española*, 7th ed. Madrid, 1968,
chs. 8–10.

A change of construction which retains the inversion is exemplified in the following :

'En buena hora nació el caballero que...'

' " Que heureux est le prince, par lequel..." ' (p. 11)

Thus inversion in the *Amadis*, whether or not it results from an imitation of the Spanish text, is one of the most important stylistic characteristics. Inverted order is used to achieve a simple narrative style, with a clear relation between elements in the sentence or paragraph. In addition there is generally a close semantic link between *invertissant* and verb ; for instance the verbs following the adverb *trop* are nearly all expressions of some form of excess, e.g. *esbahir, esmerveiller, augmenter, ennuyer, desplaire,* while twenty-one of the twenty-seven examples with the relative *où* have verbs of being or staying : *estre, se trouver, gesir, demeurer, attendre* and *sejourner*. The expressive value of inversion is not therefore exploited in this text, beyond suggesting a certain period in time, but its functional value as a means of co-ordination is of the first importance.

(iv) MARGUERITE DE NAVARRE, 'L'HEPTAMÉRON'

The frequency of inversion in the *Heptaméron*, 1.62, is the lowest of the four texts analysed, as is the number of *invertissants*, eighty-eight (table 2.08). This indicates the trend to be followed by works studied in the second half of the century, which, with the exception of du Fail, all have a form similar to that adopted by Marguerite. The proportion of inversions in key positions is almost the same as in the *Amadis* (table 2.04), and in the *Heptaméron* inversion also tends to occur in longer sentences (table 2.07). Table 2.06 shows a higher proportion of inversions having a pronoun subject than hitherto, although there are as yet no examples of compound inversion. The sentence structure appears less complex in that there are fewer examples with several inverted subjects or with a dependent clause.

An outstanding feature of this work is the frequency of the *invertissant si* in various forms, accounting for seventy-three of the inversions after a co-ordinating conjunction, the remainder having *et* (20) or *or* (6). It is also seen from table 2.09 that there is a high frequency of relative and modal adverb *invertissants*, and the five constructions listed account for 62% of all the inversions. On the other hand the verbs *être, faire* and *avoir* are found less often than in the other texts, in 21% of the examples in all (table 2.10), although a category of verbs expressing movement, the actions of coming and going, would account for a further 12% of the examples. Table 2.11 shows an increased proportion of inversions with a mobile *invertissant* in direct speech, similar to that in the *Amadis*.

Apart from a single inversion in a hypothetical clause, the immobile *invertissant* constructions are unremarkable. There is an isolated use of *quel* as a relative pronoun *invertissant* (quoted p. 31 above), which already in Old French occurred more frequently as an interrogative.[17] A feature common to this text and the *Amadis* is the small number of inversions in comparative constructions, seven and ten respectively, as against seventy-two in Rabelais and fifty-seven in Helisenne de Crenne.

The adverbial *invertissants* in this text are generally common ones, except perhaps for the temporal adverbs *depuis, incontinent, souvent, maintenant* and *de nouveau*. There are also examples of the *invertissant encore* following a subordinate clause, with a function comparable to that of *si*, e.g.

' Il luy respondit ... que, s'il n'eust crainct le jour, encores y fut-il demouré.' (p. 45)

Finally, despite the reduced number of inversions used by Marguerite, it may be noted that there is still a relatively high occurrence of participial phrase and subordinate clause *invertissants*, although both types disappear around the end of the century.

The literary structure of the *Heptaméron* is such that the narration of the framework situation may be considered on a separate level from the ' nouvelles '. Inversion is examined

---

[17] See Foulet, *Petite syntaxe*, p. 187.

below both as it occurs in direct speech, in discussions between the framework characters, and also in narrative in the constructions found in the stories related.

(a) Inversion and discussions in the ' Heptaméron '

Conversations in the *Heptaméron* are marked by simpler constructions than those in the narrative, and the structure of the inversions which occur in discussion between the storytellers is in turn less complex than in conversation within the ' nouvelles '. *Invertissants* in discussion are restricted mainly to relatives, comparatives and modal adverbs, and in particular *si* in the context of argument. Those in narrative conversations are more literary, and include *or, ainsi, au moins* and *tant*, adverbials of place and manner, infinitivals and inversions resulting from deletion and transposition operations. The form of the framework discussions are however important both for style and characterization, as noted by Jourda :

> ' Les conversations ... sont, à la fois, un document de toute première importance, et de curieux essais de style.' [18]

Examples of inversion are useful in distinguishing different types of dialogue, which is at times spontaneous and fast-moving, and at others heavy and forced, and consequently the differences in character portrayal.

The characters whose contributions to the discussion are predominantly serious, and who are noted for their *bon sens*, are also those whose language contains fairly frequent inversions and is sometimes stilted. This is particularly noticeable when the topic is religion, and the tone is more elevated, aided by Biblical references and quotations. Typical of this is the speech of Dame Oisille, the ' doyenne ' of the group, who in the introductory prologue talks of

> ' " la lecture des sainctes lettres en laquelle se trouve la vraie et parfaicte joie de l'esprit, dont procede le repos et la santé du corps." ' (p. 7)

Here the inversions with complex subjects underline the

---

[18] P. Jourda, *Marguerite d'Angoulême II*, Paris, 1930, p. 981.

seriousness of the tone and content. Later in commenting on her own ' nouvelle ' Oisille quotes the following:

> ' " Ne nous resjouissons de nos vertuz, mais en ce que nous sommes escriptz au livre de Vie, duquel ne nous peult effacer Mort, Enfert ne Peché." ' (p. 21)

This inversion, with its three stressed subjects, is certainly reminiscent of Biblical style, but since such a quotation does not exist, the style must be the character's own. The remaining inversions found in Oisille's speech all contain initial adverbial *invertissants*, when she answers arguments with characteristic *bon sens*, e.g.

> ' " Et encores ... fut bien tenu ce gentilhomme à la dame, par le moyen de laquelle il retourna entierement son cueur à Dieu." ' (p. 201)

The character of Parlamente is thought to be Marguerite's portrayal of herself, and although she too is conscious of the role of religion, it is at a much more practical level. Her speech does not aspire to direct quotation, but centres rather on her own interpretation of Biblical doctrine ; her sentences are shorter and less complex and the inversions routine :

> ' " Encores ay-je une opinion ... que jamais homme n'aymera parfaictement Dieu, qu'il n'ait parfaictement aymé quelque creature en ce monde." ' (p. 151)

It is Parlamente's idea that the company should tell stories to pass the time, and in the prologue she explains how this happens in Boccaccio. Her language here is more literary, reflecting the literary subject, and the sentences are long and more akin to the style of the narrative than of the dialogues :

> ' " Et prosmirent les dictes dames et monseigneur le Dauphin avecq d'en faire chascun dix et d'assembler jusques à dix personnes qu'ils pensoient plus dignes de racompter quelque chose, sauf ceulx qui..." ' (p. 9)

The use of the *invertissant et*, more frequent in the narrative, may also be noted.

Of the male characters, Geburon is most similar to these two women in outlook and style of discourse. Thus his conversation includes both theological interpretations and parallels between the stories told and Biblical situations, with quotations where appropriate :

> ' " En cela est verifié le dire de Nostre Seigneur : Qui se exaltera sera humilié, et qui se humiliera sera exalté." '
> (p. 185)

Here the inversion, itself Biblical in tone, is in keeping with the quotation which follows. At the end of a story told by him, Geburon includes the quotation : ' Par leurs fruictz congnoissez vous quels arbres sont ' (p. 36). It is interesting that Marguerite has here followed the Latin order of ideas of the two sources,[19] with the complement preceding the verb, without however using a *rejet* construction.

Longarine is an intermediate character in that she is gay in outlook but eminently sensible in discussion, and her speech contains more inversions in conversation than any of the others. Her sentences, besides being generally short and to the point, are often more rhythmic and balanced than most, e.g.

> ' " Je n'ay gueres veu grand feu de quoy ne vint quelque fumée ; mais j'ay bien veu la fumée où il n'y avoit poinct de feu." ' (p. 42)

This also applies when her remarks are more literary in tone, as when she prefaces a story she is about to tell with a short summary about the prince ' Amour ', in which inversions accumulate :

> ' " Et en telles mutations prent plaisir l'amoureuse divinité. Et pource que les princes n'en sont exemptz, aussy ne sont-ilz de necessité. Or, s'ilz ne sont quictes de la necessité en quoy les mect le desir de la servitude d'amour, et..." ' (pp. 202–3)

Certain dialogues are outstanding for their liveliness ; the use of inversion in short sharp sentences is exemplified in the following exchanges between Geburon and the rather more melancholy Dagoucin, whose contrasting ideas are expressed in a more complex sentence structure :

---

[19] Matt. 12, 33 : ' si quidem ex fructu arbor cognescitur ' (' Car c'est au fruit qu'on reconnaît l'arbre ').

Luke 6, 44 : ' unaquaque enim arbor ex fructu suo cognoscitur ' (' Car tout arbre se connaît à son fruit ').

' " Car, tant plus je tiens ce feu celé et couvert, et *plus* en moy croist le plaisir de sçavoir que j'ayme parfaictement." — " Ha, par ma foy, dist Geburon, *si* ne croy-je pas que vous me fussiez bien aise d'estre aymé." — " Je ne dis pas le contraire, dist Dagoucin, mais, quant je seroys tant aymé que j'ayme, *si* n'en sçauroit croistre mon amour..." ' (p. 48) Thus the inversions in conversation not only give some indication as to the character of the speaker, but reveal a concern on the part of the author for the suitability of form and content, with literary and theological discussions reflected in more elevated language.

(b) Sentence structure in the ' nouvelles '

Various critics have suggested that the style of the *Heptaméron* is at times both heavy and monotonous,[20] and the structure of many sentences containing inversion tends to justify this observation. Although it has been shown in the syntactic analysis that there are few instances of complex inverted subjects, the examples may be complicated in other ways, such as the insertion of clauses and adverbials among the main elements, and in particular the accumulation of *invertissants*.

The criticism of heaviness thus applies especially to the structure of the *invertissant*. This may be unusually long and cumbersome, particularly if it is a participial phrase or a subordinate clause :

' Sur le poinct qu'elle estoit presque toute gaingnée de le recepvoir, non à serviteur, mais à seur et parfaict amy, arriva une malheureuse fortune ; car...' (p. 71)

In the next example a subordinate clause *invertissant* is coupled with a non-finite construction, and the sentence structure is further complicated by the clauses dependent on the inverted subject :

' Et, si tost qu'elle fut levée et ensevelye, le corps mis à sa porte, actendant la compaignie pour son enterrement, arriva

---

[20] cf. Jourda : ' La monotonie du style, la lourdeur de la narration empêchent l'Heptaméron d'occuper dans l'histoire de la nouvelle française la place qu'il mérite à tant d'autres égards ', *ibid.*, p. 1003.

son pauvre mary, qui veid premier le corps de sa femme mort
devant sa maison, qu'il n'en avoit sceu les nouvelles ; '
(pp. 20–21)

Certain mobile *invertissants* such as time and place adverbials
may be elaborated by a dependent clause preceding the verb :

' Or, ung soir, apres soupper, qu'il faisoit obscur, se desroba
la dicte dame, sans appeller nulle compaignye, et entra...'
(p. 119)

In the following, a similar structure is replaced by the simple
adverb *là* in the interests of clarity :

' En ceste chambre, qui estoit sur la salle du Roy, là estoient
logées toutes les demoiselles de bonne maison...' (p. 163)

Elsewhere an independent clause or adverbial may separate
invertissant and verb, e.g.

' ... et ... entra dedans la garderobbe où, apres que le mary
fut endormy, se trouva la belle dame qui...' (p. 205)

'... et ainsy, avecq un visaige joyeulx, les œilz eslevez au ciel,
rendit ce chaste corps son âme à son Createur.' (p. 20)

A structure which is characteristic of the narrative passages
in the *Heptaméron* is the correlative construction with an
immobilized *invertissant*, e.g.

'... et, autant qu'il avoit eu le desir et d'asseurance d'estre
bien venu, autant estoit-il desesperé de s'en retourner en si
mauvais estat.' (p. 30)

An isolated example of this structure with *plus* in the framework discussions has already been quoted (p. 65 above), but
this is exceptional, although it is found quite frequently in the
more stilted speech of the characters in the ' nouvelles ', e.g.

' " Mais, ainsy comme la bische navrée à mort cuyde en
changeant de lieu, changer le mal qu'elle port avecq soy,
ainsi m'en allois-je d'eglise en eglise, cuydant fuyr celluy
que..." ' (p. 132)

In addition to the length and complex word-order of this
sentence, which contains a further inversion in a later clause,
there is also some heaviness in the repetition of *ainsi* and
cuidier. Lexical repetitions are found in other inversion
structures, e.g.

' Et, à ceste mutation de vivre, se feyt une mutation de
cueur...' (p. 176)

Here the opposition between *invertissant* and subject has some
expressive value, although this is less evident in the longer
less concise sentence below :

'... car, puisqu'elle ne povoit couvrir sa honte, couvroit-celle
ses œilz, pour ne veoir celluy qui la voyoit trop clairement...'
(p. 154)

Similarly the variation in the order of subject and verb in the
following does not wholly offset the monotony of the same
preposed adjective :

'... et en ceste longue frequentation, s'engendra une tres
grande et longue amitié.' (p. 159)

Thus the examples of inversion in the ' nouvelles ' of the
Heptaméron do reveal a tendency towards complexity and at
times heaviness, which is not always clarified by a change in
word-order.   In consequence the contrast between these
narratives and the discussions of the story-tellers is perhaps
more marked. This contrast depends in part on the type and
frequency of the inversions used by the characters, with the
style of some being closer than others to that of the narrative.

Chapter III

THE SIXTEENTH CENTURY (2)

1. SYNTACTIC ANALYSIS OF THE TEXTS
1550–1600

The texts :

J. Yver, *Le printemps d'Iver* [1]
B. Poissenot, *L'Esté* [2]
N. de Montreux, *Le premier livre des bergeries de Juliette* [3]
N. du Fail, *Les contes et discours d'Eutrapel* [4]

Table 3.01 : Inversion frequencies

JY/PRI	334 : 1·67	
BP/ES	191 : 1·53	*(mean* 1·50)
NM/BER	171 : 0·86	
NF/CD	383 : 1·92	

Table 3.02 : Percentage table to show nature of clause in which inversion occurs

	JY	*BP*	*NM*	*NF*
Main clause	38	44	34	48
Subordinate clause	58	52	58	50
Non-subordinating *invertissant* in subordinate clause	4	4	8	2
	100	100	100	100
Immobile *invertissant*	73	77	59	64
Mobile *invertissant*	27	21	39	32
Other operations	—	2	2	4
N :	334	191	171	383

[1] Tierce edition, Paris (Jean Ruelle), 1572. British Museum 12511 a 16. (JY)
[2] Paris (Claude Micard), 1583. B.N. Rés. Y² 2017. (BP)
[3] Paris (Gilles Beys), 1585. (NM)
[4] In *Propos rustiques, Baliverneries, Contes et discours d'Eutrapel*, éd. J. Marie Guichard, Paris (C. Gosselin), 1842. B.N. Y² 29486. (NF)

Table 3.03 : Percentage table to show distribution of inversions according to discourse type

	JY	BP	NM	NF
Narrative	65	73	65	58
Direct speech	33	23	35	39
Indirect speech	2	4	n	3
Free indirect speech	—	n	—	n

Table 3.04 : Percentage table to show position of inversion within the corpus examined

	JY	BP	NM	NF
Sentence initial	20	8	17	26
Paragraph initial	—	n	3	1
Chapter initial	—	—	—	n
Speech initial	1	2	n	1
Total initial	21	10	20	28
Sentence final	25	19	12	17
Paragraph final	n	—	n	2
Chapter final	—	n	—	—
Speech final	—	n	n	n
Total final	25	20	13	19

Table 3.05 : Percentage table to show position of inversion in relation to other types of discourse

	JY	BP	NM	NF
Preceding direct speech	n	—	n	n
Following direct speech	2	—	13	2
Preceding indirect speech	—	n	—	—
Following indirect speech	—	—	—	n

Table 3.06 : Percentage table to show nature of the inverted noun phrase

	JY	BP	NM	NF
Pronoun subject	20	26	17	14
Substantive subject	80	74	83	86
	100	100	100	100
2 or more subjects	6	1	6	10
S and dependent (S)	19	23	17	17

Table 3.07 : The percentage of inversions occurring in sentences of three or more clauses

	JY	BP	NM	NF
(S)—3 clauses	26	29	22	32
4 clauses	29	28	21	19
5 clauses	12	15	25	7
6 clauses	7	6	14	2
7 clauses	1	2	6	—
7+ clauses	n	—	1	n
	75	80	89	60

Table 3.08 : The ratio of inversions to *invertissants*

JY	334 : 80—4·17
BP	191 : 49—3·90
NM	171 : 39—4·38
NF	383 : 87—4·40
Total	1,079 : 146—7·39 (*mean* 4·21)

Table 3.09 : Percentage table of the most frequently occurring inversions

	JY	BP	NM	NF
Co-ordinators	15	26	1	10
Relatives	37	26	32	18
Comparatives	11	17	21	27
Indirect construction	7	7	5	3
Modal adverbs	8	6	24	10

Table 3.10 : Percentage table to show the occurrence of ' être ', ' faire ' and ' avoir '

	JY	BP	NM	NF
être	18	14	24	16
faire	11	6	12	9
avoir	2	2	2	1

Table 3.11 : Percentage table showing the distribution of direct speech *invertissants*

	JY	BP	NM	NF
Immobile *invertissant*	78	84	63	62
Mobile *invertissant*	21	16	32	33
Other operations	1	—	5	5
N :	112	44	59	149

Table 3.12 : Percentage table to show the occurrence of
adverbials and clauses in inversion constructions

	JY	BP	NM	NF
V(adv)S	7	6	2	7
(adv)VS	3	2	2	3
V(S)S	—	n	—	—
(S)VS	—	—	—	1

(i) CHOICE OF TEXTS

In the second half of the 16th century the novel is seen to be
evolving as a genre, although the predominant literary form is
still that of the *conte* or *nouvelle*. These are found either in
collections of stories or with a unifying framework analogous
to that of the *Heptaméron*, and it is from this form that the
17th-century novel emerges. The *contes* tend to be rather
more learned than in earlier works, as will be seen in the
analysis of du Fail's *Contes et discours d'Eutrapel*. This text is
little more than a collection of anecdotes, the only claim to
continuity being the presence of three shadowy framework
characters. Both Yver's *Printemps* and Poissenot's *Esté* have a
structure similar to that of the *Heptaméron*, with a division of
the framework into five and three ' days ' respectively, but
the stories tend to be longer and the background situation more
fully developed than their prototype.

As for the novel itself, the *roman de chevalerie* declines in the
course of the century to make way for a new genre, already
familiar in Spain and Italy, the *roman pastoral*. Among the
initiators of the genre in France was Nicolas de Montreux with
the *Bergeries de Juliette* (1585), the first part of which is
analysed here. The influence of Boccaccio and his imitators is
still apparent, as the work divides into *journées* which consist of
narration of the framework story, followed by a *nouvelle* told
by one of the characters. As in Yver, however, the scale is a
much larger one so that on the first day, for example, there are
forty pages of dialogue, followed by a seventy-page *nouvelle*.
On average the *nouvelle* constitutes about 60% of each day.

The four texts for this period thus represent the transition
from random collections of short stories to the novel as a

continuous narrative. In the *Printemps* the *nouvelles* constitute part of a thematic and structural whole, while Poissenot's
Esté, although an obvious imitation of Yver, is much closer to
the model of the *Heptaméron* and less carefully structured than
the *Printemps*. This text is appreciably shorter than the others,
representing only 125 pages. Then comes the new pastoral
novel, and finally a collection of *nouvelles*, du Fail's *Eutrapel*.
The last choice is a difficult one, given the comparatively large
number of such works available, but as most of these have
foreign models, du Fail seems to be the most original, both
from a literary point of view and with regard to his use of
language.

(ii) DISTRIBUTION OF THE INVERSIONS

The inversion frequency for this period shows a sharp fall in
the occurrence of the construction, with an average of $1\cdot50$ as
opposed to $2\cdot64$, and one text, the *Bergeries de Juliette*, has a
frequency only slightly above the average for each half of the
17th century. On the other hand the eight 16th-century texts
together average $2\cdot07$ which contrasts even more strikingly
with the 17th-century figure of $0\cdot80$.

Table 3.02 shows that these texts display a more marked
tendency towards immobile *invertissant* constructions than the
earlier works analysed, particularly in conversation (table 3.11).
Inversions in direct speech still constitute a large part of the
total, especially in *Eutrapel*, 39%, but to a lesser extent than
hitherto in *L'Esté*, 23% (table 3.03). While *Le printemps* and
L'Esté have a higher percentage of inversions in final position
than in initial position, the reverse is true in the other two
texts (table 3.04). There are, however, fewer inversions in
these key positions than in the first half of the century. The
occurrence of inversion seems to bear little relation in general
to changes in type of discourse (table 3.05), although a fairly
high proportion of examples in the *Bergeries*, 13%, mark the
return to narrative after direct speech, a feature previously
noted in the *Amadis* (cf. table 2.05). The sentences containing
inversion in these texts tend to be very much longer than in

the four earlier 16th-century works analysed, with an average of 76% of the examples occurring in sentences of three or more clauses, as against 51% in the previous period.

Table 3.08 shows that the overall ratio of inversions to *invertissants* is lower than in the first half of the century, and indicates a gradual loss in variety in inversion structures, particularly in the *Bergeries* where there are only thirty-nine different *invertissants*. This is also indicated below by the constructions in which inversion is found in isolated examples only, or not at all. Thus, for instance, thirty-four of the eighty-seven *invertissants* in du Fail occur only once. In the *Bergeries* there are only four types of immobile *invertissant* (co-ordinators, relatives, comparatives and indirect constructions), which account for 59% of the total inversions.

(iii) EXAMPLES

A. IMMOBILE 'INVERTISSANT'

1. *Zero : NF : 14*
   ' " On establira tant qu'on pourra officiers, *erigera l'on* nouvelles jurisdictions, *seront instituez* tant de parlemens et sieges presidaux qu'on voudra." ' (p. 139)

2. *Co-ordinating conjunctions : JY : 49 inversions, 3 ' invertissants' ; BP : 49,2 ; NM : 2,1 ; NF : 37,3.*
   '... et alors le mariage se celebra ... au contentement de toute la cité, fors de Cinthye, qui en depit s'en alla de Venise, *et* ne sceut on qu'elle devint depuis.' (NM, 55r)

3. *Relatives : JY : 124,12 ; BP : 52,5 ; NM : 54,9 ; NF : 70,10*
   ' (son sein) où deux petits montz ... traçaient et ouvroient ... un petit chemin *par où* glissoit une chesne de perles du voirre qui ...' (NM, 2v)

4. *Comparatives : JY : 37,7 ; BP : 33,10 ; NM : 36,9 ; NF : 102,6*
   ' (les soldats) font quinze fois *davantage* de maux à leur pays, *que* ne feroit le plus sanguin et carnacier ennemi...' (BP, 120v)

5. *Concessives* : *J Y* : *4,1* ; *BP* : *1,1* ; *NF* : *3,1*
'... ayant ... ouy dire que *quelque* mine *que* facent les filles,
elles sont bien aises d'estre aimées, s'estimans...' (JY, 112r)

6. *Temporal clause* : *NF* : *1,1*
'... et faire que sa femme, *lorsque* se fait l'assemblée et
concurrence des semences, ouvre la bouche et ne retienne
son haleine.' (p. 322)

7. *Causal clause* : *NF* : *1,1*
'... le consistoire des cardinaux devoit estre composé
moitié des nobles et l'autre de roturiers, *comme* entre tous
estats et assemblées populaires doit estre l'ordre ecclesi-
astic my-party et fendu en deux pieces...' (p. 147)

8. *Result clause* : *NF* : *1,1*
' "... la gendarmerie romaine ... se divisa et factionna *de
sorte que* depuis ... à veuë d'œil cheoit et tomboit une pierre
de leur bastiment, jusques au dernier de leur ruine." '
(p. 138)

9. *Hypothetical clause* : *J Y* : *3,2*
' " Las *si* avec la foy se rompoit le fil de la vie, je ne serois
ores en peine de me pleindre de celuy, qui en despit de
loyauté triomphe de mes loyalles affections." ' (54r)

10. *Correlatives* : *BP* : *1,1* ; *NF* : *2,2*
' Que *tant plus* il y songeoit, *plus* étoit-il délibéré faire
honneur à sa mémoire.' (NF, p. 324)

11. *Indirect construction* : *J Y* : *25,7* ; *BP* : *13,6* ; *NM* :
9,3 ; *NF* : *12,5*
' Mais laissons le courir, pour retourner à notre aise voir
que peut faire nostre vertueuse Fleurie, que...' (JY, 137v)

B. MOBILE ' INVERTISSANT '

1. *Attributives* : *J Y* : *9,2* ; *BP* : *4,2* ; *NM* : *11,2* ;
NF : *11,5*
'... ceste barbare et nouvelle gent, et *tels* nous appelloient-ils
aussi, regardant ce son non accoustumé d'un œil estonné
et hagard, s'est cachée...' (NF, p. 260)

2. *Adverbs—modal* : *J Y* : *27,6* ; *BP* : *12,7* ; *NM* : *41,3* ;
NF : *37,9*

' A peine le soleil avoit offusqué la clarté des estoilles ... et *à peine* pouvoit-on descouvrir les luisantes torches, dorer la voulte du ciel ... quand...' (NM, 111v)

3. *Adverbs—quantity : BP : 1,1 ; NM : 1,1 ; NF : 11,5*
' Si Combabe avoit esté tel, nous n'en sçaurions que dire, *bien* pouvons nous conjecturer, par ce qui s'ensuyt qu'il n'estoit aimé de tous...' (BP, 100r)

4. *Adverbs—temporal : JY : 5,4 ; BP : 1,1 ; NF : 7,6*
' *Incontinent* revint le clerc faisant signe de bien loing qu'on se fust approché...' (NF, p. 132)

5. *Adverbs—place : JY : 7,3 ; NM : 1,1 ; NF : 11,4*
' " *Là* vindrent aborder ces pyrates : qui ... enleverent ces deux Princesses aagées de quatre ans et moy." ' (JY, 268r)

6. *Adverbs—combinations : JY : 5,4 ; BP : 2,2 ; NF : 7,6*
' Toutefois le capitaine supplia ... que, si un jeune homme n'est un peu prout et esveillé, *malaisément et à peine* pourra-il estre bon compagnon...' (NF, p. 182)

7. *Adverbial phrase—time : JY : 4,4 ; NF : 8,4*
' *Durant ces jeux* survint une autre compagnie de Masques, d'entre lesquels...' (JY, 277v)

8. *Adverbial phrase—place : JY : 16,7 ; BP : 2,1 ; NM : 5,5 ; NF : 11,3*
'... *de l'autre bout* (de la prairie) serpentoit la mer, dont les flots...' (NM, 3v)

9. *Adverbial phrase—manner : JY : 5,2 ; BP : 2,1 ; NF : 9,4*
' "... nous provoquerons l'ire des Dieux sur nous, et *par ma temeraire entreprise* se trouvera vostre honneur grandement interessé." ' (BP, 84v)

10. *Prepositional phrase : JY : 10,3 ; BP : 8,2 ; NM : 5,2 ; NF : 7,3*
' " Or donc, puis que *de vous* depend mon bien et mon malheur, je vous supplie..." ' (NM, 146r)

11. *Direct object : JY : 1,1 ; NF : 2,2*
' " Vous jurant et protestant par le devoir qui m'oblige à vostre service (car *plus grande chose d'icy bas* ne sçaurois-je jurer) que..." ' (JY, 280r–v)

12. *Infinitival : J Y : 1,1 ; BP : 1,1*
    ' Il ne faut que doubtiez que la presence de celle, *pour à
    laquelle complaire* sont faicts tous les preparatifs du voyage,
    ne vous assiste et soulage...'' ' (BP, 81r)
13. *Participial phrase : BP : 3,2 ; NF : 3,2*
    ' On meit ordre à faire provision de toutes choses neces-
    saires à son voyage, *lequel dressé* ... fut faite levée d'une
    bonne troupe de soldats pour l'accompagner...' (BP, 77v)
14. *Preceding subordinate clause : J Y : 1,1 ; BP : 3,2 ,
    NM : 2,1 ; NF : 3,1*
    ' Or *pendant que la saincteté estoit en ces alteres*, advint un
    cas fort memorable, duquel je vous feray un compte...'
    (JY, 174v)

C. OTHER OPERATIONS

1. *Deletion : NM : 2 ; NF : 4*
   '... non plus que l'eau au forgeron, dont plus ardamment il
   allume son fourneau, et *fust* le jour ou la nuit, ils ne
   pensoient à autre chose qu'à leurs nouvelles amours...'
   (NM, 140v)
2. *Deletion and transposition : BP : 2 ; NM : 2 ; NF : 12*
   ' " Toutes les bestes brutes *tant inhumaines soient-elles*,
   n'offencent jamais l'homme, si premier il ne les pro-
   vocque...'' ' (NM, 101r)
3. *Addition and transposition : J Y : 1,1 ; BP : 1,1*
   ' *Ce n'estoit pas là*, de par Dieu, *que* gisoit son mal, les
   delices de cour ne lui estoient rien...' (BP, 93v)

(iv) DETAILS OF THE INVERSIONS

(a) Immobile ' invertissant '

Constructions with zero *invertissant* are consistently rare
throughout the periods of analysis. In the *Contes et discours
d'Eutrapel*, however, there are no fewer than fourteen examples,
twelve with a positive verb and two with a negative. As in the
examples already quoted these inversions have little in
common, and consideration of the main verb does not reveal
any useful categories. Three of the examples occur with *dire*,

one has *être* and there are three constructions with the comparable verbs *se voir* and *se trouver*. Other examples bear little resemblance to these, e.g.

 ' " Servira, dit Eutrapel, à ce propos, la response d'une belle et gentille dame de la ville de Laval..." ' (p. 212)

Whereas in the earlier part of the century inversions after co-ordinating conjunctions were the most common, this tendency is already dying out after 1550, and only two examples are found in Nicolas de Montreux. Previously *et* had been one of the most frequent *invertissants*, but now it represents a sizeable proportion in only Poissenot (twenty-five examples or 13%) and du Fail (seventeen examples or 5%), with two instances in de Montreux and six in Yver. The gradual decline in the use of this already archaic construction is accompanied by another, i.e. the increasingly limited use of the co-ordinating particle *si*. As mentioned in the previous chapter, its use gradually becomes fossilized in the construction *si est-ce que* linking two clauses, which in turn dies out in the 17th century. In Yver and Poissenot, constructions with *si* represent 12% of the inversions in each case, the majority of examples having *si est-ce que*. In Yver there is only one example of inversion after *si* alone and nine after *si* preceded by a subordinate clause, *si est-ce que* being much more common in this position. Du Fail, however, does not generally adopt the phrase and provides only two examples of it.

As shown in table 3.09, relative constructions are now those in which inversion occurs most frequently, the common *invertissants* being *que*, *où* and preposition plus *lequel*. Different *invertissants* tend to predominate in each text; for instance, Poissenot has 12% with *lequel* and 6% with *que* but few examples of *où*, while Yver has 18% with *que*, 9% with *où*, but few with *lequel*. Comparatives represent the other major class of inversions, particularly the *invertissant comme* which constitutes 12% of all the examples in de Montreux, 24% in du Fail and 8% in Yver. Except for indirect constructions other immobile *invertissants* tend to occur more sporadically than in the earlier period. De Montreux includes no other constructions at all and Poissenot has only one example of inversion in a concessive construction and one in a correlative, while Yver has four concessives and three hypothetical constructions. Thus the majority of inversions in this category are found in relatives and comparatives and to a lesser extent in co-ordinates, almost to the exclusion of all others.

(b) Mobile ' invertissant '

The most striking feature of this category is the predominance of modal adverb *invertissants* and the infrequency of formerly common *invertissants*, such as infinitivals, participial phrases and direct objects, with no example of inversion after a negative particle found in any of the four texts. Inversion after other types of adverb is relatively infrequent, and the same *invertissant* does not recur very often. Thus in du Fail there are seven inversions after six different temporal adverbs, five inversions after four in Yver, no examples in de Montreux and only one in Poissenot. This is not generally the case with modal adverbs, the most usual *invertissant* being *ainsi* (sixteen examples in du Fail, nineteen in de Montreux, ten in Yver and three in Poissenot), but never representing more than 5% of the total. Adverbial phrases and combinations of adverbs are comparatively rare as *invertissants* in these texts.

(c) Other operations

Of the other syntactic operations causing inversion in these texts, a notable feature is the number of deletion and transposition structures in *Eutrapel*. The verbs in this construction are generally *être* alone (four examples) or with a past participle (three) or with the auxiliary *avoir* (four). The remaining example, which occurs in indirect speech, uses a modal verb :

'... il protestoit d'en avoir un monitoire à fer esmoulu, luy dût-il couster bien ! ' (p. 204)

This construction generally has an impersonal or third person pronoun, although there is one instance using the second person :

' "... il faut par necessité, fussiez vous vestu de veloux verd,

que vous facies solennellement vostre entrée en prison..." '
(p. 155).

It is interesting to note that more than half the total examples
of this construction occur in direct speech and several more in
indirect speech.

2. STYLISTIC ANALYSIS OF THE TEXTS
1550–1600

(i) J. YVER, 'LE PRINTEMPS'

It has been suggested by Lohr [5] that Yver's *Printemps* has a
threefold structure, *Rahmenerzählung*, *Dialog* and *Gedicht-
sammlung*, i.e. poems serving to introduce the *nouvelles* which
are disregarded in this analysis. Closer examination, however,
suggests the following structure : the framework story, the
nouvelles and the discussions which follow each narrative, and
these may be sub-divided into the specific comments by the
narrator immediately after his story, and the general discussion
that ensues. In this text, as will also be seen in the *Esté* and the
Bergeries, the frequency of inversion in the *nouvelles* (or
histoires) is lower than in either the framework or the discussions, the latter having the highest frequency of all :

Framework 1·70
Nouvelles   1·64   (overall frequency 1·67)
Discussion 1·80

The sub-division of the discussion into narrator's monologue
and listeners' dialogue is useful in that inversion frequency in
the former is only 0·80, whereas in the latter it is unusually
high, 2·30, with an overall frequency of 1·80. This is largely
due to a concentration of inversions in the discussion on Day II,
fifteen in five pages, but in general the distribution within the
different structures is farily even over the five days, although
there is a below average frequency in the *nouvelle* of Day V.

The inversions which occur in these structures are examined
below, firstly with reference to their use in characterization in
the representation of speech, and secondly in regard to the

[5] P. Lohr, *Le Printemps d'Yver und die Quelle zu Fair 'Em'*, Diss...
München, Berlin, 1912.

criticism of Yver's style by Clouzot, ' une impression in-
déniable de monotonie '.[6]

(a) *Direct speech and characterization*

1. Conversation v. narrative

The distribution table of inversions (table 3.03) shows that
33% occur in direct speech in Yver, and 65% in narrative
(excluding indirect speech), which is the exact average of the
four texts. The examples of inversion in speech are evenly
divided between conversations which occur in the course of
the narration of a *conte* and those which are found in discussions between the story-tellers. The distribution of inversion
types within both kinds of direct speech follows the general
pattern of the whole work, as the most frequent examples are
in relative, co-ordinating and comparative constructions, in
that order. There are relatively few examples of inversion
after adverbs and adverbial phrases, but the range of these
types of *invertissant* is greater in speech in narrative than in
discussion. There is also more lexical variety in the examples
from the former category. The types of inversion which occur
in discussion are also found in narrative conversation, and the
range of *invertissants* is expanded. Thus there are four additional adverbial *invertissants*, and inversions after both direct
object and *si* (hypothetical clause) occur. From the point of
view of realistic representation of conversation, it is more
revealing to look at the inversion types that are not found in a
direct speech context. Thus while inversions in discussions are
the most common types, and those in narrative conversation
less so, those occurring less frequently in the text as a whole are
often not found at all in conversation. For example, relative
invertissants occurring in both types of speech context are :
que, lequel, où, d'où and *dont*, whereas those occurring only in
the narrative are *ce que*, preposition plus *quoy, par où*, and the
archaic preposition plus *icelluy*. The comparative *invertissants*
in speech are limited to *comme* and *ainsi que*, those involving

[6] H. Clouzot, ' Le Printemps d'Yver ', *Revue du XVIe siècle*, xviii (1931),
pp. 104–29.

more complex constructions—*aussi que, autant que, si ... que,*
and *plus ... que* being restricted to narrative. The construction
with question word *invertissants* is rare in speech (six out of
twenty-five examples), with no conversational examples of the
most common *invertissants, qui, que* and *combien*. As regards
adverbs and adverbial phrases, all the adverbial phrases of
time *invertissants* occur in narrative, as do those of place and
manner, with one exception in each case. The inversions after
the temporal adverbs *lors, adoncques* and *soudain* are found in
narrative only, but there is an example of *souvent* in conversational narrative.

Thus it seems that in this respect there is some attempt at the
realistic representation of direct speech in this text, which is in
keeping with Yver's claim of authenticity. For although the
inversions which are not found in conversation are generally
less common in the text, it is reasonable to suppose that a
sample consisting of 33% of the examples in the text would
include such *invertissants* if there were no concern with speech
presentation. The comparison between *invertissant* types found
in narration and conversation shows the clear distinction
between the two, as does the narrow range of *invertissants* in
discussions alone, all of which indicates a simpler sentence
structure in direct speech. Finally it should be noted that this
simplicity is to be equated with the restriction in range of the
invertissants rather than in the absolute frequency of inversion.
In both Yver and Poissenot there is a higher inversion rate in
discussion sections than in the general narrative or *nouvelles,*
and this may also be compared with the *Heptaméron* where the
inversion frequency in discussion is $1\cdot87$ as against $1\cdot82$ for
the whole text.

2. Speech of the characters

The distribution of inversions according to the speaker in the
framework discussions is irregular, although certain features
are common to nearly all the characters. As regards frequency,
the two most lively characters, Fleur d'Amour and Marie, also
provide the greatest number of inversions, fifteen and sixteen

respectively. The remaining three young people, Marguerite, Fermefoy and Bel-Accueil have eight, six and five respectively, while the ' Maistresse du chasteau ', who rarely intervenes, provides a single example, the construction with *c'est ... que*. From the restricted number of *invertissants* mentioned earlier, various generalizations are possible. The most striking feature is the tendency to invert after an immobile *invertissant* rather than a mobile one, which is even more pronounced in discussions. While 73% of the inversions in this text occur with immobile *invertissant* (table 3.02), the figure for the inversions in direct speech is 78% (table 3.11). In the speech of the individual characters, Fermefoy's inversions are all with immobile *invertissant*, as are all but one in the case of both Marguerite and Bel-Accueil. With Fleur d'Amour and Marie each have twelve examples with immobile *invertissant*.

As may be expected in discussion and argument in this period, constructions with the co-ordinating conjunction *si* occur in the speech of four of the characters, and inversions after *or* and *et* are also found. Inverted order after *comme* occurs in the speech of all five story-tellers, and Fleur d'Amour and Fermefoy have four examples each.

Although this section is concerned primarily with inversion in conversation, the relation between the framework character and the inversions in the story he or she relates may also be considered. Thus the high number of inversions in the speech of Fleur d'Amour and Marie is mirrored in the number of inversions in their respective *histoires*, forty-six in the case of Fleur d'Amour, an approximate frequency of 1·70, and thirty-five in Marie, approximate frequency, 1·66. The same is true in the case of Bel-Accueil and Fermefoy, both characters with few speech inversions, who have low *histoire* frequencies of 1·31 and 1·09 respectively. Marguerite, however, does not conform to this pattern, with a high *histoire* inversion rate of 1·82, although it may be argued that she tells her story on the anomalous fourth day, where there is no subsequent discussion, and the distinction between framework and other structures has become somewhat blurred.

These relationships may seem rather tenuous, but they are useful in a further context. Clouzot, following Reynier,[7] classifies the five *histoires* in the novel according to their literary genre thus stories I and IV (told by Fleur d'Amour and Marguerite) are described as *histoires chevalaresques* stories II and III (told by Marie and Bel-Accueil) as *histoires dramatiques* and the final story (by Fermefoy) as *histoire plaisante*. Taken together the *histoires chevaleresques* have an inversion rate of 1·77 and the *histoires dramatiques* one of 1·46, but the *histoire plaisante* is much lower with a frequency of 1·09, as compared with the overall *histoire* frequency of 1·64. The narrator's own conversation also has fewer inversions, four examples with *comme*, one with *si*, and one with preposition plus *ce que*. Clouzot remarks that Fermefoy represents the tradition of *conteurs satiriques* and this distinguishes him quite markedly from the other characters, his own speech fitting his role. As regards the difference in genre, the higher frequency of 1·77 for the *histoires chevaleresques* in Yver in contrast to the other forms in the same work, and also to the average frequency for the period of 1·50, may be compared with the high inversion frequency of des Essarts in the previous period, 3·25 as against the average of 2·64 for the texts analysed.

It can thus be concluded from the inversion study that there is a clear linguistic difference between the styles of the narrative and the conversations, and a further distinction between direct speech as it occurs in a narrative and in a discussion between the narrators. There also seems to be some relation between the style of the narrative and the conversation of its narrator, as well as between inversion frequency and genre, although this argument cannot be pursued beyond some general conclusions. As regards individual characterization, a greater use of inverted order seems to correspond to the liveliness of certain characters.

(b) The style of Yver

From the point of view of general word-order, the charge of

[7] G. Reynier, *Le roman sentimental avant 'L'Astrée'*, Paris, 1908, pp. 166–67.

monotony which Clouzot levels at Yver is hard to substantiate. Instead, inversion, along with other devices of word-order, plays a considerable part in sylistic variation which constitutes the *style élégant* appropriate to the aristocratic setting. The free variation in the place of the adverb, for example, is a feature of many examples of constructions with inversion, which emphasizes the inverted word-order : there are ten examples where an adverb is placed between *invertissant* and verb, and twenty-two where it is between the verb and inverted subject, which together constitute almost 10% of the inversion examples. The adverb in the following sentence is in a less usual position and counterbalances the inversion in the previous clause :

'aussi telle estoit la gehenne voluntaire que les fins Tyrans anciennement donnoient à ceux ausquels...' (135r)

The juxtaposition of direct and inverted word-orders is a common device of style throughout the modern French period, and it is most effective when the *invertissant* itself is repeated, thereby avoiding repetition of the whole structure and forming a chiasmus :

' "... qui sera cause, disoit il, que *de* ceste communication *s'ensuivra* confirmation d'amitie, et *de* ceste alliance corporelle, l'alliance des esprits *sera renforcée*." ' (331r)

As already suggested with reference to the place of the adverb, many of Yver's inversion constructions are more complex than a simple change in the position of the subject. This may be separated from its verb by an adverb or a second verb, or both,

'Avec le corps croissoit aussi et se fortifioit ce naturel amour...' (36v)

or by a form of address to the audience :

'Ainsi finirent (vertueuse compagnie) les amans, qui...' (304r)

or the verb may be separated from the *invertissant* not only by an adverb or adverbial phrase, but also by a whole clause, which may itself contain an inversion :

'Autour du lict, où reposoient ces deux amans, estoit Pistan avec Agathe et les autres damoiselles qui...' (81v)

Thus Yver makes use of both parallelism and juxtaposition of orders in the interests of variety, although this may also lead to a certain heaviness at times.

This criticism leads to a further point made by Clouzot in relation to sentence structure : ' La phrase s'allonge à n'en plus finir, bien qu'il cherche à garder le ton du récit, avec les tournures familières au conteur ' (*ibid.*, p. 123), and his conclusion as to Yver's style is that it consists of language which is ' amphigourique '.   This is certainly true of his inversions in longer sentences, although the text has again no more than an average number of inversions in sentences of more than two clauses.   Inversions may thus be used for clarity amid a profusion of subject nouns and attributes rather than clauses :

> ' là estoient pourtraites d'un art laborieux et subtil toutes sortes de fleurs, et parmy icelles toutes especes d'oyseaux, avec leurs blasons, par le moyen desquels on pouvoit faire parler des bouquets.' (314r)

Occasionally juxtapositions in one order are mirrored by those in another as in the following arrangement of verb and subject and subject and object :

> '... qui n'estoit autre chose que couver l'œuf en ton sein, duquel esclorra l'aspic mortel qui te fera piteuse recompense de ta simplette affection.' (354r)

(c) *Conclusion*

The conclusions as to the style of Yver which can be drawn from the above analysis are essentially summed up in the inversion tables, which indicate that the main features of the text coincide almost exactly with the mean for all four texts. Inversion examples show his style to be both complex from the point of view of accumulation of linguistic devices, and simple in that such devices are mainly used for clarity.   The style varies according to speaker and narrative subject matter, but not to the extent of any sustained characterization.   The inversion frequency, choice of *invertissant* and other features represent the tendencies of the period, in particular the loss of the most dislocated constructions and the concentration of inversions in other more regular structures. The word-order is thus still quite free, but the field of choice is narrowed. The verbs used in inversion constructions are unremarkable from a lexical point of view, with a tendency towards fixed, almost cliché constructions. Thus *où* co-occurs with *être* in fourteen out of the thirty examples, the remainder being largely verbs of resting or staying. Out of the sixty examples with *que*, forty are accounted for by verbs of giving or receiving, having or bringing and *faire*.

As Clouzot points out, Yver's choice is between the old language of Rabelais and the polished language of contemporary society, shown more strikingly in the works of the next century. The above syntactic and stylistic analyses show that in reality Yver appears to fall midway between two stools. The extravagance of Rabelais is avoided, while some unusual forms of inversion persist, but the device is not yet subject to the restraint found in later works in both content and type of *invertissant*. Thus the elements of the style of an earlier period are still present and only begin to disappear with the *Bergeries* and finally the *Astrée*.

(ii) B. POISSENOT, 'L'ESTÉ'

The framework situation in the *Esté* is that of three students who pass three summer days telling stories while recuperating from an illness. Each student tells a story each day, and there is a common theme for each group of three stories. The framework story is given more prominence than in Yver, occupying more than half as much space as the *contes*, and the structural divisions are less clearly defined. The frequency of inversion in each section is as follows:

Framework 1·61

Contes   1·41   (overall frequency 1·53)

Discussion 1·83

The author's attitude towards his work is essentially light-hearted, and he refers to the book several times in the preface as ' ces gayetez '. A further preface, however, (' par Jehan

Chausse son ami') opens with a sonnet containing the following lines :

   ' Heureux sont tes amis de voir ceste saison

   Par toy mistiquement, mais doctement descripte.'

and Jourda, one of the few critics of Poissenot, also takes up the notion of erudition, commenting strongly on both the learned tone of the *contes* and of the conversation of the framework characters. His final verdict on the *Esté* is a ' mélange ... d'un réalisme de bon aloi, presque classique déjà, et d'une érudition qui parfois tourne un peu au pédantisme.' [8] The analysis of the inversions will here be used to show how far this criticism of erudite writing is justified, and whether or not this seems to overshadow the light-hearted and realistic sides of Poissenot's work.

(a) *The Inversions*

The inversion frequency for this text, $1 \cdot 53$, does not suggest a style which is excessively learned, if an erudite style is to be equated with the wide use of inverted order. Indeed certain results, for example the low proportion of inversions occurring in direct speech, or the tendency for inversion to take place in shorter sentences, seem to suggest the reverse. The distribution of the inversions is, however, significant in that no fewer than 26% of the total occur in co-ordinating constructions, a figure which is in direct opposition to the general tendency at this time, and which reveals a more conservative prose style.

1. Co-ordinating constructions

Et : There are twenty-five examples of inversion after *et* in this text. Two of them occur in direct speech within a *conte* and there is also one example in free indirect speech :

   ' Si les hautes entreprises n'estoient accompagnées de beaucoup de dangers, immeritoirement le laurier et triomphe seroient la recompense des hardis entrepreneurs, *et* ne

---

[8] P. Jourda, ' Un précurseur de M. Barrès : Bénigne Poissenot et les Assassins ', *Revue du XVIe siècle*, x (1923), p. 213.

pourroit le cueur magnanime et vaillant estre discerné du lasche et poltron.' (135r)

Although it is difficult to state any definite rules for the occurrence of this inversion, it should be noted that eight of the examples have passive verbs, more than half the total number of passives which are found in inversion constructions in the text. This structure of *et* and a passive verb occurs primarily at the end of the sentence, to conclude a series of actions, stressing, perhaps, the finality :

‘ La bataille se donnant, les Allemands furent mis en route, et y fut selon aucuns Charles Ynach tué.’ (157r)

The possibility of inversion after *et* is also exploited in historical narrative, particularly in long sentences, partly for the sake of variety, and also in the interests of logical sequence :

‘ En apres de compagnie s’en allerent en un lieu appellé Boleslanie ... où le siege de l’Empereur fut dressé, et y rendit justice, *et* y fut mis un monceau de pierres, qui...’ (140v)

There are two examples of this construction where the inverted subject is the pronoun *on*, but there is no longer the regularity displayed in earlier periods in this respect, as the next examples show. In addition the inversion occurs in the narration of the framework story, whereas the direct word-order occurs in the final discussion among the characters :

‘... lequel plus on entretient *et* s’en souvient on, tant plus met on d’huille en la lampe pour...’ (55r)

‘ “ Qu’il ne soit ainsi qu’on voie ce que dit Plutarque aux preceptes de mariage, *et* on verra si je di vray ou non.” ’ (167r)

Si : There are twenty-four examples of inversion after *si* in this text, the highest number for the four texts, and of these twenty-two take the form of the expression *si est-ce que* (generally found as *si esce que*). Only four examples of the expression do not refer back to a concessive construction, three of which are used argumentatively in conversation, as in the *Heptaméron*, thus :

‘ “ C’est tresbien advisé à vous, dict Prefouché, si esce que

je ne me puis contenir que je ne vous die une chose..." '
(108v)

Of the two examples of *si* alone as *invertissant*, one functions as a routine co-ordinating construction, while the other, in sentence initial position, introduces a sentence which is further complicated by the insertion of an adverbial phrase between verb and subject, an order which occurs quite frequently in this and other texts of the period :

' Si ne laissa pour tout cela le medecin d'escrire...' (48v)

The remaining eighteen examples are very similar to those furnished by earlier texts, five of them occurring in conversation. However, whereas in the early part of the century the four items of the *si est-ce que* expression formed an indivisible unit, there are here three cases where *que* is separated from the rest, in one instance by an *incise* :

' Si est ce, dist Chasteaubrun, que pour estre d'une humeur visqueuse ... j'estime que..." ' (8v),

and in the other two examples by an adverb or adverb and *incise* :

' " Si esce toutefois, disoit il, que..." ' (58r)

The use of *toutefois* and *pourtant* in this context, which have a meaning similar to that of the particle *si* after a concessive expression, may indicate the loss of any semantic force which *si* might have been felt to have had. It is interesting that these examples occur in conversation, for if this hypothesis is correct, they may also show Poissenot's concern for realistic reproduction of speech.

2. Comparative constructions

Although Poissenot may seem to indulge rather frequently in learned comparisons, the proportion of inversions in such constructions is considerably lower than in either de Montreux or du Fail, the one being more fanciful and the other more pedantic than Poissenot. From the grammatical point of view, Poissenot has a wider range of constructions than the other three authors, with ten different *invertissants*. Variety, however, is not confined to the *invertissants*, but involves also

D

the position of the comparison in the sentence, and the nature of the comparison itself. Thus it will be seen that the constructions seem to fall into two categories, the explicit, generally having a comparative *invertissant*, and the implicit, often with a different type of inversion, which may also have an additional function in the sentence.

Unlike those in other texts analysed so far, the constructions with comparative *invertissants*, usually *comme*, are not, for the most part, placed at the end of the sentence, being short and parenthetical, and their position may at times slightly dislocate the sentence. The clause containing an inversion may thus be interposed between a verb and its dependent clause :

'... et Tite depuis surnommé les delices du peuple, qu'on attendoit, selon que dit Suetone en sa vie, devoit estre un second Neron : ' (142v),

where the parenthesis prevents the juxtaposition of two verbs and relieves the monotony of direct word-order, or as in the following :

'... (ils) s'apperçoivent, comme feit Tarquin, vieillissant à Cumes, qui ont esté ceux qui...' (72r)

This example also shows that where the inverted subject is expanded, this is not always done by means of a further finite verb, but instead more concisely with a participle which can stand next to its antecedent owing to inversion :

'... comme feit Origene interpretant ce passage trop cruement et literalement, ains qu'on...' (108r)

Sentences containing an implied comparison are more complex, and the function of the inversions is here related to structure. These comparisons are hypothetical in that one half of the comparison is of the undefined form ' celui/ceux qui...', and this is more easily expressed by means of inversion :

'... s'entrecaressans avec toutes les mignardises et folatreries que sçavent ceux qui apres un long martyre, ont atteint et cueilli le fruict tant desiré...' (75v)

Thus inversion is obviously used to enable antecedent and relative to stand together in the sentence, and the comparison loses none of its impact in grammatical obscurity.

3. Other inversions

Table 3.02 shows the comparatively small number of mobile *invertissants* in Poissenot, and this is borne out in table 3.09 which shows that only 6% of the inversions have modal adverb *invertissants*.   Several of the constructions, however, are interesting from the point of view of archaic usage. There is, for example, an instance of *malaisément* as an *invertissant* and three cases of *par aventure*, two of which occur in conversation. This suggests that Poissenot is following writers like Rabelais in such constructions, for, as already suggested, in the gradual restriction of adverbial *invertissants* it is the decline in range, not in absolute number, which is significant.

A further indication of Poissenot's linguistic conservatism is the number of participial constructions involving inversion with a non-finite verb ('... et voulant le Roy que...', 18r), which typifies earlier 16th-century writing.   It is, however, also a useful device for writers seeking conciseness on the one hand and variety of construction on the other, both of which characterize this work.

(b) *The Style of 'L'Esté'*

To sum up, the use of inversion in the *Esté*, far from being indicative of a high-flown and erudite style, generally contributes to a concise and uncomplicated one, which is entirely in keeping with the subject matter of ' ces gayetez '. In addition, inversion here is an important source of variety, as a style in which conciseness is a dominant feature risks becoming monotonous. There is variety in word-order, not only in the place of the subject, but also in that of the adverb ; there are ten examples of the adverb or adverbial phrase placed between the verb and inverted subject, and four where it is between the *invertissant* and the verb. In addition there is the variety of construction found in the different forms of comparison. This is the first text analysed in which an author has moved away from the comparative formula with few *invertissants* and little concern for variety or brevity.

There are many examples showing how Poissenot's sentences

are varied in structure, both for the sake of balance and also to
avoid monotony. This may be achieved, as in the following, by
varying both the tenses of the verb and its position in successive clauses :

> ' Finissant Prefouché son histoire, les deux autres se
> trouverent d'opinion, que d'un mal advenoit fort souvent du
> bien...' (160v)

Alternatively, inversion in a short incidental clause relieves
monotony and restores the balance, particularly when the
subject has a weighty qualifying adjective :

> ' Que si le camp se rompt et les soldats ... tombans malades ou
> s'en retournans estropiez en leur maisons, la vengeance que
> prent d'eux ceste immisericordeuse populace surpasse toutes
> les offenses et outrages, qu'elle pourroit avoir receu.' (123r)

The advantages of inversion where the subject is followed by a
dependent clause have already been shown, and this applies
equally when the subject phrase is long and involves several
items :

> ' Pour lequel debatans ambitieusement ensemble, s'enfuirent
> les factions des Orleannois, autrefois appellez Armagnacs,
> et Bourguignons et grand carnage d'hommes.' (41r)

As already suggested, Jourda's hint of a charge of pedantry
is not easily justified. On the other hand, Poissenot's attention
to historical detail is undeniable, hence the importance of an
uncluttered style, yet his references are rarely academic
indulgences.   For present purposes the most significant
stylistic feature is the linguistic simplicity of direct speech and
its generally uncomplicated structure. Thus, the work marks
an interesting advance, both in language and form, in French
narrative prose, combining elements of both the past tradition
and what is to come, as in Yver, but with a more pronounced
trend towards simplicity.

(iii) NICOLAS DE MONTREUX, 'LES BERGERIES DE JULIETTE'

The beginnings of the pastoral novel mark a definite break
with previous fictional writing, and the major changes in style

are paralleled by the difference in inversion frequencies between this text and the other 16th-century works analysed. Reynier, in his discussion of the novel prior to the *Astrée*,[9] indicates that the emerging *style précieux* depends on the avoidance of archaic and erudite expression, but the speech of the characters still tends to represent the language of the courtisan rather than the peasant, although the result is considerably more straightforward than the conversations in, for example, du Fail.

This judgement is borne out by the grammatical analysis above as regards the types of construction admitting inversion, sentence structure, and in particular frequency of inversion. Thus the different sections of the novel reveal lower frequencies than in either Yver or Poissenot, with $0 \cdot 93$ for the narrative and $0 \cdot 80$ for the *nouvelles*, the overall figure being $0 \cdot 86$. However, the fact that the proportion of inversions occurring in direct speech, 39% (table 3.03), is above average for the texts of this period does suggest that there is little attempt at the separation of narrative and conversational styles, and seems to support Reynier's observation on the unnatural speech of the characters of de Montreux.

Table 3.09 indicates that no fewer than 77% of the inversions occur in the three main construction types, co-ordinating and comparative clauses, and with modal adverb *invertissants*. This restriction on inversion constructions is underlined by the relatively small number of actual *invertissants*, thirty-eight. The results supplied by table 3.07 do not immediately suggest a simple sentence structure, as 89% of the inversions occur in sentences of three or more clauses, the most favoured length being five clauses, an exceptional feature in the 16th century, although on the other hand, table 3.06 shows a low proportion of subjects with a dependent clause, 17%.

On the question of lexis, table 3.10 shows that the *Bergeries* have by far the highest frequency of occurrence of *être* and *faire* with inverted subjects. This preference for verbs of low

[9] *Op. cit.*, pp. 318 ff.

semantic content is further emphasized in the co-occurrence of various *invertissants* and related verbs, thus, for example, *à peine* occurs with *pouvoir* in eleven of the eighteen examples. Similarly, out of the nineteen occurrences of *ainsi*, *dire* is present fifteen times, and *se plaindre* twice, all these constructions following a piece of direct speech, which indicates the narrow contextual limits of this *invertissant*. Of the thirty-six examples in comparative constructions, fourteen have the verb *être*, and a further eight have the main verb replaced by *faire*.

Inversion and the pastoral theme

It will be seen that in many respects inversion seems to be an integral part of the pastoral style. It is used almost exclusively in the interests of clarity, and is therefore subordinate in function to the major stylistic devices appropriate to the genre, such as metaphor or hyperbole. Inversion is particularly useful in description, whether of the pastoral setting, or of the sentiments of the characters. In the following example the major descriptive details are inverted after the subject :

' au milieu de la prée couloit une belle fontaine, froide comme glace, et entourée artificiellement de beaux gasons d'herbée verde ..., où...' (3v)

Ideas such as that of a shepherdess reclining beneath trees, are conventional ones in pastoral literature. In the *Bergeries* a recurring theme is underlined by the regular use of a conventional inversion, which nevertheless allows clarity and emphasis :

' elle advisa pres d'elle, deux Chevaliers armez, dont la navire ... estoit abordée au rivage d'Arcadie, non gueres loing du lieu *où se reposoit* la belle bergere.' (14r)

' Il ne fut pas si tost arresté en sa place, qu'il se mist à regarder piteusement celle *où* le jour precedent, *reposoit* sa chere Juliette, il vit les herbettes qui...' (111v)

and there are many other almost identical examples.

Inversion also plays a major role in the description of characters, as the inverted subject may be followed by an accumulation of adjectival complements without loss of clarity. This is particularly frequent after *ainsi* following direct speech, to describe the emotional state of the speaker :

> ' Ainsi disoit le triste amant, dont les yeux ruisseloient de larmes, et l'estomach bondissoit de souspirs, regardant...'
> (106v)
> ' Ainsi disoit la Magicienne, toute estincellante d'ire et de courroux, quand...' (78v)

The inclusion of poetry in the course of the novel is one of the main devices for sentimental expression, and this too may be followed by a reference to the character who sings the songs :

> ' " Et bien Rustic, voila donc des chansons, que chantoit au temps passé le pauvre Fortunio, pour moy, et non seulement il composa celle que je viens de souspirer, mais..." ' (69r)

The vocabulary of the *Bergeries* already shows marked tendencies towards *préciosité*, and this is underlined in particular by the use of relative inversions, which often seem to give the prose a rhythmic, poetic aspect, thus :

> ' "... que l'amour attise des allumettes, que luy fournissent les rayons de vos beaux yeux." ' (145v)
> ' " mes larmes sont ... indignes de laver le tombeau d'un corps où logeoit une ame si parfaite que la tienne." ' (108r)

Otherwise, of course, a relative inversion may have the sole function of ensuring comprehensibility, as in this complex example :

> ' Toutefois les dons d'esprit que la nature en recompense du tort, que leur faisoit la cruelle fortune leur avoit prestez, recompensoient ce deffaut naturel et...' (136r)

Finally inversion in combination with a precious vocabulary occurs regularly in the portrayal of characters, often through direct or indirect speech :

> ' Diane sceut alors quelle estoit la peine que souffroient ceux qui brusloient de son amour et qu'elle ne daignoit aimer...'
> (84v)

The use of inversion is also seen in the expression of such key-concepts as the personification of love,

> '... et voulut qu'ils esprouvassent la diversité de sa nature, et combien sont differents ses effects...' (3r)

the cruelty of the loved one, a secondary theme throughout the work,

> ' " n'avois je assez eu de subject de me douloir et de me
> plaindre de la cruauté que me monstroit Cliomene..." ' (75v)

and the affinity between the characters and the world of nature, underlined particularly in the similes, for example the following comparison which is highly reminiscent of Virgil :

> ' Le taureau ne porte point plus de haine au lyon, ny le
> serpent à la femme, comme faisoit Dellye à Fortunio...' (74v)

Among the most frequently occurring inversions in the *Bergeries* are those in comparative constructions, the majority connected with the learned element in the work, and these fall into three categories. First of all there are the commentaries on situations in the text, which are drawn from the pronouncements of Classical philosophers, while not reproducing an exact quotation :

> ' D'autant que comme dit Platon, l'amour est un desir
> immortel ' (138r)

The comparison, in *incise* form, may even be introduced into a borrowed metaphor :

> ' L'amour qui est, comme dit Menandre, une fureur aux
> hommes, qui corrumpt leur naturel...' (136v)

Secondly the comparison may refer to a parallel situation in history, or more often in mythology :

> ' " (contraint) d'avoir pitié de moy, de mesme que faisoit
> Narcisse devant la Nymphe Escho..." ' (8v)

Thirdly, inversion is used in similes :

> ' " Tous les hommes ne sont faits, que pour desirer, et
> presque tous leurs souhaits s'evanouissent, comme fait un
> nuau à nos yeux, quand le vent a le poussé deça delà..." '
> (123v)

The statistical analysis has shown that this text seems to have little in common with the others of its period, and the next chapter will show to what extent the *Bergeries* shares the features of the 17th-century novel, above all the *Astrée*. Of particular importance is the decline in inversion frequency, and its increasingly fossilized use in constructions such as comparisons, and those where it plays a part in expressing the main ideas of the work. There can be little doubt as to the syntactic and stylistic significance of the *Bergeries*, and Sainte-Beuve's judgement of it as ranking among '... autres insipides productions qui couraient depuis la fin du siècle' [10] does seem to do the work little justice.

(iv) NOEL DU FAIL, 'LES CONTES ET DISCOURS D'EUTRAPEL'

(a) *Inversion and narrative technique*

Unlike the other texts chosen for this period, there is in du Fail little evidence of a definite literary structure, the work being in the tradition of collections of *contes*. Nevertheless, a certain narrative technique clearly emerges and is sustained throughout, in which inversion plays a fairly important part, and which accounts for many of the examples.

The grammatical analysis has consistently shown so far that a high proportion of inversions in a text occur in initial position, generally at the beginning of the sentence, but sometimes also in the more prominent paragraph- or chapter-initial position. Du Fail is no exception, and in fact has the highest number of initial inversions for this period, 28%, although this figure is lower than in any of the texts for the previous period. In *Eutrapel* initial inversions often have the specific role of introducing a new story, which is comparable to the 'once upon a time' technique. The *invertissant* generally places the new narrative in its temporal context, thus:

'L'an mil cinq cens cinquante et trois, fut establie en ce pays de nouveau une gabele fort estrange...' (p. 288)

where the inversion begins a new chapter.

The most obvious use of inversion as a device of narrative style occurs once in du Fail, evidently as a pastiche; this archaism is a phrase familiar from the *Amadis* and medieval French prose:

'Or dit li conte, que ... le mariage fut fait...' (p. 272)

---

[10] C.–A. Sainte-Beuve, *Tableau historique et critique de la poésie française au XVIe siècle*, Paris, 1843, p. 278.

D*

Du Fail also uses inversion to introduce quotations and proverbs into his narrative, without necessarily making a break in the story :

'... comme les Avocats font quand il leur plaist : dont est venu ce mot, " De bon Advocat, mauvais Juge "...' (p. 265)

The proverb or saying may be explicitly recognized, as above, or it may form part of the narrative, often in indirect speech, with the inversion contained within it, for example the following two occurrences of the same expression :

'Lupolde ... supplia qu'à toutes fins, et à quelque prix que fust le blé, ceste consultation n'estre esventée et publiée...' (p. 147)

' Si conclurent ils neantmoins qu'il falloit avoir leur revanche à quelque pris que fust le blé...' (p. 126)

Here the use of indirect speech indicates, at least partially, the status of the expression, whose conciseness is largely attributable to the obligatory inversion of the subject. Alternatively a comparative *invertissant* may be used :

'... les restes et reliques des gens de pied retournans du camp, lesquels comme en la queue gist le venin ... voloient par terre et brigandoient...' (p. 279)

Four of the inversions after *et* serve to introduce in indirect form learned quotations which are not integrated into the narrative as easily as the presumably more popular expressions already quoted. Indeed the use of a co-ordinator as an initial *invertissant* does seem to have the reverse effect of creating a deliberate break in the story, while stressing the learned origin of the quotation, often with an exact reference :

' " Et dit sainct Augustin, Homel.j, que les faisans le contraire seront condamnez devant Dieu..." ' (p. 234)

Direct quotation, however, is rare, the only example with inversion being the following, where the origin is stated in a parenthetical construction, whose order is also followed in the quotation itself :

' " Aux beaux corps, disent les Platoniques, reposent les plus belles et heroïques ames." ' (p. 330)

Finally an inversion may be used to introduce a quotation which sums up the preceding narrative, as in :

' et en luy fut verifiée et accomplie la prophetie du roy
Charles VII ... quand il fit dire à iceluy duc bourguignon
" qu'il nourrissoit un renard qui mangeroit ses paroles." '
(p. 227)
which incidentally is reminiscent of several familiar Biblical
passages with parallel word-order (' Et cela arriva, afin que
fût accomplie cette parole de l'Ecriture, qui dit...'—Jean
XIX, 24).

(b) Du Fail and Rabelaisian syntax

Apparent similarities between the language of du Fail and
that of Rabelais have been mentioned by several critics in
various connections. Firstly there appears to be a common
desire to reproduce features of everyday conversation, chiefly
spontaneity, by means of a somewhat distorted syntax, as
Philipot states :

' Il a cherché au moins autant que Rabelais à reproduire les
mouvements capricieux et jusqu'aux tics de la conversation
rapide et régligée. Ceci est fondamental dans le style de du
Fail et nous avons là une cause importante d'obscurités.' [11]
Secondly there is the method of character portrayal itself,
although little developed by du Fail. Sahlmann notes in this
connection :

' Es findet sich bei ihm eine ähnliche Unbestimmtheit in der
Charakterisierung und eine gleiche Neigung zur Karikatur
wie bei Rabelais.' [12]
The same writer remarks on a similar attention to detail in the
two authors, and refers to du Fail as a ' Nachahmer Rabelaisi-
scher Dichtung '.[13] More specific stylistic features which might
be noted include enumerations, distortion of learned elements,
deliberate archaism and so on, often in the interests of satire,
whether of Church or Justice.

[11] E. Philipot, *Essai sur le style et la langue de Noel du Fail*, Paris, 1914,
p. 38.
[12] O. Sahlmann, *Das Leben und die Werke des Noel du Fail*, Leipzig, 1909,
p. 31.
[13] *Ibid*, p. 33.

1. Conversation

The many inversions which occur in direct speech in
Eutrapel, whether between the story-telling characters or
within the *contes*, have two striking features. Firstly, the
inversions usually occur in long sentences and are frequently
not the only examples of unusual word-order in the sentence.
As shown in table 3.12, adverbs or adverbial phrases are placed
between the *invertissant* and verb, e.g. ' "... chez lesquels
d'ordinaire repose une fureur divine, qui..." ' (p. 255) or
immediately after the verb :

> ' "... la statue de Venus en Delphes, où souloient, selon
> l'antique sottise des stoïques, respondre les âmes bien et
> deuement appellées..." ' (p. 134)

Similarly complements of the subject may precede the inverted nominal :

> ' "... et autres lieux de reputation, où se trouvoient de tous
> les environs plusieurs jeunes valets et hardeaux..." '
> (pp. 196–97)

It is, however, highly questionable whether an order such as the
following is indicative of spontaneous conversation rather than
stylistic rearrangement :

> ' " Et ainsi Lupolde, mon bon amy, fut de nostre ruyne
> payée ton extreme avarice." ' (p. 306)

The majority of speeches are, however, carefully structured,
and the clauses logically ordered :

> ' " Et combien qu'il s'en trouve quelques uns à qui telles
> entreprinses ayent heureusement succedé, si sont ils en
> tel petit nombre que, de 100, un ne vient à rencontrer le bon
> port." ' (p. 151)

The second characteristic, perhaps more typical of direct
speech, is rhetorical repetition, where the second term explains
or expands the first. In inverted constructions this may
involve the *invertissant* itself, e.g. ' en vain et pour neant '
(p. 263), the verb and subject : '... par es seule veue s'esva-
nouirent et s'en iront en fumée les noises et discords...' (p. 140),
or the verb and the adjectives qualifying the subject : '... et
là se preparent et commencerent de tresbons et heureux

mariages.' (p. 197). There is even an example where the device is applied to three different grammatical elements in one sentence :

> ' "... et lors sera tout le monde content et satisfait, chacun suivant et embrassant la condition et vocation où Dieu nous a appelez." ' (p. 144)

It is rare that the conversation consists of brief interchanges such as :

> ' " Au compte serez-vous moise ? — ' Monsieur, repond Eutrapel, belle, bonne, riche. Autre chose n'aurez-vous de moi." ' (p. 328),

or of short disconnected sentences, as in this piece of caricature :

> ' " Le temps n'est plus comme il souloit, le monde s'est apparessé ; toutesfois vient tousjours quelque peu d'eau au moulin ; s'il ne pleut, il degoute." ' (p. 136)

In general, passages of speech are long and complicated, and seem to lack the verve associated with Rabelaisian characters.

2. Parody

Du Fail's characters, in the same way as those of Rabelais, are for the most part a vehicle for ironic comment on, or parody of, contemporary figures, and in particular, in *Eutrapel*, of the legal profession. Legal language is parodied both in sentence structure and vocabulary, especially by long and archaic constructions. As regards inversion, the outstanding feature of the text, both as a stylistic device, and in statistical comparison with other texts, is the number of examples with zero *invertissant* and *et*. The former rarely occurs in contexts other than official language, and the use of the latter is certainly somewhat archaic by the end of the 16th century. Examples with zero *invertissant* are found both in narrative and direct speech, and are most effective when there is a complex or multiple subject, as in the example already quoted (p. 73) above, or :

> ' estoient lors incognus ces mots maquereux et lubriques, serviteur, maistresse ... (etc.) et telles meschancetez et drogueries, qui...' (p. 285)

It may be noted that many inversions after *et* occur in contexts where the vocabulary is a legal one, and this also suggests parody through word-order. The advantages of the construction are much the same as those with zero *invertissant*, in that there is the possibility of several subjects, dependent clauses and so on :

> ' et fut le gentil-homme, outre la privation de sa haute justice, condamné en grosses amendes.' (p. 179)

There are also many examples with other *invertissants*, such as the following, where comic effect is achieved through the incongruous, as seen already in Rabelais :

> ' "... apres quelques preface et rabrouemens et avertissemens en Droit, fut tout à propos dressé un festin pour savoir et entendre mes estudes et comme j'avois profité." ' (p. 302)

3. Other effects

If attention to detail is to be a basis for comparison between du Fail and Rabelais, it should be pointed out that their approach is completely different. The descriptive detail, which is an integral part of Rabelaisian style, whether achieved by enumeration or other devices, is almost entirely lacking in du Fail. It is perhaps the elaboration of what has already been stated, the technique described above, which gives the illusion of careful description, as in the following :

> ' si fut-il deplanté et deraciné, et plats, chapon et escueles par terre, et le porteur des presentes de chercher et tastonner, qui...' (p. 274)

Detail in du Fail consists rather of many precise references to historical precedents and learned sources, and in particular careful consideration of the law, and this is both emphasized and expressed more clearly by inversion :

> ' " Me souvient qu'aux lois etablies aux Atheniens par Solon, étoit prescrit la forme du mariage, au menu peuple de volonté, et aux nobles et autres tenant rang en la republique, de necessité." ' (p. 329)

Du Fail, like Rabelais, employs devices of accumulation and repetition, but is less extreme in doing so. In these examples inversion permits the accumulation of past participles and subjects :

   ' "... ceste belle pierre philosophale, à laquelle se sont frottez heurtez et rompus tant de gentils esprits." ' (p. 193)

   '... ils regardoient trois ou quatre tableaux ... où étoient depeints entre autres un relief d'appel, en l'autre fines esguilles, et en plusieurs l'intervention saincte Croix.' (p. 132)

Repetition is often used for comic effect, as in this example which evokes country life and thought :

   ' L'an revolu et passé, étant les bons personnages pres de leur feu, s'avisa la femme de ce qu'il y avoit justement et proprement un an qu'ils avoient épousé, fait grand'chere...' (p. 341)

The vocabulary can hardly be called Rabelaisian, although there are some exceptions, where the influence of Rabelais' rhythmic structure is also apparent :

   ' Là fit Eutrapel une sesquipedale et fort bien metrisée reverence, se tenant droit comme un jonc...' (p. 254).

In such examples inversion contributes to the balance of the sentence with stress falling on either subject or verb.

   To conclude, then, the inversions found in this text may have some structural function in the narrative as part of the story-telling technique, or alternatively may be used to help in a realistic representation of direct speech, and to parody a certain style. There are, in addition, inversions which are simply a further factor in the deviant word-order of this text, the language of which is generally complex.

Chapter IV

THE SEVENTEENTH CENTURY (1)

1. SYNTACTIC ANALYSIS OF THE TEXTS
1600–1650

The texts :

H. d'Urfé, *L'Astrée* [1]

C. Sorel, *Histoire comique de Francion* [2]

M. Le Roy de Gomberville, *La première partie de Polexandre* [3]

M. de Scudéry, *Artamène, ou Le grand Cyrus* [4]

Table 4.01 : Inversion frequencies

D'UR/AST	193 : 0·97	
SOR/FRA	161 : 0·81	*(mean 0·74)*
GOM/POL	122 : 0·61	
SCU/GC	116 : 0·58	

Table 4.02 : Percentage table to show nature of clause in which inversion occurs

	D'UR	*SOR*	*GOM*	*SCU*
Main clause	74	40	39	28
Subordinate clause	24	56	61	69
Non-subordinating *invertissant* in subordinate clause	2	4	n	3
	100	100	100	100
Immobile *invertissant*	46	57	63	69
Mobile *invertissant*	48	39	36	31
Other operations	6	4	1	—
N :	193	161	122	116

[1] ed. H. Vaganay, Strasbourg, 1925 (1ère partie, livres 1–12). (D'UR)

[2] In *Romanciers du XVIIe siècle*, ed. A. Adam, Paris, 1958 (livres I–V), pp. 66–263. (SOR)

[3] Paris, 1641. B.N. Y² 7313. (GOM)

[4] 2nd. ed., Paris, 1650 (livres I–II). (SCU)

Table 4.03 : Percentage table to show distribution of inversions according to discourse type

	D'UR	SOR	GOM	SCU
Narrative	56	61	64	62
Direct speech	44	32	34	32
Indirect speech	—	7	2	5
Soliloquy	—	—	—	1

Table 4.04 : Percentage table to show position of inversion within the corpus examined

	D'UR	SOR	GOM	SCU
Sentence initial	25	14	26	23
Paragraph initial	2	—	—	—
Speech initial	6	2	—	—
Total initial	33	16	26	23
Sentence final	17	28	28	24
Paragraph final	n	3	—	1
Speech final	2	5	—	—
Total final	19	36	28	25

Table 4.05 : Percentage table to show position of inversion in relation to other types of discourse

	D'UR	SOR	GOM	SCU
Preceding direct speech	1	n	—	—
Following direct speech	6	—	2	—
Preceding indirect speech	n	—	—	—
Following indirect speech	n	n	n	—

Table 4.06 : Percentage table to show nature of the inverted noun phrase

	D'UR	SOR	GOM	SCU
Pronoun subject	61	37	16	27
Substantive subject	39	60	84	69
Compound inversion	—	3	n	4
	100	100	100	100
2 or more subjects	1	2	9	6
S and dependent (S)	11	11	25	17

Table 4.07 : The percentage of inversions occurring in sentences of three or more clauses

	D'UR	SOR	GOM	SCU
(S)—3 clauses	21	25	39	36
4 clauses	20	19	18	16
5 clauses	14	11	14	6
6 clauses	9	13	2	2
7 clauses	6	6	—	—
7+ clauses	5	7	2	2
	75	81	75	62

Table 4.08 : The ratio of inversions to *invertissants*

D'UR	193 : 54—3·57
SOR	161 : 48—3·35
GOM	122 : 45—2·71
SCU	116 : 29—4·00
Total	592 : 100—5·92 (*mean* 3·41)

Table 4.09 : Percentage table of the most frequently occurring inversions

	D'UR	SOR	GOM	SCU
Co-ordinators	26	4	n	—
Relatives	9	26	34	31
Comparatives	2	13	9	6
Indirect construction	7	11	15	29
Modal adverbs	37	37	18	26

Table 4.10 : Percentage table to show the occurrence of ' être ', ' faire ' and ' avoir '

	D'UR	SOR	GOM	SCU
être	18	25	23	50
faire	3	9	7	10
avoir	2	n	2	3

Table 4.11 : Percentage table showing the distribution of direct speech *invertissants*

	D'UR	SOR	GOM	SCU
Immobile *invertissant*	45	37	69	70
Mobile *invertissant*	47	57	31	30
Other operations	8	6	—	—
N :	85	51	42	37

Table 4.12 : Percentage table to show the occurrence of
adverbials and clauses in inversion constructions

	D'UR	*SOR*	*GOM*	*SCU*
V(adv)S	n	5	2	2
(adv)VS	n	—	1	—
V(S)S	—	—	—	—
(S)VS	n	—	—	—

(i) DISTRIBUTION OF THE INVERSIONS

The inversion frequencies of the four texts show a tremendous drop from those of the previous century. The mean for
the half-century of $0\cdot74$ compares with the figure of $2\cdot07$ for
the 16th century as a whole. Although the frequencies have
not yet reached their lowest point, this marks the end of the
' free' word-order. While the frequencies increase again in the
19th and 20th centuries, few individual texts reach the average
of the 1550–1600 period, $1\cdot50$, and $0\cdot74$ remains an approximately average frequency for texts analysed for about 200
years, until the period of the Romantics. Throughout the
present period there is a steady decrease in inversion frequency,
although there seems to be a relative linguistic stability in the
new literary form, following the pattern first noticed in the
Bergeries de Juliette in 1585.

In table 4.02, the anomalous text is the *Astrée*, whose high
percentage of inversions in main clauses is due to the number of
examples of inversion after a co-ordinating conjunction, the
last text in which such a construction is found to any great
extent, and also the number of inversions after modal adverbs.
The 74% in main clauses is in fact the highest percentage so far,
with the exception of 75% in the *Amadis*. This also accounts
for the fact that the distribution between mobile and immobile
invertissants is more or less even, a feature of the previous
century, but not otherwise found in this period.

One may also note the sudden decrease in the inversion of
substantive subjects, with the exception of *Polexandre*, whose
figure for this construction is surpassed only by Helisenne de
Crenne.   Complementing this is the new phenomenon of
compound inversion which occurs in three of the four texts,

and enables a substantive which would have been inverted to be replaced by an inverted pronoun. The decrease in the number of inverted substantive subjects may be partially explained by the disappearance of certain *invertissants*, for example direct objects, infinitivals, hypothetical, temporal, causal and result clauses, and zero, which in the 16th century almost always occurred with a substantive. This, however, accounts for only a small proportion. More significant is the sudden increase in modal adverb *invertissants* in the 17th century, in constructions which almost invariably have a pronoun subject, although in the previous periods there were more examples with a substantive, and there seems to be a growing preference for pronominal subjects where inversion takes place, possibly because this is a clearer, less complex construction. It is perhaps significant that 17th-century grammarians who deal with inversion tend to do so under the heading of the place of the subject pronoun, and it is likely that the possibility of inversion of the pronoun only, in interrogation, has influenced other inversion constructions.

Table 4.08 shows the continual decrease in the number of *invertissants* alongside that in the number of inversions, a total of 100 as opposed to 146 in the previous period, and the ratio of the two also becomes generally lower, with the drop in frequency of occurrence. Table 4.09 reveals a change in the most frequently occurring inversions. The occurrence of co-ordinators is greatly reduced, and these are not found at all in *Cyrus*, whereas the new predominant inversion type, along with relatives, is the class of modal adverbs. Table 4.03 shows that 44% of the inversions in the *Astrée* occur in direct speech, whereas the other texts show remarkably regular proportions of 32%, 34% and 32%. Also in the *Astrée* inversion follows direct speech in 6% of the examples (table 4.05), although there are few instances in *Polexandre*, the text with the next highest proportion of speech inversions (2%), and none in the remaining texts. About half of the inversions in each text occur in one of the key positions (table 4.04). In *Polexandre* and *Cyrus* the distribution is approximately even between sentence initial and final positions, but on the other hand d'Urfé shows a marked preference for initial inversions and Sorel one for final inversions, 3% being paragraph final. It may be noted that in these two texts 8% and 7% respectively relate to direct speech constructions, whereas this constitutes a negligible proportion in the other two authors. There are more inversions in key positions in these four texts than in the previous period, but this is not nearly as many as in the first half of the 16th century.

Concerning sentence length (table 4.07), the total number of inversions in sentences of three or more clauses does not vary greatly between the texts, except possibly in *Cyrus*, where the figure is as low as 61%, and the average is about the same as that for the last fifty-year period. It is striking, however, that whereas all the inversions in *Polexandre* and *Cyrus* are in sentences of up to seven clauses, at least 6% in d'Urfé and Sorel occur in sentences of eight or more clauses, indeed examples in the *Astrée* are of ten, twelve, fifteen and twenty-two clauses.

(ii) EXAMPLES

A. IMMOBILE 'INVERTISSANT'

1. *Co-ordinating conjunctions : D'UR : 50 inversions, 2 'invertissants' ; SCU : 7,2 ; GOM : 1,1*
   ' Encore qu'ils descrivoient les faits genereux de plusieurs grands personnages, ils ne s'enflammoient point de generosité, *et* ne partoit d'eux aucune action recommandable.' (SOR, p. 233)
2. *Relatives : D'UR : 18,8 ; SOR : 40,7 ; GOM : 41,7 ; SCU : 36,7*
   ' " Je sçay que la conscience est la premiere chose *dont* se dépouïllent ceux qui veulent estre faits Citoyens de leur Republique " '. (GOM, p. 171)
3. *Comparatives : D'UR : 4,3 ; SOR : 21,7 ; GOM : 11,5 ; SCU : 8,4*
   '... il fit alors des efforts incroyables pour le suivre et pour ne le perdre pas de veuë, *comme* firent tous les Personnes

qui l'avoient suivy, dont pas un ne le pût atteindre.'
(SCU, p. 231)

4. *Concessives : SOR : 3,2 ; GOM : 3,2 ; SCU : 2,2*
' " Je luy representay que ... *pour* extraordinaire *que* fust
son infortune, il n'en devoit pas sortir par une voye si
criminelle." ' (GOM, p. 20)

5. *Correlatives : D'UR : 3,2 ; GOM : 3,1*
' *Plus* il voyait croistre le Roy, *et plus* redoubloient ses
chagrins et ses inquietudes.' (GOM, p. 259)

6. *Indirect construction : D'UR : 14,9 ; SOR : 18,9 ;
GOM : 18,9 ; SCU : 34,7*
' " O justes Dieux ! vous scavez *ce que* me couste la
Victoire et ce que j'ay fait pour ma Princesse." ' (SCU,
p. 476)

B. MOBILE 'INVERTISSANT'

1. *Attribute : D'UR : 4,2*
' *Grand* certes fut l'applaudissement de chacun, mais plus
grand la gentillesse de Clidaman, qui...' (p. 129)

2. *Adverbs—modal : D'UR : 72,12 ; SOR : 59,11 ; GOM :
26,7 ; SCU : 30,6*
' " Mais quel ferrement ? dit l'Advocat, *possible* estoit ce
une besche ". " Non Monsieur, c'estoit un glaive..." '
(SOR, p. 207)

3. *Adverbs—quantity : D'UR : 1,1 ; SCU : 2,1*
'... si l'attribuoit-on plustost à un bon natural qu'à un
amour (*tant* profite la bonne opinion que l'on a d'une
personne).' (D'UR, p. 55)

4. *Adverbs—time : D'UR : 1,1 ; GOM : 2,2*
' *Aussitôt* parut à la poupe de ce superbe vaisseau, un
jeune Turc, si beau et si charmant, qu'il pouvoit estre pris
pour une de ses merveilles qui...' (GOM, p. 2)

5. *Adverbs—place : D'UR : 1,1 ; SOR : 4,4*
' " Ouy, reprit il, *icy* se font leurs plus grandes assemblées,
tellement qu'il n'y a point de lieu dans la France qui doive
plus justement porter le nom de Parnasse." ' (SOR,
pp. 228–29)

6. *Adverbs—combinations :* $D'UR : 3,2 ; SCU : 4,2$
   ' " Et si mon Rival meurt, *plus facilement encore* vaincray-je
   l'ennemi de ma Patrie." ' (SCU, p. 470)

7. *Adverbial phrase—time :* $D'UR : 1,1 ; GOM : 2,2$
   ' " Apprend, me dit-elle, que *dans un mois* se doit executer
   la plus noire trahison que des subjets perfides puissent
   former contre leur Souverain." ' (GOM, p. 311)

8. *Adverbial phrase—place :* $D'UR : 7,4 ; GOM : 8,6$
   ' *Dessous ses pieds* s'eslevoient de gros morceaux d'osse-
   ments, dont les uns blanchissoient de vieillesse, les autres
   ne commençoient que d'estre descharnez...' (D'UR, p. 80)

9. *Adverbial phrase—manner :* $D'UR : 1,1 ; GOM : 1,1$
   ' " Si vous sçaviez que c'est d'aimer ... vous jugeriez qu'*au
   besoin* ne cognoist l'amy, mais..." ' (D'UR, p. 214)

10. *Prepositional phrase :* $D'UR : 1,1 ; GOM : 5,1$
    ' *Du pied de ces vases* naissoit une vigne d'or bronzé, qui
    rompoit le long d'une treille d'argent.' (GOM, p. 177)

11. *Direct object :* $D'UR : 1,1$
    ' " Pour ne m'enquerir de son nom et de tenir cette affaire
    secrette, *cela* feray-je volontiers." ' (p. 101)

12. *Participial phrase :* $SOR : 1,1$
    ' " *Estant retiré en sa maison*, adjousta l'Advocat, portoit il
    tousjours l'espée comme marque de sa condition." '
    (p. 207)

C. OTHER OPERATIONS

1. *Deletion :* $D'UR : 7$
   ' " De sorte que *n'eust esté* la contrainte à quoy la coustume
   m'a obligée, je ne fusse jamais venuë devant vous..." '
   (p. 185)

2. *Deletion and transposition :* $D'UR : 3 ; SOR : 3$
   ' " Monsieur *estoit il* revenu du Chastelet fort tard, il avoit
   beau dire que la faim le pressoit, elle..." ' (SOR, p. 105)

3. *Addition and transposition :* $D'UR : 1,1 ; SOR : 3,2 ;$
   $GON : 1,1$
   ' *Ce fut là que* parut l'inconstance des evenemens de la
   guerre.' (GOM, p. 153)

(iii) DETAILS OF INVERSIONS

(a) Compound inversions

Although there are no examples of compound inversion in the *Astrée*, and only one in *Polexandre*, the five examples in each of the other texts represent a proportion of 3% in Sorel, and 4% in Scudéry. With the exception of one example in Sorel, the *invertissants* in this construction are all modal adverbs. The construction is not confined to any one *invertissant*, but involves seven different adverbs. With the exception of Gomberville, where the examples of *à peine* and simple inversion occur in the narrative and those with compound inversion in conversation, there is no direct correlation between this form of inversion and the type of discourse, although the majority occur in direct speech, thus :

‘ “ *A peine* un mort a-t-il esté dans le fossé autant de temps qu'il y a que nous y avons mis nos Capitaines, quand ces deux Anges arrivent.” ’ (GOM, p. 411)

The majority are also found in initial position, but then it is the general tendency for modal adverb *invertissants* to occur initially. It is, however, an important factor in the use of compound inversion, as the repetition of the noun subject in the form of an inverted pronoun gives correspondingly greater emphasis to the beginning of the sentence.

In Sorel compound inversion takes place after two modal adverbs which are already somewhat archaic as *invertissants*, *possible* (two examples) and *paravanture*, e.g.

‘... et qu'elle en auroit de la honte, parce que *possible* Hortensius avoit il semblablement gardé un regiment de pourceaux en sa jeunesse.’ (SOR, p. 208)

This text also provides the unusual example of compound inversion within a deletion and transposition operation, already quoted (p. 111) above. The remaining example is after *encore*. The inversions in *Cyrus* occur after *à peine* (2), *aussi*, *aussi bien*, *du moins* and it is in this text that compound inversion plays the greatest part, occurring with four out of the six modal adverb *invertissants*. Also in Scudéry, the construction is paralleled by a considerable number of interrogative inversions of the same type, e.g.

' " Et *Artamene* qui ne paroist estre qu'un simple Chevalier, en pourroit-*il* concevoir la temeraire pensée...? " ' (p. 523)

(b) *Inversion in correlative constructions*

In several cases, inversions after an immobilized adverb of quantity form part of a correlative construction, in which reversal of direct word-order is important, both as regards the balance of the sentence, and also from the point of view of emphasis, where there is a change in subject, whether a new subject is introduced, or the first one repeated in pronominal form. There are three examples of this in both d'Urfé and Gomberville. In the *Astrée*, all three examples occur in direct speech, two with *autant que ... autant*, and one with *plus... plus aussi*, and in each example the original pronoun subject is retained, thus :

' " Mais puisque *plus* il va vieillissant, *plus aussi* va-t'il augmentant, je suis contraint de luy en rechercher un meilleur." ' (p. 204)

In Gomberville, all three examples are with *plus ... et plus*, only one occurs in direct speech, and in every case the first pronoun subject is replaced by a new substantive subject in the second part, as in the example quoted (p. 110) above, cf. also :

' " *Plus* je le voyois, et *plus* me croissoit l'envie de le voir." ' (p. 94)

The Gomberville correlatives constitute the only examples of inversion using an adverb of quantity in the part of the text analysed, and in d'Urfé the only other example of a non-correlative adverb of quantity is one inversion after *tant*. This suggests that with a decreasing number of inversions of this type, adverbs of quantity tend to be immobilized in a construction where inverted word-order has increased syntactic and stylistic value regarding the form of the sentence and the ideas expressed.

(c) *Modal adverbs*

The greatly increased number of inversions after a modal

adverb has already been mentioned. While such *invertissants* play a large part in each novel, although this is less true of *Polexandre*, the texts reveal quite different trends. Thus while modal adverb inversions represent 37% of the total in d'Urfé and Sorel, they include *invertissants* which are more characteristic of the 16th century than the 17th, and consequently show greater variety than the two others. The *invertissants* in these texts, which subsequently disappear, are mainly those expressing the idea of chance or difficulty. There are six examples with *malaisément* in d'Urfé, and two in Sorel, while d'Urfé has three with *difficilement*, and Sorel six with *possible* and three with *par aventure*. Such inversions are not to be found in the two later texts, except for an isolated occurrence of *possible* in Gomberville. In all, there are eighteen different modal adverb *invertissants* in the four texts, only half of which occur at all in Gomberville and Scudéry. Neither of these texts has examples of inversion after *encore*, although there are fourteen in d'Urfé and sixteen in Sorel, and this is largely due to the disappearance of the concessive constructions, analogous to those with *si* in earlier works, e.g.

' " Car *outre qu'*il est d'une des principales familles de ceste contrée, *encor* a-t-il tant de merites que la peine y sera bien employée." ' (D'UR, p. 48)

The same construction is also found to some extent with *aussi* :

' " Et *si* je l'avois attenduë avec beaucoup de peine, *aussi* la receus-je avec beaucoup de contentement." ' (p. 212)

On the other hand, examples with *à peine* (in either sense) occur regularly throughout the period, and it is *invertissants* such as this, along with, for example, *peut-être*, *du moins* and *aussi*, which will predominate. Inversion after less familiar adverbs begins to disappear, and it is the tendency for the inverted construction to be confined to certain adverbs, rather than to occur after more or less any one. Thus whereas d'Urfé and Sorel retain many adverbial *invertissants* of the 16th century and also include all those found in Gomberville and Scudéry, with the exception of *du moins*, the latter authors show a much more restricted range. There are twelve and eleven different *invertissants* in d'Urfé and Sorel respectively, as opposed to seven and six in Gomberville and Scudéry. In conclusion, although the category of modal adverbs has the highest number of *invertissants* for this period, eighteen, as compared with twelve in relatives and comparatives, and eleven in indirect constructions, this total seems likely to become lower in later periods, while the proportion of this type of inversion remains high.

2. STYLISTIC ANALYSIS OF THE TEXTS
(i) H. D'URFÉ, 'L'ASTRÉE'

The literary form of the *Astrée* expands the structures of the 16th-century works already studied. The novel consists of a narrative which is at once the framework and the central story, and which is broken up by the stories of the adventures of the main and peripheral characters, interspersed throughout with poems and letters. Although a division between the framework and the stories told is still possible, these are much more closely related in style and content than in earlier works, as even the inversion figures show. Nonetheless different stylistic features of the two types of narrative may be distinguished on this basis.

First of all, as regards the number of inversions, ninety-seven occur in the narrative, and ninety-six in the *histoires*, but as the stories represent a section nearly one-third as long again as the narrative, the latter clearly has a considerably higher inversion rate. The distribution of the inversions is similar in each section, and also close to that of the whole (see table 4.02): in the narrative there are forty-six inversions with immobile *invertissant*, forty-eight with mobile, and three from other operations, and in the *histoires* forty with immobile *invertissant*, forty-eight mobile and eight from other operations.

Although the main inversion constructions, co-ordinates, relatives and modal adverbs, are more or less evenly distributed between stories and narrative, there are certain significant differences. There are no examples of comparative *invertissants* in the *histoires*, whereas there are four in the narrative, which also has eleven examples of indirect *invertissants* as against three in the stories.   There is also a tendency for the more archaic or literary inversion constructions to occur in the stories rather than in the narrative, such as the example after a direct object, two out of the three inversions after *et*, and five with *malaisément* (only one other being found in the framework), and also examples with *seulement* and *à plus forte raison*.   There are also more examples in the stories with the co-ordinator *si* than in the framework, particularly when it occurs alone rather than in the phrase *si est-ce que* which elsewhere is the more common form at this time.

(a) The language of the 'Astrée'

Although the *Astrée* is generally regarded as the forerunner of the modern French novel, there are still many features of the 16th-century language present, which are clearly revealed by the analysis of the inversions.   Most outstanding is the number of inversions in co-ordinating constructions, 26% of the total, whereas, except for the 4% in Sorel, these are almost negligible in later texts.   Besides preserving inversion after *si* (three examples in the narrative, two with the impersonal subject pronoun *on*), d'Urfé makes extensive use of the particle *si*. Contrary to the general trend, which is for *si* to occur, if at all, in the phrase *si est-ce que*, there are thirty-one examples of *si* alone, two of *mais si* and fourteen of *si est-ce que*.   Even the latter seems excessive in view of the figures provided by other works of the period.   The two constructions divide sharply as to their distribution in narrative and direct speech.   Of the inversions after *si*, twenty occur in conversation, eight of them in initial position, and all of these eight have an argumentative function.   There are thirteen occurring in the course of the narrative, none of which are initial inversions, but function as co-ordinators following a concessive clause.   With the construction *si est-ce que*, however, there are only four examples in conversation (two initially as part of an argument) whereas there are ten examples in the narrative.   Thus although d'Urfé makes wide use of the old construction, his choice is consistent with its function, *si* being used predominantly in conversation, where it is especially effective in argument, while *si est-ce que* is hardly used at all in this context, but is reserved for the narrative and the longer, more complex constructions following concessive clauses.

Alongside *si est-ce que* after a concessive, is the use of the adverb *encore* in that context, two of the three examples being in narrative, e.g.

'" Car *outre que* je sçay que celle-cy vous est la plus difficile, *encore* nous raportera-t'elle une commodité..."'　(p. 52)

However, the fact remains that there are more 16th-century or archaic elements occurring in conversation than in ordinary narrative, at least as far as inversion is concerned, those in the framework being mostly inversions with some co-ordinating function. This may indicate the survival of archaisms in the spoken language, with a more polished style being reserved for the narrative. This problem will, however, be discussed at greater length with reference to the *Francion*.

The *Astrée*, like the other texts of the period, no longer contains inversion after a preceding subordinate clause. Instead the impersonal pronoun is found where earlier writers tended to invert, with the same effect, i.e. preserving a co-ordinating link :

' Et lors qu'il estoit entre la mort et la vie, *il* arriva sur le mesme lieu trois belles Nymphes, dont...' (p. 46)

and this may also allow inversion in the succeeding clauses.

Out of the total number of inversions in the corpus, 44% occur in conversation, and the distribution of these follows very closely that of the whole (table 4.11). Both conversation and narrative show considerable variety in *invertissants*, with twenty-seven different *invertissants* in speech alone, and fifty-four in the whole corpus. Ten of the twelve modal adverb *invertissants* are also found in direct speech, the exceptions being eight occurrences of the temporal *à peine*, which is perhaps a device of narrative, and *seulement*. Moreover direct speech accounts for four of the six examples with *malaisément*, and five of the six with *peut-être*. Thus although there is a fairly regular distribution of inversions between the two types of

discourse, certain constructions are more common to one than
to the other. Inversion is rare in direct speech in relative
constructions (five of the eighteen examples) and in indirect
constructions (four out of fourteen), but on the other hand all
three instances with comparative *invertissant* occur in speech,
and so do the three correlatives and seven of the eleven examples
of different operations of word-order, including all three
deletion and transposition examples.

Bochet,[5] in discussing the variety of dialogue in the *Astrée*,
draws a parallel with that of Marivaux. As regards inversion,
however, this is not a very fruitful comparison. In the *Paysan
parvenu* it will be seen that inversions in direct speech constitute only 28% of the whole, and these have only eighteen
different *invertissants* as opposed to twenty-seven in the
Astrée.

D'Urfé himself in his introduction states that his pastoral
characters should not speak in the style of real shepherds and
shepherdesses, but rather as the aristocracy of his own time.
This point is taken by Bochet, who says of the characters,
' Ils mettent dans tout ce qu'ils disent, de l'élégance et de la
distinction comme s'ils parlaient dans un salon '.[6]   The
predominant impression then conveyed by d'Urfé's prose,
particularly in the context of direct speech, is that of elegance.
As in the *Bergeries de Juliette*, inversion in d'Urfé is combined
with an elegant vocabulary, tending towards *préciosité*, to
indicate feeling, although the general refinement of the speech
of the characters is perhaps more striking in the *Astrée*. Some
uses of inversion in direct speech thus indicate its literary
rather than realistic character, and this is particularly true of
modal adverbs occurring initially. Often the elegant inversion
construction contrasts with the mundane content, as when a
nymph says :

' "... car pour aujourd'huy je me trouve un peu mal, et
difficilement sortiray je du lict, que sur le soir." ' (p. 125)

---

[5] H. Bochet, *L'Astrée—ses origines, son importance dans la formation de la
littérature classique*, reprinted Geneva, 1967, p. 172.

[6] *Ibid.*, p. 171.

Similarly the form of Celadon's protestations of simplicity may seem slightly incongruous :

' " Mais ... encor ne puis-je assez m'estonner de me voir entre tant de grandes Nymphes, moy qui ne suis qu'un simple Berger..." ' (p. 88)

Such inversions may also lead to a rhythmic, almost poetic sentence structure, as in the following, where the spoken sentence falls into one group of ten syllables and two of eight :

' " Malaisément (repliqua la Nymphe) peuvent avoir cognoissance/les sentiments des vaines idées/d'une malade imagination." ' (p. 160)

Obviously some types of inversion are more likely to achieve elegant effects than others, and it is the operations other than simple transposition which give a particularly elevated character to the speech. When the vocabulary is equally noble, the device is even more effective :

' "... je ne me desdiray jamais de ce que je vous ai dit, et en deussé-je douer le cœur pour gage." ' (p. 181)

An elegant construction and choice of words may be put to a specific use, such as that of conveying a compliment :

' "... encor que je ne sois point de ceste contrée, si est-ce que vostre vertu et vostre pieté envers les Dieux m'obligent à vous aimer, et...' " (p. 264)

Here the linking of subordinate and main clause underlines the contrasing content.

Thus inversion forms part of the *style élégant* in several ways, firstly in that inverted word-order in itself tends to elevate speech, secondly there are the noble overtones associated with particular constructions, especially subjunctive and hypothetical clauses, and thirdly there is the combination of inversion with a refined and specialized vocabulary such as will characterize the school of the *précieux*.

(b) Inversions and sentence structure

The rhythmic and elegant nature of d'Urfé's prose style has often been the subject of literary criticism, in particular the movement and progression within the sentence. Thus Bochet states that ' chaque phrase donne ... l'impression de quelque chose d'achevé, pour la grande satisfaction de l'oreille et de l'esprit ' (p. 162), although for this critic the greatest quality of the style of the *Astrée* is that,

> ' il fait corps avec la pensée et l'inspiration de l'auteur et s'adapte ainsi parfaitement aux personnages, à leurs sentiments, et à leur genre de vie.' (p. 178)

One of the most striking features which emerges from a stylistic consideration of the inversions in this text is their use in conjunction with direct word-order in chiastic structures. Parallel structures within the sentence are usually based on the repetition of the verb, but there is one example of parallel development of two subjects, both inverted after a single verb :

> ' Ainsi alloient discourant Lycidas et Phillis : luy infiniment fasché de la mort de son frere, et infiniment offencé contre Astrée : elle marrie de Celadon, faschée de...' (p. 69)

The more usual construction, however, involves two occurrences of verb and subject. This may be the same verb with different subjects and different order :

> ' " Si j'estois en vostre place et vous en la mienne, peut-estre vous conseilleroy-je cela mesme que vous me conseillez." ' (p. 78)

or the same subject with different verbs, although these may be cognate and virtually synonymous :

> ' " Ne faites point ce souhait, Celadon : car peut-estre ne souhaiterez-vous jamais rien de si dangereux." ' (p. 181)

Finally there is one example of parallelism where both parts of the construction contain inverted word-order :

> ' "... que ne ressens-je quelque faveur, afin que n'ayant peu mourir comme vouloit mon desespoir, je le fasse pour le moins comme le commande la rigueur d'Astrée ? " ' (p. 77).

In structures showing opposition, the contrast between direct and inverted word-order usually has the function of avoiding monotony or exact repetition. However, when the two orders are juxtaposed in sentences involving conceptual oppositions the inversion underlines them, and this, in the *Astrée*, is its more common function. Oppositions may be made completely explicit, i.e. there is a formal element present in one half of the construction such as a concessive or negative particle, or they may be contained purely in the meaning of subject and verb. There are several examples of structures where one half contains a negative statement with direct word-order, and the other a positive statement with inverted order, and it is this change in order which effectively emphasizes the negative-positive opposition :

' "... je veux bien croire pour l'amour de vous, que peut-estre il n'adviendra pas, mais peut-estre aussi adviendra-t'il." ' (p. 78)

More commonly, the opposition may be expressed by verbal phrases of quite different meaning, first in subordinate and then in main clauses, the subordinate clause generally having a concessive value :

' Car encore que je ne sceusse guere bien ce mestier, si falloit-il que je me montrasse expert en cela...' (p. 258)

In this example the particle *si* is omitted in the 1621 edition, although the juxtaposition of orders is maintained. Thirdly, the opposition may be contained in the complement or direct object, when both verb and subject are repeated :

' "... que tout ainsi que vous avez ce mal-heur contraire à vostre bon-heur, aussi avez-vous un destin si capable de vous rendre heureuse, que vostre heur ne se peut repre-senter." ' (p. 256)

And finally an example of a chiasmus where both verbs and subjects are opposed, which also achieves the effect of the author's style fitting the concept expressed :

' " Et mal-aisément parviendra la parole, où la pensée ne peut atteindre." ' (p. 145)

Although a significant proportion of inversions in this text occur in sentences of more than six clauses (table 4.07), and in some which are very much larger, the majority of these occur in the course of narrative which describes the action, rather than in direct speech, or the description of feeling and emotion. Indeed it is the tendency for strong feeling to be expressed in short, sometimes disconnected sentences. This is shown

particularly in the letters which generally convey emotion in an
almost epigrammatic style, and the same device is used in both
conversation and descriptive narrative.　Here inversion is
useful as a relief from a succession of short sentences ordered
in the same way.　The inversion may be a simple reversal of a
single-clause sentence,

' De cet Amour vint une tres-grande inimitié.' (p. 111)

The device is also very common as a short comment following
direct speech :

' A ce mot, avec le souffle s'envola son ame, et son corps me
demeura froid entre les bras.' (p. 145)

The most frequent *invertissants* in this context are, however,
modal adverbs, particularly, in direct speech, those expressing
doubt or difficulty :

' " Mais difficilement le pourrez vous aimer : au contraire..." ' (p. 263)

Very often the speaker is displaying considerable emotion, and
the emphatic effect of a short sentence with inverted word-
order represents further evidence of the correspondence
between language and thought in d'Urfé, thus :

' " Je suis tant hors de moy ... qu'à peine sçay-je ce que je
dis." ' (p. 173)

' " Car elle est devenue si jalouse de moy, qu'à peine me peut-
elle souffrir aupres de luy." ' (p. 175)

To sum up, then, inversions in the *Astrée* seem to indicate
many varied directions for stylistic investigation.　While some
linguistic elements remain from the 16th century, but soon
disappear, others are developed, such as the pastoral techniques involving cliché constructions and *préciosité*, already
foreshadowed by de Montreux.　Many features of later French
novels are introduced by d'Urfé, in particular the rhythmic
prose and balanced sentence structure, and also the language-
thought correlation.　As the form itself evolves, the old
divisions into narrative and *histoires* become increasingly
blurred, and with Sorel begin new techniques in story-telling
to replace them.

(ii) C. SOREL, 'HISTOIRE COMIQUE DE FRANCION'

The influence on Sorel of the Spanish picaresque novel has been widely acknowledged. At the end of his comprehensive study on the influence of Cervantes in France, for example, Dr. Hainsworth is able to conclude : ' Nous avons pu rattacher directement à la nouvelle espagnole celle de Sorel, de Scarron et de Segrais.' [7] Mérimée, commenting on the Spanish genre, points out that in spite of their originality the works all have similar shortcomings : ' unnatural style, intentional deformation and exaggeration of every feature and superficiality in the observation of psychological fact.' [8] It is not, then, surprising that French critics have made similar remarks about Sorel's work, and Reynier declares : ' Il manque du style.' [9] Yet in a genre that depicts for the first time popular society in its true colours, realistic representation is of the first order, although it is possible for this realism to predominate in the subject matter rather than in its expression : ' the fabliau or the picaresque tale are realistic because economic or carnal motives are given pride of place in their presentation of human behaviour.' [10]

Sorel states his literary intention quite clearly in the various prefaces to the *Francion*, maintaining primarily that both speech and action are in keeping with the characters of the novel :

> ' J'ay representé aussi naïvement qu'il se pouvoit faire, les humeurs, les actions et les propos ordinaires de toutes les personnes que j'ay mises sur les rangs.' (*Advertissement*, 1633) (p. 1262)

The use of the adverb *naïvement* here suggests a simple, economic and authentic style of narration. The later prefaces continue to emphasize reproduction of ordinary speech, with the famous claim of 1626, ' dans mon livre on peut trouver la

[7] G. Hainsworth, *Les ' Novelas exemplares ' de Cervantes en France au XVIIe siècle*, Paris, 1933, p. 237.

[8] E. Mérimée, *A History of Spanish Literature*, New York, 1930, p. 205.

[9] G. Reynier, *Le roman réaliste au XVIIe siècle*, Paris, 1914, p. 160.

[10] I. Watt, *The Rise of the Novel*, London (Penguin), 1968, p. 11.

langue Françoise toute entiere ', preceded in 1623 by the
' Advis ... touchant l'autheur de ce livre ', where Sorel says of
himself :

> '... il sçavoit bien qu'en ce lieu cy il faloit escrire simplement
> comme l'on parloit sans user d'aucune affeterie (...) : il se
> plaisoit bien plus à escrire des choses serieuses avec un
> langage coulant que non pas se contraindre pour escrire
> à la mode de son siècle.' (p. 1267)

Thus not only the conversational passages but the whole
narrative should be written in the style of everyday speech.
So following Sorel's own statements one expects the main
characteristics of the novel's style to be simplicity of presentation and lack of linguistic refinement in conversation. It is
hoped that the study of inversions will show how far this claim
is true and also what effect the introduction of the picaresque
elements of parody and irony has on the ' realistic ' narrative
style.

(a) Realism and word-order

1. Distribution of inversions

Sorel's claim to realism is borne out to some extent by the
routine nature of the majority of inversion examples and the
low proportion occurring in representation of speech. As has
already been shown the largest number of inversions occur
after relative or modal adverb *invertissants*. The latter constitute almost the total number of mobile *invertissants* (the
remainder being four adverbs of place and one participial
phrase) and this is indicative of the absence of descriptive
detail in this work. In contrast to other popular novelists of
this period, against whom Sorel's works are a conscious reaction, the overall sentence structure is relatively simple, and
deviations from direct word-order unexceptional. Thus, for
example, out of the forty inversions in relative clauses, thirty-
two have either *que* or *où* as *invertissants* which in themselves
have little, if any, stylistic value. Similarly the *invertissant*
comme accounts for the most comparative inversion constructions.

2. Direct speech

Although most of book I of the *Francion* is given over to the narration of the basic situation, the remainder of the part of the text analysed (books I–V inclusive) consists entirely of narratives by one of the characters, usually Francion. These stories are described variously as *contes* or *histoires*, but are presented much less formally than in earlier writers, so that there are, for example, often interruptions on the part of the listener. Thus the figure for inversions in direct speech (32%), a considerable drop on the *Astrée*, is somewhat misleading in that owing to the nature of the structure of the work, all but fifteen of the total inversions occur in the course of a story told by one of the characters, and of these only eight do not occur in conversation. Direct speech then is taken to mean the representation of conversation by the story teller, although both conversation and narrative are of importance in considering Sorel's realism. As there is so little actual narration by the author himself, it is difficult to differentiate between the two styles. However, it may be significant that in the course of the exposition in book I, six of the seven examples in conversation have a modal adverb *invertissant* and one the relative *que*, whereas the eight instances in the narrative are more varied : three with *où*, two with *que*, two with *encore*, and one with *ce que*. This also indicates a tendency shown throughout the work, that in general inversions in conversation seem to have a mobile *invertissant*, and those in narrative an immobile one, a structure necessarily involving subordination. Taken in conjunction with sentence length, this further indicates a simpler structure in conversation, which is an important factor in realistic presentation.

In direct speech, many of the inversions after a modal adverb occur initially, and have a simple argumentative function (cf. the examples with *si est-ce que* in conversation, which are all initial). This is especially common in the case of *aussi*, where an inversion in initial position gives weight to the supplementary remark, as in the following :

' Un de mes compagnons me vint dire alors que je le quittasse
là. " Aussi veux je, repartis je..." ' (p. 242)

The brevity of clauses with inverted order is very noticeable,
and there may be additional features of conversational style,
such as repetition or expansion of the subject :

' "...et par avanture luy aidoit elle, la mauvaise." ' (p. 104)

or a double *invertissant*, a phenomenon which is increasingly
common as inversion becomes more restricted :

' " Aussi jamais ne sortiray je d'une si precieuse chaisne." '
(p. 75)

Although colloquial speech is best seen in direct word-order, it
may also be revealed in interrogative constructions, which are
an indication of the style of the text, such as :

' " Voyla t'il pas la misere du siecle, dit le vielleux." ' (p. 102)

The non-occurrence of inversion can be an aspect of realism in
speech, and this may well be the case with the number of
instances in which the impersonal *il* is used instead of inverted word-order.

Moreover, the stylized nature of the ' realistic ' novel
becomes apparent in some of the examples of inversion. There
are constructions in conversation which it seems are improbable, given the characters who are speaking, such as inversions
with the subjunctive in hypothetical clauses and other examples where the word-order appears complex. This may be a
question of length :

' " Il exerce le sien en amusant le simple peuple par ses
paroles, et le destournant d'aller aux debauches où se perd
l'argent inutilement, et où se font les querelles et les
batteries, et moy j'exerce aussi le mien on..." ' (p. 127)

or of the position of other elements such as the adverb in :

' " Non, non, me respondit elle, ce sont des pennaches que
portent invisiblement les cocus." ' (p. 151)

And finally there is an example of the verb separated from the
invertissant by a participial phrase, the subject of which is
repeated by an object pronoun in the verb phrase, a construction which again seems incongruous in speech :

' " Ainsi leurs subjets ayans affaire de leurs personnes, les

empescheroient ils de se mettre en un si grand hasard." '
(p. 258)
Such examples are, however, infrequent, and the majority of
cases of inversion in direct speech are found in short uncomplicated sentences and supported by an otherwise completely
regular order.

3. Narrative

Unlike the *contes* or *histoires* which occurred in the course of
the works studied hitherto, the *contes* of the *Francion* are, as
has already been noted, conversational in tone. An outstanding
instance of this has been quoted above (example C2, p. 111),
which is a sort of compound inversion with zero *invertissant*,
where the *reprise du sujet* effectively expresses the spontaneous
nature of the narrative. It also emphasizes a change in subject,
as that of the previous sentence is ' elle '—his wife—and
Agathe returns to her in a later clause. Compound inversion
with such repetition is particularly useful in the introduction of
a new subject and thus occurs frequently in speech-initial
position, as in the comment of the Seigneur du Chasteau as
Francion halts his story at the close of book IV :

' " Que possible ce Raymond avoit il desrobé l'argent par
galanterie ou par necessité..." ' (p. 226)
the colloquial tone being reinforced on the one hand by the use
of the introductory *que,* and on the other by this compromise
between the two orders.

(b) *Archaism in the ' Francion '*

It is fruitless to speculate, 300 years later, whether the
archaic constructions which occur in the *Francion* were in fact
still current in the language, or are more literary forms which
the author has included. If Sorel's claim to authenticity is
accepted, it seems that archaisms form part of the popular
dialect, which is perfectly plausible, given, for example, the
numerous archaic usages which are found today in Northern
English or in the French of the *Midi*. It is noticeable that
Sorel includes various archaic features not found in the two

later texts examined for this period, which are both written in the more polished style of the great novels. Sorel in fact refers to this in 1633 :

> ' D'ailleurs comme le langage devient plus poly chaque jour, il se peut faire que l'original de nostre Autheur n'avoit pas toutes les douceurs qui sont venuës depuis.' (*Advis*)

He goes on to say that this has been remedied, and the language of his book revised, but the only change which might be of interest to the present study is the deletion of one sentence which happens to include an inversion after *encore*, although it seems highly improbable that this was the reason for its omission.

It would seem therefore that co-ordinating constructions with inversions after *si* and *et* and inversions after various modal adverbs, were still current in the first half of the century, although their greatly reduced occurrence does indicate archaic overtones, hence their proscription by the grammarians in the middle of the century. There are also, in the part of the text analysed, no fewer than twenty-six examples of the *incise* construction with *ce*, ' ce dis-je ' (out of 291 *incises*), although this usage is dying out in other texts and is condemned by the grammarians. On the other hand one can well imagine the emphatic value of this *ce*, particularly in the oral report of conversation. There are also traces of the 16th-century tendency to invert in a parenthetical construction preceding direct speech, with or without *invertissant*, e.g. ' car disoit elle : " (S) " ', which are excluded from the statistical analysis.

(c) *Parody*

The victims of Sorel's often vicious irony are in general the pedants, whether their pedantry is scholastic, literary, legal or religious, and the author frequently conveys this by means of inversion constructions in a particular style of speech. Thus, for example, he parodies a lawyer in much the same way as du Fail had done, with a proverbial expression and inversion tag :

> ' " Voyez vous, qui se faict brebis le loup le mange, comme dit le proverbe." ' (p. 159)

It might be noted that Oudin is quoted as glossing this expression as an ' idiotisme ',[11] which emphasizes the underlying parody. In the books analysed parody is directed mainly against those pedants Francion meets in school and college, and against poets, and, consequently, literary figures of the day.

The main butt for the first kind of parody is the figure of Hortensius, Francion's companion at the Collège de Lisieux, who is said to imitate the style of an unknown author he terms ' un Ciceron François'. Sorel simply reproduces part of the speech of this ' maistre Pedant ' in the following :

> ' " Hô bon homme ... sonnez moy le bransle que les Lacedemoniens dansoient à leurs sacrifices, ou la sarabande que jouoient ces Curettes, ces Corybantes, emportant Jupiter hors du Louvre de Saturne, de peur que ...' Le vielleux qui n'entendoit non plus son langage que s'il eust parlé Margajat...' (p. 199)

and the subsequent reaction of the other characters is hardly surprising. Hortensius is equally ridiculous in making love, as in the following speech referred to as ' ceste belle harangue ' :

> ' "...je doy ... essayer de transplanter cette incomparable influence du Ciel où sejourne vostre divinité, en la terre caduque où m'attachent mes deffaux " '. (p. 191)

In both these examples inversion forms part of a high-flown style which not only parodies the type of character in the novel, but also represents an attack on the language of the fashionable works of literature.

Book V describes how Francion meets a group of would-be poets who assemble in a bookshop. The bookseller's description of his clientele before Francion meets them is quoted in example B5 (p. 110) above. On their meeting, however, Francion soon discovers that ' Ils n'avoient rien, outre la politesse du langage, encore n'y en avoit il pas un qui l'eust parfaictement ' (p. 230). Thus there is a considerable anticlimax, after the mood had been set in fine style by the bookseller's speech beginning with *icy* and inversion. Following this Francion himself waxes poetic and so, again with expressive

[11] See appendix to the *Francion*, ed. Roy, Paris, 1924.

E*

inversion, makes his attack on the group even stronger:
> ' Rien n'est plus fresle qu'estoit leur amitié (...) ; rien n'est
> plus volage qu'estoit leur opinion.' (p. 233)

Incidentally one of the preoccupations of the poets is the
question of order—' il eust esté mieux ', or ' il eust mieux
esté '—and this in turn constitutes an attack on the grammarians (p. 230). Earlier, in book III, Sorel considers with
irony the rewards of poetry and literature. As a schoolboy he
had atoned for his misdeeds by reciting epigrams at dinner
and had been suitably rewarded by his guests. The comment:
> ' " O vous, miserables vers que j'ay fait depuis, encore ne
> m'avez vous jamais fait obtenir de salaire qui valust cestuy
> là, que je prisois autant qu'un Empire." ' (p. 173)

(d) *Other stylistic uses of inversion*

The comparative construction may easily become a device of
humour, depending on the degree to which the two parts of the
comparison contrast. Inversion is useful here where a sharply
contrasting subject is introduced in the second half:
> ' Quand je vis entrer Marsault, je changeay de couleur plus
> de fois que ne feroit un Cameleon en toute sa vie.' (p. 114)

Alternatively the comparison may comprise the negation of
one of a pair of opposites where the negative and direct order is
balanced by the positive and inverted order:
> ' Mais il n'estoit non plus couvert que le seroit un homme nu,
> qui n'auroit qu'un rets dessus soy.' (p. 195)

Finally Sorel also uses comparison in his satirical attacks on the
court:
> '... et se donna deux heures le jour, pour ... apprendre à
> discourir en compagnie sur toutes sortes de sujets, bien
> d'une autre façon que ne font la plus part de ceux de la
> Cour, qui tiennent des propos sans ordre, sans jugement et
> sans politesse.' (p. 251)

Inversion occurs in several instances of parody outside the
topics already mentioned. Firstly there is a criticism of the
monasteries, where Sorel makes a sarcastic comment on the
vows of poverty:

' " Quand je desiray entrer dans vos Chappelles ... j'appor-
teray un manteau doublé de pluche, en deussé je louer un
à la friperie." ' (pp. 221–22),

Secondly, inversion is found in the course of Francion's
exposition as to what constitutes nobility, using an appropri-
ately elevated style with a relative *invertissant :*

' Je leur apprenois qu'estre Noble, ... c'est avoir une ame qui
resiste à tous les assauts que luy peut livrer (la) fortune, et
qui ne mesle rien de bas parmy ses actions.' (p. 252)

Thirdly, there is a hint of satire in the use of inversions in
contexts which had occurred extremely frequently in pastoral
novels. The first example satirizes the language of noble
bergers, in both construction and vocabulary :

' Il y avoit ... deux gentils-hommes qui se plaignoient l'un à
l'autre des rigueurs dont usoit l'Amour en leur endroit '.
(p. 186)

Inversion is also used to delay and therefore heighten an
anticlimatic effect in a familiar construction :

'... et je me glissay jusques dans son lict, où couchoit encore
une vieille servante sa campagne, qu'elle y avoit laissée...'
(p. 211)

Through the study of word-order in the *Francion* it is thus
possible to show that the novel does indeed include elements of
' la langue française tout entière ', in both its learned and
popular aspects. Although inversion is less important in a
work whose main innovation is the realistic use of popular
language, it is nevertheless useful in the related aim of the
picaresque genre, that of parody and satire, and relieves the
somewhat unbalanced style with longer sentences and juxtaposed orders. In a work whose humour lies essentially in the
unexpected, this technique may be reflected in the language by
the reversal of terms, and here word-order again plays a
subsidiary, but not unimportant part. The judgement of
Sage,[12] ' le style de Sorel est inégal, souvent diffus ou lourdaud.
Mais il a des pages heureuses et d'une verve comique savour-
euse ', may equally well be applied to Sorel's use of word-order.

[12] P. Sage, *Le préclassicisme*, Paris, 1962, p. 66.

Although the majority of the text consists of direct order and routine inversions, there are nonetheless some uses of inverted order whose stylistic and comic function is indisputable.

(iii) M. LE ROY DE GOMBERVILLE, 'POLEXANDRE'

As in the *Francion* the bulk of the action in *Polexandre* is told indirectly with characters relating their own and other people's life stories so again conversation is taken to mean speech between characters in the course of various narratives as well as between protagonists. Similarly there is again a low proportion of inversions found in direct speech, as this is not the most favoured form of exposition. When direct speech has occurred, the change is sufficiently marked for there to be examples of inversion to indicate the return to ordinary narrative, a device used by d'Urfé, but not by the other two authors studied. The *invertissant* in all these cases is *à peine*, and this is also used after a stretch of indirect speech, marking a parallel change. The same adverb occurs frequently as an initial *invertissant* with a similar function of indicating a change in the course of the action, often preceded by *mais :*

' Mais à peine fut-il hors de leurs Terres, qu'ils se revolterent et couperent la gorge à tous ses officiers...' (p. 245)

Although in the 17th century there tends to be more inversion of pronoun subjects than in the previous period, Gomberville is an exception to this, such inversions representing only 16% (table 4.06). Pronoun subjects occur only after *si* and modal adverbs, with the exception of all constructions with *ainsi* and one with *au moins*. This figure is comparable to those for the novels in the style of the *romans d'aventures* of the previous century, particularly Rabelais and the *Amadis*, and there is also a certain similarity in the distribution according to the type of *invertissant*. Gomberville and Scudéry both show a high proportion of immobile *invertissants* (table 4.02), which is especially noticeable in direct speech (table 4.11), and it seems that a preference for immobile *invertissants* and substantival subjects characterizes these novels, whereas this tendency is less marked in the *conteurs* and the related pastoral and realist genres. *Polexandre* has the highest percentage of inversions with several subjects and with a dependent clause (table 4.06), together representing 34% of the total, but along with this is a shorter average sentence which will be examined below. Although there is a wide variety of *invertissants* (table 4.08) the four most common inversion types account for 76% (table 4.09), with the number of relative inversions (34%) being the highest for the period. These also occur in the longest sentences, and tend therefore to have a clear logical function in the narrative technique. Finally the fact that 30% of the inversions have the verbs *être* or *faire* (table 4.11), about the average for comparable works in the 16th century, suggests that Gomberville's prose does not rival the simplicity and consequent lack of variety of Scudéry (60%).

(a) *Description and narrative*

Wadsworth notes [13] that to Gomberville and his contemporaries the techniques of narration and description were quite distinct and required different stylistic treatment, and he points out that description is an ornamental device which is used sparingly and is mainly reserved for unusual scenes. This lack of descriptive detail is clearly shown in the inversion study. There are only eight examples which can be considered as forming part of a descriptive technique, and none of the passages is longer than a few lines. It is interesting that while, in previous texts, inversions after adverbial phrases are nearly always descriptive, as are many relative inversions, in *Polexandre* the sixteen examples of various adverbial and prepositional phrase *invertissants* are used almost exclusively in the course of action narrative, the former being mainly temporal expressions to mark progression. The two exceptions are both with a prepositional phrase *invertissant*, both are short, one or two clauses only, and in both inversion is used for the sake of clarity as the subject is followed by a dependent

---

[13] P. A. Wadsworth, *The Novels of Gomberville—a critical study of 'Polexandre' and 'Cythérée'*, Yale, 1942, pp. 72–74.

relative in one and a lengthy adjectival complement in the other, e.g.

> ' Du pied de ces vases naissoit une vigne d'or bronze, qui rampoit le long d'une treille d'argent.' (p. 177)

The other examples of descriptive inversion are all with relative *invertissants*, five with *lequel* and one with *où*. Again none of these constructions are very long, and in most cases there is some qualification of the subject. The following is a typical example of the way in which the narrative lapses briefly into description which is nevertheless essential to the action, in this case involving the key preoccupation with marine events :

> '... ils virent une autre armée composée de plusieurs grands Galions et de toutes sortes de vaisseaux tant à rames qu'à voiles, sur lesquels ondoyoient les estandars de Portugal et de Castille.' (p. 149)

As in several other episodes the inversion here represents the termination of the description and the return to narrative technique.

(b) Sentence length

As shown in table 4.07, *Polexandre* has a high proportion of inversions in shorter sentences—none are longer than seven clauses, and the most common length is three clauses (39%, the highest percentage in the four texts). In addition 26% occur in one- or two-clause sentences. This reveals a new tendency towards shorter sentences, not only those with inverted order but those in the text as a whole, which is carried even further in the *Cyrus* where 39% of the inversions occur in one- or two-clause sentences.

Short sentences are useful both in summing up what has gone before and also in stating a fact which is to be elaborated. Inversion emphasizes such key sentences, and further devices may increase the emphasis, for instance the addition of *c'est...que* :

> ' Ce fut là que parut l'inconstance des evenemens de la guerre.' (p. 153)

This sentence has a clear transitional function, and this is also brought out in the order of the following, where the adverbial phrase refers back to the previous subject and the inversion introduces the new one taken up in the next sentence :

‘ Au delà de ces peuples regne une nation aussi redoubtable pour sa beauté que pour sa valeur. Ce sont des femmes belliqueuses qui...’ (p. 240)

The low proportion of inversions in conversation has already been mentioned, and in this context, when it does occur, inversion in short sentences is an especially effective means of emphasis, as in this exclamation :

‘ “ O paix plus sanglante et plus funeste, que n’avoit esté la guerre ! ” ’ (p. 677)

The effect may also be reinforced by repetition. Here an adjective is repeated as an adverbial *invertissant :*

‘ “ La crainte possible m’empesche de bien juger ; et possible fay-je tort à la meilleure Princesse du monde.” ’ (p. 482)

The reversal of the position of the adjective is also emphatic where inversion enables the full force of the chiasmus to be appreciated :

‘ “ Hors des murs de cette ville s’achevera une si abominable action par la mort d’une Pricessse incomparable.” ’ (p. 311)

Short sentences with inverted order also tend to be found where strong emotion is expressed :

‘ “ Au moins, luy dit Bajazet, nous donnerez-vous le temps de nous resoudre à cette separation.” ’ (p. 584)

At times the language of the inversion clause shows the influence of *préciosité :*

‘ “ et cours la Mer et la Terre pour descouvrir le lieu bienheureux où regne la merveille que ce pourtrait represente.” ’ (p. 97)

The use of inversion in correlative constructions has already been mentioned, where two clauses with contrasting order are juxtaposed, the second being an expansion of the first. A similar device is used with the *invertissant à peine*, the inversion clause being expanded by *tant* and direct word-order. Here brevity is essential to the impact of the construction :

' A peine avoit-il eu la force de marcher, tant l'aise l'avoit transporté.' (p. 618)

Unlike the correlatives, inversion here takes place in the first of the two clauses, but in both constructions the clause with inverted order represents the consequence of that with direct order :

' " Plus je le voyais, et plus me croissoit l'envie de le voir " ' (p. 94)

' A peine ne sut-il y entrer tant il estoit plein de monde.' (pp. 533–34)

Thus sentence length and word-order are relevant to each other both when inversion occurs in an isolated clause, and when it is found in one of a pair, although the combination is obviously more striking in the latter case, where the additional device of the juxtaposition of two orders may be exploited.

(c) *Comparisons*

The importance of the action narrative is underlined by the lack of detailed description on the one hand, and of imagery and simile on the other. None of the 9% of inversions occurring in comparative constructions (table 4.09) involve simile or metaphor, but instead they relate either to other aspects of the narrative, different characters or events, or to some background detail. Firstly comparison serves as a brief reminder as to the setting of the story in time and place :

' "... et ma volonté ... m'impose la bien douce necessité de la servir toute ma vie, et la considerer comme quelque chose de plus grand que n'est ny l'Empire de Quasmez, ny celui de Montrezume." ' (p. 611)

Secondly, and perhaps more important, it is a means of recapitulation :

' " C'est à dire qu'il a dans le fort, une authorité aussi absolue qu'est la mienne dans le reste de l'Isle, parmy les Corsaires et sur les vaisseaux." ' (p. 169)

Unlike the previous texts analysed, then, comparisons here belong not on the imaginative plane, but on the purely functional.

In conclusion, Gomberville's style shows itself to be eminently suited to his subject matter. Simple language and logical constructions counterbalance an intricate plot, and it is the converse of the stylistic devices studied so far—brief sentences rather than complex ones, precise comparisons rather than metaphor—which produces clear, uncomplicated prose, not yet encumbered with all the features of *préciosité*, and which foreshadows the style of the Classical Age.

(iv) M. DE SCUDÉRY, 'LE GRAND CYRUS'

In most respects the tendencies already indicated in *Polexandre* are carried to the extreme in *Cyrus*. Thus the text has the lowest inversion frequency of the period, 0·58, and the least variety in *invertissants* (table 4.08), with no fewer than 92% of the examples occurring in one of the four main construction types (table 4.09). As regards sentence length (table 4.07), 39% of the inversions are in one- or two-clause sentences, again the highest number for the period, and finally the verbs *être* and *faire* account for 60% of the total (table 4.10). In comparison with the 16th century, or even with the *Astrée*, these figures reveal a tremendous reduction in variety in all aspects of the inversion construction. As in *Polexandre*, the number of inversions of a pronominal subject is lower than average, although less markedly so (table 4.06). All the subjects with dependent clauses occur in mobile *invertissant* constructions, and constitute more than half their total.

(a) The modal adverb ' invertissants '

For the first time in *Cyrus* the inversion analysis reveals a single *invertissant* with a particular function, which will recur quite often in later works, namely the use of *peut-être* in indirect speech. All the four examples in this text occur initially but are necessarily preceded by the subordinating conjunction *que* showing indirect speech, thus :

' Le Roy d'Assirie le supplia ... de se souvenir que peut-estre ne seroit-il pas inutile pour la liberté de la Princesse.' (p. 47)
Emphasis may be given by forming a double *invertissant* with

the addition of *même*. The association between a particular *invertissant* and indirect speech will be seen to be useful later in authors who make extensive use of free indirect constructions, where *que* is deleted. Here its function already seems partially to be taken over by the initial adverbs and inversion :

> ' Un procedé si hardi luy persuada qu'il y avoit sans doute quelque homme de grand cœur dans nostre vaisseau : ou *que peut-estre mesme* pouvoit il y avoir quelques-uns de ses Ennemis qui...' (p. 305)

The other occurrences of *peut-être* in this text are interesting to the extent that only three are found in a simple initial position, whereas the remaining four have a function similar to that of the now nearly obsolete *si est-ce que*, that is linking a subordinate and main clause. In three cases the preceding clause is a hypothetical one with *si*, and the fourth is a concessive :

> ' " Mais quelque ardeur que vous ayez pour la gloire, peut-estre luy ferez vous quelque jour infidelité." ' (p. 325)

One notes here the semantic contrast between the two clauses of the construction, and thus the formerly functional inversion assumes a stylistic value. Similarly one finds parallelisms such as those in the *Astrée* already described (p. 120), as in the following where the verb is repeated but the contrast lies in the two direct objects :

> ' "... et si j'en avois perdu la memoire, peut-estre auriez-vous desja perdu la vie." ' (p. 127)

The use of *à peine* as an *invertissant* may result in a chiasmus construction with inverted word-order expressing either one of two consecutive events, depending on the meaning of the adverb. Where the meaning is temporal the construction is frequently one of opposition, thus :

> ' " A peine ay-je de l'amour que j'ay desja de la jalousie." '
> (p. 361)

Here the temporal sequence is underlined by the use of *déjà*, and the word-order which is completely reversed, in addition to the conceptual opposition between love and jealousy. The remaining examples include a simple case of cause and effect, the different meaning of the adverb being underlined by the use of *pouvoir* :

'... il y eut une si grande obscurité sur toute la Terre, qu'à peine se pouvoit-on reconnoistre...' (p. 182)

Unlike the examples with *à peine*, all occurrences of *du moins*, with one exception, are in direct speech or monologue. All are in initial position, in short single-clause sentences, and there is one instance of compound inversion, where there is a substantive subject :

' " Mais du moins ... cette Innocente Princesse ne demeura-t'elle pas pas sans vengeance." ' (p. 111)

In this example, as in one other, the *invertissant* is strengthened by the addition of the conjunction *mais*, possibly indicating the conversational nature of the construction.

(b) *Restraint and elegance in ' Cyrus '*

In many respects the use of inverted order in *Cyrus* anticipates that of Madame de la Fayette in the *Princesse de Clèves* (see Chapter V). The features common to both texts are firstly the similarity between inversion constructions in narrative and dialogue, indicative of a conversational style remote from the spoken language, and secondly the use of inversion in an elegant style where clarity is of primary importance and considerable restraint is employed in exploiting the emphatic value of the device.

1. Conversational and narrative inversions

The overall analysis shows that in the whole text one inversion in three occurs in direct speech, and closer examination of the material reveals that out of the inversions with *être* or *faire* again one in three is conversational. This parallel is maintained even more noticeably with regard to sentence length. Of the short one- or two-clause sentences exactly one-third are found in conversation, as are slightly less than one-third of both the total examples of three-clause sentences and those of sentences of four or more clauses. Similarly conversation accounts for only fractionally less than one in every three

examples of both mobile and immobile *invertissant* constructions. This information may be represented as follows:

	No. in speech	Total N	Proportion (approx.)
Immobile *invertissant*	26	80	1 : 3
Mobile *invertissant*	11	36	1 : 3
(S) → 1 or 2 clauses	15	45	1 : 3
3 clauses	13	42	1 : 3
4+ clauses	8	29	1 : 4
être or *faire*	22	70	1 : 3

This curious parallelism then shows that in these respects there
is virtually no difference in style between conversation and
narrative style in *Cyrus*, and this completely supports the
impression gained on reading the novel.

2. The restrained use of inversion

The examples of modal adverb *invertissants* already quoted
have illustrated the use of inversion in simple chiastic constructions. The following seems to be the only instance in the part of
the text analysed where the juxtaposition of orders is reinforced
by a change in adjective position:

'Mais admirez, Seigneur, les bizarres effets que produisent
les passions violentes dans une ame ambitieuse qui en est
possedée.' (p. 557)

This is one of the rare examples of an elegant inversion in a
sentence of more than two clauses where the change in order is
not essential to structural clarity. It may be noted that this
example occurs in a narrative by one of the characters and
reflects the polished nature of their speech. However, in the
following, both direct and inverted orders in the relative clauses
seem necessary to preserve the overall clarity, although elegant
variation in a longer sentence is also achieved:

'... et à toutes les plaintes et à tous les cris que jettoient les
mourants ou ceux que la peur d'une mort prochaine faisoit
crier, (ils) causoient une confusion espouvantable.' (p. 14)

The majority of relative *invertissants* are employed to
prevent the separation of relative and antecedent, and thus
contribute to a logical sentence structure, e.g.

' "... car quand vous seriez Grec ou Persan, qui sont à mon advis les deux Nations de toute la Terre, ausquelles peut mieux convenir l'idée que vous nous avez donné de vostre Païs..." ' (p. 404)

Other examples permit the expression of several subjects :

' il estoit juste ... de ne se charger pas seule de l'évenement d'une affaire d'où dépendoit la perte ou la conservation de la Personne du monde la plus considerable.' (p. 156)

'... sans prevoir qu'il nous y arriveroit des choses, d'où dépendoit toute la gloire, tout le bonheur, et toute l'infortune d'Artamene.' (p. 319)

The latter with its progression in the enumerated subjects again reveals the elegance of the language used by the characters in recounting their adventures, despite the emotional content.

Although 25% of the inversions occur in final position (table 4.04), few of the examples have an important emphatic function. Inverted order may be used for clarity, as above, or to avoid an imperfect cadence, as in the following extract from a treaty :

' Que partant en mesme temps des deux villes les Combattans de part et d'autre se trouveroient au milieu de la Plaine où se feroit leur Combat.' (pp. 441–42)

One of the few interesting inversions in this position occurs also in a literary context, at the end of a letter, where the subject is the signatory :

'... et ne l'occupez plus à deffendre la vie d'un Prince, à laquelle est inseparablement attachée celle de Mondane.' (p. 435)

This variation on the use of word-order for final emphasis is particularly effective by virtue of the long adverb which precedes the subject.

The examples of inversion found in *Cyrus* are in general, however, unremarkable, and the occurrence of the device seems purely functional. While the material illustrates the evolution of some points of style in the *grands romans*, and provides some indication of the developments to be found in the Classical novel, it is too thin to permit a satisfactory stylistic analysis based on syntax alone.

Chapter V

THE SEVENTEENTH CENTURY (2)

1. SYNTACTIC ANALYSIS OF THE TEXTS
1650–1700

The texts :

P. Scarron, *Le romant comique* [1]

A. Furetière, *Le roman bourgeois* [2]

Mme de la Fayette, *La princesse de Clèves* [3]

Fénelon, *Les aventures de Télémaque* [4]

Table 5.01 : Inversion frequencies

SCA/RC	193 : 0·97	
FUR/RB	151 : 0·76	(*mean* 0·80)
LaF/PC	128 : 0·85	
FEN/TEL	124 : 0·62	

Table 5.02 : Percentage table to show nature of clause in which inversion occurs

	SCA	FUR	LaF	FEN
Main clause	13	42	9	44
Subordinate clause	87	57	88	53
Non-subordinating *invertissant* in subordinate clause	n	1	3	3
	100	100	100	100
Immobile *invertissant*	85	56	88	51
Mobile *invertissant*	13	39	12	46
Other operations	2	5	—	3
N :	193	151	128	124

[1] In *Romanciers du XVIIe siècle*, ed. Adam, Paris, 1958, pp. 532–796. (SCA)

[2] In *Romanciers du XVIIe siècle*, pp. 903–1104. (FUR)

[3] In *Romanciers du XVIIe siècle*, pp. 1107–1254. (LaF)

[4] ed. Rousseaux, Paris, 1930 (livres I–XIII). (FEN)

Table 5.03 : Percentage table to show distribution of inversions according to discourse type

	SCA	FUR	LaF	FEN
Narrative	83	81	76	72
Direct speech	9	18	19	17
Indirect speech	8	1	3	11
Free indirect speech	—	—	1	—
Soliloquy	—	—	1	—

Table 5.04 : Percentage table to show position of inversion within the corpus examined

	SCA	FUR	LaF	FEN
Sentence initial	10	32	10	27
Paragraph initial	n	4	—	9
Chapter initial	—	—	—	—
Speech initial	n	1	2	—
Total initial	11	37	12	36
Sentence final	30	19	31	32
Paragraph final	—	1	3	1
Chapter final	1	—	—	—
Speech final	n	—	3	1
Total final	31	20	37	34

Table 5.05 : Percentage table to show position of inversion in relation to other types of discourse

	SCA	FUR	LaF	FEN
Preceding direct speech	n	—	—	4
Following direct speech	—	—	—	1
Preceding indirect speech	1	—	2	—
Following indirect speech	n	—	—	—

Table 5.06 : Percentage table to show nature of the inverted noun phrase

	SCA	FUR	LaF	FEN
Pronoun subject	14	29	10	30
Substantive subject	86	70	89	68
Compound inversion	n	1	1	2
	100	100	100	100
2 or more subjects	7	5	4	2
S and dependent (S)	18	17	12	15

Table 5.07 : The percentage of inversions occurring in sentences of three or more clauses

	SCA	FUR	LaF	FEN
(S)—3 clauses	19	31	23	28
4 clauses	24	16	19	9
5 clauses	13	7	10	2
6 clauses	15	1	9	2
7 clauses	8	1	5	—
7+ clauses	7	—	5	—
	—	—	—	—
	86	56	71	41

Table 5.08 : The ratio of inversions to *invertissants*

SCA	193 : 35—5·51
FUR	151 : 44—3·43
LaF	128 : 22—5·82
FEN	124 : 35—3·54
Total	596 : 67—8·90 (*mean* 4·58)

Table 5.09 : Percentage table of the most frequently occurring
inversions

	SCA	FUR	LaF	FEN
Relatives	51	30	62	19
Comparatives	19	13	6	3
Indirect construction	12	10	19	28
Modal adverbs	13	28	11	32

Table 5.10 : Percentage table to show the occurrence of ' être ',
' faire ' and ' avoir '

	SCA	FUR	LaF	FEN
être	19	23	27	28
faire	20	18	6	3
avoir	3	9	8	3

Table 5.11 : Percentage table showing the distribution of
direct speech *invertissants*

	SCA	FUR	LaF	FEN
Immobile *invertissant*	67	59	92	43
Mobile *invertissant*	33	33	8	52
Other operations	—	8	—	5
	—	—	—	—
N :	18	28	25	71

Table 5.12 : Percentage table to show the occurrence of
adverbials in inversion constructions

	SCA	FUR	LaF	FEN
V(adv)S	7	5	2	4
(adv)VS	n	1	1	—

(i) DISTRIBUTION OF THE INVERSIONS

For the first time the average inversion frequency for the two
periods is virtually the same, with $0 \cdot 80$ as opposed to $0 \cdot 74$ in
the first half of the century. The overall reduction in inversion
coincides with the standardization of its use, as shown in
table 5.09. Here it is clear that the major constructions
admitting inversion account for nearly all the examples in the
four texts, the figure being as high as 95% in Scarron and 98%
in Madame de la Fayette. The category of co-ordinating
constructions has now disappeared from the table of common
inversion types, and is replaced by the class of modal adverbs,
some of which take over the function of the co-ordinators. In
nearly every case, the exception being Fénelon, the most
frequently occurring *invertissants* are relatives, often a feature
of the logical arrangement of items. The fact that the inversions show even less variety than in the previous period is
underlined by the continued reduction in number of *invertissants*, giving an average of $4 \cdot 58$ inversions to each *invertissant*,
as opposed to $3 \cdot 41$ in the first half of the century (table 5.08).
In addition the four texts for this period provide only sixty-
seven *invertissants* between them, in contrast to the total of
100 noted in the previous chapter, although the number of
inversions has actually increased by four.

As regards the position of the inversions in the sentence
(table 5.04) the texts again tend to show a marked preference
for either initial or final position, although the distribution in
Fénelon is approximately equal. Scarron and La Fayette,
however, have far more inversions in final position, whereas
Furetière prefers initial position although to a lesser extent.
One may also note in Fénelon the unusually high proportion of
inversions, 9%, in paragraph initial position. Since immobile

invertissants are more likely to occur in final position than mobile ones, which are found in either position although more probably initially, the two texts with a small proportion of initial inversions, Scarron and La Fayette, also have few examples of mobile *invertissants* (table 5.02). In Furetière and Fénelon, however, where there are more inversions in initial than in final position, the proportion of mobile *invertissants* is much higher, 39% and 46% respectively, and the distribution between both immobile and mobile *invertissants* and initial and final positions is altogether more even.

The number of inversions in direct speech (table 5.03) in these texts is considerably lower than the 35% average of the previous period, the average proportion now being around 16%, and most of these have an immobile *invertissant* (table 5.11). Although in Fénelon 4% of the inversions are in a position preceding direct speech (table 5.05), this introductory device is not generally used in the other texts.

From the point of view of style it may be worth noting that the two Classical texts have fewer inverted subjects which consist of more than one noun or which have a dependent clause than do the two earlier works (table 5.06), while also showing a greater variety of verbs in inversion constructions (table 5.10).

(ii) EXAMPLES

A. IMMOBILE ' INVERTISSANT '

1. *Co-ordinating conjunctions : FUR : 1 inversion, 1 ' invertissant '*
   ' " *Si* est-ce que pourtant (dit Collantine à Belastre), puisque vous en avez tant fait qu'il faut que..." ' (p. 1096)
2. *Relative conjunctions : SCA : 99,8 ; FUR : 45,7 ; LaF : 80,7 ; FEN : 24,6*
   ' " Le rang d'aîné *qu'*avait le Dauphin, et la faveur du roi *qu'*avait le duc d'Orléans, faisaient entre eux une sorte d'émulation..." ' (LaF, pp. 1130–31)
3. *Comparatives : SCA : 36,8 : FUR : 20,7 ; LaF : 7,4 ; FEN : 4,3*

' Il paraît toujours doux ... toujours appliqué à donner les ordres *comme* pourrait faire un sage vieillard appliqué à régler sa famille et à instruire ses enfants.' (FEN II, 89)

4. *Concessives : SCA : 4,2 ; FUR : 3,1 ; LaF : 3,1*
' " Il faut m'en aller à la campagne, *quelque* bizarre *que* puisse paraître mon voyage." ' (LaF, p. 1191)

5. *Temporal clause : SCA : 2,1 ; FUR : 1,1*
' *Tant que* dura la Comedie, Ragotin luy cria de mesme force qu'il s'assist et...' (SCA, p. 768)

6. *Correlatives : FEN : 1,1*
' " *Autant que* Minerve est au-dessus de Mars, *autant* une valeur discrète et prévoyante surpasse-t-elle un courage bouillant et farouche." ' (I, 211)

7. *Indirect construction : SCA : 23,7 ; FUR : 15,7 ; LaF : 23,4 ; FEN : 35,6*
' Mais comme Vollichon estoit plus formaliste, il dit qu'il vouloit voir plus précisément *en quoi* consistoient ses effets, et il...' (FUR, p. 957)

B. MOBILE ' INVERTISSANT '

1. *Attributives : FUR : 8,1 ; FEN : 4,1*
' *Tel* entre ceux-là est l'Astrée...' (FUR, p. 1006)

2. *Adverbs—modal : SCA : 25,7 ; FUR : 50,7 ; LaF : 14,4 ; FEN : 40,6*
' " Vous ne songez peut-estre pas que vous ne faites que passer par Seville, et peut-estre ne sçavez-vous pas aussi que je ne trouverois pas bon que..." ' (SCA, p. 775)

3. *Adverbs—time : FUR : 1,1 ; FEN : 1,1*
' ... et *aussi-tost* arrivoient force jeunes gens de toutes conditions qui y estoient plutôt attirez pour voir Lucrece que pour divertir l'avocate.' (FUR, p. 918)

4. *Adverbs—place : FUR : 1,1 ; FEN : 2,1*
' *Là* s'éleve avec ordre un bûcher, qui ressemble à un bâtiment régulier.' (FEN II, 99)

5. *Adverbs—combinations : FEN : 3,1*
' " *Encore même* n'a-t-il pas le vrai courage d'un simple soldat." ' (I, 254)

6. *Adverbial phrase—place : FUR : 3,3 ; LaF : 1,1 ; FEN : 5,4*
' *Après elle*, venaient la Reine Dauphine, Madame cœur du Roi, Madame de Lorraine et la Reine de Navarre, leurs robes portées par des princesses.' (LaF, p. 1214)

7. *Prepositional phrase : FUR : 3,3 ; FEN : 2,2*
'... et *à sa poultre* estoient attachées plusieurs cages pleines d'oyseaux qui avoient appris à siffler sous lui.' (FUR, p. 954)

C. OTHER OPERATIONS

1. *Deletion and transposition : SCA : 2 ; FUR : 5*
'... parce qu'il n'estoit pas encore assez en colere et qu'il luy en falloit pour se resoudre à se battre, *ne fût-ce* qu'à coups de poing.' (SCA, p. 536)

2. *Addition and transposition : SCA : 2,1 ; FUR : 3,3 ; FEN : 3,3*
' *C'est* là *que*, sur le midi, arrive une caravane de demoiselles à fleur de corde, dont les meres...' (FUR, p. 905)

(iii) DETAILS OF THE INVERSIONS

(*a*) *Co-ordination*

It has already been shown that inversion after a co-ordinating conjunction had begun to disappear by the end of the 16th century. Thus the device is no longer used either to link two main clauses, or a subordinate and main clause which are in hypothetical, concessive or temporal relation to each other, and there is also the absence of inversion after a preceding subordinate, essentially a co-ordinating device. However, although inversions after *et* and *si* no longer occur, there are other *invertissants* which fulfil a similar function. Thus a simple co-ordinating conjunction may be strengthened and emphasized by a modal adverb and inverted word-order. In Scarron all three occurrences of the *invertissant encore* are found after *et*, uniting two main clauses. Also in Scarron are two examples of *au moins* having the same connecting function as *si est-ce que* after a subordinate hypothetical clause :

‘ “ Et si cela n'a pas fait grand effet sur vous, au moins aurez-vous veu par là que je sçay tenir ma parole...” ’ (p. 561)

Another instance of a co-ordinator being replaced by a modal adverb is in sentence initial position. In the 16th century co-ordinating conjunctions, in particular *si* and *et*, were found at the beginning of a sentence which generally introduced information supplementing that conveyed by the previous sentence, thereby connecting the two. Now this function is taken over by certain modal adverbs, particularly *aussi* and *encore*. In Furetière for example there are eleven occurrences of *aussi* and seventeen of *encore* in initial position. La Fayette has five examples of *aussi* initially. In Fénelon there are three occurrences of the combination *encore même*, all of them sentence initial (see p. 148 above). Thus by the end of the 17th century modal adverb *invertissants* serve both to reinforce co-ordinating conjunctions and to replace former co-ordinating *invertissants* in certain circumstances.

(b) *Constructions with two orders*

The chiasmus construction where direct and inverted orders are juxtaposed is a familiar one, and has already been discussed with reference to the style of various texts. A number of such constructions are found in the texts of this period which reveal the extent to which choice of order is limited. For example two constructions may be exactly the same as to *invertissant*, subject and verb, but if the subject is repeated in pronoun form inversion is not generally possible. The following is therefore a grammatical rather than a stylistic chiasmus, because neither of the indirect constructions admits an alternative order :

‘... après qu'on m'eut demandé où estoit Sophie, je demanday aussi où elle estoit...’ (SCA, p. 747)

The same applies where the second subject and verb are

different, if one subject is the impersonal *on*, although in this
example from *Télémaque* the sentence acquires balance and
rhythm from the necessary change in order :

> ' Télémaque ... demanda à la deesse à qui étoit ce vaisseau
> et à quoi on le destinoit.' (I, 146)

In certain indirect questions, then, direct order is obligatory
if they are not to become plain interrogatives. In relative
constructions, where most conjunctions are identical to
interrogative *invertissants*, inverted order with pronoun subject
might well imply direct interrogation, so the author is again
obliged to maintain direct order, in spite of the fact that the
substantive subjects with the same verb may be inverted in the
same context :

> ' Le bruit que nous faisons et que faisoient les brutaux et les
> yvrognes ... fit sortir d'une salle basse le Seigneur du
> Chasteau...' (SCA, p. 679)

Finally there are constructions where both subjects are
substantives and could both be inverted equally well :

> ' Les efforts que le petit homme avoit fait (*sic*) ... et ceux que
> faisoient le Destin et l'Olive l'enfloient encore davantage.'
> (SCA, p. 704)

The choice of inverted order is here determined by the main
verb which immediately follows the second relative clause, so
the chiasmus again appears to be more syntactic than
stylistic, given the lack of comprehensibility which is likely
to ensue from direct order. There remain two chiasmus
constructions in the *Princesse de Clèves*, both of which show
plainly that in certain circumstances choice of order is completely free, thus :

> '... elle n'eût pas dû aller dans un lieu où était le Vidame ;
> elle partit pour aller à Chambord, où la Cour était alors.'
> (p. 1225)

(c) *Mixed constructions*

There are several examples in these texts of mixed constructions, those which include both elements for avoiding inversion

and the inversion itself. Thus in Scarron one finds the construction *peut-être que* followed by an inversion as if after
peut-être:

> ' "Peut-estre que vous ne la trouverez-vous pas telle,
> mais..." ' (p. 680)

In Fénelon there is what seems to be a mixed interrogative, a
construction with elements of both direct and indirect
questions:

> ' Dites-nous donc qui est-ce que nous pouvons choisir pour
> notre roi.' (I, 120–21)

2. STYLISTIC ANALYSIS OF THE TEXTS

(i) P. SCARRON, 'LE ROMANT COMIQUE'

Scarron's famous work is the antithesis of the two *grands
romans* analysed in chapter IV, and satirizes many distinctive
features of both their language and content. The *Roman
comique* also contrasts with the earlier work in a similar genre,
the *Francion*, in form if not in content, as Scarron's *style
burlesque* and his presentation of *bourgeois* life and language
constitute a more subjective realism, as Reynier puts it: ' Son
style est très loin de l'impersonnalité que réclame le pur
réalisme '.[5] The inversion analysis of the *Roman comique*
showed, like the *Francion*, the highest frequency for the period,
and inversions figure quite prominently in the details of
Scarron's style which differ from previous works. The main
topic of interest is the *style burlesque* with its correspondence
between form and content, and thus the use of a *langue
bourgeoise*, in addition to the satire on earlier novels, although
one should perhaps consider first of all the general narrative
technique.

(a) *Inversion and the narrative technique*

The *Roman comique* introduces for the first time in French
literature what has been called the self-conscious narrator,[6] a

---

[5] *Le roman réaliste au XVIIe siècle*, p. 297.

[6] cf. W. C. Booth, ' The self-conscious narrator in comic fiction ', *Publications of the Modern Language Association of America*, lxvii (1952), pp. 163–85.

technique used more extensively eleven years later in Furetière's *Roman bourgeois*. The most obvious realization of this comes to the reader when the narrator looks forward to the action which is about to take place, and inversion is frequently used in these transition devices at the end of a chapter. Although there are only a couple of inversions in this text which occur in chapter-final position, there are several more which come in the course of the concluding sentence without actually falling at the end. Inversion is most effective when it allows the final subject to conclude the chapter, as in the following intervention by the narrator, where the noun clause has a co-ordinating function, containing in it the whole of what is to come:

'... et fit descendre Destin dans la cuisine de l'hostellerie, où se passoit ce que vous allez voir dans le suivant chapitre.' (p. 692)

Inversion can also be found in parentheses in a similar capacity, and in this sentence, the penultimate in the chapter, it underlines the opposition between the story teller in the novel and the narrator himself:

' Vous allez voir cette histoire dans le suivant chapitre non telle que la conta Ragotin, mais comme je la pourray conter d'aprés...' (p. 552)

There is also a hint of self-parody in another of Scarron's chapter endings, this one referring back then looking forward as the more high-flown language together with an inversion contrasts with the simpler form of expression and direct order, which precedes it:

' Tandis que le bruit de tant de personnes ... diminue peu à peu et se perd dans l'air , de la façon à peu prés que fait la voix des Echos, le Cronologiste fidelle finira le present chapitre...' (p. 710)

There are other interventions on the part of the narrator using inversions, which have a different purpose. In the next example he comments on his own writing, this time ending a chapter with an emphatic co-ordinating inversion:

' Car, sur mon honneur, cette description m'a plus cousté que tout le reste du livre, et encore n'en suis-je pas trop bien satisfait.' (p. 642)

Finally from time to time he reveals his own literary intention, with the implication of condemning certain features of other writers,

> ' Je ne vous diray point si les flambeaux que tenoient les Demoiselles estoient d'argent.' (p. 559)

and also :

> 'Je ne vous diray point exactement s'il avoit soupé, et s'il se coucha sans manger, comme font quelques faiseurs de Romans, qui reiglent toutes les heures du jour de leurs Heros...' (p. 555)

where his ideas are made fully explicit, and inversion usefully stresses the main criticism.

The self-conscious narrator is not, however, necessarily omniscient, and this may be conveyed by various speculative statements. In the following example the use of *peut-être* as an *invertissant* stresses this factor :

> '... car il en fut esveillé et peut-estre en pesta-t-il en son âme, mais...' (p. 673)

The 17th-century *roman de mœurs* exemplified in the *Roman comique* contains a certain amount of detailed description in addition to the all-pervading satire, a mixture which has frequently been commented on by critics, e.g. Sage :

> ' Scarron, s'il grossit le trait, reste un narrateur véridique. Son livre se fonde sur une observation fidèle des hommes et des professions qu'il évoque à nos yeux,' [7]

and Reynier :

> ' Ce qui étonne, c'est de trouver une part de vérité dans un livre écrit ainsi avec une intention ironique par le plus fantaisiste des hommes...' [8]

Although space does not permit the full investigation of Scarron's descriptive technique here, one aspect of it alone will be sufficient to show his use of inversion in such contexts.

---

[7] *Le préclassicisme*, p. 224.
[8] *Le roman réaliste*, p. 266.

Scarron is among the first authors to show any interest in the dress or appearance of his characters, an important factor in realistic writing. This example shows how the inverted subject is expanded for this purpose. Scarron is comparing a loaded carriage to a pyramid,

> '... au haut de laquelle paroissoit une Demoiselle habillée moitié ville, moitié campagne.' (p. 532)

Alternatively the costume itself, and in this case its particular function in the story, may be stressed by inversion :

> ' La femme ... le surprit ... par sa beauté ... et par un air majestueux que ne put cacher aux yeux de ceux qui l'admirerent un méchant habit d'Esclave.' (pp. 728–29)

Where costume is the main point of interest a comparative *invertissant* may be used to introduce supplementary detail, in this case detail of contemporary custom :

> '... le méchant habit de mon valet ... me rendoit bien different de ce que je paroissois avec le mien, qui estoit plus beau que ne l'est d'ordinaire celui d'un escolier.' (p. 690)

Finally as regards narrative technique, a work which is concerned with both everyday realism and satire must depend on unambiguous expression for its effect. Morillot notes ' Ce style est fait de simplicité et de vérité '.[9] It has already been shown how inversion has the joint role of emphasis and clarity in descriptive detail. It has also been seen above (table 5.06), that 25% of the inversion constructions have several subjects, or subjects with a dependent clause, the highest proportion for the period, and indicative of the use of inversion for the sake of clarity. It may be also noted that out of a total of ninety-eight examples with relative *invertissants* no fewer than thirty-four of the subjects are proper nouns. This is a further indication of the tendency to place important subjects in inverted position wherever possible, to give them due weight and to avoid any potential confusion or disordered expression, thus :

> ' Tous les Comediens l'un aprés l'autre suivirent exactement l'ordre qu'avoit donné la Rancune, et ne respondirent point à ce que leur dit Ragotin ou...' (p. 623)

[9] P. Morillot, *Scarron, étude biographique et littéraire*, Paris, 1888, p. 395.

(b) The ' style burlesque '

The technique of the 17th-century *burlesque* writers in France is described by Bar [10] as the ' recherche systématique de la variété et de l'inattendu ' which is achieved by such means as archaism and foreign or dialectal terms. He notes also the occurrence of inversion :

' Elle est extrêmement fréquente et l'on en trouve toutes les formes possibles. Le but visé est sans doute ... de faire rire par surprise.' (p. 320)

although the syntactic analysis has shown that while Scarron's work has an above average inversion frequency, this is not outstanding, nor are there very many different *invertissants* (table 5.08). In the *Roman comique* comparative *invertissants* are often used to convey the unexpected, while other inversions may be employed for emphasis in the course of *burlesque* description.

Comparison depends for its effect firstly on the degree of difference between the two things compared, and consequently on the appropriateness of such a parallel. It has already been shown how inversion may be used to underline one half of the construction, and such emphasis becomes essential in the comparisons in this text, where the two terms are very different and the appropriateness of the comparison questionably a result of the technique of degradation. Thus one frequently finds a comparison based on the human-animal opposition, e.g.

' Un petit Ours nouveau-né, qui n'a point encore esté léché de sa mere, est plus formé en sa figure oursine que ne le fut Ragotin en sa figure humaine aprés...' (p. 765)

Here the humour lies in the contrast ' oursine ' and ' humaine ', but it is inappropriate to the extent that a baby bear is being compared to a human adult. The idea is taken further in comparisons between a single human being and a whole class of animals :

' Cependant l'Organiste ... qui estoit fort colere, comme sont tous les animaux imbarbes, dit...' (p. 622)

[10] F. Bar, *Le genre burlesque en France au XVIIe siècle*, Paris, 1960, p. xxxiii.

'... sur lesquelles il (Ragotin) avoit accoustumé de s'asseoir, comme font tous les autres animaux raisonnables.' (p. 643)

Another comparative device is for the second item to consist of a general or generic term, which may be purely descriptive,

'... sur le lict qui estoit haut sur les siennes (jambes), comme sont tous les licts à l'antique...' (p. 686)

or again to some extent inappropriate :

'Rancune ... dormait aussi paisiblement qu'auroit fait un homme de bien, et ...' (p. 546)

The effect of inversion in such constructions is to stress the supposed general validity of the comparison, as in :

'... elle estoit tres succulente, comme sont toutes les femmes ragottes.' (p. 706)

Finally Scarron uses comparatives in satirizing the *grands romans* :

'Je ne croy pas que deffunct Phaëton de malheureuse, memoire ait esté plus empesché aprés les quatre chevaux fougueux de son Pere que le fut alors nostre petit advocat sur un cheval doux comme un asne.' (pp. 642–43)

Here the *burlesque* element lies in the opposition between Phaëton and the 'chevaux fougueux' and the 'petit advocat' with his 'cheval doux comme un asne', both of which are in emphatic position owing to the comparative *invertissant*.

In presenting a picaresque style of life, the concepts which are elevated by writers in the old tradition are inevitably reduced to a lower level, and reference is made to facts of everyday life which would have been unacceptable to such authors. Death, for example, is now treated with the accent on its material aspects rather than on the spiritual. In the first example the obligatory indirect *invertissant* emphasizes this material side, and in the second the inversion in parentheses brings out the irony and underlines whose death is referred to :

' " Il a voulu sçavoir à quoy monteroit son enterrement, et mesme l'a voulu marchander avec moy le jour que je l'ay confessé." ' (p. 695)

'Le corps de l'hoste fut porté à sa derniere demeure et l'hostesse, nonobstant les belles pensées de la mort que luy

devoit avoir données celle de son mary, ne laissa pas de
faire payer en Arabe deux Anglois qui alloient de Bretagne
à Paris.' (p. 704)

A co-ordinating conjunction reinforced by a modal adverb
invertissant may also stress the introduction of an incongruous,
and therefore humorous or even pathetic statement :

' Il en fit un acte de contrition tel quel, et encore luy fallut-il
donner parole qu'il ne serait point ensevely dans un autre
drap que celuy qu'il avoit choisi.' (pp. 695–96)

Having thus lowered the tone of one of the most important
concepts of contemporary writing, Scarron uses the same means
to question the bases of the art itself :

' le peuple et la plus grande partie du monde ne sçavoient
point à quoy estoient bonnes les regles severes du Theatre.'
(p. 645)

References to the easy-going life of the comedians are at
times given added impact by the use of inversion. It has been
noted several times that certain verbs tend to co-occur with
certain *invertissants*, to the extent that in the pastoral genre,
for instance, *où* and *coucher* or *reposer* is almost a cliché. It
therefore comes as something of a shock if the inverted subject
is out of keeping with the earlier contexts, and this underlines
the comic effect of the idea, for example, of numerous people
sharing one bed :

' et ayant passé la plus grande partie de la nuict à coudre et à
découdre, (il) se coucha dans le lit où dormoient Ragotin et
la Rancune.' (p. 709)

Alternatively the unelevated subject in inverted position may
give a hint of anti-climax :

' La pauvre Caverne se trouva si mal qu'elle se coucha dans
un des licts de la chambre où estoient leurs hardes.' (p. 665)

Thus the syntax of the *style burlesque* serves to highlight the
ideas which characterize the comic genre, while a richer
vocabulary, in conjunction with non-rhetorical constructions,
contrasts sharply with the elegant style of contemporary
writers.

(c) The ' langue bourgeoise '

The language of the characters of the *Roman comique*, or indeed of its narrator, is coloured by vivid terms taken from the popular vocabulary, mainly nouns and adjectives, and along with this is found an increased dependence on verbs of low semantic content, and their necessary repetition if rhetorical devices are to be avoided. In many cases a change in word-order is the only factor averting monotony from continual repetition, whether the same verb is used or near synonyms. In the first example the verb *faire* occurs four times, and in the second there are four verbs of saying in half the complete sentence :

' (ils) ... faisoient leur Cour, alloient au cours ou en visite, et faisoient tout ce que font les jeunes gens de leur condition en cette grande ville, qui fait passer pour compagnars les habitans des autres villes du Royaume.' (p. 605)

'... et ne respondirent point à ce que leur dit Ragotin, ou changerent de discours autant de fois qu'il voulut parler de la nuit precedente.' (p. 623)

Alternatively auxiliaries may recur in rapid succession :

' " Aussy d'abord que je vous ay veu, vous ay-je connu comme si je vous avois nourry." ' (p. 572)

In conversation one also finds the accumulation of clauses, a feature of natural speech, and here inversion frequently helps to preserve some sort of order (cf. table 5.07), as in the following, where it distinguishes the key sentence from the tirade which precedes it :

' " Je m'empescherois bien de vous dire des choses qui peuvent vous deplaire, mais je ne m'acquiterois pas de tout ce que je vous dois si je ne vous découvrois tout ce que je sçay de Dom Fernand, en une affaire d'où depend le bonheur ou le malheur de vostre vie." ' (p. 653)

(d) Inversion and satire

The place of inversion in Scarron's satirical attack on the style of the *grands romans* has already been referred to in connection with the *style bourgeois*. Comparison, for example,

is a common way of satirizing the extremes of emotion extolled
by earlier novelists :

> ' Dom Carlos fut si consolé de mes paroles que sa joye le
> transporta aussi fort qu'avoit fait sa douleur.' (p. 733)

However, the most usual form of satire which involves inversion is the use of words or structures beloved of the *précieux*.
In the case of the former, the inverted subject is the target for
satire :

> ' Il se trouva à l'assignation embelly et parfumé où l'at-
> tendoit l'Ambassadrice du matin.' (p. 779)

Alternatively it is the whole inversion construction which is
borrowed from the eloquent writers and placed in a key
position :

> ' " Il ne tiendra qu'à vous ... de finir une vie aussi malheu-
> reuse qu'est la vostre." ' (p. 740)

Scarron also uses the device of implicit comparison, characterized by the relative *invertissant que*, but only to follow it by
a humorous anti-climax :

> ' Ils l'ont démasquée, l'ont reconnuë, et, avec toute la joye
> *que* font paroistre ceux qui trouvent ce qu'ils cherchent, l'ont
> emmenée apres avoir donné quelques coups à celuy qui la
> conduisoit.' (p. 717)

Extremes of feeling and affection are satirized in terms similar
to those used by serious authors :

> ' On peut aisément se figurer les caresses que se devoient
> faire deux filles qui s'aymoient beaucoup, et mesme apres les
> dangers où elles s'estoient trouvées.' (p. 726)

Inversion is also to be found in a parenthesis which contradicts
the idea expressed in the main clause, and the juxtaposition of
the inverted subject and the rest of the sentence has, in the
next example, both a comic effect and a satirical reference to
the great literary heroes :

> ' Je me jettay sur luy, nonobstant la foiblesse que m'avoit
> laissée ma pâmoison, et avec une adresse vigoureuse...'
> (p. 735)

Finally the satirical effect may lie in the incongruity of both
vocabulary and construction with the situation :

' C'est en un de ces Tripots là ... que j'ay laissé trois personnes comiques, recitant la Mariane devant une honorable compagnie, à laquelle presidoit le sieur de la Rappiniere.' (p. 536)

In the *Roman comique*, then, inversion assumes an additional stylistic function, that of parody of the elegant style of which it was an integral part with some archaic effect. Moreover its frequent occurrence in a work of this kind underlines its usefulness both in maintaining clear, unambiguous expression, and in emphasizing important ideas, whether these are points of realistic detail, or objects of satire, or are introduced for other comic effects.

(ii) A. FURETIÈRE, 'LE ROMAN BOURGEOIS'

(a) The 'anti-roman'

Although the stylistic contrast between the earlier ' heroic ' novels and the *Roman bourgeois* is very marked, Furetière's style does not depend on syntactic means for its effect. Indeed it is characterized by the absence of those syntactic features which were so important in the *grands romans*, and inversion itself has hardly any stylistic functions. However it does happen that constructions with inverted order are the vehicle for irony or parody of the heroic style, particularly in the *Historiette de l'amour esgaré* (pp. 983–1002), whose Classical subject, that of the infant Cupid, allows the author plenty of scope. There is, for example, the comparative construction, familiar from works of the previous century, which is given an ironic twist :

'... ainsi le tesmoigne Pline, qui peut-estre est un faux tesmoin.' (p. 985)

Another familiar construction, this time an attributive adjective *invertissant* draws attention to an apparently Classical name :

' Archelaïde, (tel estoit le nom de cette dame) estoit une femme parfaitement accomplie...' (p. 993)

Indeed it seems that parentheses, with inverted order, are

particularly useful in bringing out the irony of the sentence of which they are a part :

'... car il n'y a point de dieu, tant fabuleux soit-il, que l'hypocrisie ne choque horriblement.' (p. 990)

Again inversion may be used in conjunction with elements of a *précieux* vocabulary :

'... il ne laissa pas de ... faire toutes les grimaces et les emportemens que font les amans passionnez qui languissent...' (p. 1007)

Finally, the concessive construction is well suited to be a vehicle for irony, with the possibility of oppositions of content, as well as word-order, between the two parts of the construction :

' Quelque clairvoyant que soit son esprit, il ne sera jamais persuadé de ses deffauts.' (p. 990)

(b) The self-conscious narrator

The presence of the narrator in the *Roman bourgeois* is much more obtrusive than in Scarron's *Roman comique*, and is perhaps a corollary to Furetière's professed *anti-roman* intentions.[11] The author's interventions account for quite a number of the inversion examples, as he tends to use two main devices which necessarily involve inversion. The first is the use of indirect constructions in appealing to the reader, and the second is the use of comparatives, generally the cliché-like *comme* and inversion, in referring to other writers.

Indirect questions where there is no possibility of direct word-order may serve as a comment on the action, thus :

' Mais encore lecteur ... je serois bien aise de vous faire deviner quel fut le succes de ces plaidoyries et qui fut le plus opiniastre de Collantine ou de Charroselles.' (p. 1104)

In the following, Furetière is criticizing novelists who indulge in unnecessary detail :

' De sorte que je ne veux pas mesme vous dire comme est faite cette église, quoy qu'assez celebre.' (p. 905)

---

[11] cf. Booth: ' one is made to feel that the order of events is transformed merely to portray the whimsical narrator and thus to parody conventional narration ' (*op. cit.*, p. 168).

The comparative constructions make this criticism more explicit, and the effect of the inversion, although very common, is to emphasize the object of criticism, which is usually expanded by a dependent clause :

> ' car je ne vous veux point surprendre, comme font certains autheurs malicieux qui ne visent à autre chose...' (p. 923)

The opposition between the negative intention of the author and the positive actions of others is thus underlined. Then there is a comparative inversion in parentheses where the irony lies in the coupling of the two inverted subjects :

> '... si ses sujets ne se mangeoient les uns les autres (comme font les loups et les poëtes) ... elles ne pourroient pas les nourrir ny les loger.' (p. 984)

Furetière also employs comparatives to comment on the language he has used, or attributed to his characters, thereby stressing certain aspects of the bourgeois language :

> '... qui sont les grands chemins par où l'honneur bourgeois va droit à Versailles, comme parlent les bonnes gens.' (p. 937)
>
> ' Il la ramassa avec une fourchette ... et lui dit ... comme font plusieurs personnes maintenant, qu'il lui demandoit un million d'excuses.' (p. 959)

(c) Documentation

As witness to the objective and realistic nature of his novel, Furetière frequently introduces various types of documents, letters, catalogues and the like, which, according to Goebel ' unterstreichen den dokumentarischen und protokollarischen Charakter des Romans '.[12] The inversions which occur within such documents are highly stereotyped, according to the style of the item represented. Thus, for example, the *table de chapitres* of a work entitled *Somme dédicatoire*, quoted in full near the end of the novel, contains six *que invertissants* and one with *où*, all of which contribute to the succinct style of chapter headings, e.g.

' Divers avantages qu'ont les historiens sur les poëtes et

---

[12] G. Goebel, *Zur Erzähltechnik in den ' Histoires comiques ' des 17. Jahrhunderts*, Berlin, 1965, p. 217.

romanciers, et des belles occasions qu'ont ceux-là d'obliger plusieurs personnes.' (p. 1092)

Inversion is used in the same way, conveying documentary succinctness, in catalogues, inventories and a will, and nearly all the *invertissants* here are relatives. The exception is a temporal conjunction which is found in the *Estat et rooles des sommes* (pp. 1095–96), a parody of Chapelain's list of pensions, and which likewise has a formal tone :

' Nota que cela s'entend de pension par chacun an, tant que durera la composition, pourvu que ce soit sans fraude.' (p. 1095)

A feature of such inversions is that they usually relate to a noun which has no verbal antecedent :

' De l'usage du helescopophore, ou de certaines lunettes dont se servent les grands, qui...' (*Catelogue*, p. 1085)

' Premierement, un lit où estoit gisant ledit deffunt, consistant en...' (*Inventoire*, p. 1077)

The formal, legalistic tone which often accompanies inversions with a passive verb is found in the reading of a will (pp. 1078–79), whose parodied style is clearly recognizable, in spite of the fact that many of the ' vaines formalités ' are said to have been omitted, since ' ce style des notaires ... ne fait que gaster du parchemin ' (p. 1078) :

' Je donne et legue à Claude Catharinet ... mon grand Agenda ou mon Almanach de disners, dans lequel sont contenus les noms et les demeures de toutes mes connoissances avec les observations...' (p. 1078)

Finally the same construction occurs in the course of a conversation between Lucrece and her *marquis*, where the same language is used in referring to a document as presumably would be in quoting from it :

' " Il y auroit pareillement en ce greffe une pancarte ou tableau où seroient specifiez par le menu les manieres et les regles pour s'habiller, avec..." ' (p. 934)

In these examples, then, inversion is used in the course of parody, because it is clearly identifiable with certain documentary styles.

(d) Conclusion

Inversion in the *Roman bourgeois* is thus confined, in its stylistic function, to the expression of certain types of irony, or to the characterization of the language of documents or of the narrator. The study of word-order in this text proves only that the *style bourgeois* depends on non-syntactic effects. The analysis of inversions occurring in direct speech is unfruitful, beyond showing that the vast majority are in book II, which is devoted to conversations between literary figures. It appears from this that the language of the bourgeois characters does not generally allow deviation from direct order, except in indirect constructions. The inversions in speech do include a couple of comparatives where the intention seems to be satirical. Thus Charroselles (the ill-disguised Sorel) is satirized by his pretentious speech :

> ' "... et j'aurois plustost dit *donrois* au lieu de *donnerois* comme faisoient les anciens qui usoient de la syncope." '
> (p. 1070)

and Collantine represents the bourgeois idea of literature :

> ' "... j'aime generalement tous les vers poëtiques, et surtout les quatrains de six vers, tels que sont ceux qui sont pour moi." ' (p. 1071)

However, the conclusion remains that this isolated example of the bourgeois novel, a specialized form of comic writing, is a protest not only against the traditional novel form, but also against stylistic syntax, at least as far as word-order is concerned.

(iii) MME. DE LA FAYETTE, ' LA PRINCESSE DE CLÈVES '

The elegance and simplicity of the style of the *Princesse de Clèves* is reflected in certain syntactic features revealed by the analysis of the inversions. While the frequency of inversion in the novel, $0 \cdot 85$, is slightly higher than the average for this period (table 5.01), the number of *invertissants*, twenty-two, is unusually low (table 5.08), which results in the high ratio of 5.82 inversions to each *invertissant*. The only other texts in this study with so few *invertissants* are all by 18th-century writers : Duclos (24), Diderot (19) and Prévost (19). Thus the inversions in this novel are found to occur very regularly, and table 5.09 shows that 98% belong to the four main categories of which no fewer than 62% are relatives as compared to 51% in Scarron and only 19% in the other writer representing French Classicism, Fénelon. Although the majority of inversions occur in sentences of three or more clauses, 71% (table 5.07), the structures are generally simple in that interposed adverbials are found in only 3% of the examples (table 5.12), and the proportion of inverted subjects with dependent clauses, 12%, is lower than in the other three texts (table 5.06).

Many of the inversions in relative clauses are fixed cliché constructions, and there is little variety in the verbs which occur. Thus out of the forty examples with the *invertissant que*, eighteen have the verb *donner*, while other predictable verbs, *causer*, *faire* and *avoir* account for all but seven of the remainder. The constructions with *où* are even more limited, with *être* figuring in nineteen of the twenty-four examples. There is a marked tendency for relative inversions to occur in final position, particularly in emphasizing the expression of emotions, e.g.

' la peine que lui donnait l'affection de ce prince.' (p. 1124)
'... par la douleur que lui donnait cette pensée.' (p. 1141)
The extent to which such constructions may be said to characterize the style of this novel is examined below.

Inversion and restraint in ' La Princesse de Clèves '
1. Narrative
In Madame de la Fayette's presentation of the historical background to her novel, inverted word-order is employed as is usual in descriptive technique, to emphasize or clarify lengthy or complex subjects. The occurrence of four subjects, all names of important characters at court, after an adverbial phrase of place has already been quoted (p. 148) above. Similarly inversion is frequently used in the presentation of characters where a relative clause qualifies the inverted subject :

'... elle mena toutes ses filles, parmi lesquelles était Mlle de Pisseleu, qui a été depuis la duchesse d'Etampes.' (p. 1129)

In the following example the emphasis provided by inversion is important in the transition from the description of the heroine and her surroundings to her feelings for the subject of the portrait :

'... et (elle) s'en alla proche d'une grande table vis-à-vis du tableau du siege de Metz, où était le portrait de M. de Nemours.' (p. 1227)

In addition, inversion is used quite often in chiastic constructions in description, e.g.

'... et sur les cinq heures on en partit pour aller au Palais, où se faisait le festin, et où le Parlement, les Cours Souveraines et la Maison de la Ville étaient priés d'assister.' (p. 1214)

The restrained elegance of the style of Madame de la Fayette becomes perhaps fully apparent in considering the second level at which the novel progresses, that of psychological analysis. Despite the emotional subject, inversion in an analytical style has similar functions to those already mentioned, clarity and emphasis, in addition to ensuring a rhythmic sentence structure. Thus, for instance, an inversion with two long subjects concludes a paragraph :

'... et peu d'hommes ... ont ressenti en même temps la douleur que cause l'infidelité d'une maîtresse et la honte d'être trompé par une femme.' (p. 1233)

The following constitutes a chiasmus which retains the logical order of elements :

'... elle ne lui avait pas fait la même impression que venait de faire la conversation qu'elle avait eue avec lui...' (p. 1250)

The frequency of cliché constructions in this context has already been noted, and this, together with a general lack of qualification, contributes further to the attenuated style. Stressed subjects are mostly unexpanded by a complement or dependent clause, as in the following extract from a letter :

' J'ai joui de tout le plaisir que peut donner la vengeance.' (p. 1171)

There is thus considerable restraint in the treatment of

inversion as an emphatic device. In the following example the contrast between the two epithets *obligeant* and *austère* is brought out by the word-order in a sentence where the vocabulary itself is rather neutral :

' Peut-être que des regards et des paroles obligeantes n'eussent pas tant augmenté l'amour de M. de Nemours que faisait cette conduite austère.' (p. 1021)

2. The speech of the characters

The language of the dialogue in *La Princesse de Clèves* reveals self-restraint on the part of the speaker similar to that already noted in the narrative, as well as the polished style of elegant conversation. Thus in Madame de Clève's conversation with M. de Nemours after the death of her husband the highly emotional content is couched in elegant, rhythmic prose, with inversion contributing to the balance of the sentence :

' " Il n'est que trop véritable que vous êtes cause de la mort de M. de Clèves : les soupçons que lui a donnés votre conduite inconsidérée lui ont coûté la vie, comme si vous la lui aviez ôtée de vos propres mains." ' (p. 1245)

The careful structure indicates perhaps a certain remoteness from the spoken language and a lack of spontaneity on the part of the characters. The combination of inverted word-order and precious vocabulary produces a similar impression, as in this extract from one of the heroine's soliloquies :

' " Et veux-je enfin m'exposer aux cruels repentirs et aux mortelles douleurs que donne l'amour ? " ' (p. 1191)

The speech of M. de Nemours, whether in monologue or conversation, is characterized by the same rhythmic structure as in the following example where inversion avoids an imperfect cadence, stresses the subject and lends variety to the sentence :

' " J'avoue ... que l'on ne peut être ... plus affligé que je le suis de l'infidelité que m'a faite le Vidame de Chartres..." ' (p. 1206)

The monologues are more emotional, but with inversion nevertheless preserving clarity, as in the following :

' " Quoi! je serai aimé de la plus aimable personne du
monde, et je n'aurai cet excès d'amour que donnent les
premières certitudes d'être aimé que pour mieux sentir la
douleur d'être maltraité! " ' (p. 1230)

Inverted order both disposes of a subject which is slightly
longer than usual, as well as stressing the opposition *être
aimé—être maltraité*.

Finally one of the rare moments of extreme emotion in
conversation, where M. de Nemours begs the heroine to listen
to him, is similarly marked by an inversion whose function is
both one of rhythm and of clarity:

' "... si ce n'est par bonté, que ce soit ... pour vous délivrer
des extravagences où m'emporterait infailliblement une
passion dont je ne suis plus le maître." ' (pp. 1242–43)

This example is also one of the few instances in which an
adverbial, the lengthy *infailliblement*, separates verb and
subject in the inversion clause. In this sentence relatives and
antecedents occur in logical sequence, despite the emotive
content, and in such conversations it seems true to say, as
Rousset has observed in the soliloquies: ' on ne lit ici que les
pensées claires à l'instant où elles naissent à la clarté.' [13]

3. The ' récits '

The *récits* which arise quite naturally out of the conversation
do not differ greatly from the narrative, although the reader is
constantly reminded of the context, either by the story-teller's
comments or his use of the second person in addressing his
audience. Eleven inversions are found in the four *récits* and
they are mostly isolated occurrences, with the exception of the
first story. This contains six inversions in about four pages, a
much higher frequency than usual. The second *récit*, while
twice as long as the first, has only two inversions. A possible
explanation of this is that the first story, told by Madame de
Chartres about Diane de Poitiers, is largely factual and impersonal, with four relative *invertissants* and two comparatives,

---

[13] J. Rousset, *Forme et signification* (*Essais sur les structures littéraires de
Corneille à Claudel*), Paris, 1964, p. 42.

whereas the second, told by M. de Clèves about Sancerre, involves the speaker himself, so it is nearly all in the first person and in a slightly less formal style, the two inversions both being after *ce que*. The remaining *récits* are both told by Madame la Dauphine about the English court, and have one inversion in each. As the *récits* represent a short respite from the main action for the protagonists, it is not surprising that these inversions have little emotional significance. Most of them are of this descriptive type, as in example A2 quoted (p. 146) above. Although the emphasis in the following is perhaps more subjective, the inversion also facilitates the expression of a complex subject:

' " Jamais il n'y a eu une si grande haine que l'a été celle de ces deux femmes." ' (p. 1130)

Unlike the conversations, stories and monologues in, for example, Scudéry, those of Madame de la Fayette form an integral part of the structure of the novel. This unity is reinforced by a common style which is characterized primarily by simplicity and restraint. As seen above, the occurrence of inversion constructions is modified accordingly, with certain unelaborate sentence structures predominating, whose use is confined mainly to ensuring clear and rhythmic prose. Thus inversion is a device whose resources typify the dominant characteristics of Madame de la Fayette's style as summed up by Dédéyan: ' la simplicité, la concentration de l'intérêt, et l'équilibre.' [14]

(iv) FÉNELON, ' TÉLÉMAQUE '

The inversion frequency in *Télémaque* is the lowest of the four texts, as well as being among the lowest in all ten periods, although the analysis reveals an average number of different *invertissants* (table 5.07). The most striking feature shown above is the small proportion of inversions occurring in sentences of three or more clauses, 41% (table 5.06), of which 28% are in sentences of three clauses only. This is well below

[14] C. Dédéyan, *Madame de Lafayette*, Paris, 1955, p. 114.

the average proportion in any period, and few individual texts show a lower occurrence. Consistent with the use of shorter sentences is the predominance of modal adverb *invertissants* over relatives (table 5.08), the latter being unusually infrequent. The fact that 28% of the examples are found in indirect constructions reflects the tendency for inversion to occur in more routine structures and also the relatively high proportion in indirect speech, 11% (table 5.03). Also indicative of simple inversion structures is the number of examples having the verb *être*, 28% (table 5.09).

While *Télémaque* provides instances of every type of mobile *invertissant* represented in the texts analysed in this period, there are no examples of inversion in temporal clauses, and only one deletion and transposition operation, a concessive construction. Thus the inversions which do occur tend to be fairly common ones, in a simple sentence structure, and their use in the Classical style of Fénelon is examined below.

(*a*) *Inversion and Fénelon's Classical style*

Inversion is relevant to Fénelon's Classical style in two respects. Firstly it is used to emphasize names from, or allusions to, Classical Antiquity or to facilitate their expression, and secondly it is to be found in various rhetorical constructions which befit the content of the work. Thus inverted order often stresses names which may be qualified by a complement or relative clause:

'D'un autre côté paraissait Mars avec une fierté rude et menaçante.' (II, 30)

'Après eux venaient des Tritons, qui sonnaient de la trompette avec leurs conques recourbées.' (I, 91)

The *invertissant* may be underlined by the operation of addition:

'C'etait là que régnait le vieux Aceste, sorti de Troie.' (I, 15)

Alternatively the Classical allusion may be contained in the complement following the inverted subject:

' " Ils continuèrent à parler ... de cette heureuse paix dont jouissent les justes dans les Champs-Elysées, sans crainte de pouvoir la perdre." ' (I, 90)

Inversion in the following permits the succession of antecedents and relatives, with the last two relatives both having either a Classical antecedent or subject:

'... les nations qui habitent ..., sur le sommet d'Acratas, où règne un hiver que les zéphirs n'ont jamais adouci.' (I, 19)

The emphatic property of inversion is also exploited in comparative structures, e.g.

' "... et faire voir on vous ... un roi aussi digne de régner que le fut jamais Ulysse lui-même." ' (I, 13)

In the next two examples the verb as well as the subject is emphasized, and in each case constitutes something of a cliché:

' Ainsi fleurissait la nouvelle ville d'Idoménée sur le rivage de la mer.' (I, 198)

' On voyait s'élever ... de flammes semblables à ces feux souterrains que vomit le mont Etna.' (I, 270)

Although the rhetorical use of inverted order has a limited role in *Télémaque*, it is of some importance in chiastic structures and to a lesser extent in epic simile and enumerations. The opposition of two orders in chiasmus may involve the repetition of an element which constitutes the *invertissant* in the inversion clause, or of some other element in the sentence. The two instances of the former quoted below are used to different effect:

' "Autant que Minerve est au-dessus de Mars, autant une valeur discrète et prévoyante surpasse-t-elle un courage bouillant et farouche." ' (I, 211)

' Télémaque ... comprend à peine ce qu'il vient d'entendre; à peine peut-il croire qu'il ait entendu ces hautes prédictions.' (I, 205–6)

The first chiasmus stresses a parallel which relates the two sentences to each other and the elements within them, the opposition Minerve-Mars being echoed by that of *valeur-courage*, each qualified by two postposed adjectives. The second example also constitutes a parallelism in that the same idea is expressed in each, with the rearrangement of items echoing this. After the repetition of *à peine* a pronoun is substituted for the substantival subject, and *pouvoir croire* replaces *comprendre*. This example represents a restatement in the second part of the chiasmus, while in the previous instance the two clauses are related by a formal correlative.

In the next example, the change in word-order serves to stress the dependent infinitive:

> ' " Il y a vingt ans qu'ils font gémir tous les hommes de bien et qu'à peine ose-t-on même gémir, tant leur tyrannie est cruelle." ' (II, 25)

In the frequent indirect constructions, direct and inverted orders may again be contrasted and thus prevent monotony where there is generally no syntactic choice involved, as in the example quoted above (p. 150), and:

> ' " Jugez quelle fut ma surprise et combien je versai de larmes ... quand je vis..." ' (II, 53)

In both cases the change of interrogative pronoun and word-order results in a balanced and varied sentence structure.

The comparisons in *Télémaque* draw mainly on familiar objects and ideas and may be stressed by inversion. The following is an explicit comparison reminiscent of Virgilian epic simile:

> ' "... le grand Hercule ... devant qui les autres héros n'étaient que comme sont les faibles roseaux auprès d'un grand chêne, ou comme les moindres oiseaux en présence de l'aigle." '
> (II, 44)

The next is based on an object rather than natural phenomena, while also having Classical overtones:

> ' Semblable à un vase précieux, mais fêlé, d'où s'écoulent toutes les liqueurs les plus délicieuses, le cœur de ce grand capitaine ne pouvait rien garder.' (II, 78)

In both instances inversion emphasizes the *comparant* and lends variety to the sentence.

Inversions in descriptive passages in *Télémaque* are generally employed for clarity and emphasis, e.g.

> ' " A la porte du temple est sans cesse une foule de peuples qui viennent faire leurs offrandes." ' (I, 80)

an unusual feature of this example being the interposed adverbial which delays the subject. In some examples the preoccupation with Antiquity may lead to *préciosité*, e.g.

'Mais quand il vit l'urne d'or où étaient renfermées les cendres si chères ... il versa un torrent de larmes.' (II, 104)

Elsewhere inverted order permits rhetorical repetition, as in this use of several verbs,

' " Elle était bordée par un grand amphithéâtre d'un gazon frais sur lequel était assis et rangé un peuple innombrable." '
(I, 102)

or even enumeration, where there are a number of complements after the inverted subject, e.g.

'... on voyait une rivière où se formaient des îles bordées de tilleux fleuris et de hauts peupliers, qui portaient leurs têtes superbes jusque dans les nues.' (I, 7)

(b) *Inversion in the expression of moral purpose*

In this text certain non-comparative *invertissants* are used where a general analogy is drawn from a particular example for the purpose of moral teaching. Thus modal adjectives and adjective attributes, among others, seem to assume a comparative function. An example with the *invertissant ainsi* makes this clear :

'Ainsi tomberont tous les rois qui se livrerent à leurs désirs et aux conseils des esprits flatteurs.' (I, 208)

Here the *invertissant* is both co-ordinating and comparative in function, and it is the latter element which may be stressed by the addition of *c'est ... que* as in,

' " C'est ainsi ... que parlent ces hommes sages, qui n'ont appris la sagesse qu'en étudiant la simple nature." ' (I, 181)

The moral may also be drawn by the use of a similar *invertissant*, the adjective *tel* :

' " Telle est la condition des rois les plus éclairés et les plus vertueux." ' (I, 258)

The example of a correlative construction with inversion in the second clause (quoted p. 171, above) also assumes a didactic function. A different way of showing moral values and

involving inversion is the appeal to an audience by the use of
the verb *voir* or of *voilà* with the *invertissant ce que :*

' "... et voilà ce que fait le traître Amour, qui paraît si
doux ! " ' (I, 150)

In all the above examples the inversion construction co-
ordinates by referring back to the preceding clause or sentence
from which a general conclusion is to be drawn, and is at the
same time a means of comparison. Clarity is achieved by the
fact that complements or dependent clauses are allowed to
follow on from the inverted subject to which they belong.

Thus inversion in *Télémaque* is seen to enhance the French
Classical style in that it provides a clear and balanced sentence
structure while giving emphasis to description and comparison,
and syntactic variety in oppositions. The emphatic properties
of certain *invertissants* also at times reflect the didactic intention of the work. Many other inversions which occur in short
sentences, have a primarily co-ordinating function in the
narrative, with the *invertissant* related to the previous topic,
thus :

' " De ce rocher sortait une fontaine claire." ' (II, 52)

' " Là coulent mille divers ruisseaux d'une eau claire, qui
distribuent l'eau partout." ' (I, 58)

The examples quoted perhaps illustrate the unobtrusive nature
of the inversions in *Télémaque*, although the contexts in which
they occur are nevertheless characteristic of Fénelon's style.

CHAPTER VI

THE EIGHTEENTH CENTURY (1)

1. SYNTACTIC ANALYSIS OF THE TEXTS
1700–1750

The texts :

A.-P. Lesage, *Histoire de Gil Blas de Santillane* [1]
Abbé Prévost, *Manon Lescaut* [2]
P. Marivaux, *Le paysan parvenu* [3]
C. P. Duclos, *Histoire de Mme. de Luz* [4]
        Les confessions du comte de xxx [5]
        Acajou et Firphile [4]

Table 6.01 : Inversion frequencies

LES/GB	111 : 0·55	
PRE/ML	51 : 0·33	*(mean 0·52)*
MAR/PP	149 : 0·75	
DUC/	86 : 0·43	

Table 6.02 : Percentage table to show nature of clause in which inversion occurs

	LES	PRE	MAR	DUC
Main clause	38	27	58	36
Subordinate clause	62	73	42	63
Non-subordinating *invertissant* in subordinate clause	—	—	—	1
	100	100	100	100
Immobile *invertissant*	59	67	39	57
Mobile *invertissant*	32	13	52	37
Other operations	9	20	9	6
N :	111	51	149	86

[1] ed. Bardon, Paris (Garnier), 1955 (analysis to bk IV ch 5 inc.). (LES)
[2] ed. Deloffre and Picard, Paris (Garnier), 1965 (length *c.* 66,000 words). (PRE)
[3] ed. Deloffre, Paris (Garnier), 1959. (MAR)
[4] In *Œuvres*, Paris (Didier), 1855. (DUC)
[5] In *Romanciers du XVIIIe siècle II*, ed. Etiemble, Paris (Bibl. de la Pléiade), 1965, pp. 199–301.

Table 6.03 : Percentage table to show distribution of inversions according to discourse type

	LES	PRE	MAR	DUC
Narrative	56	71	66	76
Direct speech	42	25	28	22
Indirect speech	1	4	3	2
Free indirect speech	—	—	2	—
Soliloquy	1	—	1	—

Table 6.04 : Percentage table to show position of the inversion within the corpus examined

	LES	PRE	MAR	DUC
Sentence initial	31	25	21	34
Paragraph initial	4	2	12	7
Chapter initial	1	—	—	—
Speech initial	—	—	2	—
Total initial	36	27	35	41
Sentence final	37	37	16	31
Paragraph final	1	4	5	6
Chapter final	1	—	—	—
Speech final	—	2	1	—
Total final ·	39	43	22	37

Table 6.05 : Percentage table to show position of inversion in relation to other types of discourse

	LES	PRE	MAR	DUC
Preceding direct speech	—	4	—	1
Following direct speech	1	2	—	—
Preceding indirect speech	—	—	1	—
Following indirect speech	—	—	—	—

Table 6.06 : Percentage table to show nature of the inverted noun phrase

	LES	PRE	MAR	DUC
Pronoun subject	25	25	45	27
Substantive subject	71	73	52	71
Compound inversion	4	2	3	2
	100	100	100	100
2 or more subjects	2	6	2	2
S and dependent (S)	12	4	15	10

Table 6.07 : The percentage of inversions occurring in sentences
of three or more clauses

	LES	PRE	MAR	DUC
(S)—3 clauses	28	29	25	43
4 clauses	16	16	25	6
5 clauses	5	4	12	5
6 clauses	—	2	5	2
7 clauses	—	2	1	—
	49	53	68	56

Table 6.08 : Ratio of inversions to *invertissants*

LES	111 : 25—4·44
PRE	51 : 19—2·69
MAR	149 : 37—4·03
DUC	86 : 24—3·58
Total	397 : 55—7·22 (*mean* 3·69)

Table 6.09 : Percentage table of the most frequently occurring
inversions

	LES	PRE	MAR	DUC
Relatives	39	22	26	36
Comparatives	3	6	5	2
Indirect construction	14	33	5	9
Modal adverbs	24	20	42	29

Table 6.10 : Percentage table to show the occurrence of ' être ',
' faire ' and ' avoir '

	LES	PRE	MAR	DUC
être	31	47	21	23
faire	3	2	7	5
avoir	4	2	6	2

Table 6.11 : Percentage table showing the distribution of
direct speech *invertissants*

	LES	PRE	MAR	DUC
Immobile *invertissant*	60	54	27	47
Mobile *invertissant*	31	15	56	37
Other operations	9	31	17	16
N :	47	13	41	19

Table 6.12: Percentage table to show the occurrence of
adverbials and clauses in inversion constructions

	LES	PRE	MAR	DUC
V(adv)S	6	—	1	6
(adv)VS	1	—	—	—
V(S)S	—	—	—	—
(S)VS	—	—	3	2

(i) DISTRIBUTION OF THE INVERSIONS

With the first 18th-century period the inversion frequency
reaches its lowest, 0·52, as compared with 0·74 and 0·80 in the
texts of the previous century, after which the trend is reversed.
The period includes the work with the fewest inversions, *Manon
Lescaut*, which has only fifty-one examples, and a frequency of
0·33, the novel being about three-quarters the standard
length. These texts also have the fewest *invertissants*, fifty-five
different ones in all, and an average of twenty-six per novel, as
compared with thirty-four and forty-four in the two previous
periods, and this decrease is also halted in the next fifty years.
In these four texts the number of inversions correlates with the
number of *invertissants*, the fewest occurring in Prévost and
the most in Marivaux.

The rise of compound inversion noted in the second half of
the 17th century, which accounted for an average 3% of the
examples in each text then, is continued in both 18th-century
periods (table 6.06). There also appears a new phenomenon,
the tendency to insert clauses between *invertissant* and verb,
which will become increasingly marked. The overall decrease
in direct speech inversion continues (table 6.03), although the
proportion for the previous period, an average of 16% seems to
have been abnormally low. Of these examples fewer have an
immobile *invertissant* (cf. table 2.11), whereas the proportion
of mobile *invertissants* remains about the same (table 6.11).
On the other hand there is a dramatic increase in inversions
resulting from other syntactic operations, namely deletion and
transposition or addition and transposition, and this is most
marked in the direct speech examples, where the proportion is

considerably higher than in the general corpus in all four texts. On average such inversions represent 18% of the direct speech examples in each text, as compared to the overall average of 11%. Also concerning direct speech, the tendency to invert after a conversational passage which characterized the 16th century and still persisted in the 17th, has now disappeared, the examples for the whole century representing 1% in Lesage and 2% in Prévost (table 6.05).

There is also a continued decrease in the length of the sentence containing inversion (table 6.08), with very few examples exceeding five clauses. Inversions in sentences of three or more clauses average 57% of the examples. Finally as regards the type of *invertissant*, now that co-ordinating *invertissants* are extinct, modal adverbs are near to becoming the most common type, representing an average of 29%, as compared to the 31% of relatives, which is a drop of 10% on the previous period. A contributory factor is perhaps also a marked reduction in comparative inversions (table 6.09).

(ii) EXAMPLES

A. IMMOBILE 'INVERTISSANT'

1. *Relative conjunctions : LES : 43 inversions, 7 ' invertissants' ; PRE : 11,4 ; MAR : 39,6 ; DUC : 31,5*
   ' La confusion que j'avais de me voir si mal équipé modérait la joie *qu'*ont ordinairement les prisonniers de recouvrer la liberté.' (LES II, 48)
2. *Comparatives : LES : 3,1 ; PRE : 3,3 ; MAR : 8,4 ; DUC : 1,1*
   ' J'étais bien sûr qu'après un éclat *tel que* l'avait dû causer ma fuite de Sainte-Sulpice, il me traiterait beaucoup plus rigoureusement.' (PRE, p. 57)
3. *Concessives : LES : 5,2 ; PRE : 3,1 ; MAR : 3,2 ; DUC : 9,2*
   ' *Toute* indiscrète *qu'*était la mère, elle nous servit pourtant à merveilles.' (MAR, p. 103)

4. *Indirect construction* : *LES* : *15,4* ; *PRE* : *17,5* ; *MAR* : *8,4* ; *DUC* : *8,4*

' " Vous voyez *jusqu'où* va ma confiance : puissiez-vous ne m'en faire repentir ! " ' (DUC/CON, p. 281)

B. MOBILE 'INVERTISSANT'

1. *Attributes* : *LES* : *7,1* ; *MAR* : *5,1* ; *DUC* : *2,1*

' *Telle* fut l'origine des petites maisons qui se multiplièrent dans la suite, et cessèrent d'être des asiles pour le mystère.' (DUC/CON, p. 234)

2. *Adverbs—modal* : *LES* : *27,6* ; *PRE* : *10,3* ; *MAR* : *63,7* ; *DUC* : *25,5*

' *Ainsi* mourut la plus belle, la plus malheureuse, et j'ose dire encore, la plus vertueuse et la plus respectable de toutes les femmes.' (DUC/LUZ, p. 150)

3. *Adverbs—time* : *MAR* : *2,1*

' " Voyons : d'abord il me vient une dame, *ensuite* arrive un garçon, je les reçois tous deux... " ' (p. 229)

4. *Adverbs—place* : *MAR* : *1,1*

' *Ici* se dissipèrent toutes ces enflures de cœur dont je vous ai parlé, toutes ces fumées de vanité qui m'avaient monté à la tête.' (p. 265)

5. *Adverbs—combinations* : *MAR* : *2,2* ; *DUC* : *2,1*

' Et s'il faut tout dire, *peut-être aussi* voulais-je voir ce qui arriverait de cette aventure, et tirer parti de tout.' (MAR, p. 87)

6. *Adverbial phrase—time* : *LES* : *1,1*

' Il survint ensuite deux comédiens, Constance et Celinaura ; et *un moment après* parut Florimende, accompagnée d'un homme qui avait tout l'air d'un " Señor cavallero " des plus lestes.' (II, 184)

7. *Adverbial phrase—place* : *MAR* : *2,2*

' *Après ces messieurs*, venait un jeune homme d'une assez belle figure.' (p. 190)

8. *Prepositional phrase* : *MAR* : *2,1* ; *DUC* : *3,1*

' " *De la perte de l'honneur* naissent des malheurs trop certains " ' (DUC/LUZ, p. 78)

C. OTHER OPERATIONS

1. *Deletion : MAR : 1*
   ' " *Viennent* tous les présidents du monde et tous les greffiers du pays, voilà ce que je leur dirai, fussent-ils mille " ' (p. 122)

2. *Deletion and transposition : LES : 7 ; PRE : 4 ; MAR : 8*
   ' " *Le cours du sang est-il ralenti*, elle le précipite ; *est-il* trop rapide, elle en arrête l'impétuosité." ' (LES II, 82)

3. *Addition and transposition : LES : 3,2 ; PRE : 3,2 ; MAR : 5,4 ; DUC : 5,4*
   ' Elle ignorait, et moi aussi, que *c'était* sur elle-même *que* devait tomber toute la colère du Ciel et la rage de nos ennemis.' (PRE, p. 194)

(iii) DETAILS OF THE INVERSIONS

(a) Reduction of ' invertissants '

At the time when inversion is least common, the examples are mostly confined to the four main types. The immobile *invertissant* constructions are reduced to four, with no examples of zero or temporal *invertissants* or of the other less common subordinating conjunctions. Within these constructions there are few different *invertissants*, for example, the comparisons in all four texts are limited to *comme, tel que* and *plus que*. Similarly there are only eight different relative pronouns : sixty of all the 124 examples have the *invertissant que*, half as many have *où*, and the examples of preposition and *lequel* are reduced to five, with none at all in Marivaux and Duclos. Thus even the *invertissants* which are found throughout the period of analysis are considerably reduced at this time.

With the exception of modal adverbs, the adverbial mobile *invertissants* are restricted to isolated examples. Adverbs of quantity and adverbial phrases of manner are not found ; the only adverbs of time and place occur sporadically in Marivaux and there are few instances of combinations. Apart from these there are eight adverbial and prepositional phrase *invertissants* in all the texts. Although there are numerous modal adverb inversions, there are only nine different *invertissants*. Most common are *aussi* (forty examples, of which twenty-four are in Marivaux) and *peut-être* (twenty-nine, thirteen in Marivaux), and *à peine* with thirteen occurrences each of restrictive and temporal uses. The others are *ainsi* (2), *encore* (8), *du moins* (6) and *aussi bien* (2), the last two in Marivaux only, and also twelve examples of *au moins* in Duclos. There are no other mobile *invertissants*, but the sudden increase in other operations results in a total of thirty-six examples from the four texts.

(b) *The position of other elements in inversion constructions*

The separation of verb and subject, or of *invertissant* and verb, by an adverb, adverbial phrase or clause, tends to emphasize the fact of inversion, one order stressing the inverted subject, and the other stressing both subject and verb. In these texts both Lesage and Duclos interpolate adverbs between verb and subject (6% of the examples in each), but this is rarely the case in Marivaux (1% of the examples). In Prévost there is, moreover, no such separation. While these figures are similar to those for earlier periods, the situation regarding the position of adverbs other than the *invertissant* is rather different. In the 16th century the freedom of word-order means that the order adverb-verb-subject after an *invertissant* is relatively common, but this frequency soon diminishes, with the result that the 17th century yields only isolated examples in each text, and in this period there is still only a single example of an adverbial phrase in Lesage which is quite unexceptional :

'Elle m'emmena même de la chambre du chanoine dans une garde-robe, où, parmi plusieurs habits, était celui de mon prédécesseur.' (p. 72)

Even more rare is a clause in this position, with occasional examples in the 16th century and a single one in d'Urfé in the 17th. In Marivaux and Duclos, however, such constructions account for 3% and 2% of the whole respectively, and these proportions increase in the texts of the next period. The following quotation from Marivaux, which furthermore occurs in conversation, is typical :

> ' " Aussi bien, après le service que vous avez tâché de nous rendre, serions-nous mortifiées de ne connaître qu'en passant un aussi honnête homme que vous." ' (p. 209)

It may be concluded that individual texts show certain preferences with regard to this aspect of word-order. In Prévost there is no separation by adverbials of any elements in the inversion construction, and only a very few instances where a dependent infinitive precedes the subject. In Lesage subject and verb are the only items liable to separation either by adverb or infinitive, with one exception. In the two later texts, however, all items are separable, and it is notable that only clauses, not adverbs, are placed between *invertissant* and verb. It might also be noted that inversions in Marivaux and Duclos occur in longer sentences (table 6.07) and that many of the inverted subjects have dependent clauses (table 6.06), possibly indicating a greater awareness of the stylistic potential of word-order on the part of these two authors.

(c) Direct speech

Although only an average 28% of the inversion examples in each text are found in direct speech, it would be surprising, given the reduction in inversion types, if these examples did not follow the main distribution quite closely. Indeed if tables 6.02 and 6.11 are compared it is clear that in Lesage the correspondence between the operational distribution in direct speech and in the text is exceptionally close. In this work each inversion type contains conversational examples in strikingly even proportions, the number of occurrences of immobile *invertissants* in direct speech being unusually high for this period. The three remaining texts, however, all have some inversion construction which does not occur in direct speech, concessive clauses in Prévost and attributes in Duclos, while in Marivaux there are similarly no attributes, and the only adverbial *invertissants* to occur in conversation are modal adverbs.

2. STYLISTIC ANALYSIS OF THE TEXTS

(i) A.-P. LESAGE, 'GIL BLAS'

(a) *Sentence length in Lesage*

An unmistakable feature of Lesage's writing is his short sentences, as noted, for example, by Dédéyan : ' La phrase courte et ailée a fait aussi son entrée, et contribue à donner à l'art de Lesage un brillant de plus.' [6] This is already clear from table 6.07, only 49% of the inversions being found in sentences of three or more clauses, and this is the first text studied in which no inversion occurs in a sentence of more than five clauses (cf. also Voltaire, Diderot and Laclos, in the next section). While Voltaire's style is generally the most succinct, the analysis in chapter VII will show slightly more inversions in longer sentences than in Lesage, although a greater number of these are three-clause sentences. *Gil Blas* may also be compared with the *Roman bourgeois* on this point. In the former there are 8% fewer inversions than the average for the period in longer sentences : similarly in Furetière there are 56% in sentences of three or more clauses (of which only 2% occur in sentences of more than five clauses), as compared with the average of 64% for that period. The shortest inversion sentences, however, have been found in Fénelon (table 5.07), with a total of 41% in sentences of three or more clauses, and the low proportion in Lesage may be the result of French Classical influence.

The distribution of multi-clause sentences, with or without inversion, suggests that these tend to occur at moments of crisis or important developments throughout the work. In this case a change in word-order underlines the deviation from the average length of a sentence, while at the same time linking the clauses more coherently. This is exemplified in the following extract from book I, where Gil Blas is contemplating his escape from the robbers, and here the inversion brings some relief in the string of conditionals ; the sentence is preceded

[6] C. Dédéyan, *Lesage et ' Gil Blas '*, Paris, 1965, t. 2, p. 494.

by two single-clause sentences, and followed by three equally short ones :

> ' S'ils m'eussent vu fuir, ils se seraient mis à mes trousses, et m'auraient bientôt rattrapé, ou peut-être auraient-ils fait sur moi une décharge de leurs carabines, dont je me serais fort mal trouvé.' (p. 28)

Exactly the same pattern is found when Gil Blas' conversation with Doña Mercia suffers an unwelcome interruption :

> ' J'allais lui demander quel parti elle voulait prendre dans la conjoncture où elle se trouvait, et peut-être allait-elle me consulter là-dessus, si notre conversation n'eût pas été interrompue.' (p. 44)

A similar function is fulfilled by an inversion found at the end of a paragraph, although the sentence is only slightly longer than average, describing the escape of Gil Blas and Doña Mercia :

> ' Nous eûmes beaucoup de peine à la lever, ou plutôt, pour en venir à bout, nous eûmes besoin de la force nouvelle que nous prêta l'envie de nous sauver.' (pp. 36–37)

Inversions in key positions are however generally in short sentences and without any special significance beyond linking sentences, paragraphs or chapters.   Thus chapter eight of book III opens :

> ' Tel fut l'histoire que don Pompeyo raconta, et que nous entendîmes...' (p. 173)

Chapter five of book IV closes with a three-clause sentence and inversion which perhaps stresses the idea of a natural break :

> ' J'approuvai cette pensée, et, laissant le seigneur don Felix avec son page, je me retirai dans un cabinet où était mon lit.' (p. 236)

(b) Direct speech in ' Gil Blas '

The number of direct speech inversions found in this text, 42%, (table 6.03), is the highest of those analysed so far, with the exception of the *Astrée* (44%), and in the later periods is surpassed only by Diderot (48%). All the *invertissants* which are in the narrative also occur in conversation, except for the

G

one example of an adverbial phrase of time and a single occurrence of *ainsi*. Certain *invertissants* which are associated with narrative technique tend to occur most frequently in this context, for instance all but one of the thirteen examples of *où*, the example of *ainsi*, and six out of the seven of *tel*. Otherwise just over half the modal adverb *invertissants* are conversational as are two-thirds of the indirect *invertissants*. As a result Deloffre's comment in this respect presents little surprise:

' Les personnages de Le Sage ... discourent plutôt qu'ils ne dialoguent.' [7]

An indication of the lack of differentiation between the language of narrative and conversation is found in the robber chief Rolando's explanation to Gil Blas of how he has been captured. Contrary to the general distribution two inversions occur here in quick succession, followed a little later by a third. It is noticeable that although the two sentences containing inversion are separated by a single-clause sentence, and the sentences of the immediate context are also short, these two are considerably longer, the first opening with the only conversational example of the *invertissant tel* :

' " Tel est ce souterrain, que les officiers de la sainte Hermandad viendraient cent fois dans cette forêt sans le découvrir. L'entrée n'en est connue que de moi seul et de mes camarades. Peut-être me demanderas-tu comment nous l'avons pu faire sans que les habitants des environs s'en soient aperçus." ' (p. 15)

The subsequent inversion is a relative which concludes a three-clause sentence, and although unremarkable in itself, its appearance in this type of conversation seems unlikely :

' " Les uns demeuraient dans les cavernes, et les autres firent plusieurs souterrains, du nombre desquels est celui-ci." ' (p 16)

Many of the remaining inversions in direct speech confirm this impression. They may be divided into two types, those where the construction seems unduly literary or elevated, and

[7] F. Deloffre, *Une préciosité nouvelle : Marivaux et le Marivaudage*, 2nd. ed. Paris, 1967, p. 220.

those where inversion is coupled with highly emotional content. Some constructions are suited to the character in question, as for example, the hypothetical constructions pronounced by Dr. Sangrado (example C2, p. 181). Similarly the learned comparison made by the valet Fabrice may be an indication of the scholastic aspirations of the barber's son :

' " Jamais, comme dit Cicéron, il ne doit se laisser abattre jusqu'à ne se plus souvenir qu'il est homme." ' (p. 64)

Less likely perhaps is this lengthy sentence in the course of Laure's uncharitable remarks about the actress Rosarda :

' " Si, depuis qu'elle a des amants, elle avait exigé de chacun d'eux une pierre de taille pour en bâtir une pyramide, comme fit autrefois une princesse d'Egypte, elle en pourrait faire élever une qui irait jusqu'au troisième ciel ! " ' (p. 181)

The use of concessive *invertissants* in direct speech gives an elevated tone to the conversation which is not always appropriate, for example the money-lender's claim :

' "... et peu s'en faut même, quelle que soit aujourd'hui la misère, que je ne me fasse un scrupule de prêter au denier cinq." ' (p. 148)

There is the same tendency in conversation as elsewhere for inversion to occur in long sentences placed among much shorter ones. Such constructions also tend to have considerable emotional content. However, the examples in which inverted order serves to highlight strong feelings are not necessarily those in the longest sentences. Thus Don Ambrosio says to Doña Mercia :

' " Je sens approcher ma dernière heure. A peine m'êtes-vous rendue, qu'il faut vous dire un éternel adieu." ' (p. 52)

and similarly Enrique's mistress :

' " Et peut-être, hélas ! répondrez-vous à leur attente, même aux dépens de vos plus doux vœux." ' (p. 207)

Earlier in the same speech, however, inversion occurs in a longer sentence, and enables the conclusion of the relative clause depending on the inverted subjects to occupy a position in line with subsequent indirect objects, which thus heightens the emotional effect :

' " Soit pressentiment, soit raison, je sens s'élever dans mon
cœur des mouvements qui m'agitent et *que* ne peut calmer
toute la confiance que je dois à vos bontés. Je ne me défie
point de la fermeté de vos sentiments ; je ne me défie que
de mon bonheur." ' (p. 207)

In conclusion, although there are many inversions in direct
speech, there are few whose function is different from their
narrative equivalents. Occasionally elevated speech corresponds to a pretentious speaker, although quite often this is not
the case. Just as inversion in the narrative is often found in
longer sentences in isolation, this also happens in conversation,
usually with additional emotive force.

(c) Other characteristics of the style of ' Gil Blas '

In a work of this nature consisting of numerous episodes
related in brief and concise sentences, inversion as a means of
liaison is virtually absent. However, according to Bardon, the
distinguishing qualities of Lesage's style are ' le naturel, la
vivacité et ... la vitesse,' [8] and it does happen that at times
inversion helps to achieve a fast-moving narrative, namely
when it occurs in a clause which represents some sort of
opposition to that which precedes it, e.g.

' "... le point d'honneur nous oblige à payer avec exactitude.
Aussi ne payons-nous pas les autres religieusement." '
(pp. 145–46)

Inversion may underline a humorous idea :

' " Doña Manuela de Sandoval ... est actuellement sans
laquais ; elle n'en a qu'un d'ordinaire, encore ne le peut-elle
garder un jour entier." ' (p. 68)

On the other hand the opposition may lie in a semantic
contrast between the verbs in each clause ;

' " Fi donc ! madame, m'écriai-je, pouvez-vous haïr ce
qu'aiment les femmes hors du commun ? " ' (p. 158)

Inversion resulting from deletion and transposition produces a
more obvious chiastic construction :

---

[8] Introduction, p. xix.

' S'ils louaient une pièce, je l'estimais ; leur paraissait-elle mauvaise, je la méprisais.' (pp. 188–89)

Such inversions readily underline a moralizing tone :

' " Un homme d'esprit est-il dans la misère, il attend avec patience un temps plus heureux." ' (p. 64)

However the *invertissants* used most effectively in drawing moral conclusions are *tel* and *ainsi*, as in the following chapter ending :

' Ainsi périt le seigneur don Mathias de Silva, pour s'être avisé de lire mal à propos des billets doux supposés.' (p. 177)

It may also be stressed by the addition of *c'est ... que :*

' " C'est ce que pratiquent si heureusement nos maîtres ; et c'est ainsi qu'on doit user tout homme qui vise à la réputation d'esprit distingué." ' (p. 152)

Like those of *picaresque* writers, the descriptions in Lesage refer to the material details of everyday life, rather than to its natural background. As Bardon notes :

' il s'intéresse ainsi aux objets qui accompagnent l'existence ; il en dit la forme, la matière, la couleur avec le scrupule d'un maître hollandais.' (p. x)

Evidence of this from the inversions is provided only by the relative constructions. In some cases the relative introduces the object of interest, e.g.

' Elle portait une longue robe d'une étoffe de laine la plus commune, avec une large ceinture de cuir, d'où pendaient d'un côté un trousseau de clefs et de l'autre un chapelet à gros grains.' (p. 70)

and in others the inversion introduces an explanation for their introduction :

' J'aperçus bien des choses précieuses dans ce cabinet qu'éclairaient une grande quantité de bougies.' (p. 167)

Finally in one example, inversion is used in the course of description with a subject followed by a dependent clause expanding the description :

' J'y trouvai une trousse où étaient deux rasoirs qui semblaient avoir rasé dix générations ... avec une bandelette de cuir pour les repasser et un morceau de savon.' (p. 103)

In spite of the relatively high number of inversions for this period (111), word-order is far from being a key feature of Lesage's style. As a natural consequence of the new sentence length, inversion is not generally used to link clauses and is found only occasionally for emphasis in an important position. Change in word-order is, however, employed as an additional emphatic device, for example where critical events are related in unusually long sentences, both in the narrative and in conversation, where inversion may also underline the characteristics of the speaker.

(ii) ABBÉ PRÉVOST, 'MANON LESCAUT'

Manon Lescaut has the lowest inversion frequency and the fewest *invertissants* of all the texts in this study, in a period in which the average inversion frequency of the texts chosen is also at its lowest. In syntax and style it has several affinities with *Gil Blas*, in particular the short sentence technique discussed above (pp. 184–85). Thus table 6.07 shows that 53% of the inversions occur in sentences of three or more clauses, only 4% more than Lesage. In both texts pronoun subjects account for 25% of the inversions (table 6.06). Prévost's novel, however, has fewer inversions in direct speech (25%) (table 6.03), a higher proportion of examples of other syntactic operations, and an unusually high frequency of the verb *être*, which figures in 47% of the examples (table 6.10), the second highest proportion in the study (cf. 50% in *Cyrus*). The exceptionally small number of inverted subjects with a dependent clause, 4% (table 6.06), is a further indication as to the brevity of Prévost's writing. It seems therefore that as in the previous text inversion does not play a very important stylistic role in *Manon Lescaut*, and the examples will only be examined with reference to the thematic importance of the inverted subject and, in the case of direct speech, to the context in which they arise.

(a) *Inversion and the main themes*

Manon Lescaut is a work which portrays in various guises strong human emotions, and as Sgard states: 'Les deux amants jouent surtout avec ce qui leur fait peur, avec leurs craintes ou leurs remords '.[9] These themes of fear and remorse, and similarly of malevolent fate and of the torments of love, are sometimes emphasized by a change in word-order. Thus as des Grieux considers the possibility of his death after killing Synnelet he says,

' Quelque pressante que fût cette crainte, elle n'était pas la plus forte cause de mon inquiétude.' (p. 195)

where the main idea gains emphasis from its position and stands next to the following subject pronoun. In another concessive construction the subject, referring to the author's feelings, is in a strong position in relation to the following clauses and is balanced by the four emotions which conclude the sentence :

' Cependant, de quelque nature que fussent les miens, il est certain qu'il devait y entrer de la douleur, du dépit, de la jalousie et de la honte.' (p. 69)

It is interesting to note that this construction was changed after the 1731 edition, in which there was no inversion : ' de quelque nature que les miens fussent.' An example of important ideas in parallel positions at the end of each clause is the following, where this is produced by a relative *invertissant :*

' Je n'eus pas plutôt quelque relâche du côté de cet accablement où m'avait jeté la confusion, que je retombai dans les tourments de l'amour.' (p. 83)

The addition of *c'est ... que* and transposition may result in a parallelism between the stressed element which has become the *invertissant* and the inverted subject, a device which is particularly effective when there are several subjects :

' Elle ignorait, et moi aussi, que c'était sur elle-même que devait tomber toute la colère du Ciel et la rage de nos ennemis.' (p. 194)

Inversion is also found in expressing the transition between two themes or emotional states. In the following, the rational, the idea of escaping alone, gives way to the emotional, reunion

---

[9] J. Sgard, *Prévost romancier*, Paris, 1968, p. 243.

with Manon. The inverted subject, which also stresses the idea of reason, is repeated in pronominal form to introduce in the next clause the more powerful emotion :

> ' Quelque solide que me parût ce raisonnement, il ne put l'emporter, dans mon esprit, sur un espoir si proche de mettre Manon en liberté.' (p. 105)

The paragraph following the death of Synnelet opens with des Grieux's feelings, his elevated conception of victory being emphasized by inversion on the one hand, and the idea of a ' combat mortel ' on the other, but this at once gives way to the more mundane concern for the consequences, expressed in simpler, direct terms :

> ' Malgré la joie que donne la victoire après un combat mortel, je réfléchis aussitôt sur les conséquences de cette mort.' (p. 195)

Finally, an inversion introduces the last sentences of des Grieux's narrative before he again addresses himself directly to the author, the *invertissant* presenting almost as an afterthought the loss of consciousness which is related to the novel's important *leitmotif* of dreams and semi-consciousness :

> ' Aussi ne demeurai-je pas longtemps dans la posture où j'étais sur la fosse, sans perdre le peu de connaissance et de sentiment qui me restait.' (p. 201)

(b) *Inversions in direct speech*

Three of the four examples of inversion through deletion and transposition occur in conversation, and in each case they are used to give some idea of the character who is speaking. The first example is in the opening conversation between des Grieux and the author, who has already formed some opinion as to the latter's birth and education, which a rhetorical construction such as this clearly illustrates, as does the vocabulary :

> ' '' Les sollicitations, l'adresse et la force m'ont été inutiles ; j'ai pris le parti de la suivre, dût-elle aller au bout du monde.'' ' (p. 13)

The next occurrence comes when des Grieux is talking to a

porter at the *Hôpital Général* and posing as a stranger, another occasion on which a more elevated style is required :

‘ “... il fera du moins quelque chose pour une fille aimable, ne fût-ce que par l'espérance d'avoir part à ses faveurs.” ’ (p. 99)

Lastly the construction is used by Manon, but only when she is relating the speech of G . . . M . . ., her social superior :

‘ “ Qu'il valait mieux ... vous envoyer là votre nouvelle amante, ne fût-ce que pour vous empêcher de vous y morfondre pendant toute la nuit.” ’ (pp. 146–47)

and this distinctive construction with its imperfect subjunctive is thus a useful indication of both character and situation.

In their introduction to the Garnier edition of *Manon Lescaut*, Deloffre and Picard draw attention to the device used extensively in *burlesque* works, the contrast between language and situation :

‘ Ce n'est pas le langage élevé et noble du héros qui semble déplacé dans sa bouche ; ce sont les circonstances avilissantes où il se trouve qui paraissent indignes de lui.’ [10]

This irony is nowhere more striking than in the reunion scene at La Salpêtrière, witnessed by M. de T. The inversion with which des Grieux begins his reply heightens the effect of noble language already conveyed by M. de T.'s choice of words and verb form :

‘ “ Il n'y a point de sort glorieux auquel je ne préférasse une maîtresse si belle et si passionnée.” “ Aussi mépriserais-je tous les empires du monde, lui répondis-je, pour m'assurer le bonheur d'être aimé d'elle.” ’ (p. 103)

In discussing the conversations in the novel, Sgard suggests that ‘ Les plus beaux dialogues ... sont ceux de personnages qui ne parlent pas la même langue,’ [11] and it is true that in certain dialogues such oppositions are effectively conveyed by stylistic means. For example in the conversation between des Grieux and G . . . M . . . the speech of the latter is characterized as

---

[10] p. cxl.
[11] *Op. cit.*, p. 276.

bourgeois, whereas des Grieux replies in elevated tones, the inversion occurring in an unusually long seven-clause sentence, which again expresses considerable emotion :

> ' " Mais, si vous connaissez la force de l'amour, si vous pouvez juger de ce que souffre un malheureux jeune homme à qui l'on enlève tout ce qu'il aime, vous ne trouverez peut-être pardonnable de..." ' (pp. 155–56)

In the argument between des Grieux and Tiberge (pp. 90–93), the differences between the two characters are underlined by the juxtaposition of direct and indirect speech. This extract is preceded by what Tiberge is reported to have said, and des Grieux's argument is emphasized by his direct question which puts words into Tiberge's mouth, as well as by the inversion, and the oppositions *tourmente/corps* and *bonheur/âme* :

> ' " Direz-vous, comme font les mystiques, que ce qui tourmente le corps est un bonheur pour l'âme ? " ' (p. 91)

Later in the debate des Grieux uses *c'est ... que* to emphasize the idea he is rejecting :

> ' " J'avoue, repris-je, qu'elle n'est pas juste ; mais prenez-y garde, ce n'est pas sur elle que porte mon raisonnement." '
> (p. 91)

Finally, in conversation with his father des Grieux uses a compound inversion to stress his elevated feeling for him, before opposing him in simpler terms ;

> ' " Aussi le Ciel m'est-il témoin que j'ai pour vous tous les sentiments du fils le plus tendre et le plus respectueux. Mais ... il me semble que votre rigueur est extrême." '
> (p. 171)

Although inversion is not an integral part of Prévost's style and frequently does not occur where an alternative order is possible (table 6.09 shows that one-third are grammatical inversions, being part of indirect constructions), its function is one of stylistic emphasis rather than of syntactic liaison. This emphasis may be contrastive, as in certain dialogues, either between two characters or between a character and his surroundings, or thematic, as in the portrayal of emotions and the linking of important themes.

(iii) P. MARIVAUX, ' LE PAYSAN PARVENU '

The syntactic tables above show that the *Paysan parvenu*
is clearly different in structure from the other three texts.
The inversion frequency of $0\cdot75$ is 20% higher than that of
Gil Blas (table 6.01), and there are twelve more *invertissants*,
with this text providing thirty-seven out of the total fifty-one
in all four works (table 6.08).   Inversions in Marivaux also
occur in longer sentences, indicating a more flexible sentence
structure and a style freed from the constraints of Classicism.
This is also suggested by the lexical variety of verbs in inversions (table 6.10 shows that *être* has the lowest frequency in
this text, 21%) and by the number of different mobile *invertissant* constructions which constitute 52% of the examples
(table 6.02).   Although there are few cases of inversion after an
adverbial phrase, modal adverb *invertissants* account for 42%
of the total inversions (table 6.09), a figure equalled only by
Diderot and Laclos in the next period, with whom the Marivaux text has much in common.

In his brief discussion of inversion in Marivaux after certain
adverbs, Deloffre [12] states that Marivaux follows modern usage
in inverting after *aussi, sans doute, peut-être, encore* and *du
moins*, and with isolated examples of other adverbs.   He does
not, however, mention *à peine* (fifteen examples in this text
alone), *aussi bien* and *ensuite* (two examples each) and *ici* and
là (one example of each, the latter with *c'est ... que*).   He adds
that ' à l'imitation de la langue parlée, l'inversion n'apparaît
pas après *aussi* et *du moins* si ces mots sont détachés par la
diction et constituent un élément rythmique ' (*loc. cit.*), but in
the *Paysan parvenu* there are many counter-examples to the
instances of direct order cited by Deloffre, e.g.

' " Oui, monsieur, du moins me le dit-elle, et assurément je ne
l'empêcherai pas." '   (p. 126)

Examples of inverted word-order may to a considerable
extent reveal the exploitation of various linguistic devices
which constitute *le marivaudage*.   In particular mention should

---

[12] *Op. cit.*, p. 482.

be made of those relating to narrative technique, to the presentation of direct and indirect speech, sentence structure, and the many forms of word play, especially on social and comic themes, all amounting to a specific conception of the dramatic role of language.

(a) *Inversion and the personal narrative*

It has already been seen in chapter V how the intervention of the narrator in two 17th-century texts was limited to comments on the literary structure of the work, and that these were frequently characterized by inversion. In *Gil Blas* the personal narrator is indicated by little more than the appropriate syntactic changes, with no question of deviation from the action of the novel. *Le paysan parvenu*, however, takes the form of an autobiographical memoir in which the narrator is also the principal actor and commentator, and his intervention in either of his roles as story-teller or commentator is more frequent and more complex.

Firstly, like the narrator of the *Roman comique*, Jacob refers occasionally to the structural divisions of the novel, namely at the end of parts I and III and the beginning of parts II and V. The opening sentence of part V links it to the preceding section, and by means of an inversion the subject of the new section is placed in the emphatic and logical position :

‘ J'ai dit dans la dernière partie que je me hâtai de me rendre chez Mme Remy, où m'attendait Mme de Ferval.’ (p. 221) Within these main divisions Marivaux uses similar devices to link different types of narrative, as in the following example, occupying a single paragraph, which forms the transition between a long speech and the continuation of the action :

‘ Voilà par où finit l'officier, et je rapporte son discours à peu près comme je le compris alors.’ (p. 202) Secondly the narrator intervenes to comment on his own technique. This is generally done with reference to an implied criticism by the reader. This may be a trivial matter, as in the next example where the long description of Madame de Ferval is resumed, following Jacob's apology for its length :

' Venons à la physionomie que composait le tout ensemble.'
(p. 142)

On the other hand it may refer to a complicated rhetorical device. The following is a comment on the use of allegorical prosopopœia, in terms of which Jacob describes his mental struggle between honour and cupidity, and this apology is inserted between the two speeches :

' On trouvera peut-être les représentations que me faisait l'honneur un peu longues, mais c'est qu'il a besoin de parler longtemps...' (p. 27)

Moreover the intervention may amount to an apology for the basic technique of the work, as in the following extracts which account for the discrepancy in time between the meeting which is recounted and the information contained in the accompanying description which could not have been simultaneous :

' Telle était donc la dame d'auprès de qui je sortais ; je vous la peins d'après ce que j'entendis dire d'elle dans les suites...' (p. 143)

' Pour faire ce portrait ... il ne m'en a coûté que de me ressouvenir de tous les discours que nous tint cette bonne veuve...' (p. 77)

In the first case inversion permits the transition from the subject of the portrait to the narrator and his technique, by means of the dependent relative clause. In the second the passage is from the portrait and the writer's technique back to the subject, by the same means.

Thirdly the memoir form permits the simultaneous inclusion of the main character's thoughts and his comments on the action, without the more obvious and disruptive intervention of an omniscient narrator. When Jacob the actor introduces comments on his actions, the tone is even more apologetic than the narrator commenting on his narrative. This may be underlined by the use of *invertissants* expressing doubt or concession which often occupy a key position indicating the change in the role of the author. In the course of part I, the following paragraph opening introduces Jacob's personal feelings and reflexions on the previous episode :

' Peut-être fis-je mal en prenant l'argent de Geneviève ; ce n'était pas, je pense, en agir dans toutes les règles de l'honneur.' (p. 22)

Later Jacob tries to excuse his lack of feeling on the death of Geneviève's husband by sympathizing with her, and the paragraph ends with his true reason stressed by inversion :

' Aussi était-ce ma bienfaitrice.' (p. 38)

In relating Jacob's thoughts, Marivaux's narrative technique allows them to take a direct form when they and the action are simultaneous :

'... et le lendemain des noces je fus tout surpris de me trouver marié ; avec qui ? du moins est-ce avec une personne fort raisonnable, disais-je en moi-même.' (p. 194)

Here the reader is addressed, and the tense of the inversion clause changes to one of direct discourse. This key sentence concludes the paragraph after which Jacob continues to describe his wife. Jacob's retrospective comments, however, continue the normal tense sequence. The next example, although not itself in a key position, illustrates the use of a double *invertissant* which introduces the reflexion and expresses the reluctance with which Jacob admits his motives :

' Et s'il faut tout dire, peut-être aussi voulais-je voir ce qui arriverait de cette aventure, et tirer parti de tout.' (p. 87)

Jacob's remarks, whether spontaneous or reflective, are also frequently used as moral comments. The following again concludes a paragraph after which the action narrative is resumed :

'... et c'est la forme la plus dangereuse que puisse prendre le diable pour tenter une jeune fille un peu coquette, et par-dessus le marché, intéressée.' (p. 18)

(b) Inversion and conversation

In this text most of the *invertissants* occur in both narrative and conversation. Although hitherto this has been taken to indicate little concern on the part of the author to differentiate between the two styles, in Marivaux it would seem to suggest a conversational style in the narrative, rather than the reverse, as is also implied by the lack of certain types of inversion. From the familiar tone of many of the conversations the proportion of 28% of the inversions in direct speech seems surprisingly high (table 6.03). This colloquial tendency is reflected in all sentence types, and contrasting structures are often found, as for example the popular interrogative forms ' D'où vient est-ce que...' (p. 212) and ' D'où vient que je vous en parle ?' (p. 237). There are, however, many examples of Marivaux's stylistic use of a more formal word-order to be found in conversational passages, as will be illustrated below.

The forms of inversion other than transposition after an immobile or mobile *invertissant* tend always to give a rhetorical flavour to conversation especially when the imperfect subjunctive is used. The following example from part V, in which Madame de Ferval's suitor pleads his love for her, is particularly effective, not least because of the simple comment by the hidden narrator which immediately follows it, and makes the speaker seem ridiculous :

> ' " Ne m'aimassiez-vous qu'un jour, ces beaux yeux noirs qui m'enchantent ne dussent-ils jeter sur moi qu'un seul regard un peu tendre, je me croirais encore trop heureux." '
> (p. 128)

It also brings out the underlying satire on earlier works in which such declarations were commonplace. Jacob himself employs similar terms to declare his love for Mlle Habert, which contrasts with the simple language she has previously used to him ; this is perhaps additionally effective because of the difference in their ages, since the speech characteristics might be expected to have been reversed :

> ' " La seule pensée m'en fait mourir d'aise ; viennent tous les présidents du monde et tous les greffiers du pays, voilà ce que je leur dirai, fussent-ils mille, avec autant d'avocats." '
> (p. 122)

The only other occasion on which Jacob uses this type of construction is also in addressing Mlle Habert, and both the language and the underlying intention contrast with the idea of the ' honnête garçon ' expressed at the end of the speech :

' "... et n'y eût-il que le chirurgien qui était vis-à-vis la maison ... je serais bien aise de le voir pour lui montrer que je suis plus honnête garçon qu'il ne s'imagine." ' (p. 158)

Repetition is a feature of natural speech which may be highlighted or alleviated by a change in word-order. In the following there is obligatory direct order in the clause with a pronoun subject and inverted order in that with a noun subject, thus giving variety to two nearly synonymous expressions :

' " D'ailleurs, je n'ai point vu le dessein de votre livre, je ne sais à quoi il tend, ni quel en est le but." ' (p. 200)

Where the subject is the same in each clause, inversion is equally desirable as in this example where the change of tense and of subject position emphasize the affirmatory nature of the second verb :

' " Elle me parut extrêmement jolie, aussi l'est-elle." ' (p. 257)

Inversion is used in direct speech, just as in the narrative, to stress certain oppositions, although to a lesser extent. As in the *Astrée*, inversion is especially effective in the contrast of subjects where the same verb occurs :

' "... il faut le plus souvent sacrifier ce qu'on veut à ce que veulent les autres, et cela me dégoûtait." ' (p. 95)

However where the subject is an unstressed pronoun, emphasis may equally well be placed on the contrasting verbs ;

' "... qu'on hâte de la secourir, elle se meurt, peut-être la sauvera-t-on." ' (p. 145)

(c) *Inversion as an emphatic device*

An important theme in the *Paysan parvenu* is the portrayal of *les dévots*. Inversion is found in this context either to stress their peculiarities or to pass cynical judgement on them. In the first case the following example contrasts the *dévote* and an ordinary woman. The addition of *c'est ... que* emphasizes the change of manner adverbial and the inversion stresses the different subject :

' Quand une femme vous aime, c'est avec amour qu'elle vous le dit ; c'était avec dévotion que me le disait la mienne, mais avec une dévotion délicieuse.' (p. 163)

Alternatively a routine liaison inversion may be used to link the description of the characters and the author's comment, which in this instance represents a contrast in content and style :

> 'Tels sont ceux que j'appelle des dévots, de la dévotion desquels le malin esprit a tout le profit...' (p. 48)

Jacob's observations are often made more pointed by the use of compound inversion :

> 'Aussi sa dévotion en avait-elle augmenté de moitié, sans en être apparemment plus méritoire...' (p. 246)

The use of *aussi* in an independent clause has a very strong reinforcing effect in the text. In the next example a rather absurd generalization is given a particular application in Jacob's description of Catherine :

> 'Il faut bien des attentions pour faire un pain comme celui-là ; il n'y avait qu'une main dévote qui pût l'avoir pétri ; aussi était-il de la façon de Catherine.' (p. 49)

In presenting emotional situations, Marivaux sometimes uses inversion in order that words with emotional content may fall in a comparable position in each phrase, e.g.

> 'Si j'avais peur, c'était par un effet de l'émotion que m'avait causée mon accident, car je ne songeai point à craindre pour ma vie.' (p. 147)

Here the relative *invertissant* allows the subject to take a position related to *avoir peur*, *émotion* and *craindre pour ma vie*. In the next extract another relative inversion enables *état* and *douleur* to assume related positions :

> 'Dans la triste expérience qu'elle en fit alors, je crois que l'étonnement où la jetait son état lui sauvait la moitié de sa douleur.' (p. 38)

The use of *c'est ... que* and inversion as an emphatic device has already been noted (p. 200 above), where the *invertissant* is an adverbial phrase of manner contrasting with a previous one. This addition is also used to form an *invertissant* from a preposition and pronoun with a similar function of stress. In the first example this structure echoes that of the first clause :

' La compagnie était chez madame : on m'y attendait, et ce
fut aussi chez elle que me mena mon guide.' (p. 124)

The inversion not only reinforces the expression of Jacob's
destination, but also provides the thematic link with the next
paragraph which describes his entrance. The *invertissant* in
the second example not only refers back to the subject of the
opening clause, but contrasts with the prepositional phrase that
follows :

' Il y a bien des amours où le cœur n'a point de part, il y en
a plus de ceux-là que d'autres même, et dans le fond c'est
sur eux que roule la nature, et non pas sur nos délicatesses
de sentiment qui ne lui servent de rien.' (p. 230)

Here the addition of *c'est ... que* stresses the appropriate element of the opposition while the inversion results in the important subject being placed in a strong position, also perhaps
contrasting with irony *la nature* and the *délicatesses de sentiment*. Thus this particular operation of word-order has a
double emphatic function, firstly in stressing the element
which becomes the *invertissant* and consequently in stressing
the now inverted subject.

Chiastic constructions with contrasting word-order occur
frequently in this text. The following sentence consists of two
parallel chiastic structures and also illustrates the use of
peut-être as an *invertissant* in indirect thought passages :

' Il avait surpris le secret de ses meurs, peut-être se vengerait-
il si on le rebutait, peut-être se tairait-il si on le traitait avec
douceur.' (p. 231)

The increase in certain syntactic features represented in this
text is thus seen to be accompanied by an extension of their
function. For example the number of modal adverb inversions
(cf. table 6.09) is due in part to the use of *peut-être* and *aussi*
in introducing the narrator's comments in passages of both
direct and indirect speech. The number of other inversion
operations in speech (table 6.11) is accounted for by certain
emphatic devices in the case of *c'est ... que*, and by instances of
parody in direct speech in others. Other inversions may also
play a part in suggesting a discrepancy between language and

context, and lastly relative inversions continue to ensure both liaison and harmony, e.g.

'Geneviève ... déguisa la petite satisfaction que lui donnait ma préférence d'un souris qui signifiait pourtant: Je te remercie; mais...' (p. 12)

It seems then that Deloffre is over-simplifying when he says:

'On ne doit pas s'attendre à voir Marivaux rechercher des effets de surprise par le bouleversement de l'ordre normal des mots.' [13]

(iv) c. p. duclos, 'romans'

While the literary value of the works of Duclos is perhaps debatable, the texts studied represent the average occurrence of most features figuring in the syntactic analysis. Possible exceptions are the lower proportion of conversational inversions (22%) (table 6.03), although as in the *Princesse de Clèves*, this may be a characteristic of the short novel form, and, like Marivaux, fewer inversions in which the verb is *être* (table 6.10). In other points of sentence structure the two *romans* and the *nouvelle* tend to conform to the norm for the period. The style of Duclos has been compared to that of Madame de la Fayette [14] and also to Marivaux and Laclos; le Bourgo, for example, claims: '*Les Confessions du comte xxx* forment le trait d'union entre le *Paysan parvenu* et les *Liaisons dangereuses*'.[15] Certain features of the syntactic analysis do seem to confirm this, although in other respects they appear unrelated. In sentence length for example, Duclos falls midway between the other two in the decreasing number of inversions in sentences of three or more clauses (68%–56%–42%). In all three texts the verb *être* has a similar frequency in inversion constructions (21%–23%–22%). They all have an equally low proportion of more than one subject in the inverted noun phrase (2%), whereas the number of inverted subjects

[13] *Op. cit.*, p. 479.

[14] By P. Meister, *Charles Duclos*, Geneva, 1956, pp. 175 ff.

[15] L. le Bourgo, *Duclos, sa vie et ses ouvrages*, Bordeaux, 1902, p. 160.

with a dependent clause shows a steady decline (15%–10%–8%). In Duclos the inversions with stylistic relevance have characteristics common to both Madame de la Fayette and Marivaux, and it will be seen later how far Laclos conforms to this pattern. As in Lesage and Prévost, the low inversion frequency in Duclos makes it difficult to associate inversion with a particular device of style, but as in earlier works inversions in this text contribute to several different stylistic effects.

(a) *Inversion and the analytic technique*

The study of contemporary mœurs which constitutes an important aspect of the novels of Duclos is expressed in a form of language which Meister calls ' un outil analytique ' [16] and which reveals the 18th-century *préciosité* already noted in Marivaux. The object of this analysis is ' l'amour-goût ... composé de désir et de vanité ', which, according to le Bourgo, ' est analysé minutieusement dans les romans de notre auteur '.[17] Comments of this nature, whether made by the narrator or by the characters themselves, fall into four categories according to whether they are wholly general, confined to a particular context, or move from the general to the particular or vice versa. In each case there are instances of inversion balancing or linking parts of the observation. The following general precept concludes the exposition of the *conte Acajou et Zirphile*, in which inversion underlines the relation between subject and object :

' Quelque aveugle que soit l'amour-propre, on connaît bientôt ses défauts quand l'intérêt s'en mêle.' (p. 280)

The concessive inversion may be used to similar effect when the terms are strictly context-bound :

' " Quelque violente que soit ma passion pour vous, je sens qu'elle me rend malheureux." ' (LUZ, p. 67)

The order in this construction may be compared with that of a later extract from the same work, where the direct order of the

---

[16] *Op. cit.*, p. 234.
[17] *Op. cit.*, p. 156.

concessive contrasts with the necessarily inverted order of the interrogative :

> ' " Quelque chimérique que cet état paraisse à la plupart des hommes, peuvent-ils y préférer un commerce languissant, où souvent le dégoût succède au plaisir ? " ' (p. 80)

This function of inversion, to balance two specific states, is by far the most common in the text studied. A progression from particular to general may be marked by a change in word-order, as in the following where the *invertissant que* begins the generalization :

> '... il me salua avec cette espèce de timidité qu'éprouve tout honnête homme qui a une grâce à demander ou à recevoir.' (CON, p. 273)

The reverse of this is less common, and only exemplified in a wider and usually non-analytical context, with inversion marking a progression in the narrative rather than in sentimental description. For example, when the Comte de xxx considers the necessity of a new conquest, his thoughts move from the general nature of the choice to a particular subject :

> ' On était attentif au choix que j'allais faire : de ce choix seul pouvaient dépendre tous mes succès à venir. Madame de Limeuil me parut d'abord la seule femme digne de mes soins.' (CON, p. 247)

A little later he follows a few general references to Senecé's mistress by a more detailed description :

> ' Ce chef-d'œuvre que m'avait vanté Senecé, était une femme d'environ quarante ans, qui avait encore des restes de beauté, sans avoir jamais eu d'agréments.' (CON, p. 258)

In both these instances inversion marks a change : in the first the end of the generalities, in the second the beginning of particular details.

(b) *Inversion in conversation between men and women*

The nineteen inversions which occur in direct speech in Duclos are all found in the two *romans*, twelve in the *Histoire de Madame de Luz*, and seven in the *Confessions*. The interest of these examples centres on whether the conversation is

between various men and the heroine in the first story, or
between different women and the hero in the second. In the
first one five examples occur in the speech of Madame de Luz
addressing her admirers, and seven in the speech of the men
talking to her, whereas in the second all but two of the inversions are spoken by the count's mistresses in conversation
with him.

It is in the conversations in which the hero or heroine is
addressed by admirers of the opposite sex that inversions
occur together with elements of *préciosité*, which suggest that
this is associated with a particular kind of speech, namely the
language of courtship. Thus, for example, in the conversation
between the Marquise de Valcourt and the count, the language
of the Marquise emphasizes not only the difference in sex, with
the *précieux* terms in which the subject is expressed, but also
perhaps the age difference, as the older speaker uses a rhetorical
device to stress the subject of the proposition :

> ' " (L'amour) ... est le seul principe de nos plaisirs, c'est en
> lui que se trouve la source de nos sentiments et de la
> délicatesse." '   (CCN, p. 201)

The language of the admirers of Madame de Luz, however, is
more down to earth, while still retaining a number of extrava-
gances emphasized or balanced by inversion, as in the next two
examples, the first spoken by Thurin and the second by
Saint-Geran :

> ' " Vous voyez, madame, ce que peuvent vos charmes,
> puisqu'ils me font violer mon devoir." '   (LUZ, p. 107)

> ' " Mais quelle que soit ma passion pour vous, je ne voudrais
> pas vous devoir au malheur d'un ami, et, ce qui est encore
> plus respectable pour moi, d'un homme qui vous est cher." '
> (LUZ, p. 117)

Certain types of inversion are also favoured by speakers
according to their sex. Of the six occurrences of *peut-être* as an
invertissant, five are in the speech of women, perhaps because
it conveys a more appropriate hesitancy in delicate matters.
In the following example where Madame de Selve declares her

feelings for the Comte de xxx, the double *invertissant* stresses a feminine lack of self-control :

> ' " Je ne suis plus en état de combattre un penchant qui m'a entraînée ; peut-être même n'en aurais-je ni la force ni la volonté." ' (CON, p. 281)

On the other hand four of the five concessive inversions occur in the speech of men, perhaps because it is more suited to chiastic and other rhetorical forms of expression. Thus M. de Thurin says to Madame de Luz :

> ' Et, quel que soit le service que je vous rends aujourd'hui, je me trouverai encore chargé de la reconnaissance." '
> (LUZ, p. 95)

An exception to the general tendency for the most striking inversions to occur in the speech of characters addressing the hero or heroine is found in the *Histoire de Madame de Luz*, where the heroine uses several inversions in reflecting on the nature of love. However, these examples are less exceptional in that the speech is more of a soliloquy, although Saint-Geran is present, and its theme is the difference between men and women in love :

> ' " Les hommes ... n'ont en aimant qu'un intérêt, c'est le plaisir ou une fausse gloire ; nous en avons un second ... qui est l'honneur et la réputation : c'est de là que dépend notre vrai bonheur. De la perte de l'honneur naissent les malheurs trop certains." ' (LUZ, p. 78)

Both inversions are emphatic, placing the subject in a very strong position, and this in turn gives rise to a contrast between *bonheur* and *malheurs*.

Finally it should also be noted that an important feature of the conversations in the novels, the theme of remorse, is also emphasized through inversion. In the first example there is a contrast between the count's recognition of his failings and his lack of remorse, which is stressed in Madame de Selve's speech by the *invertissant peut-être* :

> ' " Je vois ... que vous commencez à connaître vos torts ; mais peut-être ne vous reprochez-vous pas tous ceux que vous avez, et qui m'ont été les plus sensibles." ' (CON, p. 296)

The second example is spoken by the heroine's confessor and inversion repeats the idea of crime, as do the adjective *criminelle* and the Biblical quotation about the repentant sinner which follows :

' "... dirai-je mes crimes ou mes malheurs ? "

" Ne craignez rien ... quelles que soient les fautes que vous ayez commises, vous ne sauriez être bien criminelle avec autant de romords. Le ciel est plus sensible à ..." ' (LUZ, p. 135)

This also increases the irony because the priest himself succumbs to the charms of Madame de Luz soon afterwards.

(c) *Inversion and abstract nouns*

In many respects the language of Duclos' works is closely linked to the subject matter, as noted with reference to *préciosité* in conversation. A further point of contact is his treatment of abstract ideas, as Meister points out :

' La sécheresse inévitable que le maniement continu de l'abstraction implique s'y trouve parfois aérée par des traits d'esprit et des jeux de mots.' (*op. cit.*, p. 234)

Inversions may be used in this respect to achieve a balance of abstract nouns while adding precision to the sentence :

' Rien n'égala l'étonnement que me donna cette impudence.' (CON, p. 265)

The abstracts are generally different, with the verb indicating their relationship, as in this very similar example :

' Mais rien n'approche de la douleur que lui causa cette nouvelle.' (CON, p. 283)

but there are also instances where inversion both stresses a contrast and avoids the immediate repetition of an abstract idea :

' Il est vrai que, pour éviter un certain pédantisme que donne souvent l'étude, on avait imaginé le secret d'être savant sans étudier.' (AZ, p. 307)

A significant feature of all the examples of this kind is that the verb in the inversion clause is either *causer* or *donner*, so in each case inversion is used to emphasize a cause and effect relation between abstracts.

(d) Conclusion

Although in this work the results obtained by syntactic analysis are unremarkable, and there are only eighty-six examples of inversion in all, it seems that those which do occur have a more readily defined purpose than those in at least the first two 18th-century texts analysed. Because of the nature of the author's style there are few examples where inversion is essential to the composition and comprehension of the sentence. As only 2% of the examples have more than one inverted subject (table 6.06), constructions such as the following are isolated :

' Nous montâmes dans un appartement où régnaient à l'envi
la simplicité, là propreté et la commodité.' (CON, p. 229)
Similarly the only example of inversion after *ainsi* (quoted above, p. 180, ex. B2) is one in which the subject is extremely complex, and the context, the death of the heroine, of the first importance. With routine stylistic inversions reduced to a minimum it is clear why this text has a low ratio of inversions to *invertissants* (table 6.08) considering the number of the latter (cf. the ratio of 4·44 in Lesage with twenty-five *invertissants* as opposed to 3·58 in Duclos with twenty-four). Although the text itself is unpromising as literature, the details of its word-order are perhaps more rewarding than in the case of its illustrious contemporaries.

Chapter VII

THE EIGHTEENTH CENTURY (2)

1. SYNTACTIC ANALYSIS OF TEXTS
1750–1800

The texts :

F. de Voltaire, *Romans et contes* [1]

J.-J. Rousseau, *Julie, ou la Nouvelle Héloïse* [2]

D. Diderot, *Jacques le fataliste* [3]

P. Choderlos de Laclos, *Les liaisons dangereuses* [4]

Table 7.01 : Inversion frequencies

VOL/RC	123 : 0·62	
ROU/NH	209 : 1·05	*(mean 0·68)*
DID/JF	73 : 0·37	
LAC/LD	132 : 0·66	

Table 7.02 : Percentage table to show nature of clause in which inversion occurs

	VOL	ROU	DID	LAC
Main clause	34	39	63	52
Subordinate clause	66	58	33	48
Non-subordinating *invertissant* in subordinate clause	—	3	4	—
	100	100	100	100
Immobile *invertissant*	63	54	32	44
Mobile *invertissant*	31	37	60	50
Other operations	6	9	8	6
N :	123	209	73	132

[1] ed. Bénac, Paris (Garnier), 1949. (VOL)

[2] ed. Pomeau, Paris (Garnier), 1960, parts I and II. (ROU)

[3] In *Œuvres romanesques*, Paris (Garnier), 1951. (DID)

[4] Paris (Garnier), 1959. (LAC)

Table 7.03 : Percentage table to show distribution of inversions according to discourse type

	VOL	ROU	DID	LAC
Narrative	51	97	49	98
Direct speech	38	3	48	2
Indirect speech	10	n	3	—
Soliloquy	1	—	—	—

Table 7.04 : Percentage table to show position of the inversion within the corpus examined

	VOL	ROU	DID	LAC
Sentence initial	15	29	41	36
Paragraph initial	8	5	7	2
Chapter initial	—	n	—	—
Speech initial	—	n	1	—
Total initial	23	35	49	38
Sentence final	45	33	29	38
Paragraph final	2	2	—	4
Chapter final	—	—	—	—
Speech final	1	—	1	—
Total final	48	35	30	42

Table 7.05 : Percentage table to show position of inversion in relation to other types of discourse

	VOL	ROU	DID	LAC
Preceding direct speech	—	—	3	1
Following direct speech				
Preceding indirect speech		no examples		
Following indirect speech				

Table 7.06 : Percentage table to show nature of the inverted noun phrase

	VOL	ROU	DID	LAC
Pronoun subject	21	27	49	39
Substantive subject	74	69	44	55
Compound inversion	5	4	7	6
	100	100	100	100
2 or more subjects	2	4	1	2
S and dependent (S)	10	13	12	8

Table 7.07 : The percentage of inversions occurring in sentences of three or more clauses

	VOL	ROU	DID	LAC
(S)—3 clauses	38	31	30	25
4 clauses	7	16	16	14
5 clauses	6	6	5	3
6 clauses	—	1	—	—
	51	54	51	42

Table 7.08 :   Ratio of inversions to *invertissants*

VOL	123 : 33—3·73
ROU	209 : 50—4·18
DID	73 : 19—3·84
LAC	132 : 39—3·38
Total	537 : 78—6·88 (*mean* 3·78)

Table 7.09 :   Percentage table of the most frequently occurring inversions

	VOL	ROU	DID	LAC
Relatives	27	36	5	27
Comparatives	13	3	3	3
Indirect construction	22	12	12	10
Modal adverbs	23	27	49	42

Table 7.10 :   Percentage table to show the occurrence of ' être ', ' faire ' and ' avoir '

	VOL	ROU	DID	LAC
être	30	21	38	22
faire	6	4	4	5
avoir	5	5	3	4

Table 7.11 :   Percentage table showing the distribution of direct speech *invertissants*

	VOL	ROU	DID	LAC
Immobile *invertissant*	53	40	29	33
Mobile *invertissant*	38	40	60	33
Other operations	9	20	11	33
N :	47	5	35	3

Table 7.12 : Percentage table to show the occurrence of adverbials and clauses in inversion constructions

	VOL	ROU	DID	LAC
V(adv)S	2	9	1	6
(adv)VS	—	3	1	1
V(S)S	—	—	—	—
(S)VS	1	3	—	6

(i) DISTRIBUTION OF THE INVERSIONS

With the frequency of inversions now increasing, their occurrence is more than $0·60$ in all the texts except Diderot $(0·37)$. The number of *invertissants* is also greater, the four texts yielding seventy-eight, as opposed to fifty-five in those of the first half of the century, although the Diderot novel is again exceptional, with only nineteen. While there are very few inversions in direct speech in Rousseau and Laclos, undoubtedly a feature of epistolary form (table 7.03), these represent an exceptionally high proportion in Voltaire and Diderot, 38% and 48% respectively, although their distribution is quite different (table 7.11). The latter constitutes the highest proportion of conversational inversions of all the texts analysed in this study. There are, however, no examples of inversion in free indirect speech in any of the texts in this period.

The average length of the sentence containing inversion continues to decrease (table 7.07) with approximately 50% of the inversions in the four texts occurring in one- or two-clause sentences, and 50% in sentences of three or more clauses. Relative *invertissants* are the most common in Voltaire and Rousseau (table 7.09) but in Diderot they form only 5% of the total, the lowest proportion in any text. Instead there is in *Jacques le fataliste* the highest occurrence of modal adverb *invertissants*, 49%, and such inversions account for 60% of those in direct speech. Almost as many inversions after modal adverbs are found in Laclos (42%).

The separation of *invertissant* and verb by an independent clause noted in the previous chapter (table 6.12), characterizes a number of the examples in Laclos (6%) and to a lesser extent in Rousseau (3%) (table 7.12). Although this becomes a more common feature of word-order in later works, none of those analysed reveal such a high precentage as *Les liaisons dangereuses*. Compound inversions represent about 5% of the examples in each text (table 7.06) and this remains the average for succeeding periods.

(ii) EXAMPLES

A. IMMOBILE ' INVERTISSANT '

1. *Relative conjunctions :*   *VOL: 33 inversions, 6 ' invertissants ', ROU : 76,11 ; DID : 4,2 ; LAC : 36,5*
' Telle est la situation cruelle *où* me plongent le sort qui m'accable et mes sentiments qui m'élèvent et ton père qui me méprise, et toi qui fais le charme et le tourment de ma vie.' (ROU, p. 54)

2. *Comparatives : VOL : 16,3 ; ROU : 5,2 ; DID : 2,1 ; LAC : 4,3*
' La ferveur de l'aimable prêcheuse me servit *mieux que* n'aurait pu faire mon adresse.' (LAC, p. 49)

3. *Concessives : VOL : 1,1 ; ROU : 5,2 ; DID : 9,2 ; LAC : 4,2*
' *Quelque* sort *que* m'annonce un transport dont je ne suis plus maître, quelque traitment que ta rigueur me destine, je ne puis plus vivre dans l'état où je suis...' (ROU, p. 32)

4. *Temporal clause : LAC : 1,1*
' Songez donc ... que *depuis* dix jours *que* dure mon exil, je n'ai passé aucun moment sans m'occuper de vous...' (LAC, p. 118)

5. *Indirect construction : VOL : 27,7 ; ROU : 26,9 ; DID : 8,4 ; LAC : 13,6*
' " Cruel homme ! j'ignore *quelle* sera la durée de mon tourment ; mais j'éterniserai le tien..." ' (DID, p. 633)

B. *Mobile ' invertissant '*

1. *Attributes : VOL : 1,1 ; ROU : 13,1 ; DID : 6,1 ; LAC : 4,1*

' " Dis-moi comment celui qui a écrit le grand rouleau a
pu écrire que *telle* serait la récompense d'une action
généreuse ? " ' (DID, p. 572)

2. *Adverbs—modal : VOL : 28,5 ; ROU : 56,10 ; DID :
   36,5 ; LAC : 55,9*
   ' *Inutilement* voudrions-nous y suppléer par lettres...'
   (LAC, p. 86)

3. *Adverbs—quantity : DID : 1,1*
   ' *Autant* en fit la monture de Jacques, car il y avait entre
   ces deux animaux la même intimité qu'entre leurs
   chevaliers.' (DID, p. 508)

4. *Adverbs—temporal : VOL : 2,2 ; ROU : 2,2 ; LAC : 2,2*
   ' *Ensuite* vint une armée de moines défilant deux à deux,
   blancs noirs gris ... puis marchait le bourreau.' (VOL/SCA,
   p. 91)

5. *Adverbs—place : LAC : 1,1*
   ' *Là* finit mon histoire.' (LAC, p. 95)

6. *Adverbs—combinations : LAC : 1,1*
   ' Il vous laisse le champ libre ... *peut-être même* ne se
   relèvera-t-il jamais du coup que je lui ai porté.' (LAC,
   p. 189)

7. *Adverbial phrase—time : DID : 1,1*
   ' *Dans ce moment* survinrent les petits enfants de cette
   femme, ils étaient presque nus, et...' (DID, p. 571)

8. *Adverbial phrase—place : VOL : 4,3 ; ROU : 3,3 ;
   LAC : 1,1*
   ' *Entre ces solives* est une planche en travers sur laquelle le
   dieu s'assied, et *sur le devant* pend un morceau de grosse
   toile barbouillée, qui...' (ROU, p. 227)

9. *Prepositional phrase : ROU : 3,2 ; LAC : 1,1*
   ' Et *de la surprise* où jettent ces nouvelles manières naît
   cet air gauche qu'on reproche aux étrangers.' (ROU,
   p. 214)

10. *Subordinate clause : VOL : 3,1*
    ' *Tandis qu'il parlait au ministre* entre brusquement la
    belle dame chez qui Babouc avait dîné.' (VOL/le M, p. 78)

C. OTHER OPERATIONS

1. *Deletion and transposition* : *VOL* : *4* ; *ROU* : *10* ; *DID* : *5* ; *LAC* : *3*
   ' " Voyez, *eussiez-vous* encore cent lieues à faire, vous n'en boirez pas de meilleur de toute la route." ' (DID, p. 611)

2. *Addition and transposition* : *VOL* : *4,3* ; *ROU* : *10,7* ; *DID* : *1,1* ; *LAC* : *5,4*
   ' Comme *c'est* ordinairement à la promenade *que* se passent nos petits rendez-vous, le temps affreux ... ne m'en laissait pas espérer.' (LAC, p. 226)

(iii) DETAILS OF THE INVERSIONS

(a) Types of construction

With one notable exception, the types of inversion found in these texts are very similar to those of the preceding period. There is little change in immobile *invertissants* apart from a general increase in the number of indirect constructions, and in particular more comparatives in Voltaire, and the only difference with regard to other syntactic operations is that there is no example of deletion here, although all four texts have deletion and transposition, as opposed to three in the first half of the century. Among the adverbial constructions, however, there are considerably more examples of inversion after modal adverbs, 175 in all, as compared with 125 in the last four texts. Other adverbial *invertissants* occur sporadically as before, although inversion after an adverbial phrase of place has again become more common, occurring in three out of the four novels analysed.

The important change in the pattern of inversion types is the return of inversion after a subordinate clause, a form fairly common in the 16th century, but which has not been found in any of the works studied since 1600. All three examples are in the Voltaire text, and the *invertissant* in each case is a temporal clause, the most common one in the 16th-century examples. In two of the examples the verb in the inversion clause is *arriver*, and in the third, *entrer*, both being verbs found with zero *invertissant* in texts of later periods.

The increase in modal adverb inversions does not coincide with a much larger number of *invertissants*. In Diderot, where they form 49% of the total, nearly all the examples are with *aussi, encore, à peine* and *peut-être*. Different *invertissants* are also rare in the other texts, although there is an occurrence of *à plus forte raison* in Rousseau, and of *en vain, pourtant* and *inutilement* in Laclos, the text which also provides the temporal adverb *invertissant rarement*. Similarly, although there is a notable increase in inversion in comparative constructions in Voltaire, these are divided between two main *invertissants, comme* (9) and *plus que* (6), with one example of *aussi que*.

(b) Position of the inversions

The texts in both halves of the 18th century show a closer relation between inversion and the paragraph (table 7.04), although this is most marked in the 19th and 20th centuries. In this period the inversions which conclude paragraphs are not of outstanding interest, the majority being indirect constructions, with a few adverbial *invertissants* whose function is to place the subject in an important position from which it might be developed. However, opening the paragraph with an inversion is a fairly frequent narrative device in all the texts except Laclos, and the types of *invertissants* used are attributive adjectives, and modal and temporal adverbs.

The use of *tel* is a common linking device in sentence initial position, and is even more effective at the beginning of a paragraph, as in Rousseau (four examples) and Diderot (one example) :

' Telle fut à la lettre la conversation du chirurgien, de l'hôte et de l'hôtesse.' (DID, p. 526)

The adverb used most frequently in this position is *à peine*, with temporal meaning, of which there are eight examples in Voltaire and three in Diderot. The narrative value of these inversions is clear, as in the following example, where the temporal clause marks a progression in the story, with the compound construction emphasizing the subject, which is in pronominal form in the preceding paragraph :

H

' A peine Candide fut-il dans son auberge, qu'il fut attaqué d'une maladie légère...' (VOL/CAN, p. 190)
Similarly it may have the familiar connecting function :
' A peine eut-il fait cette réponse, qu'on entendit le bruit d'un cabriolet qui...' (DID, p. 681)

2. STYLISTIC ANALYSIS OF THE TEXTS
1750–1800

(i) F. DE VOLTAIRE, ' ROMANS ET CONTES '

The *contes* which have been analysed for this study, with the number of inversions they contain, are the following :
Zadig (37)
Le monde comme il va (10)
Memnon ou la sagesse humaine (3)
Les deux consolés (2)
Histoire des voyages de Scarmentado (5)
Micromégas (10)
Histoire d'un bon Bramin (2)
Le blanc et le noir (12)
Jeannot et Colin (3)
Candide (39)

(a) *Inversion and the satirical intention*

Voltaire uses inversion in the service of both literary and social satire, although it is perhaps more striking in the former, in contexts where inversion had become predictable in earlier writers. The most important forms of satire which concern word-order, are firstly the use of quotations, secondly certain literary devices including types of description and *préciosité*, and thirdly ironic social comment.

1. Quotations

The use of inversion with *comme,* or alternatively with various relative *invertissants* in presenting a quotation is a familiar device, and one which lends authenticity to the statement. This is constantly exploited by Voltaire, to obtain a variety of satirical nuances. In the first place the very convention of literary quotation may be satirized by excessive precision. The following extract not only gives the exact reference, but also follows it by the original Greek, obviously ridiculous in a *conte* of less than twenty pages :

> ' " L'âme est une entéléchie, et une raison par qui elle a la puissance d'être ce qu'elle est. C'est ce que déclare expressément Aristote, page 633 de l'édition du Louvre." ' (MIC, p. 111)

On the other hand the quotation may be wholly unremarkable, both in its content and its origins, as in the speech of the Marquise de la Jeannotière :

> ' " Il est bon qu'un jeune seigneur puisse briller dans l'occasion, comme dit monsieur mon mari." ' (J/C, p. 133)

Alternatively a presumably familiar quotation may be placed in a satirical context. This remark, attributed to Fontenelle, occurs in the course of a condemnation of the study of all history except contemporary events :

> ' Toutes les histoires anciennes, comme le disait un de nos beaux esprits, ne sont que des fables convenues.' (J/C, p. 131)

With yet another shift of emphasis, the inversion clause may reveal specific satire, as in the brahmin's imitation of the language of Pascal :

> ' " Je me trouve dans un point entre deux éternités, comme disent nos sages, et je n'ai nulle idée de l'éternité." ' (BB, p. 114)

The frequent reference to a higher authority in *Zadig* generally takes the form of direct quotation. Here inversion is used to give an illusion of authenticity :

> ' Le moment où l'on se trouve et celui où l'on se sépare, sont les deux plus grandes époques de la vie, comme dit le grand livre du Zend.' (ZAD, p. 47)

and also to characterize the language of the quotation itself :

> '... suivant ce grand précepte de Zoroastre ; " Quand tu manges, donne à manger aux chiens dussent-ils te mordre." '
> (ZAD, p. 3)

Elsewhere a similar inversion has a slightly different function, balancing an absurd situation, two philosophers on Saturn's rings, by a *bona fide* scientific observation, with a facetious opposition between *illustre* and *petit* :

> ' Ils sautèrent d'abord sur l'anneau, qu'ils trouvèrent assez plat comme l'a fort bien deviné un illustre habitant de notre petit globe.' (MIC, p. 101)

2. Literary devices

In the rare love scenes, Voltaire parodies the technique of the *grands romans*, which, where inversion occurs, is exemplified by relative *invertissants*, as in this ironic account of Zadig's feelings for his wife :

> ' Jamais bouche plus ravissante n'exprima des sentiments plus touchants par ces paroles de feu qu'inspirent le sentiment du plus grand des bienfaits et le transport le plus tendre de l'amour le plus légitime.' (ZAD, p. 4)

This familiar language, however, becomes more concise to meet the demands of the Voltairean sentence, to which inversion is an important contributory factor :

> ' Celui-ci, dans le même temps, la défendait avec toute la force que donnent la valeur et l'amour.' (ZAD, p. 4)

The same is true of natural descriptions, with relative *invertissants* forming part of the condensed style, and, where the verb is often *être* (cf. table 7.10), balancing phrases with no verb at all :

> ' Et au bout de ces allées, une rivière, le long de laquelle sont mille maisons de plaisance, avec des jardins délicieux.' (BN, p. 122)

Descriptions may also be used to convey an ironic comment on their realism, as in the following chain of simple sentences with a connective inversion :

> ' Ils remuèrent une large pierre, et jetèrent à droite et à gauche une terre dont s'exhalait une odeur empestée ; ensuite on vint poser un mort dans cette ouverture, et on remit la pierre par-dessus.' (LeM, p. 69)

Finally, Voltaire adds an ironic footnote concluding with an inversion which stresses the satirical choice of subject:

> 'Mlle Catherine Vade n'a jamais pu trouver l'histoire du perroquet dans le portefeuille... C'est grand dommage, vu le temps auquel vivait ce perroquet.' (BN, p. 128)

3. Ironic comments

Inversion underlines the irony in Voltaire's writing again through its occurrence in familiar constructions, but in a less usual relation to other terms. Thus this common use of a relative inversion where the subject is followed by a dependent clause, serves in fact to stress the contradiction:

> 'Cette belle personne lui conta, de l'air le plus naïf et le plus touchant, tout le mal que lui faisait un oncle qu'elle n'avait point.' (MEM, p. 82)

Similarly an inversion after *tel*, commonly used to sum up previous sentences, introduces an ironic comment on them in the course of legal satire:

> 'On ne lui permit pas de parler, parce que ses tablettes parlaient; telle etait la loi de Babylone.' (ZAD, p. 12)

The emphatic position of an inverted subject may in turn lead to an anti-climax, as in the following, where the subject recurs in pronominal form:

> 'Un peu de vin pris modérément est un remède pour l'âme et pour le corps. C'est ainsi que pense le sage Memnon; et il s'enivre.' (MEM, p. 83)

Here both the difference in word-order and the two forms of the subject underline formally the contrasting content of the two sentences.

(b) Linguistic devices in Voltaire's sentence structure

At a time when inversion is still widely condemned, it may seem surprising that it is an important feature of Voltaire's style, with its compactness and fast-moving sentences. However, as far as simplicity is concerned, it has already been seen that inversion of the subject, far from complicating the style, contributes to its simplification, which is a valuable device when the main emphasis is elsewhere. As regards movement, Voltaire's apparent lack of connectives for the sake of rapidity has been widely noted,[5] but again inversion is a more subtle and less obtrusive means of liaison than perhaps a co-ordinating conjunction. In this example, the seemingly disconnected sentences are linked firstly by repetition of the verb in the inversion clause, and secondly by that of the personal pronoun. Inversion, besides preserving the rhythm of the sentence, renders the first repetition a little less obvious :

> ' Il vit une maison où régnaient tous les plaisirs. Téone régnait sur elle ; elle savait parler à chacun son langage.'
> (LeM, p. 79)

The devices of which inverted order is an essential part, are chiefly those of repetition and opposition, together with a few stylistic details examined in the next section.

Sentences may be linked by repetition of one or more of their components, with inverted order either stressing or concealing this. The repeated element may be the verb, as above, or both the verb and the subject, with the chiasmus ensuring movement and variety :

> ' On m'a élu roi en Corse ; on m'a appelé " Votre Majesté ", et à présent à peine m'appelle-t-on " Monsieur " '. (CAN, p. 210)

Less obvious is the repetition of related concepts, as in the following series of adjectives—*superbe, auguste, élevé* :

> ' Le roi, la reine, les infants, les infantes, étaient sous un dais superbe. Vis-à-vis cette auguste famille était un autre trône mais plus élevé.' (SCA, p. 91)

The two sentences again form a chiasmus, with the result that all the important ideas are closely interrelated. In the next example, the juxtaposition of the proper name and noun in apposition follows from inversion, and is then expanded, with the two qualities united by virtue of the repeated anteposition of the adjectives :

---

[5] e.g. G. Lanson ; ' V. rejette toutes ces lourdes façons d'exprimer les dépendances logiques, et de matérialiser, par des mots-crampons, les rapports des idées ' (*L'art de la prose*, 9th ed., Paris, 1911, p. 155).

' Vis-à-vis sa maison demeurait Arimaze, personnage dont la méchante âme etait peinte sur sa grossière physionomie.' (ZAD, p. 11)

The juxtaposition of irreconcilable concepts is a common feature of satirical writing, and although this is not normally achieved by inversion in Voltaire, the change in order often permits emphasis to fall on such ideas. In the first example these form the inverted subject, with an unusual co-occurrence of noun and adjective, and in the second they form the antecedent of the relative *invertissant*, with inversion delaying the appearance of the next stressed item :

' " Ne manquez pas, dit Candide, de leur représenter quelle est l'humanité affreuse de faire cuire des hommes, et combien cela est peu chrétien." ' (CAN, p. 173)

' ... Sirien ... se mit à rire pour la seconde fois de l'excès de petitesse dont étaient les habitants de notre globe.' (MIC, p. 104)

(c) *Voltaire's affinities with the style of Rabelais*

A detailed comparative study of the satire of Voltaire and Rabelais has shown many points of contact,[6] and although no reference was made to word-order in the two authors, some uses of inversion are strikingly similar. Particular points of Voltaire's style involving inversion which may be compared to Rabelais' usage are the attention to quantitative detail, exaggeration and enumerations, as well as the extensive use of quotation already examined above. As Miss Flowers points out (*op. cit.*, p. 90), Voltaire in his satire makes greater use of stylistic devices than Rabelais, such as the ironic after-thought which follows his quotations.

The use of comparative *invertissants* highlights these devices, while ensuring a clear sentence structure. Thus in an example from *Micromégas* reiterating the theme of man's insignificance, inversion clarifies an unusually long sentence, as the separation

[6] R. C. Flowers, *Voltaire's Stylistic Transformation of Rabelaisian Satirical Devices*, Washington, 1951.

of verb and subject and the postposition of the latter permits
it to be followed immediately by its relative clause :

> ' ... en prenant la taille des hommes d'environ cinq pieds,
> nous ne faisons pas sur la terre une plus grande figure qu'en
> ferait sur une boule de dix pieds de tour un animal qui
> aurait à peu près la six cent millième partie d'un pouce en
> hauteur.' (pp. 105–6)

A similar structure, again with a comparative inversion, is the
following, where the relative is replaced by a hypothetical
clause, which constitutes a typically ironic comment by
Voltaire :

> ' ... une enceinte de montagnes plus roides qu'une contre-
> scarpe, et plus hautes que n'aurait été la tour de Babel si
> elle avait été achevée, barra entièrement la caravane ...'
> (BN, p. 121)

Inverted order in Rabelais is generally found when the
subject is expanded into a whole list of items, and similar
enumerations are found in Voltaire, e.g.

> ' Ensuite vint une armée de moines défilant deux à deux,
> blancs, noirs, gris, chaussés, déchaussés, avec barbe, sans
> barbe, avec capuchon pointu, et sans capuchon.' (SCA,
> p. 91)

A change in order may also create parallelisms, as in the
following example of enumerated adjectives :

> ' Près de sa maison, qui était belle, ornée et accompagnée
> de jardins charmants, demeurait une vieille Indienne, bigote,
> imbécile et assez pauvre.' (BB, p. 114)

Voltaire's treatment of these stylistic devices naturally avoids
the excesses and extremes of Rabelais, but nonetheless the two
writers make the same use of inversion in often very similar
contexts, an indication of the far-reaching stylistic significance
of word-order in French prose.

(ii) J.-J. ROUSSEAU, ' LA NOUVELLE HÉLOÏSE '

The two epistolary novels of this period differ greatly in
language and style, despite their common form, and a detailed
comparison of the use of inversion by the two writers concludes

the section on Laclos. It will be seen, however, that while inversion in Laclos primarily distinguishes the styles of different correspondents in the novel, in Rousseau the construction also plays a part in the more general style of the author. The examples discussed below relate firstly to the language of the two main characters, and secondly to the lyricism of Rousseau, including his sentimental language and the presentation of his doctrine.

(a) Inversion in the language of the correspondents

1. The styles of Julie and Saint-Preux

The frequency with which the two main characters use inversion in their letters is as follows: Julie averages 1·5 inversions per letter, and Saint-Preux 2·9. Although Saint-Preux writes only one more letter than Julie in the sections analysed, his inversions account for well over 50% of the total and these of Julie for about 29%, the remainder occurring in the letters of the three other writers. The distribution of the main inversions in Saint-Preux corresponds almost exactly to that of the total. Thus of his 117 examples 35% are relatives (whole work 36%), 12% are indirect constructions (12%) and 30% modal adverbs (27%) (cf. table 7.09). The inversions found in Julie's letters have a less regular distribution, and are therefore more interesting, since she differs from the other protagonists as regards her youth and emotional situation, although her speech is less ingenuous than that of Laclos' Cécile. Of the examples from Julie's letters, 43% have relative *invertissants*, but only 18% follow modal adverbs. There are fewer indirect constructions, but three comparatives (the only other examples being one each in Saint-Preux and Edouard), and more attributes. In comparing the language of Julie and her lover, it should be noted that all the examples of operations other than simple transpositions are found in their writing, with seven examples of deletion and transposition by Saint-Preux and three by Julie, and nine examples of addition and transposition by Saint-Preux and just one by Julie.

H*

2. Identity of the recipient

Although there is less variety in the style of a single correspondent than in Laclos, depending on the identity of the
addressee, certain changes in tone are at times clearly perceptible. While there is little evidence of this from the type of
inversions which occur, a change in frequency is often significant. Two letters by Saint-Preux may be cited as examples,
numbers XXI and XXIII of Book II, both dealing with aspects
of Parisian life, but the first addressed to Julie and the second
to Madame d'Orbe. The letter to Julie, an account of Parisian
women, contains eleven inversions in ten and a half pages,
whereas that addressed to his cousin, a description of the
Opéra, has sixteen inversions in only six pages.

From the opening of the letter to Julie, characterized by
exclamations, interrogatives, short sentences and similar
emotional devices, the identity of the recipient is quite clear,
although this becomes less obvious as the subject develops.
The second letter is almost exclusively descriptive, and contains several learned references and philosophical speculations.
There are undoubtedly slight concessions made to Julie's
youth in the first letter, as is shown by the different types of
comparisons, a simple classroom simile in the one, and more
complex parallels with the Classical and Italian theatre in the
other.

However, despite the difference in frequency, similar inversion constructions are used in both letters, the four main types
with the addition of two examples of other operations in the
letter to Julie, and with predictably two adverbial phrases of
place in the other. With one exception, the inversions in this
letter to Madame d'Orbe are either descriptive or critical, while
those to Julie occur in the description of people or customs,
with no tendency to philosophical generalization.

Thus although the identity of the recipient may be deduced,
at least at times, from the style of writing, the criterion as
regards word-order seems to be frequency rather than type of
inversion, and this only applies when the author in his
enthusiasm does not succumb to more elaborate language. The

letter to Julie, for instance, opens with predominantly direct order in short declarative sentence, together with other simple means of expressing emotions. This simplicity continues through the beginning of the main theme, as the following inversion, with its clear logical structure, shows :

‘ Commençons par l'éxtérieur : c'est à quoi s'en tiennent la plupart des observateurs.’ (p. 211)

Then the writer forgets his recipient and begins to use more complex structures, indicated by the following examples with more clauses and compound inversion :

‘ Les femmes de la ville ont mieux aimé renoncer à leurs couleurs naturelles et aux charmes que pouvoit leur prêter *l'amorose pensier* des amants, que de rester mises comme des bourgeois.’ (p. 214)

‘ Aussi, comme le grand fléau de tous ces gens si dissipés est l'ennui, les femmes se soucient-elles moins d'être aimées qu'amusées.’ (p. 216)

In the letter to Madame d'Orbe, however, this style is used consistently throughout, e.g.

‘ Aussi l'ancien Labérius ne put-il reprendre sa place au cirque parmi les chevaliers romains, tandis que le nouveau en trouve tous les jours une sur les bancs de la Comédie-Françoise parmi la première noblesse du pays.’ (p. 227)

(b) *Inversion and Rousseau's style*

1. Lyricism

In discussing Rousseau's style, Mornet [7] describes the *Nouvelle Héloïse* as ‘ la premiere œuvre vraiment lyrique de notre littérature.’ Inversions with a lyrical subject are found both in descriptions of nature and in the presentation of the lovers' preoccupation with music. In the first case inverted order is functional, facilitating a particular mode of expression, and in the second it is emphatic. Thus where natural scenes are depicted, relative *invertissants* are followed by a verb of

---

[7] D. Mornet, *La Nouvelle Héloïse de J. J. Rousseau, étude et analyse*, Paris, 1950, p. 58.

high expectation and low semantic content, with consequent emphasis on the antecedents and subjects, e.g.

> ' Parmi les bosquets naturels que forme ce lieu charmant ...'
> (p. 29)
> ' Près des coteaux fleuris d'où part la source de la Vevaise...'
> (p. 75)

A rustic scene may be introduced by an adverbial phrase *invertissant :*

> ' Autour de l'habitation principal dont M. d'Orbe dispose, sont épars assez loin quelques chalets, qui de leurs toits de chaume peuvent couvrir l'amour et le plaisir, amis de la simplicité rustique.' (p. 75)

An example of a relative *invertissant*, where the verb is closely related to the subject, is used to facilitate the presentation of the idea of a sympathetic natural divinity, which occurs at the end of one of Saint-Preux's letters to Julie :

> ' Et comme la Divinité tire tout son bonheur d'elle-même, les cœurs qu'échauffe un feu céleste trouvent dans leurs propres sentiments une sorte de jouissance pure et délicieuse...' (p. 193)

At the climax of Saint-Preux's letter devoted to Italian music, and the experience it held for him, the highly emotional subjects are both stressed by the repeated use of *c'est ... que* and inversion :

> ' Mais c'est de la seule mélodie que sort cette puissance invincible des accents passionnés ; c'est d'elle que dérive tout le pouvoir de la musique sur l'âme.' (p. 92)

A description which is less passionate, but which exemplifies the rhythmic use of inversion with lyrical context, occurs in Saint-Preux's letter on the Opéra :

> ' A ces beaux sons, aussi justes qu'ils sont doux, se marient très-dignement ceux de l'orchestre.' (p. 230)

Here, as well as the choice of verb, each element related to the order of the sentence is put to highly lyrical use, i.e. the separation of *invertissant* and verb, the inversion itself, and the further separation of verb and subject.

2. Sentimental language

The distinctive ' langage du cœur ' of the *Nouvelle Héloïse*, like the sentimental language of d'Urfé and of the *Précieux*, employs relative *invertissants* in order to emphasize certain elements. Many of the examples are found in Julie's letters, whose style reveals more clearly the influence of 17th-century writers. In the following, inversion introduces three important subjects :

> ' Je t'en conjure, mon tendre et unique ami, tâche de calmer l'ivresse des vains désirs que suivent toujours les regrets, le repentir, la tristesse.' (p. 20)

This use of relatives is, however, more striking in a style which makes frequent use of nominal syntax, as does that of Saint-Preux :

> ' Puisse le ciel les combler du bonheur que méritent leur sage et paisible amour, l'innocence de leurs mœurs, l'honnêteté de leurs âmes ! ' (p. 193)

In Julie's writing there are structures which have become sentimental clichés, again reminiscent of the *Précieux*, where a verb of high expectation follows a relative *invertissant* in conjunction with a key subject :

> '... n'empoisonne point, par d'injustes reproches, l'innocente joie que m'inspire un si doux sentiment.' (p. 38)

> ' Je ne parle point de ce tour vif et de ces expressions animées qu'inspire la force du sentiment.' (p. 187)

Although similar devices are to be found in the letters of Saint-Preux, these do not necessarily appear as clichés, often because of the changing rhythm caused by the repetition of certain items. Thus there is the example A1 (p. 214 above) where a succession of inverted subjects are followed by dependent clauses. Elsewhere it may be the repetition of prepositional phrases which in the following disguise a well-worn association of *s'allumer* and *flamme*, which is also relieved by the insertion of an adverbial and the clause which follows the inverted subject :

> ' C'est du premier regard de tes yeux, du premier mot de ta bouche, du premier transport de mon cœur, que s'alluma

dans lui cette flamme éternelle que rien ne peut plus éteindre.'
(p. 180)

The opposing forces of vice and virtue are a recurrent theme
in the novel, and again it is the relative inversion construction,
often used to achieve effects of contrast and balance, which
emphasizes these ideas. A particular feature of such constructions is that they tend to occur at the end of the sentence,
e.g.

'Je crains cette force terrible que doit avoir l'exemple
universel et continuel du vice.' (p. 175)

'Nous n'avons pas besoin de chercher ce qu'exigeroit en
pareil cas la vertu.' (p. 204)

Other important themes are stressed by chiastic structures, as
in the following association of crime and punishment:

'Quel que soit mon châtiment, il me sera moins cruel que
le souvenir de mon crime.' (p. 240)

Juxtaposition of two orders may be reinforced by contrasting
adjective positions:

'Ce chaos ne m'offre qu'une solitude affreuse où règne un
morne silence.' (p. 180)

Alternatively the contrast may lie in the two inverted subjects
as in the next example, where the inversion clause expands
the idea expressed in the preceding clause, both being introduced by the same relative conjunction:

'C'est peut-être la ville du monde où les fortunes sont le plus
inégales, et où règnent à la fois la plus somptueuse opulence
et la plus déplorable misère.' (pp. 181–82)

The example of contrasting verbs and subjects but with a
single *invertissant* has already been quoted (p. 214 above,
example A3 in the syntactic analysis).

3. The presentation of Rousseau's doctrine

Comparative inversions may be introduced to refute an
argument as follows:

'L'attaque et la défense, l'audace des hommes, la pudeur
des femmes, ne sont point des conventions, comme le pensent
les philosophes...' (p. 88)

However, where inversion occurs in the course of a philosophical discussion, it is generally to facilitate expression or to emphasize a particular point. Thus the attributive *tel* may be used to sum up the preceding argument :

' Telle est la loi sacrée de la nature, qu'il n'est pas permis à l'homme d'enfreindre...' (p. 148)

Alternatively, the *invertissant encore* introduces and emphasizes an additional point in debates :

' Nous renoncerons pour jamais à l'histoire moderne ... encore n'est-ce que parce que ...' (p. 27)

This, it will be remembered, is the device used by Marguerite de Navarre in presenting the discussions in the *Heptaméron*.

Thus the constructions involving inverted word-order in the *Nouvelle Héloïse*, by virtue of their frequency, are inevitably of stylistic importance. To a certain extent inversion characterizes the correspondents and their attitude towards the reader, but this is less true of Rousseau than of Laclos, as will be seen later. The device is however an important part of an inherited form of sentimental expression, and Rousseau also makes extensive use of it both in presenting his own philosophy, and in the structure of his sentences, where inversion is a key factor in achieving rhythm and balance of lyrical subjects, as well as a logical order in the expression of philosophical ideas.

(iii) D. DIDEROT, ' JACQUES LE FATALISTE '

The main features of Diderot's style are already indicated in the syntactic analysis above, and contrast sharply with the other three texts. Apart from the low number of inversions (73) and *invertissants* (19) (table 7.08), the analysis reveals a predominance of mobile *invertissants* (60%) (table 7.02), particularly modal adverbs (49%) (table 7.09), and table 7.04 shows that a large proportion of the inversions occur in initial position (49%). Also along with a tendency for inversion to occur in shorter sentences (49% are in single- or two-clause sentences), it may be noted that 38% have the verb *être* (table

7.10), and that there is little separation of the main items by adverbials (table 7.12).

Since the form of *Jacques le fataliste* is essentially that of a dialogue,[8] and since the author is concerned with realistic presentation,[9] the low inversion frequency is to be expected, and this is also consistent with the high proportion of examples which occur in direct speech (48%). Inversion may therefore be studied with regard to the two narrative techniques, that of the author and of his characters, and their relation to the sentence structure and fast-moving style of the novel.

(a) The narrative technique

All the inversion types which occur in the narrative are also found in dialogue, with the exception of the comparatives (two examples of *comme*) and the adverb *autant*, all three of these inversions occurring in the narrative style of the author, not of the characters. Each comparative introduces a facetious quotation for which the author interrupts either the narrative or the dialogue of his characters. The following, which concludes a long aside to the reader, falls between the Master exhorting Jacques to proceed with his story, and the latter's continuation of it, producing an effect of alienation :

' C'est, comme le disait un officier à son général le grand Condé, qu'il y a un fier Bigre, comme Bigre le charron ; de plats Bigre, comme une infinité d'autres.' (p. 702)

Other types of inversion are not peculiar to either dialogue or narration, or to the narrative style of any one character or the author. The *invertissant tel* has the familiar summing-up function, generally at the beginning of the paragraph or sentence, where it links a new theme to the preceding one, often a description or conversation :

' Telle fut à la lettre la conversation du chirurgien, de l'hôte et de l'hôtesse.' (p. 526)

---

[8] cf. J. Smiétanski, ' Jacques le fataliste ... est un vaste dialogue, ou plus exactement une juxtaposition de dialogues ', *Le réalisme dans ' Jacques le fataliste '*, Paris, 1965, p. 142.

[9] cf. Smiétanski, *ibid.*, p. 148.

Occasionally, however, the sentence which contains the construction in its opening clause may also conclude a paragraph, and here the additional liaison function is lacking:

> ' Et telle est la différence de deux hommes braves par caractère, mais dont l'un est sage, et l'autre a un grain de folie.' (p. 610)

There are three examples of inversion preceding direct speech, and in each case it is the *invertissant aussi* which is used. It will be remembered that absolute inversion preceding speech was common practice in the 16th century, and here the *invertissant* has a similar function of stressing the change in type of speech. The three examples occur in the narratives of the author,

> '. Jacques ... avait en aversion les redites. Aussi disait-il quelquefois à son maître...' (p. 608)

of the hostess,

> ' Elle étouffait d'indignation et de rage ; aussi répondit-elle au marquis, d'une voix tremblante et entrecoupée...' (p. 633)

and Jacques,

> ' Mon parrain Bigre avait vraiment de l'amitié pour moi ; aussi lui répondis-je avec franchise...' (p. 695)

but it is perhaps most effective in the last example, the only instance of the inverted subject differing from that of the preceding clause.

(b) *The style of ' Jacques le fataliste '*

The two stylistic features of this text to which inversion contributes are, as suggested above, the rapidity of both narrative and dialogue, and realism in the representation of speech, and to a certain extent the two are complementary.

Compound inversion, particularly in a key position, is effective in both. The following example opens a short narrative paragraph which links two dialogues, The temporal *invertissant* indicates the time lapse and the compound inversion, together with the short sentences, stresses the new subject and begins the movement:

'A peine Jacques fut-il couché, qu'il s'endormit profondément.' (p. 559)

In the following, the inversion clause depends on *c'est* ... *que*, which in turn refers back to an earlier object :

'Mais ce que je ne vous laisserais pas ignorer ... c'est qu'à peine le maître de Jacques eut-il fait cette impertinente réponse que...' (p. 508)

This use of *ce que* or *ce* gives a conversational style to the narrative, and in the next example it both expands the original idea and effects a contrast between inverted and direct order :

'Le premier serment que se firent deux êtres de chair, ce fut au pied d'un rocher qui tombait en poussière.' (p. 604)

The various narratives of the characters in the novel provide examples of inversion used in the interests of rapidity. This technique of short sentences juxtaposed, often with inverted order replacing connectives, and preventing monotony, has already been noted in earlier texts. Again *à peine* is a convenient *invertissant*, providing a temporal connective, with the change in order adding contrast to the string of clauses :

'Elle lui paraît jolie : il la suit ; à peine est-il entré, que le guet survient.' (p. 675)

When the story moves less urgently, the sentence may be supplemented by dependent clauses, as in Jacques' narrative :

'A peine furent-ils séparés, qu'ils sentirent le besoin qu'ils avaient l'un de l'autre ; ils tombèrent dans une mélancolie profonde.' (p. 550)

However, these are not always present, and the next example shows inversion which permits the pronominal form of the subject to follow its antecedent, instead of the more usual relative pronoun :

'Dans ce moment survinrent les petits enfants de cette femme, ils étaient presque nus, et les mauvais vêtements de leur mère montraient toute la misère de la famille.' (p. 571)

Repetition on the one hand and economy on the other are equally characteristic of normal speech, and both are to be found in the conversation of Diderot's characters. In the examples of the former, inversion again provides a contrast to the preceding sentence, several elements of which are repeated :

' " Je baisai sa jambe, j'y attachai la jarretière que j'avais retenue ; et à peine était-elle attachée, que Jeanne sa mère entra." ' (p. 773)

Alternatively economy and concern for movement may lead to the omission of the *invertissant* in a second clause with analogous order :

' " Aussi dormait-il la veille d'une action sous sa tente comme dans sa garnison, et allait-il au feu comme au bal." ' (p. 504)

There are few inversions in indirect speech, which may seem surprising in a novel where all the main characters tell stories, but which is explained by the fact that in most cases direct speech is reported in its original form. Thus an inversion construction is not made more complicated by embedding it as a subordinate clause :

' " Un valet entre et demande ' N'est-ce pas ici que loge un pauvre homme, un soldat qui... ? ' " ' (p. 580)

and also loses nothing of its original impact, as in the following exclamations :

' " ' Epouser ! cela serait bien dur, aussi ne l'appréhendé-je pas ' " ' (p. 766)

The most frequent conversational *invertissant* is the adverb *peut-être* whose value in characterizing a certain type of dialogue has been noted elsewhere. In this text it is used particularly in presenting the philosophy of its hero, e.g.

' " C'est un cheval perdu, et peut-être est-il écrit là-haut qu'il se retrouvera." ' (p. 521)

In the following example from a speech by Jacques, the inversion both provides variety, stresses the co-ordinating conjunction, and introduces reported speech, although this is again in direct form :

' "... il ne me dit pas un mot, il semble me méconnaître, et peut-être à present se dit-il en lui-même avec un sentiment de mépris..." ' (p. 562)

Thus inversion, although not a key factor in Diderot's style, often contributes to its main effects. Conversation is realistic because of the sparing use of inverted order, and also because when it does occur it supplements the necessary effects of both economy and repetition. Finally, as in other works characterized by a rapid flow of short sentences, inversion contributes to their movement and avoids tedium, a possibility which is acknowledged elsewhere by Diderot himself.[10]

(iv) P. CHODERLOS DE LACLOS, 'LES LIAISONS DANGEREUSES'

It has been widely acknowledged by literary critics that the *Liaisons dangereuses* comprise as many styles as there are correspondents.[11] The distribution of the inversions of the novel also suggests a different use of word-order by each writer, and it seems preferable to examine the use of inverted order in the letters of each character in turn, and thus to arrive at an assessment of the style of each. The text has been analysed up to letter 102 inclusive, and inversions occur in letters written by six characters.

(a) The Vicomte de Valmont

Valmont is the most prolific correspondent in the *Liaisons*, with fifty-one letters in all, out of a total of 175, and in the part of the work analysed the proportion is about the same, thirty-six out of 102. These letters contain seventy-nine inversions, giving a frequency of $2 \cdot 14$ per letter. Moreover the frequency for the letters addressed to the other main correspondent, the Marquise de Merteuil, rises to $2 \cdot 60$, or fifty-six inversions in twenty-one letters, as compared with $1 \cdot 9$ or twenty-one inversions in eleven letters, in those to the Présidente.

The most common types of inversion used by Valmont are relatives, followed by twelve examples of *peut-être* as *invertis-*

---

[10] ' Nous avons gagné, à n'avoir pas d'inversions, de la netteté, de la clarté, de la précision, qualités essentielles au discours ; et ... nous y avons perdu de la chaleur, de l'éloquence et de l'énergie ', *Lettre sur les sourds et muets*, ed. P. H. Meyer, Geneva, 1965, pp. 66–67.

[11] e.g. L. Versini, *Laclos et la tradition*, Paris, 1968, pp. 313 ff. and J. Rousset, *op. cit.*

sant. In addition there are a number of unusual features revealed by the analysis, such as the adverb *inutilement* with inversion (example B2, p. 215 above), and similarly *rarement*, which gives a slightly archaic and intellectual flavour to the style. Many of the examples of *peut-être* are used to convey concealed commands, as in the letter to Danceny:

'Peut-être feriez-vous bien de lui écrire.' (p. 202)

In a further example, one of only three in direct speech, this technique is subtly reversed:

'"Eh! peut-être l'action dont vous me louez aujourd'hui perdrait-elle tout son prix à vos yeux, si vous en connaissiez le véritable motif."' (p. 49)

Valmont is reporting verbatim his first conversation with the Présidente, and attributes to himself this complex sentence. There is furthermore an opposition between the verb in the intervening clause, and that of the inversion clause which follows it, *louer* and *perdre prix.* A further feature of Valmont's carefully worked style is his use of deletion and transposition, the only character to do so. Two of the three examples are, however, so similar in their terms, with the juxtaposition of *devoir, être digne,* and *refuser,* that his sincerity is suspect:

'"Dût ma confiance me nuire auprès de vous, vous en êtes trop digne, pour qu'il me soit possible de vous la refuser."' (p. 49)

'Et dussiez-vous me refuser toujours un bonheur que je désirerai sans cesse, il faut vous prouver au moins qui mon cœur en est digne.' (p. 137)

It is in the letters to the Présidente that Valmont's artificial style and, in the words of Versini, his 'galanterie précieuse' [12] are most apparent. Thus he uses relative inversions to achieve parallelisms of either related or opposing concepts, a device noted earlier in the *Astrée*:

'Enfin ce jour arriva où devait commencer mon infortune; et par une inconcevable fatalité, une action honnête en devient le signal.' (p. 75)

---

[12] *Op. cit.,* p. 343.

' Et ce sentiment pur, que ne troublait point alors l'image
de votre douleur, suffisait à ma félicité.' (p. 52)

A less elegant device, but perhaps one better suited to the
female reader, is the immediate repetition which is made more
acceptable with the inverted order of the dependent clause :

'... je l'épiais dans vos regards ; dans ces regards d'où partait
un poison d'autant plus dangereux qu'il était répandu sans
dessein, et reçu sans méfiance.' (p. 75)

Valmont's use of rhetorical devices, interrogation and exclamation, seem as semantically limited as the examples of
deletion and transposition above, thus :

' Savez-vous jusqu'où peut aller mon désespoir ? non.'
(p. 118)

' Qui sait jusqu'où peut aller votre pouvoir ! '' (p. 185)

The language used in pursuit of Madame de Tourvel suggests
a return to the 17th century :

' En vain m'accablez-vous de vos rigueurs désolantes ; elles
ne m'empêchent point de m'abandonner entièrement à
l'amour...' (p. 101)

Versini suggests that Valmont is most natural in his correspondence with the Marquise de Merteuil, and some inversions
indeed indicate a more familiar tone. However, the narrative
parts of Valmont's letters to her are by contrast written in a
much more intellectual style, similar to that in which he
addresses the Présidente throughout. Thus relative inversions
supplement simple descriptions, and others introduce a careful
analysis of developing love :

'... armé de ma lanterne sourde et dans la toilette que
comportait l'heure et qu'exigeait la circonstance, j'ai rendu
ma première visite à votre pupille.' (p. 216)

'... j'observais, non sans espoir, tout ce que promettaient à
l'amour son regard animé, son geste devenu plus libre, et
surtout ce son de voix qui...' (p. 48)

Midway between the two styles are the ironic comments
Valmont introduces into his narrative, where inversion highlights opposing concepts conveyed in a simple sentence
structure :

' Ce que n'a pu la vertu tant vantée, l'esprit de ruse l'a produit sans effort.' (p. 230)

The familiar style, where inversion is less common, is characterized by irony and exclamations, and also by repetition :

' Peut-être, pendant que je vous écris, s'occupe-t-elle déjà de cette douce idée ! ' (p. 228)

' Personne ne sait rien, personne ne désire de rien savoir : à peine en aurait-on parlé, si j'avais consenti qu'on parlât d'autre chose.' (p. 231)

The stylish descriptions are replaced by ironic ones, indicated by devices such as parentheses and also by impersonal forms, such as the following combination of a compound inversion and passive verb :

' A peine le baiser a-t-il été donné, que la main a retrouvé sa force pour échapper, et que...' (p. 95)

Thus Valmont's style comprises both the rhetorical and the familiar, but although he makes full use of techniques developed by the *Précieux* writers, he does so dispassionately, in the interests of dissimulation, where the style is elevated, and of irony where it is not.

(b) *The Marquise de Merteuil*

Although the Marquise uses inverted word-order nearly as much as Valmont, all but one of the examples occur in the twelve letters to the Vicomte, and therefore may only characterize her attitude towards him. Le Hir sums up her language thus : ' Sa langue et son style nous offrent un merveilleux équilibre de qualités classiques ',[13] and as regards word-order, the unremarkable inversions, generally having a connective function, and the concise sentences in which they occur are certainly reminiscent of Madame de la Fayette. The predominant inversions are modal adverbs (twelve examples) followed by relatives (seven examples), and both are used, as well as for functional purposes, to bring out a light irony and in the course of analytic description.

[13] Introduction to the Garnier edition, p. xxx.

The ironic attitude of the writer focusses both on herself and
Valmont, their acquaintances and society in general. For
example she comments thus on Valmont's romantic intentions,
with an ironic afterthought introduced by *aussi* :

'Il faut qu'elle se donne, me dites-vous : eh! sans doute il
le faut ; et aussi se donnera-t-elle comme les autres, avec
cette différence que ce sera de mauvaise grâce.' (p. 25)

She is equally detached in regard to her own behaviour :

'J'y joignis, par une seconde réflexion, l'air qu'autorisait
mon âge ; et jamais il ne me jugea plus enfant...' (p. 177)

Here inversion allows the topic to be taken up in the next
sentence, but in the opposite sense, resulting in the opposition
âge—enfant. Alternatively a chiasmus permits the contrast
between the irony and experience of the Marquise, and
Valmont's self-esteem :

'Peut-être surmonterez-vous cet obstacle, mais ne vous
flattez pas de le détruire.' (p. 15)

The perspicacity of the Marquise is directed both at the
characters of other people, and at the situations about which
she writes. For example she escapes the suspicion of one of
her lovers by presenting him with her key :

'C'est par cette adresse que j'ai prévenu les réflexions
qu'aurait pu lui faire naître la propriété, toujours suspecte,
d'une petite maison.' (p. 28)

Inversion emphasizes the source of the supposed anxiety, and
the beginning of the Marquise's train of thought. Elsewhere
she instructs Valmont in attention to detail, and inversion
again forms part of a logical sequence :

'A ces précautions que j'appelle fondamentales, s'en
joignent mille autres, ou locales, ou d'occasion, que la
réflexion et l'habitude font trouver au besoin ; dont le
détail serait minutieux...' (p. 181)

To conclude, the style of the Marquise de Marteuil does contrast with that of the other characters in its use of word-order.
Here it is part of a sustained Classical style, whereas elsewhere
it is exploited to a greater or lesser extent to convey a transient
style or attitude.

(c) *Présidente de Tourvel and Madame de Volanges*

The fourteen letters written by the Présidente contain only eight inversions, whereas the four by Madame de Volanges have five. In each case the distribution of examples is uneven, although both use similar types of construction. There is only one instance of an immobile *invertissant*, an indirect construction, in each, the remainder being predominantly modal adverbs.

The inversions in the correspondence of the Présidente are interesting in that they reveal a complete change of tone with each recipient and each situation. Four of the inversions occur in three letters to Valmont, and four in one letter to Madame de Rosemonde. Each set of letters is significant, firstly because of the difference in tone, and secondly because of the concentration of inversions in the first letter of each series. Thus the first letter to Valmont has two inversions, although there are none at all in the next four, the remainder occurring in subsequent letters, numbers 67 and 78. Similarly letter 102, the first of the correspondence between the Présidente and Madame de Rosemonde, has four inversions, while the remaining eight letters, not included in this analysis, have five inversions between them, with never more than one in a letter.

The examples in the letters to Valmont all have the *invertissant peut-être*, two being compound inversions, and all showing the restraint which Versini notes as characterizing this correspondence (*op. cit.*, p. 325). In two instances the *invertissant* is separated from the verb by an intervening clause, a device which contrasts strongly with the shorter, simpler sentences favoured in more emotional contexts. Thus in letter 26 the Présidente seeks to explain her conduct to Valmont :

> ' Oui, j'ai pleuré, je l'avoue ; peut-être aussi les deux mots, que vous me citez avec tant de soin, me sont-ils échappés.' (p. 55)

The examples in the opening letter to Madame de Rosemonde mark a change in style. Here the tone is highly emotional, corresponding to the author's confession of her love, and the same *invertissant* is used in an exclamation, and is repeated with direct order, rather than the longer compound construction :

> ' Ah ! si je l'avais combattu avec plus de soin, peut-être eût-il pris moins d'empire ! peut-être alors ce départ n'eût pas été nécessaire.' (p. 237)

As indicated in the above example, a recurrent metaphor in this letter is the idea of fighting, and this is highlighted by an inversion in the following :

> ' J'étais sans puissance et sans force ; à peine m'en restait-il pour combattre, je n'en avais plus pour résister.' (p. 236)

As the downfall of the Présidente continues, her letters to her *confidente*, while becoming increasingly emotional, are at times almost lyrical in tone, with a hint of *préciosité*. This is exemplified by the inversions which occur in the two concluding letters of the series (both excluded from the syntactic analysis). Firstly letter 139, where she is convinced of Valmont's sincerity :

> ' A cet état de douleur et d'angoisse, ont succédé le calme et les délices. O joie de mon cœur ! ' (p. 328)

and secondly, latter 143 opens with the expression of final disillusion :

> ' Le voile est déchiré, Madame, sur lequel était peinte l'illusion de mon bonheur.' (p. 336)

The return of inversion in these two instances, after only sporadic and unexceptional occurrences of the device, helps to heighten the effect of the victim's emotional style. Thus the inversion examples confirm in every respect the judgement passed by Versini :

> ' La Présidente est une précieuse, la langue de la dévotion est encore une langue mondaine, élégante et poétique.' (*op. cit.*, p. 325)

Three of the four inversions in the correspondence of Madame de Volanges occur in a single letter. A fifth example, an unexceptional use of *où* followed by *être*, is found in a letter to the Marquise. The others, however, show clearly the character's sententious nature, and her preference for an oratorical style. Two of the three examples in letter 32 to the Présidente, which is important not least because it introduces the idea of a *liaison dangereuse*, are of the *invertissant tel*, both having a moralizing quality, and also concluding a paragraph, e.g.

> ' Tel serait cependant l'aspect sous lequel vous montrerait une liaison intime avec M. de Valmont, quelqu'innocente qu'elle pût être.' (p. 65)

The other example is of the use of *c'est ... que*, which gives both relief to a lengthy sentence, and emphasis to a complex subject, and contributes to the patronizing style of the whole letter :

> ' Cette vérité me paraît d'autant plus nécessaire à croire, que c'est d'elle que dérive la nécessité de l'indulgence pour les méchants comme pour les bons, et que...' (p. 64)

The remaining example is of *aussi*, also in a longer complex sentence, in the first letter between the two women.

(d) *Cécile and Danceny*

The epistolary style of Cécile Volanges is characterized above all by a naïve spontaneity, and her youth is vividly conveyed by a conversational tone and dislocated syntax. It is not surprising, therefore, that there are only four examples of inversion in her letters, two in eleven letters to Sophie, and two in six letters to Danceny, and these only when her style is beginning to mature. The letters to Sophie containing inversion (numbers 16 and 61) are the fifth and tenth in the series, and those to Damceny (82 and 94) are the fifth and sixth. It may be noted that the remaining two letters to Danceny, composed by Valmont, have no inversions, which perhaps indicates how closely the girl's style is imitated. The four invertissants are *où*, *peut-être*, *encore* and *au moins*, and the constructions have little stylistic value. The last example does, however, suggest the naïve enthusiasm peculiar to this writer :

> ' Si vous vouliez, nous nous aimerons tant ! et au moins n'aurions-nous de peines que celles qu'on nous fait ! ' (p. 211)

In contrast to Cécile's *style familier*, the language of Danceny has something of a Classical flavour, in spite of the occasional jargon noted by Versini (*op. cit.*, p. 319). According to Le Hir, ' la langue et le style de Danceny sont ceux de l'Amant pâle, dévoré d'amour, avec parfois une affectation d'antithèses et de pointes ' (p. xxiii). Unlike the other characters, the inversions here are more evenly distributed, six in eight letters to Cécile and two in one letter to Madame de Volanges, although there are none in the three letters to Valmont analysed. In the remainder of the book there are two inversions in two letters to Madame de Rosemonde, one in a letter to Valmont, and six in three letters to the Marquise de Merteuil. There is no evidence of any change of style in the various correspondences, although there is an unusual concentration of inversions, four in all, in the first letter to the Marquise, in which Danceny declares his love for her. Unlike the other correspondents, Danceny favours immobile *invertissants*, particularly relatives, the most common exception being *peut-être*.

Of the six examples in the letters to Cécile, three are concerned with practical details of the lovers' situation, and they are all in letter 65, e.g.

'... et ce sera par lui que passera notre correspondence mutuelle.' (p. 133)

Of the remainder, the first shows a logical Classical structure, and the second a somewhat facile language :

' J'ai vu se fixer sur moi ces yeux charmants, qu'embellissait encore l'expression de la tendresse.' (p. 63)

' Puis-je encore parler de bonheur ? peut-être est-il perdu pour moi, perdu pour jamais.' (p. 210)

The same contrast between the elevated and the commonplace is shown in the letters to Cécile's mother, the first example being a sentimental inversion cliché, and the second a less complicated and well-balanced sentence :

'... je ne crains pas d'ajouter que celui (le sentiment) que m'a inspiré Mademoiselle votre fille est tel qu'il peut vous déplaire, mais non vous offenser.' (p. 130)

' Je ne prétends pas blâmer une démarche qu'autorise, peut-être la sollicitude maternelle.' (p. 131)

Thus the epistolary novel, first popularized in France by Rousseau, is perfected by Laclos, and the differences between them are clearly shown through the study of their word-order. While there are the beginnings of individual characterization through inversion in the *Nouvelle Héloïse*, this is exploited to the full in the *Liaisons*. Inverted order marks not only the style of an individual, but also a character's changing attitudes to the other protagonists, besides maintaining its now traditional functions of ensuring clarity and continuity, conveying emphasis, and other effects of stylistic importance.

Appendix : Rousseau and Laclos

The inversion frequency in Rousseau is 1·05, with fifty *invertissants*, as opposed to 0·66 and thirty-nine in Laclos. In the one 54% of the inversions occur in sentences of three or more clauses, as compared with only 42% in the other (table 7.07), and 17% of the inverted noun phrases in Rousseau consist of several subjects or a subject with a dependent clause, as against 10% in Laclos (table 7.06). Although the texts share most types of inversion, the majority in Rousseau occur in the more complicated subordinate clause constructions, while the reverse is true of Laclos. Thus, for example, 36% of the inversions in Rousseau have relative *invertissants* and 27% modal adverbs, while the figures for Laclos are 27% and 42% (table 7.09). Similarly operations of deletion and transposition, or addition and transposition account for twice as many examples in Rousseau. The literary distribution of the inversions follow similar patterns. In Rousseau the correspondents, with the exception of Julie, make an approximately equal use of inversion, but this contrast is hardly comparable to that of the letters in Laclos. The use made of inverted order by the protagonists in each work may be compared as follows :

Saint-Preux : 2·9 inversions per letter ; Valmont 2·1
Julie   : 1·5 inversions per letter ; Cécile 0·2
Claire   : 2·6 inversions per letter ; Marquise de
                                   Merteuil 1·9

Thus in each work the hero uses inversion most, while in Laclos the naïve mistress hardly uses it at all. This contrast is less marked in Rousseau, where inverted order is also a fairly distinctive feature of Julie's style (sixty examples in forty letters). The Marquise in Laclos uses inversion slightly less than Valmont, as does Rousseau's Claire, compared with Saint-Preux. Other correspondents in Laclos all average well below one inversion per letter, although in Rousseau the distribution is more uneven, for instance, ten examples in three letters by Edouard.

Chapter VIII

THE NINETEENTH CENTURY (1)

1. SYNTACTIC ANALYSIS OF THE TEXTS
1800–1850

The texts :

F.-R. de Chateaubriand, *Atala*
René
Les Natchez (I–X) [1]

Mme de Staël, *Corinne* [2]

A. de Vigny, *Cinq-Mars* (I–XX) [3]

Stendhal, *Le rouge et le noir* (1er livre) [4]

H. de Balzac, *Le Père Goriot* [5]

Table 8.01 : Inversion frequencies

CHA/	268 : 1·34	
STA/COR	187 : 0·94	
VIG/CM	164 : 0·82	(*mean* 1·08)
STE/RN	145 : 0·73	
BAL/PG	310 : 1·55	

Table 8.02 : Percentage table to show nature of clause in which inversion occurs

	CHA	STA	VIG	STE	BAL
Main clause	46	38	34	39	26
Subordinate clause	54	62	66	60	74
Non-subordinating *invertissant* in subordinate clause	n	—	n	1	n
	100	100	100	100	100
Immobile *invertissant*	45	57	67	61	73
Mobile *invertissant*	54	35	33	33	24
Other operations	1	8	n	6	3
N :	268	187	164	145	310

[1] In *Œuvres complètes III*, Paris (Garnier), 1929. (CHA)]
[2] ed. Charpentier, Paris, 1841. (STA)
[3] In *Œuvres complètes II*, Paris (Gallimard), 1948. (VIG)
[4] ed. Martineau, Paris (Garnier), 1957. (STE)
[5] ed. Castex, Paris (Garnier), 1960. (BAL)

Table 8.03 : Percentage table to show distribution of inversions according to discourse type

	CHA	STA	VIG	STE	BAL
Narrative	77	69	70	83	76
Direct speech	21	29	30	13	24
Indirect speech	2	2	n	3	—
Soliloquy	—	—	—	1	—

Table 8.04 : Percentage table to show position of the inversion within the corpus examined

	CHA	STA	VIG	STE	BAL
Sentence initial	29	30	19	27	22
Paragraph initial	17	4	8	10	2
Chapter initial	—	—	n	1	—
Speech initial	2	1	2	1	1
Total initial	48	35	29	39	25
Sentence final	23	30	30	27	35
Paragraph final	10	1	4	9	5
Chapter final	—	n	n	1	n
Speech final	1	2	4	2	1
Total final	34	33	38	39	41

Table 8.05 : Percentage table to show position of inversion in relation to other types of discourse

	CHA	STA	VIG	STE	BAL
Preceding direct speech	2	—	1	1	1
Following direct speech	9	2	1	1	—
Preceding indirect speech	—	—	—	1	—
Following indirect speech	—	—	—	—	—

Table 8.06 : Percentage table to show nature of the inverted noun phrase

	CHA	STA	VIG	STE	BAL
Pronoun subject	7	15	9	15	11
Substantive subject	91	81	89	77	82
Compound inversion	2	4	2	8	7
	100	100	100	100	100
2 or more subjects	4	6	7	3	6
S and dependent (S)	18	16	10	12	13

Table 8.07 : The percentage of inversions occurring in sentences
of three or more clauses

	CHA	STA	VIG	STE	BAL
(S)—3 clauses	19	28	23	30	28
4 clauses	8	12	15	11	19
5 clauses	3	4	7	2	6
6 clauses	3	2	2	1	4
7 clauses	—	—	—	—	1
7+ clauses	—	1	—	—	—
	—	—	—	—	—
	33	47	47	44	58

Table 8.08 : Ratio of inversions to *invertissants*

CHA	268 : 56—4·79
STA	187 : 56—3·34
VIG	164 : 43—3·81
STE	145 : 39—3·72
BAL	310 : 51—6·08
Total	1,074 : 113—9·59 (*mean* 4·35)

Table 8.09 : Percentage table of the most frequently occurring
inversions

	CHA	STA	VIG	STE	BAL
Relatives	34	42	49	43	53
Comparatives	3	2	7	4	11
Indirect construction	5	9	8	8	7
Modal adverbs	19	14	12	19	15

Table 8.10 : Percentage table to show the occurrence of ' être ',
' faire ', and ' avoir '

	CHA	STA	VIG	STE	BAL
être	18	27	19	26	21
faire	n	4	4	3	4
avoir	1	2	n	1	2

Table 8.11 : Percentage table showing the distribution of direct
speech *invertissants*

	CHA	STA	VIG	STE	BAL
Immobile *invertissant*	66	62	73	64	65
Mobile *invertissant*	34	31	25	21	27
Other operations	—	7	2	15	8
	—	—	—	—	—
N :	56	55	49	19	74

I

Table 8.12 : Percentage table to show the occurrence of
adverbials and clauses in inversion constructions

	CHA	STA	VIG	STE	BAL
V(adv)S	11	7	8	8	6
(adv)VS	1	1	1	2	n
V(S)S	—	—	n	—	—
(S)VS	2	n	1	2	3

(i) DISTRIBUTION OF THE INVERSIONS

Although the texts of the preceding fifty years showed the
number of inversions beginning to increase, the works after
1800 have by comparison a high rate of inversion, and the
average frequencies for the 19th and 20th century periods vary
by only $0 \cdot 19$. However, whereas earlier periods revealed few
differences in frequency between individual texts, particularly
from 1600 to 1750, the inversions in the novels in the last two
centuries tend to have either a very high or a relatively low
frequency of occurrence, the highest being $1 \cdot 55$ in Balzac, and
the lowest $0 \cdot 44$ in Sarraute. In the first half of the 19th century, however, the lowest frequency of $0 \cdot 73$ in Stendhal is
already higher than the average for each of the 18th-century
periods. Although Chateaubriand is the first author to resume
frequent use of inversion, this is not necessarily a characteristic
of the Romantic writers. An influential pre-Romantic writer,
Bernardin de Saint Pierre, in 1787 used only seventy-three
inversions in *Paul et Virginie*, giving a comparable frequency of
$0 \cdot 75$, which exactly fits the pattern of the period 1750–1800.

Corresponding to the higher inversion frequency is the rise
in number of the *invertissants*, with an average of forty-nine
per text, again the highest since the end of the 16th century.
As regards type of inversion, the analysis reveals a reversal of
the trend noted in the previous century, with relative inversion
constructions again becoming more frequent at the expense of
modal adverb *invertissants*. The latter account for an average
of only 16% of the total inversions in each text, as opposed to
35% in the previous period, while relatives now account for
44%, as against 29% in the last four texts analysed. The
average proportion of inversions in direct speech is the same as

in the preceding period, 23%. On the other hand the low number of examples with *être* and the other common verbs, 26%, and the tendency for the majority of inversions to occur in one- or two-clause sentences, may both be indicative of a change in style in the 19th century. As will be seen below, the main inversion types are all represented in the texts of this period, although certain constructions such as inversion in temporal clauses, or after a subordinate clause or adverbs of time and quantity, occur only sporadically. Inversion is not found in causal, result, purpose, substantival or hypothetical clauses.

(ii) EXAMPLES

A. IMMOBILE 'INVERTISSANT'

1. *Zero : CHA : 1 ; STA : 3 ; VIG : 1 ; STE : 1*
 ' " Je fus distrait de ces pensées par un grand bruit qui se fit à une porte. *Entrent* aussitôt deux guerriers qui se tenoient en riant sous le bras." ' (CHA, pp. 249–50)

2. *Relatives : CHA : 92 inversions, 8 ' invertissants ' ; STA : 78,7 ; VIG : 81,9 ; STE : 63,6 ; BAL : 164,9*
 ' D'ailleurs son mollet charnu, saillant, pronostiquait, autant que son long nez carré, des qualités morales *auxquelles* paraissait tenir la veuve, et *que* confirmait la face lunaire et naïvement niaise du bonhomme.' (BAL, p. 28)

3. *Comparatives : CHA : 9,5 ; STA : 4,2 ; VIG : 11,2 ; STE : 6,4 ; BAL : 33,6*
 ' " Tel est l'esprit des deux cultes ; mais notre catholicisme romain est *moins* sombre cependant *que* ne l'était celui du Nord." ' (STA, p. 75)

4. *Concessives : CHA : 5,1 ; STA : 5,3 ; VIG : 2,1 ; STE : 5,3 ; BAL : 7,2*
 ' " Mais, *tout* aimable *qu'*est Corinne, je pense comme Thomas Walpole ; ' que fait-on de cela à la maison ? ' " ' (STA, p. 172)

5. *Temporal conjunctions : STA : 1,1 ; VIG : 1,1 ; STE : 1,1 ; BAL : 1,1*

' A six heures, le corps du père Goriot fut descendu dans sa
fosse autour de laquelle étaient les gens de ses filles, qui
disparurent avec le clergé *aussitôt que* fut dite la courte
prière due au bonhomme pour l'argent de l'étudiant.'
(BAL, p. 308)

6. *Correlatives : STE : 2,1*
   ' " C'est bien d'un curé que l'on peut dire : *tant* vaut
   l'homme, *tant* vaut la place ", disait-il aux élèves qui
   faisaient cercle autour de lui.' (p. 186)

7. *Indirect construction : CHA : 14,4 ; STA : 16,6 ;
   VIG : 13,4 ; STE : 11,7 ; BAL : 21,7*
   ' " Cela peut être d'un grand poids dans la balance de nos
   destins." — " Je cherche *combien* y pèse le cœur d'un
   roi ", reprit Cinq-Mars.' (VIG, p. 259)

B. MOBILE ' INVERTISSANT '

1. *Attributes : CHA : 31,5 ; STA : 5,1 ; VIG : 6,1 ;
   STE : 13,1 ; BAL : 3,2*
   ' *Moins rapide* est l'hirondelle effleurant les ondes, moins
   léger le duvet du roseau qu'emporte un tourbillon.'
   (CHA, p. 198)

2. *Adverbs—modal : CHA : 38,5 ; STA : 27,7 ; VIG :
   19,6 ; STE : 27,6 ; BAL : 48,5*
   ' *A peine* quelques mots et d'amour et de la mort dirigent-
   ils de temps en temps la réflexion, mais plus souvent le
   vague de la musique se prête à tous les mouvements de
   l'âme...' (STA, p. 212)

3. *Adverbs—quantity : VIG : 1,1*
   ' " Eh bien, nous pouvons la lui arranger ; *autant* vaut
   cette application qu'une autre à présent." ' (p. 105)

4. *Adverbs—time : CHA : 3,1 ; STA : 1,1 ; VIG : 2,2*
   ' *Ici* partit et s'élança jusqu'aux voûtes l'explosion des
   cris du peuple.' (VIG, p. 80)

5. *Adverbs—place : CHA : 14,5 ; STA : 1,1 ; VIG : 1,1 ;
   STE : 1,1 ; BAL : 6,2*
   ' *Partout* brille l'acier, *partout* flottent les drapeaux de la

France :   drapeaux immortels couverts de cicatrices...'
(CHA, p. 195)

6. *Adverbs—combinations : STA : 5,2 ; VIG : 1,1*
   ' *Peut-être aussi* croyait-elle que ... leur voix avait un
   accent qui trahissait leur affection mutuelle, et que...'
   (STA, p. 98)

7. *Adverbial phrase—time : CHA : 2,2 ; BAL : 1,1*
   ' *Le lendemain matin* régnait à Paris un de ces épais
   brouillards qui l'enveloppent et l'embrument si bien que...'
   (BAL, pp. 46–47)

8. *Adverbial phrase—place : CHA : 31,12 ; STA : 23,13 ;*
   VIG : 20,9 ; STE : 5,4 ; BAL : 15,12
   ' *Au delà, sur la rive gauche*, serpentent cinq ou six vallées
   au fond desquelles l'œil distingue fort bien de petits
   ruisseaux.' (STE, p. 7)

9. *Adverbial phrase—manner : VIG : 2.2*
   ' " *Avec un chef de vingt-deux ans* s'est conçue, même et va
   s'exécuter la plus vaste, la plus juste, la plus salutaire des
   entreprises." ' (VIG, p. 272)

10. *Prepositional phrase : CHA : 12,2 ; STA : 3,2 ; VIG :*
    2,1 ; BAL : 1,1
    ' Mais *à ce repos* est unie la profondeur de sentiments qui
    caractérise le christianisme.' (STA, p. 188)

11. *Subordinate clause : STE : 1,1*
    ' Pour que rien ne manquât au triomphe de M. de Renal,
    comme Julien récitait, entrèrent M. Valenod, le possesseur
    des beaux chevaux normands, et M. Charcot de Maugiron,
    sous-préfet de l'arrondissement.' (STE, p. 32)

C. OTHER OPERATIONS

1. *Deletion and transposition : STA : 3 ; VIG : 1 ; STE :*
   7 ; BAL : 8
   ' *Une action lui semblait-elle* admirable, c'était celle-là
   précisément qui attirait le blâme des gens qui l'environ-
   naient.' (STE, pp. 41–42)

2. *Addition and transposition : CHA : 2,2 ; STA : 12,8 ;*
   STE : 2,2 ; BAL : 2,2

' " Vous sentez que *c'est* au milieu des arts et sous un beau ciel *que* s'est formé ce langage mélodieux et coloré." '
(STA, p. 63)

(iii) DETAILS OF THE INVERSIONS
(a) *Types of immobile and mobile ' invertissants '*

The six examples of zero *invertissant* are unevenly distributed among four texts, but all have one feature in common, the presence of an adverb between verb and subject, which generally stands in a close semantic relation to the verb. It may be noted that the three examples from de Staël and the one from Stendhal all have the combination *venir* and *ensuite*, also a feature of inversion in English (' next comes . . .'). All the examples except the Stendhal (' Vinrent ensuite les anecdotes ', p. 187) have a complex subject, mostly including a dependent clause, thus :

' Reste donc debout ce duc de Bouillon, à qui son Sedan donne de l'orgueil.' (VIG, p. 108)

Two examples, in Stendhal and de Staël, constitute paragraph openings, and in addition to the Vigny construction quoted above, two occur in conversation, both being in de Staël, e.g.

' " Viennent ensuite, continua Corinne, les tableaux dramatiques tirés de quatre grands poëtes." ' (STA, p. 198)

Thus although the absolute construction is becoming more common, its use is restricted to specific verbs, mostly in closely definable narrative and syntactic contexts.

Despite the increase in relative constructions, the *invertissants* remain the same, with the relative pronoun *que* occurring most frequently in every text. With the exception of Balzac, there is little use made of inversion in comparative clauses, although it might be noted that while this author uses a greater range of *invertissants*, more than half the examples have the verb *être*, whereas in other authors, in particular Chateaubriand and Vigny, there is much more variety in the verbs used. Although there are only four examples of inversion in a temporal clause, one in each text except Chateaubriand, the *invertissants* are all different. However, apart from the Balzac example quoted above (p. 252) where the verb has no temporal value, each verb has a strong semantic link with the *invertissant*, thus in de Staël *tant que* is followed by *durer*, and in Vigny and Stendhal *quand* and *lorsque* are followed by *venir* and *arriver* respectively. The example from Balzac is exceptional both in the use of the less usual conjunction *aussitôt que* and of the verb *dire*, in its passive form.

Where the *invertissant* is an attributive adjective, this has hitherto almost always been *tel*, followed by the verb *être*. However, in Chateaubriand the analysis of *Les Natchez* reveals a number of different *invertissants*, and also, in the case of *tel*, a variety of verbs. This also happens in the *Père Goriot*, where the construction ' Divers en sont les effets ' occurs (p. 114). The most common alternative to *tel* as an attributive *invertissant* is an adjective preceded by an adverb of quantity, as in the example B1, p. 252 (above). Other examples in Chateaubriand include :

' Moins ravissant étoit dans l'antiquité ce mode de musique...' (p. 234)

and

' Bien différents s'élèvent dans une riante prairie, au milieu des ruisseaux et des doux ombrages, ces monceaux d'herbes et de fleurs...' (p. 317)

The use of *tel* with descriptive verbs is mainly, but not wholly, confined to natural descriptions or comparisons. Inverted order may be juxtaposed with direct order, to produce a chiasmus, which may be due to a syntactic consideration, as in the following, where the substitution of the pronoun ensures direct order in the second clause :

' Tels se pressent les deux guerriers, tels ils s'étouffent dans leurs bras serrés par les nœuds de la colère.' (p. 224)

Other verbs used in this construction include *croître, se montrer* and *paraître*.

The remaining mobile *invertissants* are predominantly modal adverbs, and these are unexceptional, with little difference between the texts. The most notable feature in this sphere is the infrequent occurrence of other types of adverbs and adverbial phrases, except for the fourteen adverbs of place in Chateaubriand and the comparatively large number of adverbial phrases of place in all the texts except Stendhal which has only five. Again in Chateaubriand there is little use of *être*, which occurs in only two of the thirty-one examples of inversion after the latter, and slightly more frequently in Vigny and Balzac, although it is present in nearly all the examples from *Corinne*.

(b) *Other operations*

In discussing the style of another work by Chateaubriand J.-M. Gautier quotes as a particular instance of inversion the deletion and transposition operation, which he states is an alternative to a temporal or conditional clause.[6] All the examples he uses have verbs in the indicative and a pronominal subject, except for ' Le ciel était-il serein, je traversais le grand Mail '. Although no such examples are found in the three works of Chateaubriand analysed here, they do occur in other texts, and an example with a substantive subject, and thus in the form of a compound inversion, is quoted on p. 253 (ex. C1). A further example is in the *Père Goriot* :

' Un étranger se présentait-il, elle lui vantait la préférence que monsieur Goriot ... lui avait accordée.' (p. 29)

The use of the imperfect indicative stresses the temporal rather than the hypothetical element, although the latter seems to take precedence when the present tense is used :

' Quitte-t-on sa maîtresse, on risque, hélas ! d'être trompé deux ou trois fois par jour.' (STE, p. 72)

The majority of examples of this operation, however, still have verbs in the imperfect subjunctive, although the increasing use of indicative forms does have the effect of lightening the sentence, as Gautier observes with reference to the *Mémoires*.

With the exception of Madame de Staël, the authors selected for this period make little use of the addition and transposition operation, there being no examples in Vigny, and two each in

---

[6] J.-M. Gautier, *Le style des ' Mémoires d'outre-tombe ' de Chateaubriand*, Geneva, 1959, p. 148.

Chateaubriand, Stendhal and Balzac. Of the twelve examples in *Corinne*, which contain eight different *invertissants*, all but one occur in the narrative. Nine of them are in sentence-final position and thus have a certain rhythmic function, especially where the subject has a complement or a preposed adjective, or both, as in the following:

'... mais ce n'est pas ainsi qu'est faite la funeste imagination des âmes sensibles.' (p. 14)

Similarly there are only three examples where the construction is quite simple, the others having several subjects, or a subject with a dependent clause, an adverb separating verb and subject, or a passive verb phrase (five examples), e.g.

' C'est dans les Thermes de Caracalla qu'étaient placés l'Hercule Farnèse, la Flore et le groupe de Dircé.' (p. 96)

In addition, in all four cases where the *invertissant* is the adverb *là*, there is a parallel structure with direct order, following, or in one example preceding, the structure containing inversion:

' C'est là que se promenaient les orateurs de Rome, en sortant du Forum ; c'est là que César et Pompée se rencontraient comme de simples citoyens, et qu'ils...' (p. 95)

' C'est là qu'on apprend à sentir Homère et Sophocle ; c'est là que se révèle à l'âme une connaissance de l'antiquité qui...' (p. 185)

Thus it seems that in this one text the addition and transposition operation has a fairly important syntactic role in conjunction with other features of syntax, and also a stylistic role, when inherent features of emphasis and rhythm assume an additional contrastive function.

2. STYLISTIC ANALYSIS OF THE TEXTS

(i) F.-R. DE CHATEAUBRIAND, ' RENÉ ', ' ATALA ' AND ' LES NATCHEZ '

The types and distribution of inversions are very similar in the joint analysis of *René* and *Atala* and in that of *Les Natchez*. In each there are more constructions with mobile *invertissants*

I*

(table 8.02), and the most common types of inversion are relatives and modal adverbs (table 8.09). With the exception of zero *invertissant* and concessive constructions, every type of inversion in *Les Natchez* had already occurred in *René* or *Atala*, although there are sometimes here only isolated examples of structures which become very frequent in the later work. In the two short books all but two of the thirteen examples in direct speech occur after relative or modal adverb *invertissants*, every example but one of the latter being *peut-être*. In *Les Natchez*, with the exception of the eleven place adverbials, every type of inversion includes a number of conversational examples, although again the majority are relatives and inversions after *peut-être* constitute most of the modals. In the analysis of *Les Natchez* certain inversion constructions show a wholly disproportionate increase in occurrence, in particular comparatives (eight examples to one), attributes (twenty-five to six) and adverbial phrases of place (again twenty-five to six), all of which are important constructions in the work. However, in the overall analysis of Chateaubriand's inversions the proportion of the total represented by *René* and *Atala* as compared to *Les Natchez* is in the ratio of two to seven, that is three and a half times as many inversions in the latter as in the two early books.

As shown in table 8.07, the majority of inversions in these texts occur in one- or two-clause sentences, with only 33% found in sentences of three or more clauses. On the other hand certain features of word-order are found more often in Chateaubriand than in the other writers of this period, namely inverted subjects with a dependent clause (table 8.06) and the occurrence of an adverb between verb and inverted subject (table 8.12). It may also be noted that despite the number of inversions after place adverbials, the occurrence of *être* in inversion constructions (table 8.10) is lower than in the other texts, where these *invertissants* are less frequent. It will be seen in ensuing sections that these facts are directly related to the prose style of Chateaubriand.

INVERSION IN POETIC PROSE

(a) *Natural description and sentence structure*

The descriptive passages in Chateaubriand's novels contain a wide variety of sentence structures. The alternation of different sentence lengths has already been noted by Gautier :

' L'art de Chateaubriand consiste à faire suivre une phrase courte et statique, ou bien une énumération, d'une phrase plus longue, que suit parfois une véritable période.' [7]

Although the majority of inversions occur in short sentences, others are often found in very complex structures. This is exemplified by a number of place adverbial *invertissants* which contain a further inversion clause embedded within them, e.g.

' Par delà ces globes où sommeillent les âmes qui n'ont point encore subi la vie mortelle se creuse la vallée où elles doivent revenir pour être jugées, après leur passage sur la terre.' (NAT, p. 230)

In such instances where a clause is placed between *invertissant* and verb, considerable emphasis falls on the subject when it does occur. In the next example a rhythmic cadence is achieved both by delaying the subject and by virtue of its formation, with a lengthy preposed adjective ; inversion also links the subject to that of the subsequent sentence :

' Les sauvages ont raconté que sous les ombrages de la Floride, dans une île au milieu d'un lac qui étend ses ondes comme un voile de gaze, coule une mystérieuse fontaine. Les eaux de cette fontaine...' (NAT, p. 307)

A further instance of the development of the subject in this way exemplifies the use of contrasting orders in shorter sentences :

' Deux collines le bornoient au septentrion et au midi ; il ne s'ouvroit qu'à l'occident, où s'élevait un grand bois de sapins. Les troncs de ces arbres ... ressembloient à de hautes colonnes, et ...' (ATA, p. 46)

Alternatively a short sentence with direct order may be

[7] *Ibid.*, p. 129.

followed by a longer more rhetorical structure, such as the following :

' Je m'assieds sur un rocher. D'un côté s'étendent les vagues étincelantes, de l'autre les murs sombres du monastère se perdent confusément dans les cieux.' (REN, p. 94)

Many of the inversions after place adverbials contain subjects with the dependent relative clauses already mentioned, and in the following the *invertissant* is also separated from the verb by a relative clause :

' Dans un champ du soleil, dans des prairies dont le sol semble être de calcédoine, d'onyx et de saphir, sont rangés les chars subtils de l'âme, chars qui se meuvent d'eux-mêmes, et qui sont faits de la même manière que les étoiles.' (NAT, p. 228)

(b) *Enumeration and repetition*

Many of the inversion constructions in which there is more than one subject exemplify Chateaubriand's use of enumeration, where the subject or complement is expanded in some detail. This ranges from a simple list of subjects,

' "... il regretta l'humble lit que lui avait creusé la nature, les oiseaux, les fleurs, les arbres et les ruisseaux, jadis modestes compagnons de son paisible cours." ' (REN, p. 96)

to a whole string of clauses :

' Alors s'expliquèrent pour moi plusieurs choses que je n'avois pu comprendre : ce mélange de joie et de tristesse qu'Amélie avoit fait paroître au moment de mon départ ... le soin qu'elle prit de m'éviter à mon retour, et...' ' (REN, p. 92)

In some instances, where the main clause has direct order, inversion has a less important function, that of lending variety to the clauses which follow, e.g.

' " Je visitai celle (chambre) où ma mère avoit perdu la vie en me mettant au monde, celle où se retiroit mon père, celle où j'avois dormi dans mon berceau, celle enfin où..." ' (REN, p. 89)

There is also one unusual example of enumeration in which a

list of subjects and objects follow a compound inversion, where
the repeated verb is understood :

' " A peine le fils connoît-il le père, le père le fils, le frère la
sœur, la sœur le frère ! " ' (REN, p. 89)

Inversion is also used in the repetition of complete structures,
as in the following, where the *invertissants* are the same, and
the verbs semantically very similar :

' Là paroissent les sept anges avec les sept coupes pleines de
la colère de Dieu ; là se tient la femme assise sur la bête
de couleur écarlate...' (NAT, p. 230)

Such constructions may also be linked closely to their lyrical
content, as in the following example where the description
appeals to different senses with each new relative clause :

'... je vous préfère encore ces tombeaux aériens du sauvage,
ces mausolées de fleurs et de verdure que parfume l'abeille,
que balance le zephyr et où le rossignol bâtit son nid et fait
entendre sa plaintive mélodie.' (ATA, p. 66)

Alternatively the repetition of a structure may stress a single
change, such as the shift in emphasis from aural to visual
description :

' On entend le bruit des chaînes et les roulements de la
pesante artillerie. Partout brille l'acier, partout flottent les
drapeaux de la France.' (NAT, p. 195)

(c) *Vocabulary*

The extension of poetic vocabulary to prose and the resulting
lexical variety, is reflected in several aspects of the inversion
analysis. The low occurrence of *être* in attributive constructions
has already been mentioned (p. 255 above), and there are
parallel examples of a wider range of verbs in other inversion
structures, particularly where the *invertissant* is a place
adverbial, which is now frequently followed by a reflexive verb :

' " A quelque distance s'offroit une grotte dont l'entrée étoit
fermée per des framboisiers." ' (NAT, p. 280)

' Au-dessus des flots de l'armée se hérissoient les baïonnettes,
telles que ces lances du roseau qui tremblent...' (NAT, p. 302)

In other contexts an unusual co-occurrence of verb and subject

may find striking emphasis in inversion, as in the following
treatment of abstract subjects :

> ' Ainsi durant une nuit d'hiver brille une solitude où des
> tribus canadiennes célèbrent la fête de leurs génies.' (NAT,
> p. 199)
> ' Dans ces abîmes flottent des visions comme celle qui...'
> (NAT, p. 234)

Along with the low frequency of *être* there are few examples of
highly predictable verbs after a given *invertissant*. In the
following comment after a speech, Chateaubriand selects a less
usual combination with which to resume the narrative :

> ' Ainsi retentirent dans l'éternité ces paroles qui tombèrent
> de Soleil en Soleil, et descendirent ... jusqu'aux abîmes de la
> terre.' (NAT, p. 318)

(d) *Inversion and sound contrasts*

Sound, and in particular natural sound, is a *leitmotif* in all
three texts, and this is often stressed by inverted order. The
contrast between two sounds, or between a sound and some
other phenomenon, is frequently conveyed by the juxtaposition
of two orders. Thus in the following, inversion introduces an
enumeration, and the chiastic structure opposes the darkness
and noise :

> ' " Alors le grand Esprit couvre les montagnes d'épaisses
> ténèbres ; du milieu de ce vaste chaos s'élève un mugisse-
> ment confus formé par le fracas des vents, le gémissement
> des arbres, le hurlement des bêtes féroces, le bourdonne-
> ment..." ' (ATA, p. 39)

In *René* Chateaubriand, like Proust, uses sound to awaken
early memories and related ideas, which may again be introduced by an inversion :

> ' " Tout se trouve dans les rêveries enchantées où nous
> plonge le bruit de la cloche natale : religion, famille, patrie, et
> le berceau et la tombe, et le passé et l'avenir." ' (REN, p. 75)

Closely related to devices of enumeration are inversions which
either precede or follow lengthy comparisons involving sounds.
In the next example, the *invertissant* of the final clause reminds

the reader that the construction is comparative, and inverted
order stresses the nature of the simile, the movement and
sounds of nature compared with those of human behaviour :

> ' " Comme on voit les flots de la mer se briser pendant un
> orage, comme en automne les feuilles séchées sont enlevées
> par un tourbillon, ... comme un grand troupeau de cerfs
> brame au fond d'une forêt, *ainsi s'agitoit et murmuroit* le
> conseil." ' (ATA, p. 31)

Such inversions may, however, have a purely rhythmic function, in avoiding a *cadence mineure* :

> ' Le son que rend l'essieu d'or du monde en tournant sur
> lui-même.' (NAT, p. 229)
> ' " Les sons que rendent les passions dans le vide d'un cœur
> solitaire ressemblent au murmure que..." ' (REN, p. 83)

Invertissants which seem to play an individual role in this
type of comparison are prepositional phrases, the adjective
attribute *tel*, and the adverb *ainsi*. There seems to be only
one comparative clause *invertissant* of note, which occurs in the
opening sentence of *Les Natchez*, and which contains the
important opposition between the sounds of nature (*airs*) and
those familiar to humans, besides presenting the theme of
solitude. The use of *chanter* here is also significant and will be
mentioned again below :

> ' A l'ombre des forêts américaines, je veux chanter des airs
> de la solitude tels que n'en ont point encore entendu des
> oreilles mortelles.' (NAT, p. 189)

The preposition of the indirect object of a verb such as
succéder is particularly effective in emphasizing this type of
opposition, and it may be noted that this inversion generally
concludes a sentence. A relation between the sounds of man
and of nature is stated in the first example, with inversion
indicating the change of topic as the paragraph ends. In the
second example there is also a change of theme, as natural
sound is contrasted with its absence :

> ' A mesure que le bruit des hommes s'affoiblit, celui du
> désert augmente, et au tumulte des voix succèdent les
> plaintes du vent dans la forêt.' (ATA, p. 33)

' La mer fixe ses flots ; tout mouvement cessa, et au bruit des glaces brisées succéda un silence universel.' (NAT, p. 285)

Such inversion structures are not confined to this particular opposition, but are also used in contrasting light and dark, or natural and human characteristics, e.g.

' Mais bientôt à une clarté perpétuelle succéda une nuit sans fin.' (NAT, p. 285)

The attributive adjective *tel* is generally used to introduce natural sound in the course of a comparison, and in *Les Natchez* the inversion clause in this context is invariably followed by a temporal clause which locates the comparison more precisely, e.g.

' Les décharges des mousquets et des batteries font de la colline un effroyable chaos. Tels sont les mugissements, les ténèbres et les lueurs de l'Etna, lorsque le volcan se réveille.' (NAT, p. 311)

Finally there is an inversion following direct speech in which two human sounds are contrasted :

' Ainsi parle ou plutôt ainsi chante Adario, et les sauvages lui répondent par des hurlements.' (NAT, p. 304)

Here the replacement of the original verb by *chanter* underlines the author's preference for this word, which is reserved for lyrical and generally mystical passages, and assumes a value besides that of pure sound. This quality is emphasized here by the contrasting noise of the savages.

In addition to the features of Chateaubriand's style discussed above, inversion figures in a number of other devices. One example is its occurrence in a style which is highly reminiscent of Biblical prose :

' Un chant séraphique leur annonce le lieu où réside la Vierge qui renferma dans son flanc celui que l'univers ne peut contenir.' (NAT, p. 233)

The role of adjectives is also important, and anteposition is often related to inversion of the subject of which it is a part :

' A cet exercice des armes succèdent de savantes manœuvres.' (NAT, p. 200)

Thus, in conclusion, the high frequency of inversion in the works of Chateaubriand is clearly an indication of a new style of prose-writing. This is borne out by closer analysis of the examples, which are shown to differ from those of the last century, both in the choice of vocabulary and sentence structure, and the use of syntactic devices for rhythmical purposes.

(ii) MADAME DE STAËL, 'CORINNE'

Despite her professed aversion to the construction,[8] the frequency of inversion in Madame de Staël's *Corinne* is closest to the average for the texts of this period. Along with the previous text, it has the highest number of *invertissants* (56) (table 8.08), and consequently the lowest ratio of inversions to *invertissants* (table 8.08). Again, like Chateaubriand, the most common inversion types account for a relatively low proportion of examples, 67% (table 8.09). The major *invertissants* which do not occur in the text are adverbs of quantity and adverbial phrases of time and manner. On the other hand there are twelve examples of addition and transposition, eight of which contain adverbial *invertissants*. Table 8.10 shows that this variety in construction is offset by the highest occurrence of *être* in the five texts, 27%. Inversions are found in sentences of much the same length as those of Vigny and Stendhal (table 8.07), although there are rather more inverted subjects with dependent clauses (table 8.06). The inversions which have some bearing of the lyrical style of the novel are perhaps less striking than those connected with its Italian setting, both of which will now be considered.

(a) *The lyricism of Madame de Staël*

As already noted in the case of Rousseau (chapter VII), Madame de Staël's use of word-order has various stylistic functions in the expression of lyrical themes. For instance inverted order stresses topics in a lengthy digression on the

---

[8] ' Les inversions ne conviennent guère aux langues modernes ' (*De l'Allemagne*), quoted by S. Ullmann, *Style in the French Novel*, p. 149.

relation between music and sentiment in Book IX. In the following example, musical rhythm is linked with fleeting emotion, the first idea being emphasized by inversion :

> ' Le cœur bat plus vite en l'écoutant : la satisfaction que cause la régularité de la mesure, en rappelant la brieveté du temps, donne le besoin d'en jouir.' (p. 210)

A little later, a musical comparison is used to stress the idea of perfect emotion which is inevitably followed by sorrow. As before inversion emphasizes the musical element, and also forms a transition from the simile to the situation of the two characters :

> ' C'est un bien-être trop grand pour la nature humaine ; et l'âme vibre alors comme un instrument à l'unisson, que briserait une harmonie trop parfaite.' (p. 211)

Themes of religion, art and emotion are interwoven throughout the novel. In the following, the introduction of a religious theme is heightened by a lyrical metaphor, with inversion stressing both verb and object :

> ' " Je ne vous ai jamais entretenu de mes sentiments religieux ; permettez qu'aujourd'hui je vous en parle, peut-être dissiperai-je ainsi les nuages que j'ai vus s'élever dans votre esprit." ' (p. 228)

Elsewhere religious feeling mingles with the description of pagan ruins, and Classical or Christian works of art. An example of an indirect object *invertissant* links two such themes :

> '... l'on ne connaissait plus ... cette unité d'existence, ce naturel dans la manière d'être, qui tient encore du repos antique, Mais à ce repos est unie la profondeur de sentiments qui caractérise le christianisme.' (p. 188)

The liaison function of inversion is exploited here, both in the repetition of *repos*, and in the fact that the position of the verb reinforces the idea of unification. Another example occurs in the speech of Corinne as she talks of Saint Peter's, Rome :

> ' " Il y a quelque alliance des religions antiques et du christianisme dans l'effet que produit sur l'imagination l'intérieur de cet édifice." ' (p. 81)

and in this instance the intervening adverbial is stressed as well
as the delayed subject. The emphatic function of inversion in
this context is seen in Oswald's account of his impression of
Christian painting :

' " Ma plus forte objection ... contre les sujets chrétiens ...
c'est le sentiment pénible que fait éprouver l'image du sang,
des blessures, des supplices, bien que le plus noble enthousiasme ait animé les victimes." ' (p. 191)

Inverted order here permits the emphasis of a subject with
enumerated elements which express similar ideas.

Several examples in direct speech from Book X (entitled
La semaine sainte) show how inversion is used either to ennoble
the style, as in the first example by Corinne, or to emphasize a
familiar ideal as in the second by Oswald :

' " Je reconnais dans l'homme quelque chose de désintéressé,
et dût-on multiplier trop les magnificences religieuses, j'aime
cette prodigalité des richesses terrestres pour une autre
vie..." ' (p. 232)

' " Corinne, comment pourrait-on se préparer par cette
disposition aux sacrifices sans nombre qu'exige de nous le
devoir ? " ' (p. 234)

A similar idea is also stressed by inversion in an earlier speech
by Oswald, with the subject concluding a paragraph :

' "... et l'on n'est pas, comme chez nous, longtemps absorbé
dans les pensées et les sentiments que fait naître l'examen
rigoureux de sa conduite et de son cœur." ' (p. 231)

Finally the Italian setting is also an important part of the
lyricism of *Corinne*, and underlies the following opposition in
which both elements are stressed by inversion, but with the
two subjects emphasizing the second idea more strongly :

' " Il ne faut pas non plus, pour les goûter (les arts), la gaîté
qu'inspire la société, mais la sérénité que fait naître un beau
jour, un beau climat." ' (p. 191)

In the next example, inversion after the addition of *c'est ... que*
underlines an important idea in Corinne's discussion of the
musical qualities of the Italian language, with the two key
adjectives in final position :

' " Vous sentez que c'est au milieu des arts et sous un beau ciel que s'est formé ce langage mélodieux et coloré." ' (p. 63)

(*b*) *Descriptive technique in* ' *Corinne* '

Inversion is employed in two ways in the descriptive passages of *Corinne*, firstly to ensure clarity and the logical sequence of ideas, and secondly to emphasize important details, often with a didactic intention. In examples of the first type, the *invertissants* are generally place adverbials, and the construction often has several subjects, or a subject followed by a dependent clause :

' A quelque distance, des deux côtés de l'obélisque, s'élèvent deux fontaines dont l'eau jaillit perpétuellement et retombe avec abondance en cascade dans les airs.' (p. 79)

Alternatively the subject may be repeated in the subsequent sentence :

' Dans l'intérieur du sanctuaire du Panthéon sont les bustes de nos artistes les plus célèbres : ils décorent les niches où...' (p. 75)

The following is the only example in which a clause separates *invertissant* and verb, and the inverted order here maintains a logical sentence structure :

' Au fond de la salle où elle fut reçue, étaient placés le sénateur qui devait la couronner et les conservateurs du sénat.' (p. 37)

The emphatic inversion structure which occurs most frequently is *c'est ... que* and a place adverbial :

' C'est sur le mont Aventin que furent placés les temples de la Pudeur patricienne et de la Pudeur plébéienne.' (p. 94)

The adverb *là* may be employed to sum up preceding description, and the repetition of this construction in the following example is additionally effective in that it forms a chiasmus :

' C'était là qu'existaient la maison de Salluste et celle de Pompée ; c'est aussi là que le pape a maintenant fixé son séjour.' (p. 97)

This use of contrasting orders to lend variety to the description is not uncommon, and in the following the more emphatic construction again precedes the one with direct order :

> ' C'est là que se promenaient les orateurs de Rome, en sortant du Forum ; c'est là que César et Pompée se rencontraient comme de simples citoyens, et qu'ils...' (p. 95)

Emphatic inversion with a didactic function is also exemplified in the following :

> ' " La mesure des vers, les rimes harmonieuses, ces terminaisons rapides, composées de deux syllabes brèves dont les sons glissent en effet, comme l'indique leur nom (' sdruccioli '), imitent..." ' (p. 145)

> ' " C'est d'ici ... que l'on devrait apercevoir Saint-Pierre, et c'est jusqu'ici que les colonnes qui le précèdent devaient s'étendre : tel était le superbe plan de Michel-Ange." '
> (p. 78)

both these inversions occurring in the speech of Corinne. The inclusion of an Italian word in the first example is both instructive and evocative, and is stressed by the explanatory clause introduced by the *invertissant comme*. The comment introduced by *tel* in the second argument is made more emphatic by the preposed adjective.

(c) *Other uses of inversion : conclusion*

While no more than an average proportion of inverted subjects occur in key positions in this text (table 8.04), the use of this emphatic device is fairly marked in *Corinne*. For instance, the following examples are typical of many constructions in which the proper names of the protagonists are stressed in this way :

> ' Il (Oswald) ne comprenait pas comment une seule personne pouvait réunir tout ce que possedait Corinne.' (p. 56)

> ' A ce nom, Corinne se troubla visiblement, et refusa d'une voie (*sic*) émue ce que désirait Oswald.' (p. 140)

Thus inversion permits the opposition between one character and the other, and the frequent repetition of such structures is also suggestive of their involvement with each other. It is noticeable that Madame de Staël repeats proper names where other writers might use a pronoun, and inverted order does to a certain extent prevent this tendency from becoming monotonous. The following sentence opens a paragraph, which increases the emphasis on the name of Oswald, while the order of the clauses and the final inversion gradually builds up a link between the characters:

> ' Oswald était tellement absorbé dans ses réflexions, des idées si nouvelles l'occupaient tant, qu'il ne remarqua point les lieux antiques et célèbres à travers lesquels passait le char de Corinne.' (p. 36)

There is one example of an inversion concluding a chapter in this novel:

> ' Mais ces paroles obligeantes se perdirent dans les airs au milieu de ... tout ce bruit de départ, quelquefois triste, quelquefois enivrant, selon la crainte ou l'espoir qu'inspirent les nouvelles chances de la destinée.' (p. 241)

This is a particularly effective device in that the stressed subject may be said to contain the elements of the development of the remainder of the novel.

The inversions which occur in conversation in the course of this novel do not differ significantly from those in the narrative. There are twice as many spoken by Corinne (32) as by Oswald (16), the rest occurring in the speech of minor characters. In addition to the examples already quoted above (p. 269), the following instances of zero *invertissant* may be noted in the speech of Corinne:

> ' " Vient ensuite celle (époque) où les talents et la gloire n'attiraient que la malheur et l'insulte." ' (p. 197)

> ' " Viennent ensuite, continua Corinne, les tableaux dramatiques tirés de quatre grands poëtes." ' (p. 198)

Just as the occurrence of inversion in this text is no more than the average for this period, so there seems to be little of outstanding interest in the way in which the device is employed. Its function in the style of Madame de Staël is primarily emphatic, and thus inversion stresses lyrical themes and aspects of the background of the novel, sometimes underlining the didactic intention. The lack of any very distinctive use of word-order reflects perhaps the clear, but unexceptional, style of the authoress.

(iii) A. DE VIGNY, 'CINQ-MARS'

The analysis of the three middle novels of this period, that is *Corinne, Cinq-Mars*, and *Le rouge et le noir*, shows that they all share a fairly low inversion frequency, between the high rates of Chateaubriand and Balzac (table 8.01). There are also similarities in sentence length, all three texts having an approximately equal number of inversions in longer sentences, as compared with the short constructions of Chateaubriand and the much longer ones of Balzac (table 8.07). However, Vigny and Chateaubriand, the two major Romantic writers, share a low occurrence of *être* in inversion structures (table 8.10).

Despite the fact that there are fewer inversions in *Cinq-Mars*, this novel has the highest proportion of speech examples of the five, 30% (table 8.03), 73% of which have an immobile *invertissant*, as compared with 67% in the whole work. There is also a marked tendency for inversion to occur in final position (38%) as opposed to initial position (29%), although in de Staël and Stendhal the distribution is almost even (table 8.04). Table 8.08 shows that in *Cinq-Mars*, as in *Le rouge et le noir*, there is a comparatively low range of *invertissants*, and the majority of examples, 49%, occur in relative constructions (table 8.09).

(a) *The technique of the historical novel*

As in other forms of the novel, the presence of the author is here occasionally stressed by the use of inversion. In the following examples, the *invertissant* introduces an explanatory aside :

> ' Des archers à barbe pointue ... renfermaient dans cette double ligne deux lignes pareilles de pénitents gris ; du moins donnerons-nous ce nom, connu dans quelques provinces du midi de la France, à des hommes revêtus d'une longue robe de cette couleur, qui...' (p. 53)

Elsewhere inversion is used to emphasize the change of subject:

> ' A présent que la procession diabolique est entrée dans la
> salle de son spectacle, et tandis qu'elle arrange sa sanglante
> représentation, voyons ce qu'avait fait Cinq-Mars au milieu
> des spectateurs en émoi.' (p. 56)

The author's presence which has already been indicated by the
opening conjunction is reintroduced by the antecedent *voyons*,
and this simple concluding structure contrasts with the
preceding clauses, in which subordination and adjective
position are both effective. However, uses of inversion which
are more typical of this genre are found in passages which
suggest an interpretation of history, linking the events of the
novel to a generalization or to a specific point in time, and also
in descriptive passages, whether factual or fanciful.

An inverted subject with a dependent clause is often used as
a transitional device in narrative, and in the next example it
links historical detail and Vigny's interpretation of it, by
means of a reference to his source of information:

> '... et le Cardinal écrivit à la hâte cet ordre, que les manuscrits
> contemporains nous ont transmis, et que pourrent imiter les
> diplimates de nos jours, qui...' (p. 144)

A more direct link is effected in the following, where the author
uses this transition to introduce a generalization:

> ' Cependant la maladie du Roi jetait la France dans un
> trouble que ressentaient toujours les Etats mal affermis aux
> approches de la mort des princes.' (p. 238)

Such a generalization may be emphasized, both by the length
of its inverted subject and its final position in the paragraph,
as in the first example, and by the length of the dependent
clause, also concluding a paragraph, as in the second:

> ' Ce devait être quelques-uns de ces changements occultes,
> d'où naissent, dans les monarchies sans base, des bouleverse-
> ments effroyables et de longues et sanglantes dissensions.'
> (p. 186)

> '... et vivant encore, on le regrettait déjà, comme si chacun
> eût désiré de recevoir la confidence de ses peines avant qu'il
> n'emportât avec lui le grand secret de ce que souffrent ces

hommes placés si haut qu'ils ne voient dans leur avenir que
leur tombe.' (p. 239)

Such emphasis may also be used to effect when awareness of
future events is expressed through the premonitions of the
characters. In the next examples the key word concludes
firstly a sentence and secondly the whole speech :

' " Vous assisterez peut-être à ces conseils où se règle la
destinée des nations." ' (pp. 154–55)

' " Je compte ... sur un coup de dés. Si sa volonté peut cette
fois durer quelques heures, j'ai gagné ; c'est un dernier
calcul auquel est suspendue ma destinée." ' (p. 235)

Much of the background detail is introduced by means of
routine adverb of place *invertissants*, often opening a paragraph, thus :

' Devant une très petite table entourée de fauteuils dorés,
était debout le roi Louis XIII, environné des grands officiers
de la couronne ; son costume était fort élégant.' (p. 119)

Inversion may also enhance historical detail by contrastive
stress,

' Les révoltes de l'Angleterre et celles de l'Espagne et du
Portugal faisaient admirer d'autant plus le calme dont
jouissait la France.' (p. 185)

or by emphasizing the feelings of the protagonists :

' Le ministre ... descendit de cheval péniblement et en jetant
quelques cris involontaires que lui arrachaient ses douleurs ;
mais il les dompta et s'assit sur l'affût d'une canon.' (p. 144)

In the next example the detailed nature of the comparison is
underlined both by the repetition of the verb and by its
change of tense :

' Louis XIII vint se placer à ses côtés, mais il vint comme
vient l'élève adolescent forcé de reconnaître que son maître
a raison.' (p. 140)

In the following, the main theme is colour, and the stylistic
effect lies in the contrast between *blancheur éclatante* and the
couleur brune, effected firstly by stressing the latter through
inversion, and secondly by chiasmus ; although the nouns
and adjectives are in parallel positions, the actual idea of

colour is conveyed in the substantive in the first phrase and in the qualifying adjective in the second :

> ' Mais la blancheur éclatante de son visage, que relevait encore la couleur brune de son capuchon, attirait d'abord tous les regards ; ses yeux noirs semblaient porter l'empreinte d'une profonde et brûlante passion.' (p. 53)

(b) *Direct speech*

Much of the dominant theme of *Cinq-Mars*, the social importance of the aristocracy, is conveyed through the speech of the various characters. As already mentioned (p. 271) there is a fairly high proportion of inversions in conversation, and these examples reveal the noble, idealized style of many of the speakers, which contrasts with the conversation of the lower classes. The rhetoric of such speech is, however, at times somewhat improbable, and the number of ' elegant ' inversions in conversation suggests the unreal nature of the characters concerned.

The novel's ideal is often expressed through the words of *Cinq-Mars*, frequently couched in high-flown and unnatural language, as in the following hypothetical construction :

> ' " Ma pensée entière, la pensée de l'homme juste, se dévoilera aux regards du Roi même s'il l'interroge, dût-elle me couter la tête." ' (p. 155)

Even when revealing his idealist sentiments in a series of short sentences, the hero lapses into a more rhetorical tone with a somewhat literary inversion :

> ' " L'horreur que m'inspire cet homme est passée dans mon sang." ' (p. 235)

Other factors, such as the separation of verb and subject and the elaboration of both verb and subject appear in his speech on youth and destiny, e.g.

> ' " Avec un chef de vingt-deux ans s'est conçue, même et va s'exécuter la plus vaste, la plus juste, la plus salutaire des entreprises." ' (p. 272)

The rhetoric of *Cinq-Mars* is echoed by that of de Thou, as seen in examples (p. 273) above.

The minor characters often reflect, through their syntax, the social superiority of the person whom they address. There is, for example, the formula ' Si tel est votre bon plaisir ' (pp. 116 and 160). A monk speaking to Richelieu uses the following elegant structure, in which the stressed subject concludes his speech :

' " Si Monseigneur veut se souvenir de mes conseils donnés à Narbonne, il conviendra que j'avais un juste pressentiment des chagrins que lui causerait un jour ce jeune homme." ' (pp. 159–60)

In his turn the Cardinal opens his remarks to the king with an inversion :

' " Derrière cette colline, Sire, sont en colonne six régiments de dragons et les carabins de La Roque." ' (p. 142)

Elsewhere, a nun says to Richelieu :

' " Sous votre cuirasse doit battre un noble cœur." ' (p. 168)

When talking among themselves, soldiers and others use a more natural form of dialogue, and inversion, when it does occur, is of a routine nature, although in the following example it also aids an opposition between subjects :

' " Ah ! ah ! est-il bête ! ... il écoute ce que disent les bourgeois."
" ... "
" Tu ne sais donc pas ce que disait ma mère blanc bec ? reprenait gravement le plus vieux..." ' (p. 164)

Comments on current speech are also common, whether they are facetious,

' "... je te prierais de voyager avec moi sur le fleuve de Tendre, comme disent les grandes dames de Paris..." ' (p. 166)

or critical from a political point of view :

' " Nous autres, vieux compagnons d'armes du feu roi, nous entendons mal la langue que parle la Cour nouvelle, et elle ne sait plus la nôtre." ' (p. 12)

(c) *Narrative style*

While many of the inversions in *Cinq-Mars* are similar to those already noted in the poetic prose of Chateaubriand, it will be seen from the examples below that in the narrative prose of Vigny they are used to quite different stylistic effects. Whereas the inversions in descriptive passages in Chateaubriand and the use of various rhetorical constructions all contribute to a poetic prose style where considerations of harmony and rhythm predominate, the same structures in *Cinq-Mars* indicate instead a style which is carefully contrived as a vehicle for its historical content, but which at the same time is not lacking in rhythm and artistic value.

Adverbial phrase *invertissants*, which in Chateaubriand and de Staël were frequently used in natural or artistic description, are here seen as marking progressions in the factual narrative. In the following there is an unusual accumulation of inversions to stress the entrance of the main characters in a new scene, giving a somewhat majestic note :

'... lorsque ... l'obscurité dans laquelle était l'église cessa tout à coup ; ses deux grandes portes s'ouvrirent et, à la lueur d'un nombre infini de flambeaux, parurent tous les juges et les ecclésiastiques entourés de gardes ; au milieu d'eux s'avançait Urbain...' (p. 82)

The next example, inverted order permits a lengthy subject as well as stressing the temporal sequence in a rapid succession of scenes :

' Le jour commençait à poindre, et l'on vit que, du bout de l'île Saint-Louis, accourait en effet une foule d'hommes, de femmes et d'enfants de la lie du peuple, poussant au ciel et vers le Louvre d'étranges vociférations.' (p. 191)

A similar construction is also used to great effect in a very different context, the portrayal of King Louis at Chambord in ch. XIX :

' Entre ses yeux et les pages qu'il s'efforçait de lire, passaient de brillants cortèges, des armées victorieuses, des peuples transportés d'amour : il se voyait puissant, combattant, triomphateur, adoré.' (p. 239)

The inversion here appears to be necessary only to introduce a triple subject, with changes in adjective position varying the structure. However, the clause between *invertissant* and verb, with its direct order, provides an additional contrast between reality and the King's ideal, the pathos of which becomes apparent in the concluding sentence, related by its subject to the interposed clause.

As in Chateaubriand, inverted order may stress certain lexical items, for instance in the following paragraph opening :

'Ainsi se termina cette échauffourée, qui semblait pouvoir enfanter de grands malheurs ; personne n'y fut tué.' (p. 193)

In the next example the inversion clause concludes a paragraph in which the stressed features give a brief but effective indication of the type of character speaking :

'"J'ai tous les noms et signalements" dit avec empressement le juge secret, inclinant jusqu'au fauteuil sa grande taille et son visage olivâtre et maigre, que sillonnait un rire servile.' (p. 161)

Finally, a subject stressed both by its inverted position at the beginning of a paragraph, and by the anteposition of the adjective, serves to sum up the preceding narrative, and introduces a renewed progression in time :

'Le rire qu'avait excité la sanglante plaisanterie du vieux ministre durait encore, lorsque la porte du cabinet s'ouvrit, et un page annonça plusieurs courriers qui arrivaient...' (p. 105)

To conclude, however, the affinity between the style of Vigny and that of the two earlier authors is reflected in a number of examples which obtain similar effects in parallel contexts. Thus an indirect object *invertissant* in a chiastic structure echoes the contrast in content, as in the sound oppositions of Chateaubriand (pp. 263–64 above) :

'L'orage semblait donc entièrement apaisé, et aux agitations violentes de la matinée succédait un calme fort doux.' (p. 125)

Again reminiscent of Chateaubriand are the relative inversions in the course of natural description, as in that with which the novel opens :

'Des vallons peuplés de jolies maisons blanches qu'entourent

des bosquets, des coteaux jaunis par les vignes ou blanchis
par les fleurs du cerisier ... des jardins de roses d'où sort tout
à coup une tour élancée, tout rappelle la fécondité de la
terre.' (pp. 27–28)

Vigny also uses relative *invertissants* to introduce occasional
artistic references, which, because of their infrequency, are
perhaps more effective than those of Madame de Staël :

'... et son regard ... devint sublime comme celui du jeune
évangeliste qu'inventa Raphaël, car la lumière s'y réfléchis-
sait encore.' (p. 265)

'... et le gros livre glissa sur sa robe jusqu'au coussin de
velours où s'appuyaient ses pieds, et où reposèrent molle-
ment la belle Astrée et le galant Céladon, moins immobile
que...' (p. 211)

(iv) STENDHAL, 'LE ROUGE ET LE NOIR'

The frequency of inversion in *Le rouge et le noir* is the lowest
of the five texts, and there are also fewer *invertissants* (39).
Thus although relative constructions account for an average
proportion of the inversions (table 8.09), there are only six
invertissants represented. Similarly, while the same table
shows that this text, along with Chateaubriand, has the
highest proportion of inversions after a modal adverb (19%),
as in the other texts there are only a small number of *invertissants* in this category. Although the text contains a few less
usual examples of inversion, such as that after a subordinate
clause (see p. 253 above), many constructions commonly
found with inverted order do not occur, such as time adverbials
and prepositional phrases, and there are few *invertissants*
which are adverbial phrases of place.

Stendhal does not include many inversions in conversation,
and these occur in the lowest proportion of the five texts
(table 8.03). Furthermore the context of the examples tends
to be quite simple, with few inversions occurring in sentences
longer than four clauses (table 8.07) and only 3% of the
examples have more than one subject. An outstanding feature,
however, is the proportion which occupy key positions with

respect to the paragraph (table 8.04), a characteristic also noted in the analysis of Chateaubriand. On the other hand, the initial analysis of word-order shows little in common with the style of Balzac in this respect, there being an unusually high inversion frequency in *Le Père Goriot*, and an average rate of occurrence of various features which are found less commonly in Stendhal.

(a) *Inversion in a documentary style*

The documentary features of *Le rouge et le noir* are not confined to details of contemporary society, although these are of course frequently introduced and inversion is often used in this context, for example where it facilitates enumeration :

'... ce qui surnageait des innombrables mensonges, sottes interprétations, discussions ridicules ... dont avaient été l'objet successivement le roi, l'évêque d'Agde, le marquis de la Molle, les dix mille bouteilles de vin, le pauvre tombé de Meirod ... ce fut l'indécence extrême d'avoir " bombardé " ... Julien Sorel...' (p. 112)

The device is, however, more closely related to content and its stylistic value is consequently more apparent, in two other aspects of Stendhal's style, namely his treatment of description and his explicitness in the portrayal of emotion. It will be noted that in nearly all the following examples, inversion occurs at the beginning or end of the sentence, its position being indicative of its emphatic function.

The passages of natural description in the novel are generally short and serve as background to the action, and inversion may be used to underline the topographical setting, thus :

'... Julien poursuivait son chemin gaiement au milieu des plus beaux aspects que puissent présenter les scènes de montagnes. Il fallait traverser la grande chaîne au nord de montagnes.' (p. 71)

In the same way it may stress human presence and thus curtail a possible poetic digression :

' Enfin il atteignit le sommet de la grande montagne, près duquel il fallait passer pour arriver, par cette route de traverse, à la vallée solitaire qu'habitait Fouqué, le jeune marchand de bois son ami.' (p. 72)

In physical description, inverted order may emphasize a visual contrast as in the following where colour predominates :

'Entre ces joues rouges et ce front blanc, brillaient deux petits yeux noirs faits pour effrayer le plus brave.' (p. 169)

In the presentation of emotions, Stendhal uses familiar inversion constructions to render these explicit. In both of the following examples a cliché construction explains the cause of the emotion, and its agent is the subject of subsequent sentences :

'Madame de Rênal s'approcha, distraite un instant de l'amer chagrin que lui donnait l'arrivée du précepteur. Julien ... ne la voyait pas s'avancer.' (p. 26)

'Cette résistance intérieure fut le premier sentiment pénible que lui causa Julien. Jusque-là le nom de Julien...' (p. 35)

Inversion constructions may also act as introductory comments,

'Après des combats affreux, Madame de Rênal osa enfin lui dire, d'une voix tremblante, et où se peignait toute sa passion...' (p. 77)

or again as an aside in the course of the description of ideas :

'Les âmes qui s'émeuvent ainsi sont bonnes tout au plus à produire un artiste. Ici éclate dans tout son jour la présomption de Julien.' (p. 193)

The most common *invertissant* in such commentaries is, however, *tel*, which may indicate the presence of the author, besides having explanatory force. In the first example the author's comment forms a parenthesis within the main construction, and in the second two *tel* clauses are integrated into the narrative :

'Tel était l'effet de la force, et, si j'ose parler ainsi, de la grandeur des mouvements de passion qui bouleversaient l'âme de ce jeune ambitieux.' (p. 64)

'On rit beaucoup, on admira ; tel est l'esprit à l'usage de Verrières. Julien était déjà debout, tout le monde se leva malgré le décorum ; tel est l'empire du génie.' (p. 141)

The comparative *tel que* has a similar function, but here it introduces comments on contemporary institutions, with inversion ensuring an emphatic position :

'Etrange effet du mariage, tel que l'a fait le XIXe siècle ! ' (p. 155)

'Ce sentiment apprécie la "justice distributive", telle que nous la donnent nos tribunaux, à sa valeur et même au-dessous de sa valeur.' (p. 182)

Allusions to historical detail are also emphasized as in the next parenthesis which comprises a complete paragraph :

'Le lecteur, qui sourit peut-être, daignerait-il se souvenir de toutes les fautes que fit, en mangeant un œuf, l'abbé Delille invité à déjeuner chez une grande dame de la cour de Louis XVI.' (p. 180)

Finally there is a reference to regional characteristics where the subject occupies a key position and is expanded in the subsequent sentence :

'Il ne l'écouta pas moins avec cet air de tristesse mécontente et de désintérêt dont sait si bien se revêtir la finesse des habitants de ces montagnes. Esclaves du temps de la domination espagnole, ils...' (p. 15)

This attention to detail, devoid of extravagance, seems to bear out, along with the examples above, Bardèche's comment on Stendhal's technique :

'Alors toute cette documentation sur la province, aussi importante que chez Balzac, et peut-être même plus diverse, plus riche, n'est pas pour le lecteur qu'une documentation.' [9]

and in this word-order is important in its function of objective emphasis on the key elements.

(b) *Inversions in key positions*

The liaison function of inversion in this text is stressed by its frequent occurrence at the beginning or end of an important unit of speech, particularly the paragraph (table 8.04). There

---

[9] M. Bardèche, *Stendhal romancier*, Paris, 1947, p. 219.

K

are two types of liaison effected in this way, the first being temporal, mainly involving the *invertissant à peine*. The verbs in nearly all these examples represent movement or a change in state, and the predicate is underlined by inversion and contrasts with the action of the subsequent clause, e.g.

' A peine M. Castanède fut-il remonté chez lui, que les élèves se divisèrent en groupes.' (p. 187)

This change, however, may be emotional rather than physical, as in the following :

' A peine fut-elle délivrée de la crainte d'être surprise par son mari, que l'horreur que lui causait cette boîte fut sur le point de la faire décidément se trouver mal.' (p. 58)

The second type of liaison concerns the association of objects or places. Thus the petition mentioned in chapter XIX is followed by a marginal note ; the *invertissant* at the beginning of the paragraph refers back to the one, and the subject introduces the other :

' En marge de cette pétition était une apostille signée " De Meirod " et qui commençait par cette ligne...' (p. 112)

An adverbial phrase *invertissant* may also be used to resume the narrative after a digressive paragraph, as in the following, where the author's attention is diverted from the main action by the description of a door, which recurs in the *invertissant* opening the new paragraph :

' Cet ouvrage avait l'air fait de la veille.

Devant la porte étaient réunies à genoux vingt-quatre jeunes filles, appartenant aux familles les plus distinguées de Verrières.' (p. 108)

In the following liaison inversion the subject which concludes the paragraph is repeated in the new one, where it is developed at greater length :

' Julien la regarda froidement avec des yeux où se peignait le plus souverain mépris.

Ce regard étonna Madame Derville, et...' (p. 56)

There is an inversion with a similar function in sentence final position later in the novel, marking the end of a straightforward narrative passage. The sentence which develops the inverted subject is in free indirect construction, and this in turn leads to the expression of the thoughts of the Abbé Pirard :

> ' Il ne savait pas que M. Pirard avait reçu et jeté au feu quelques lettres timbrées de Dijon, et où, malgré les formes du style le plus convenable, perçait la passion le plus vive. De grands remords semblaient combattre cet amour.' (p. 177)

Thus inversions in important positions, whether initial or final, have a clear co-ordinating function, which also at times relates to the overall style of the work.

(c) *Emphasis on contemporary themes and local colour*

Although Stendhal's ' génie de pamphlet ' [10] is not fully revealed by the inversion examples, there are nonetheless instances of contemporary issues receiving stress from inverted order, such as the following parenthesis concerning Biblical exegesis :

> ' (Julien venait de lui parler, sans être interrogé à ce sujet, du temps " veritable " où avaient été écrits la Genèse, le Pentateuque, etc.) ' (p. 172)

The Napoleonic *leitmotif* is naturally important, and occasionally references to battle themes and imagery are highlighted by inversion. Thus in this example the logical subject, tales of war which impressed the young Sorel, is given full emphasis by its position in the sentence, the grammatical subject being neatly disposed of by means of inversion :

> ' Plus tard il écoutait avec transport les récits des batailles du pont de Lodi, d'Arcole, de Rivoli, que lui faisait le vieux chirurgien-major.' (p. 23)

Lexical choice may also be stressed by word-order. The importance of Italian for local colour in the *Chartreuse de Parme* has already been noted,[11] and some evidence of this persists in *Le rouge et le noir*. For instance the learned *mezzo-termine* for

---

[10] Bardèche, *Ibid.*, p. 192.
[11] S. Ullmann, *Style in the French Novel*, ch. 1.

moyen terme is brought out both by inversion, and by its
position at the end of a paragraph :

> 'Il voulait cacher l'admiration que lui donnait le savant
> mezzo-termine inventé par le précepteur de ses enfants.'
> (p. 41)

In the same way Stendhal indicates contemporary attitudes to
certain words, as in the following, which also concludes a
paragraph :

> 'Les enfants étaient ravis de ce seul mot "cabaret", que
> prononce avec tant de plaisir la pruderie moderne.' (p. 145)

Political ideas may be expressed in this way, as well as the
many references to the commercial interests of the various
characters of the liberal Fouqué :

> '"... il vaut mieux gagner cent louis dans un bon commerce
> de bois, dont on est le maître, que de recevoir quatre mille
> francs d'un gouvernement, fût-il celui du roi Salomon."'
> (p. 213)

The second is indicated by the frequent association of a
relative *invertissant* and a verb such as *coûter* or *offrir*; the
first example stresses the commercial aspects of the Church,
and the second those of society :

> 'Plus tard il entra dans les fonctions de Julien de vérifier les
> comptes de ce qu'avait coûté cette cérémonie.' (p. 107)

> '"J'allais au petit théâtre de San-Carlino, où j'entendais une
> musique des dieux : mais ô ciel ! comment faire pour réunir
> les huit sous que coûte l'entrée du parterre ?'" (p. 152)

As in the earlier texts analysed, inversion occurs sporadically
in *Le rouge et le noir* in various other stylistic functions. In the
following, for instance, the juxtaposition of two orders reflects
the opposing concepts expressed :

> 'Telle princesse ... prête infiniment plus d'attention à ce que
> ses gentilshommes font autour d'elle, que cette femme si
> douce, si modeste en apparence, n'en donnait à tout ce que
> disait ou faisait son mari.' (p. 36)

There are instances of emphasis on inverted subjects in closely
similar contexts, a device also used by Balzac, e.g.

' Un coup violent fit voler dans le ruisseau le livre que tenait Julien ; un second coup...' (p. 17)

' En passant, il regarda tristement le ruisseau où était tombé son livre...' (p. 17)

Thus inverted word-order is, in addition to its other stylistic functions, a convenient means of expression in a primarily documentary style, where emphasis is frequently achieved by position in the sentence, as Stendhal recognized,[12] but it is in Balzac that these devices are exploited to the full. In the *Père Goriot* a more extensive use of inversion will emphasize those aspects of literary technique already present in Stendhal, and others which have not yet been fully developed.

(v) H. DE BALZAC, 'LE PÈRE GORIOT'

The 310 inversions in *Le Père Goriot* represent the highest frequency for the period. The author's partiality for inverted order is further revealed by an analysis of his longer *Splendeurs et misères* [13] where there are at least 400 inversions. More than half the inversions in the *Père Goriot* are relatives (table 8.09), and the number of *invertissants* which occur is about average for these texts (table 8.08). The detailed analysis of the constructions shows that these do not differ greatly from the other contemporary novels, except in that Balzac has the highest occurrence of inversion in comparative structures (table 8.09) and also in longer sentences (table 8.07). A feature which will have some stylistic importance is the high proportion of inversions in final position, particularly at the end of a sentence, 35% (table 8.04). More important, however, is the distribution of the inversions in speech, 24% of the total, as compared with the overall distribution, and this will be examined along with other features of Balzac's style, namely the relation between structure and content, and his descriptive technique.

---

[12] ' Il y a souvent une physionomie dans la position des mots, qu'aucune traduction ne saurait rendre ' (*La Chartreuse de Parme*) quoted by Ullmann, *Ibid.*, p. 146.

[13] See Ullmann, *Ibid.*, ch. 4.

(a) *Inversion in direct speech*

1. Distribution

The number of inversions in conversation is about average for the period, and their distribution largely coincides with that of all the inversions for the texts as regards the basic operations. Within these categories, however, there is considerable variation. For instance whereas constructions with relative *invertissants* account for 53% of the total examples, they represent only about 30% of those in conversation. On the other hand the 11% comparative inversions in the novel, already shown to be unusually high, is easily surpassed by the proportion in direct speech, nearly 20%. There are also more inversions in indirect constructions and after modal adverbs in conversation, 18% and 23% respectively, as compared with 7% and 15% in the text as a whole. The types of *invertissant* not found at all in direct speech include concessives, temporal clauses, attributives, prepositional phrases and adverbial phrases of place, of which there are fifteen examples in the text. Thus in spite of the greatly reduced number of relative inversions, there is in general less variety in the conversational examples, with the four main inversion types accounting for 91% as against 86% in the narrative.

2. Characters

The characters in whose speech inversion is most frequent are Vautrin (sixteen examples), Eugène de Rastignac (ten), Delphine (eight) and Goriot, who along with Madame Vauquer and Madame de Beauséant has five examples. Of the remainder twenty-one examples are spoken by women and fifteen by men, the extra one being a comment attributed to the reader. The most interesting examples are of course those found in the speech of Vautrin, which clearly indicate the various aspects of his character, and further suggest that certain types of inversion are not to be associated with elevated speech. Thus for instance the familiar construction of a relative inversion whose subject has a dependent clause appears couched in argotic terms :

' " Vous ne patouillerez pas longtemps dans les marécages où vivent les crapoussins qui nous entourent ici." ' (p. 181) Elsewhere Vautrin uses terms which are far from literary in conjunction with a more formal construction, thus :

' " Je parierais ma tête contre un pied de cette salade que vous donnerez dans un guêpier chez la première femme qui vous plaira, fût-elle riche, belle et jeune." ' (p. 124)

The style of Vautrin's speech also serves as a subtle indication of underlying deception, as in the following where inversion introduces an ironic comment :

' " Un forçat de la trempe de Collin, ici présent, est un homme ... qui proteste contre les profondes déceptions du contrat social, comme dit Jean-Jacques, dont je me glorifie d'être l'élève." ' (p. 226)

Irony is made more explicit in the next compound inversion :

' " Aussi l'honnête homme est-il l'ennemi commun. Mais que croyez-vous que soit l'honnête homme ? " ' (pp. 124–25)

Another side of Vautrin's character is revealed in more conventional language through his comments on contemporary society. In one passage an apparently exotic comparison is stressed by the final inversion, although here too there is an element of irony :

' " Paris ... est comme une forêt du Nouveau-Monde, où s'agitent vingt espèces de peuplades sauvages ... qui vivent du produit que donnent les différentes classes sociales ; vous êtes un chasseur des millions." ' (p. 128)

It might also be noted that Vautrin's philosophy is summed up in a single passage in which all three examples in the text of the *invertissant là* are found :

' " Certes, là est la vertu dans toute la fleur de sa bêtise, mais là est la misère (...). Voilà la vie telle qu'elle est ... sachez seulement vous bien débarbouiller ; là est toute la morale de notre époque." ' (p. 125)

Finally there are three examples of other inversion operations in his speech, all of which contain ironic references to women, as in the example quoted above and in the following :

' " Et la femme se trouve si heureuse et si belle aux heures où

elle est forte, qu'elle préfère à tous les hommes celui dont la force est énorme, fût-elle en danger d'être brisée par lui." '
(pp. 120–21)

Thus the syntax of Vautrin is revealing in that the same construction may be used to very different effects, while in each case the terms correspond to an aspect of the speaker's character.

The inversions in the speech of the other main characters also indicate several of the ideas for which they stand. For example the comparisons used by Eugène suggest a parallel between the academic and the student of life :

' " En deux mots, ce brigand m'a dit plus de choses sur la vertu que ne m'en ont dit les hommes et les livres." ' (p. 133)

In other constructions one idea may be emphasized rather than the other :

' " Il serait donc aussi fort que l'était Auguste, roi de Pologne ? " se dit Eugène quand la barre ronde fut à peu près façonnée.' (p. 46)

Eugène is also the only character besides Vautrin to use deletion and transposition structures, suggesting perhaps a linguistic affinity with one of Vautrin's many aspects.

By contrast all four of the relative inversions in Goriot's speech have an emphatic function, the subjects generally being of importance in his life. Two of them are in a strong final position, and all bring out a certain pathos, e.g.

' " Ceci ... est le premier présent que m'a fait ma femme, le jour de notre anniversaire." ' (p. 27)

' " Ce n'est rien en comparaison de la douleur que m'a causée le premier regard par lequel Anastasie m'a fait comprendre que je venais de dire une bêtise qui l'humiliait." '
(p. 290)

The remaining inversion, after a comparative *comme*, is unexceptional.

The inversions in the conversation of other characters may have contrasting functions. Thus two examples from Madame de Beauséant show firstly in general terms a parallel structure with contrasting orders, reinforced by a change in adjectival position, and secondly a direct unrefined attack, the subject being stressed by compound inversion :

> ' " Vous sonderez combien est profonde la corruption féminine, vous toiserez la largeur de la misérable vanité des hommes." ' (p. 93)

> ' " Aussi, madame de Nucingen laperait-elle toute la boue qu'il y a entre la rue Saint-Lazare et la rue de Grenelle pour entrer dans mon salon." ' (p. 93)

(b) Relations between syntactic structure and content

The frequency of inversion in final position has already been noted, and this structure is used to emphasize certain important themes and devices of Balzac's novel. In his descriptions, for instance, selected details are stressed in this way, e.g.

> ' Bientôt la veuve se montre attifée de son bonnet de tulle sous lequel pend un tour de faux cheveux mal mis (...) Sa face vieillotte, grassouillette, du milieu de laquelle sort un nez à bec de perroquet.' (p. 12)

In the next example, the repeated inversion construction underlines the idea expressed in the verb :

> ' Aussi le spectacle désolant que présentait l'intérieur de cette maison se répétait-il dans le costume de ses habitués, également délabrés.' (p. 18)

However, this sentence structure is put to its best advantage when the subject is the enigmatic Vautrin. Thus in the following the mysterious effect is heightened by the retarded subject :

> ' Des gens moins superficiels que ne l'étaient ces jeunes gens emportés par les tourbillons de la vie parisienne, ou ces vieillards indifférents à ce qui ne les touchait pas directement, ne se seraient pas arrêtés à l'impression douteuse que leur causait Vautrin.' (p. 23)

The next example is similar, but the subject receives added stress by virtue of being at the end of a paragraph :

> ' Rastignac fut alors sanglé comme d'un coup de fouet par le regard profond qui lui lança Vautrin.' (p. 113)

K*

This emphatic device is employed again as the mystery unfolds :

> ' Poiret s'avança vivement entre elle et Vautrin, comprenant qu'elle était en danger, tant la figure du forçat devint férocement significative en déposant le masque bénin sous lequel se cachait sa vraie nature.' (p. 221)

The position of the adjective in conjunction with inversion of subject and verb may also emphasize the content, as in the next example where the word-order establishes a relation between the verb and the anteposed adjective :

> ' Il regarda cette chambre où respirait la voluptueuse élégance d'une riche courtisane.' (p. 167)

In the following the same nominal structure is the subject of one inversion clause and the antecedent of another, the meaning of the qualifying adjective being enhanced by its unusual position :

> ' A travers les mille pensées qui s'élevaient dans son cœur, perçait un tumultueux mouvement de volupté qu'excitait l'échange d'une jeune et pure chaleur.' (p. 207)

It may be noted here that these anteposed adjectives which frequently occur in inversion clauses often assume considerable stylistic significance, although Mayer maintains that they are generally banal and of little semantic value.[14] On occasions, however, many such possibilities are lost in the thoroughly entangled structure of the Balzacian sentence :

> ' Peut-être l'insouciante générosité que mit à se laisser attraper le père Goriot, qui vers cette époque était respectueusement nommé monsieur Goriot, le fit-elle considérer comme un imbécile qui ne connaissait rien aux affaires.' (p. 26)

(c) Descriptive and narrative technique

At the beginning of the novel, historical detail and various comments by the author are introduced, along with the main themes and characters. A compound inversion, expressing a

---

[14] G. Mayer, La qualification affective dans les romans d'H. de Balzac, Paris, 1940, pp. 10–11.

particular theme, may thus contain a further inversion presenting a different detail :

' Aussi, vers la fin du mois de novembre 1819, époque à laquelle éclata ce drame, chacun dans la ¦pension avait-il des idées arrêtées sur le pauvre vieillard.' (p. 39)

Later the author uses a parenthesis with direct order, which contrasts with inversion in the next sentence :

' A peine ce couple " morganatique ", jolie expression allemande qui n'a pas son équivalent en français, avait-il atteint la porte, que le comte interrompit sa conversation avec Eugène.' (p. 73)

References to Balzac's own technique occur frequently in various structures at the start of the novel, and in the following this develops into a vivid image which is again emphasized by the choice of order and adjectives :

'... (l'odeur de pension) pue le service, l'office, l'hospice. Peut-être pourrait-elle se décrire si l'on inventait un procédé pour évaluer les quantités élémentaires et nauséabondes qu'y jettent les atmosphères catarrhales...' (p. 11)

The end of this section is made fully explicit, with an inversion structure concluding a chapter :

' Ici se termine l'exposition de cette obscure, mais effroyable tragédie parisienne.' (p. 105)

In the physical description of various characters, certain features may be thrown into relief by their position after the verb, especially when there is a dependent clause or lengthy subject :

' Habituellement vêtu d'un habit bleu-barbeau, il prenait chaque jour un gilet de piqué blanc, sous lequel fluctuait son ventre piriforme et proéminent, qui faisait rebondir une lourde chaîne d'or garnie de breloques.' (p. 26)

The same is true of the presentation of emotion, which is emphasized below by the repetition and expansion of the inverted subject :

' Le vieillard oubliait de manger pour contempler la pauvre jeune fille dans les traits de laquelle éclatait une

douleur vraie, la douleur de l'enfant méconnu qui aime son
père. (p. 66)

Contrast in tone may also be marked by inversion in final
position :

'Chacun s'en allait à sa fantaisie, suivant le degré d'intérêt
qu'il prenait à la conversation, ou selon le plus ou le moins
de pesanteur que lui causait sa digestion.' (p. 175)

Inversion may portray inner thought, rather than direct
description :

'Ses yeux s'attachèrent presque avidement entre la colonne
de la place Vendôme et le dôme des Invalides, là où vivait
ce beau monde dans lequel il avait voulu pénétrer.' (p. 309)

Although *Le Père Goriot* has comparatively few inversions
after adverbial expressions of place, much of the description
depends on these and on relative *invertissants*. They tend to
accumulate in certain descriptive passages, which may have a
highly concentrated effect :

'Derrière le bâtiment est une cour large d'environ vingt
pieds, où vivent en bonne intelligence des cochons, des
poules, des lapins, et au fond de laquelle s'élève un hangar à
serrer le bois. Entre ce hangar et la fenêtre de la cuisine se
suspend le garde-manger, au-dessous duquel tombent les
eaux grasses de l'évier.' (pp. 9–10)

Frequently descriptive passages are linked to details of the
characters, thus :

'Le long de chaque muraille, règne une étroite allée qui
mène à un couvert de tilleuls, mot que madame Vauquer ...
prononce obstinément " tieuilles ", malgré les observations
grammaticales de mes hôtes...' (p. 9)

Repetition of inverted order may contribute to the progression
in the narrative or emphasize certain descriptive details :

'Au-dessus de ce troisième étage étaient un grenier à étendre
le linge et deux mansardes où couchaient un garçon de
peine, nommé Christophe, et la grosse Sylvie, la cuisinière.'
(p. 17)

'Ses petites mains potelées, sa personne dodue ... sont en
harmonie avec cette salle où suinte la malheur, où s'est

blottie la spéculation, et dont madame Vauquer respire l'air chaudement fétide sans en être écœurée.' (p. 13)

While only a few aspects of Balzac's technique have been discussed in relation to word-order, it is clear that the frequent inversions do in many cases form part of a highly expressive style, despite Riffaterre's dismissal of their importance.[15] Although the main function of inversion in *Le Père Goriot* is undoubtedly one of emphasis, the technique and its stylistic effect vary with each aspect of the *Comédie humaine* they serve to stress.

[15] ' Le chiffre élévé ... n'étonnera pas si l'on pense au caractère cherché et surchargé, souvent prétentieusement, de son style... ', *Le style des* ' *Pléiades* ' *de Gobineau,* p. 98.

Chapter IX

THE NINETEENTH CENTURY (2)

1. SYNTACTIC ANALYSIS OF THE TEXTS
1850–1900

The texts :

G. Flaubert, *Madame Bovary* [1]

E. and J. de Goncourt, *Germinie Lacerteux* [2]

V. Hugo, *Quatrevingt-treize* [3]

E. Zola, *Germinal* [4]

G. de Maupassant, *Bel-Ami* [5]

Table 9.01 : Inversion frequencies

FLA/MB	131 : 0·66	
GON/GL	151 : 1·01	
HUG/93	289 : 1·45	*(mean 0·89)*
ZOL/GER	136 : 0·68	
MAU/BEL	128 : 0·64	

Table 9.02 : Percentage table to show nature of clause in which inversion occurs

	FLA	*GON*	*HUG*	*ZOL*	*MAU*
Main clause	38	25	36	49	19
Subordinate clause	60	75	63	49	81
Non-subordinating *invertissant* in subordinate clause	2	—	1	2	—
	100	100	100	100	100
Immobile *invertissant*	60	75	58	43	81
Mobile *invertissant*	34	23	35	52	18
Other operations	6	2	7	5	1
N :	131	151	289	136	129

[1] In *Œuvres I*, ed. A. Thibaudet and R. Dumesnil, Paris (Gallimard), 1951, pp. 327–535. (FLA)

[2] Paris (Flammarion), 1921. (GON)

[3] In *Romans III*, Ed. du Seuil, Paris, 1963, pp. 418–548. (HUG)

[4] *Livre de poche* (1968), pp. 7–280. (ZOL)

[5] Paris (Garnier), 1959. (MAU)

Table 9.03 : Percentage table to show distribution of inversions according to discourse type

	FLA	GON	HUG	ZOL	MAU
Narrative	80	99	89	88	86
Direct speech	11	1	11	2	11
Indirect speech	4	—	—	1	2
Free indirect speech	3	—	—	9	1
Soliloquy	2	—	—	—	—

Table 9.04 : Percentage table to show position of the inversion within the corpus examined

	FLA	GON	HUG	ZOL	MAU
Sentence initial	26	20	16	31	9
Paragraph initial	4	5	17	—	11
Chapter initial	—	1	1	—	—
Speech initial	1	—	n	1	—
Total initial	31	26	34	32	20
Sentence final	27	30	23	31	24
Paragraph final	9	7	10	9	16
Chapter final	—	1	n	—	1
Speech final	2	—	2	1	5
Total final	38	38	35	41	46

Table 9.05 : Percentage table to show position of inversion in relation to other types of discourse

	FLA	GON	HUG	ZOL	MAU
Preceding direct speech	2	1	n	5	3
Following direct speech	—	—	1	—	—
Preceding free indirect	—	—	—	1	1
Following free indirect	—	—	—	1	—

Table 9.06 : Percentage table to show nature of the inverted noun phrase

	FLA	GON	HUG	ZOL	MAU
Pronoun subject	12	4	4	26	1
Substantive subject	86	93	95	66	98
Compound inversion	2	3	1	8	1
	100	100	100	100	100
2 or more subjects	8	17	6	2	10
S and dependent (S)	11	11	14	7	9

Table 9.07 : The percentage of inversions occurring in sentences of three or more clauses

	FLA	GON	HUG	ZOL	MAU
(S)—3 clauses	34	33	25	19	29
4 clauses	15	12	9	8	15
5 clauses	2	5	4	2	5
6 clauses	1	1	3	1	1
7 clauses	1	—	2	—	—
7+ clauses	—	—	—	—	1
	53	51	43	30	51

Table 9.08 : Ratio of inversions to *invertissants*

FLA	131 : 42—3·12
GON	151 : 36—4·20
HUG	289 : 53—5·45
ZOL	136 : 40—3·40
MAU	129 : 33—3·90
Total	836 : 105—7·96 (*mean* 4·01)

Table 9.09 : Percentage table of the most frequently occurring inversions

	FLA	GON	HUG	ZOL	MAU
Relatives	47	67	50	38	58
Comparatives	4	3	3	1	10
Indirect construction	6	3	3	3	12
Modal adverbs	11	6	6	29	1

Table 9.10 : Percentage table to show the occurrence of ' être ', ' faire ' and ' avoir '

	FLA	GON	HUG	ZOL	MAU
être	12	11	26	5	2
faire	4	8	7	—	9
avoir	2	9	1	1	6

Table 9.11 : Percentage table showing the distribution of direct speech *invertissants*

	FLA	GON	HUG	ZOL	MAU
Immobile *invertissant*	43	100	78	—	73
Mobile *invertissant*	43	—	12	100	20
Other operations	14	—	10	—	7
N :	14	1	32	3	15

Table 9.12 : Percentage table to show the occurrence of
adverbials and clauses in inversion constructions

	FLA	GON	HUG	ZOL	MAU
V(adv)S	27	17	12	5	12
(adv)VS	4	1	2	10	1
V(S)S	—	—	n	—	—
(S)VS	2	3	n	4	—

(i) DISTRIBUTION OF THE INVERSIONS

The average inversion frequency for these five texts, 0·89,
represents a slight decline on the previous period, and it may
be noted that while inverted constructions are very common in
both Hugo and the Goncourts, the frequencies in Flaubert,
Zola and Maupassant are all lower, between 0·65 and 0·68
(table 9.01). Similarly the total number of *invertissants* is
smaller, 105, as compared with 113 in the first half of the
century. There are very few examples of inversion in conversation, an average of 7% in each text, with the Goncourts and
Zola, having only 1% and 2% respectively. Table 9.03 also shows
that with the popularity of the *style indirect libre*, 3% of the
examples in Flaubert and 9% in Zola occur in this type of discourse. The average frequency of *être, faire* and *avoir* in inversion constructions continues to fall, although table 9.10 shows
that the occurrence of *être* is still high in Hugo (26%), a proportion not found in any of the later texts analysed.

Table 9.12 reveals the increasing freedom of word-order,
with all the texts except Zola showing a high frequency of the
order verb-adverb-subject. On the other hand the Zola
examples are unusual in that in 10% of them an adverb
precedes the verb and subject, and in a further 4% a clause is
in this position. The analysis of *Germinal* reveals several other
anomalies, for example the equal distribution of inversions
between main and subordinate clauses (table 9.02), the high
proportion of pronoun subjects and compound inversion
(table 9.06) and the tendency for inversion to occur in short
sentences (table 9.07) with a corresponding reduction in
examples with several inverted subjects or dependent clauses

(table 9.06). A significant proportion of examples preceding direct speech, 5%, and the high frequency of modal adverbs (table 9.09), may also be mentioned.

(ii) EXAMPLES

A. IMMOBILE 'INVERTISSANT'

1. *Zero : FLA : 3 ; GON : 1 ; HUG : 1*
   ' "... Vu l'article 17 de la loi du 30 avril...,
   Sont mis hors la loi..."
   Il fit une pause et reprit :
   " Les individus désignés sous les noms et surnoms qui suivent." ' (HUG, p. 510)

2. *Relatives : FLA : 62 inversions, 6 'invertissants' ; GON : 101,8 ; HUG : 144,8 ; ZOL : 51,6 ; MAU : 75,7*
   ' Toutes ces voitures chargées d'amour, *sur qui* semblaient voltiger des caresses, jetaient sur leur passage une sorte de souffle sensuel, subtil et troublant.' (MAU, p. 221)

3. *Comparatives : FLA : 5,2 ; GON : 4,3 ; HUG : 8,2 ; ZOL : 2,1 ; MAU : 13,2*
   ' Huit jours entiers, elle roula cette idée et ce mot : la Justice ! la Justice *telle que* se la figure l'imagination des basses classes, quelque chose de terrible, d'indéfini, d'inévitable...' (GON, pp. 215–16)

4. *Concessives : FLA : 1,1 ; HUG : 4,1*
   ' *Quelle que* fût pour la corvette la nécessité de ne pas être aperçue, il y avait une nécessité plus impérieuse encore, le sauvetage immédiat.' (HUG, p. 430)

5. *Temporal clause : FLA : 3,1 ; GON : 2,2 ; HUG : 1,1 ; ZOL : 2,2 ; MAU : 1,1*
   ' Mais, *à mesure que* se serrait davantage l'intimité de leur vie, un détachement intérieur se faisait qui la déliait de lui.' (FLA, p. 362)

6. *Indirect construction : FLA : 8,4 ; GON : 5,2 ; HUG : 9,4 ; ZOL : 4,3 ; MAU : 16,7*
   ' Et quand elle fut partie, il murmura ... sans chercher dans les replis de son cœur *d'où* lui venait, ce jour-là, cette opinion : " Elle est gentille, tout de même." ' (MAU, p. 90)

B. MOBILE 'INVERTISSANT'

1. *Attributes : FLA : 2,1 ; HUG : 17,1*
' " Ah ! c'est là la question ! *Telle* est effectivement la
question : That is the question ! comme je lisais dernière-
ment dans le journal." ' (FLA, p. 516)

2. *Adverbs—modal : FLA : 15,5 ; GON : 9,4 ; HUG :
17,4 ; ZOL : 44,5 ; MAU : 1,1*
' Et puis, quelle raison donnerait-il dans les visites, quand
on l'interrogerait ? *Peut-être*, cependant, s'était-il trompé
en quelque chose ? Il cherchait, ne trouvait pas.' (FLA,
p. 493)

3. *Adverbs—quantity : FLA : 1,1 ; ZOL : 3,2 ; MAU : 1,1*
' *Au plus* toucheraient-ils huit centimes, et c'était deux
centimes que leur volait la Compagnie...' (ZOL, p. 174)

4. *Adverbs—temporal : FLA : 1,1 ; GON : 1,1 ; HUG :
3,3 ; ZOL : 3,3 ; MAU : 8,2*
' *Alors* commença l'interminable défilé des assistants.'
(MAU, p. 362)

5. *Adverbs—place : FLA : 5,3 ; GON : 4,4 ; HUG : 12,4 ;
ZOL : 5,4 ; MAU : 1,1*
' Ce terrain, ces croix, ce prêtre disaient : *Ici* dort la Mort
du peuple et le Néant du pauvre.' (GON, p. 278)

6. *Adverbs—combination : ZOL : 1,1 ; MAU : 1,1*
' *Puis, derrière*, suivait la queue des mineurs, une cinquan-
taine d'ombres à la file.' (ZOL, p. 185)

7. *Adverbial phrase—place : FLA : 18,11 ; GON : 15,7 ;
HUG : 34,12 ; ZOL : 10,6 ; MAU : 10,9*
' *Au-dessus de la porte*, où seraient les orgues, se tient un
jubé pour les hommes, avec un escalier tournant qui
retentit sous les sabots.' (FLA, p. 389)

8. *Prepositional phrase : FLA : 2,2 ; GON : 6,2 ; HUG :
20,2 ; ZOL : 4,2*
' *De ce chaos d'ombre et de cette tumultueuse fuite de nuages*,
sortaient d'immenses rayons de lumière parallèles aux lois
éternelles.' (HUG, p. 471)

C. OTHER OPERATIONS

1. *Deletion and transposition :* $FLA : 5 ; GON : 2 ; HUG :$ $2 ; MAU : 1$
   ' Mais *arrivait-il* un malheur, une nouvelle de mort, une tristesse dans la maison ; *un enfant tombait-il malade,* Madame de Verandeuil l'apprenait toujours à la minute...' (GON, pp. 36–37)

2. *Addition and transposition :* $GON : 1,1 ; HUG : 18,8 ;$ $ZOL : 7,5$
   ' *C'est* par la Convention *que* s'ouvrit la grande page nouvelle et que l'avenir d'aujourd'hui commença.' (HUG, p. 465)

(iii) DETAILS OF THE INVERSIONS

(a) *Immobile ' invertissant '*

Absolute inversion (zero *invertissant*) becomes increasingly common in the 19th century, although this does not emerge from the texts analysed. Whereas, for example, there is only one occurrence of the construction in *Germinie Lacerteux* (' Vint le moment où...'), Ullmann's study of *Manette Salomon* has revealed no fewer than seven examples, all with verbs of movement.[6] It will be noted that the example from *Quatre-vingt-treize* quoted above (p. 298) represents a legalistic style and is followed by a lengthy subject. The three examples in Flaubert all take the form ' Venait ensuite...'. Absolute inversion is discussed by Cressot, who explains it by its relation to the preceding sentence, that is as an example of thematic liaison. He stresses its frequency of occurrence, suggesting that ' chez nombre d'écrivains modernes (ce tour) est devenu une véritable manie.' [7]

The other significant development with regard to immobile *invertissant* constructions is the occurrence of temporal clause *invertissants* in all five texts, and the variety of terms employed, the analysis revealing six different *invertissants*. The verbs are not solely confined to those expressing length of time (e.g. *tout le temps que* and *durer* in the Goncourts and Hugo) or to

---

[6] *Op. cit.*, p. 167.
[7] *La phrase et le vocabulaire de J.-K. Huysmans*, p. 97.

those indicating initiation of an action (*maintenant que* and *commencer* in Zola and *quand* and *arriver* in Flaubert) ; in addition to the Flaubert example quoted above (p. 298), the following is found in Maupassant :

'Lorsque fut dissipé le premier étonnement, après les premières larmes versées, on s'occupa de tous les soins et de toutes les démarches que réclame un mort.' (p. 176)

(b) Mobile ' invertissant '

The occurrence of inversion in subordinate clauses of time is reflected by the frequency of the construction after temporal adverbs, which is again found in all five texts, and particularly in Maupassant. The sixteen examples from the texts use eight different *invertissants*, the most striking of which, *parfois* and *brusquement*, are quoted in the stylistic analysis below. The other structures all have verbs of movement, with the possible exception of an example in Hugo where this is conveyed in the dependent relative :

'Tout à coup, dans cette paix profonde, éclata un éclair qui sortit de la forêt, puis un bruit farouche.' (p. 509)

The range of the verbs and *invertissants* used is, however, notable and marks a clear development in this period.

Apart from constructions favoured by individual authors, such as the seventeen examples of inversion after *tel* in Hugo, the other important feature of the analysis is the use of modal and quantity adverb *invertissants* in free indirect speech in Flaubert and Zola. Both the examples of these inversions quoted above (p. 299) occur in this context, and in Zola all three adverbs of quantity followed by inversion are found in free indirect style. The only modal adverb *invertissant* in this style is *peut-être* in both texts, which is particularly effective in stressing the developing thought processes.

2. STYLISTIC ANALYSIS OF THE TEXTS
(i) G. FLAUBERT, 'MADAME BOVARY'

Although the inversion frequency in *Madame Bovary* is among the lowest for this period, the analysis nevertheless clearly indicates a sentence structure which is generally more complex than that of the other texts. Similarly, although there are few inversions, the constructions in which they occur are more varied. The novel has more different *invertissants* than all the others except Hugo, resulting in a low ratio of inversions to *invertissants* (table 9.08), the lowest since Prévost, and fore-shadowing the variety which is to be found in the more modern texts in this study.

The most striking feature of sentence structure revealed by the analysis is the fact that in no fewer than 27% of the examples, the inverted subject is separated from the verb by an adverbial (table 9.12). In a further 4% of the cases an adverbial separates the *invertissant* and verb, and in 2% a whole clause is in this position. Although the number of examples with more than one inverted subject is not unduly high (table 9.06), two have four subjects, and two more have six. In three of these four examples an adverb precedes the first subject, e.g.

' Jeanne Darc (*sic*), Héloïse, Agnès Sorel ... pour elle, se détachaient comme des comètes sur l'immensité ténébreuse de l'histoire, *où saillissaient* encore ça et là, mais plus perdus dans l'ombre et sans aucun rapport entre eux, Saint Louis avec son chêne, Bayard mourant, quelques férocités de Louis XI, un peu de Saint-Barthélemy, le panache du Béarnais, et toujours le souvenir des assiettes pointes où Louis XIV était vanté.' (p. 359)

The sentences in which inversion occurs tend to be longer than average, and table 9.07 shows that 53% of the examples are found in sentences of three or more clauses, the highest figure for the period, and second only to Balzac in the 19th-century texts (58%), the average for each half of the century being 46%.

The results obtained by the analysis of inversion in *Madame Bovary* confirm in some respects the features observed by Ullmann in the *Education sentimentale*,[8] while also indicating a more extensive use of the device in the later novel. Apart from the greater frequency of the construction (135 inversions in the *Education* as opposed to 131 in parts I and II of *Madame*

[8] *Op. cit.*, pp. 161 ff.

Bovary only), there also appears to be more variety in its use. For example inversions after the relative *où* represent 18% of the total in *Madame Bovary* as against 25% in the later work, and place adverbials also account for 18% in the former, as opposed to 25% in the latter. Similarly of the eight temporal clause inversions in the *Education*, seven are constructed with *quand*, whereas the three examples in *Madame Bovary* also include the conjunction *à mesure que*. The stylistic function of inversion appears to be similar in both novels. Ullmann notes the use of the construction in presenting the psychological order of perception, and this is the central feature of Flaubert's descriptive technique discussed below.

(a) *Inversion and descriptive technique*

Thibaudet has defined Flaubert's style as ' composition par tableaux ',[9] and this technique is clearly revealed in his descriptive passages. These may, as the critic suggests, consist of a series of pictures rather than a dramatic progression, but on the other hand more detailed descriptions also involve the isolation and progressive examination of one of these *tableaux*. In both types of description inversion is an important means of emphasis, and its liaison function is also exploited in the second.

The first type of description is illustrated in particular by Flaubert's use of comparatives, and in the introduction of certain *leitmotive* such as gastronomic details. As in the other texts analysed in this chapter, there are few examples of inversion in comparative clauses in *Madame Bovary*, but with the exception of one routine construction (' comme dit Saint Paul ', p. 426), all have the same descriptive function, that of introducing a familiar natural image, to contrast with a preceding expression of the protagonist's emotions. Thus in the following examples inversion emphasizes both this opposition and the picture itself, especially when this concludes the sentence :

'... et le chagrin s'engouffrait dans son âme avec des

[9] A. Thibaudet, *Gustave Flaubert*, 2nd ed., Paris, 1935, p. 230.

hurlements doux, comme fait le vent d'hiver dans les
châteaux abandonnés.' (p. 437)

'... il lui semblait qu'une abondance subite se serait détachée
de son cœur, comme tombe la récolte d'un espalier quand on
y porte la main.' (p. 362)

Inversion in more prolonged descriptions, such as that of
Emma's wedding breakfast, for example, tends on the other
hand to have the function of adding variety, while also stressing
a particular item:

'... puis se tenait au second étage un donjon en gâteau de
Savoie, entouré de menues fortifications en angélique,
amandes, raisins secs, quartiers d'oranges.' (p. 351)

The following is especially effective because of its chiastic
structure, along with the parallel between the two subjects—
a drink qualified by its container:

' Aux angles, se dressait l'eau-de-vie, dans les carafes. Le
cidre doux en bouteilles poussait sa mousse épaisse autour
des bouchons et tous les verres ... avaient été remplis de
vin...' (p. 350)

The second type of description, the detailed examination of a
tableau, and the part played by inverted order is fully exemplified by the presentation of Yonville (pp. 388–91) in the course
of which eight inversions occur close together, with three pairs
of one inversion clause embedded within another. The opening
sentence of the passage demonstrates Flaubert's technique of
seizing on a detail and building up a description from it, as if
approaching a picture and giving an account of it:

' Au bas de la côte, après le pont, commence une chaussée
plantée de jeunes trembles, qui vous mène en droite ligne
jusqu'aux premières maisons du pays. Elles sont encloses
de haies...' (p. 382)

Inversions with functions of emphasis and of liaison are
exemplified in the following, and also in example B7
(p. 299 above):

'Puis, à travers une claire-voie, apparaît une maison blanche
au-delà d'un rond de gazon que décore un Amour le doigt
posé sur la bouche.' (p. 390)

Inversion may also link two aspects of description, the overall picture and a detail of it, as in the example below, where the inverted subject in sentence final position concludes one and begins the other with its repetition in pronominal form :

'Pour arriver chez la nourrice, il fallait ... suivre, entre des maisonnettes et des cours, un petit sentier que bordaient des troènes. Ils étaient en fleur et les véroniques aussi...' (p. 408)

Finally two examples of description where the inversions have slightly different functions. In the first the inverted subject constitutes not so much a detail as all that can be discerned, and is expanded in a series of visual impressions in the order in which they strike the observer :

'Et de tous ces grands carrés noirs bordés d'or sortaient, çà et là, quelque portion plus claire de la peinture, un front pâle, deux yeux qui vous regardaient, des perruques se déroulant sur l'épaule poudrée des habits rouges, ou bien la bouche d'une jarretière en haut d'un mollet rebondi.' (p. 368)

In the second, concerning a barrel-organ, the inversion concludes a description of the figures on the instrument by restoring them to their proper perspective, before returning to the subject of the organ-grinder :

'... sur l'orgue, dans un petit salon, des danseurs haut comme le doigt, femmes en turban rose, Tyroliens en jaquette ... tournaient entre les fauteuils, les canapés, les consoles, se répétant dans les morceaux de miroir *que* raccordait à leurs angles un filet de papier doré. L'homme faisait aller sa manivelle...' (p. 384)

Flaubert's pictures, although detailed, are not strikingly colourful, and black and white predominate. It is notable that when colour reference is emphasized by inversion, the subject is almost invariably at the end of a sentence, in spite of the variety of contexts, e.g.

'Une tuméfaction livide s'étendait sur la jambe, et avec des phlyctènes de place en place, par où suintait un liquide noir.' (p. 489)

'... tandis qu'un souffle fort écartait ses narines minces et relevait le coin charnu de ses lèvres, qu'ombrageait à la lumière un peu de duvet noir.' (p. 503)

'... devant l'attelage que conduisaient au trot deux petits postillons en culotte blanche.' (p. 360)

The two main colours may be contrasted, either with each other,

'... la longue ligne des voiles blancs, que marquaient de noir çà et là les capuchons raides des bonnes sœurs inclinées sur leur prie-Dieu.' (p. 425)

or with an unspecified colour :

'... une mécanique compliquée recouverte d'un pantalon noir, que terminait une botte vernie.' (p. 497)

Thus inversion in Flaubert's description has various uses, which are all aspects of its main function as described by Ullmann : ' the pictorial effect achieved by detaching the subject from its background '.[10] It may underline certain thematic oppositions, as in the above references to colour, introduce successive *tableaux*, or provide variety and liaison in descriptive progressions. In spite of the fairly low frequency of the construction in *Madame Bovary*, inversion is, therefore, an integral part of Flaubert's style. As Riffaterre puts it :

' Flaubert en use d'une manière si définie, en particulier comme élément de style descriptif, qu'on ne peut avoir de doute sur le caractère intentionnel du procédé.' [11]

(b) The structure of the inverted subject

The emphatic value of inversion often contributes to the effect of another syntactic device, such as that of nominalization. In the following the nominalization which forms the first of three inverted subjects, is stressed both by its position and by the parallel structure of the other two subjects :

' Ils avaient ... ce teint blanc que rehaussent la pâleur des porcelaines, les moires du satin, le vernis des beaux moubles, et qu'entretient dans sa santé un régime discret de nourritures exquises.' (p. 371)

[10] *Op. cit.*, p. 163.
[11] *Op. cit.*, p. 97.

The elliptical subject in the next example, although showing a different structure, is also stressed by inversion at the end of a sentence :

'... et sa casquette de cuir ... laissait voir, sous la visière relevée, un front chauve, qu'avait déprimé l'habitude de casque.' (p. 393)

Related to the above examples of nominal syntax is the emphasis on abstract and collective noun subjects. Thus two abstract subjects are inverted in parallel structures in the following :

' Dans leurs regards indifférents flottait la quiétude de passions journellement assouvies ; et à travers leurs manières douces perçait cette brutalité particulière, que communique la domination de choses à demi faciles, dans lesquelles...' (p. 372)

The first, more complex, subject receives emphasis from its position in a single-clause sentence, while the second introduces a series of dependent clauses ; in both structures inversion lends emphasis to the verb as well as the subject. A metaphorical collective subject is stressed in the next example, and again the construction is mirrored by inversion in the dependent relative :

'... tandis que le long des murs s'étendait une abondante batterie de cuisine, où miroitait inégalement la flamme claire du foyer...' (p. 338)

A collective noun may also have a depersonalizing effect, the subject being expanded, somewhat ironically, by a succession of sentences with the pronoun subject *on* :

' Venait ensuite la société des duchesses : on y etait pâle ; on se levait à quatre heures.' (p. 378)

A further variation in the structure of the subject stressed by inversion is the use of one physical detail for the whole picture, a technique related to Flaubert's descriptive style discussed above, e.g.

'... alors à travers elles (les clartés), comme dans les feux de Bengale, s'entrevoit l'ombre du pharmacien accoudé sur son pupitre.' (p. 390)

'On avait brodé cela sur quelque métier de palissandre ... où s'étaient penchées les boucles molles de la travailleuse pensive.' (p. 377)

This device culminates in the famous description of Catherine Leroux, where the person is replaced by a wholly abstract concept, which is emphasized by inversion and concludes a paragraph :

'Ainsi se tenait, devant ces bourgeois épanouis, ce demi-siècle de servitude.' (p. 463)

Finally two less striking, but equally relevant occurrences of inverted abstract subjects, the first being an unusual presentation of speech, and the second a device avoiding an unbalanced sentence structure :

'Alors commença l'éternelle lamentation : " Oh ! si..." ' (p. 418)

'... et (ils) portent enfin, à soixante ans, quand vient l'âge des rhumatismes, une brochette en croix, sur leur habit noir ...' (p. 381)

(c) *Inversions in direct speech : conclusion*

With a decreasing proportion of inversions in direct speech in this period, conversational occurrences may be all the more effective in the characterization of the speaker. This is exemplified firstly in the speech of Homais, and secondly in the presentation of various minor and incidental characters. The deletion and transposition operation is used in both instances. In the first example it characterizes the speaker, the *curé*, while in the second it seems somewhat inappropriate when spoken by Homais addressing Charles Bovary, perhaps because this conversation follows closely on the first :

' " Cependant, ne serait-ce que ces personnes de sexe différent réunies dans un appartement en chanteur ... tout cela doit finir par engendrer un certain libertinage d'esprit..." ' (p. 525)

' " Enfin, croyez-moi, conduisez madame au spectacle, ne serait-ce que pour faire une fois dans votre vie enrager un de ces corbeaux-là, saperlotte ! " ' (p. 526)

Other inversions of Homais indicate the chemist's pretensions to learning, with the appropriate emphasis on either subject or verb :

' " Ainsi, vous n'êtes pas sans savoir l'effet singulièrement aphrodisiaque que produit le ' nepeta cataria ', vulgairement appelé herbe-au-chat, sur la gent féline." ' (p. 516)

It may also stress the exploitation of clichés, a device noted by Brombert [12] in relation to this character, thus :

' " A peine sentiras-tu, peut-être, une légère douleur." ' (p. 485)

Inversions in key positions emphasize still further the nature of the speaker. The first example concludes the speech of the *proviseur* in the opening chapter, and the second, in initial position, is part of the councillor's address at the *Comices* :

' " Si son travail et sa conduite sont méritoires, il passera ' dans les grands ', où l'appelle son âge." ' (p. 327)

' " Qu'y vois-je ?   Partout fleurissent le commerce et les arts." ' (p. 455)

Although the frequency of inversion is not especially high in *Madame Bovary*, it is clear that the occurrence of the construction is closely linked to particular thematic or stylistic effects. While, as noted by Thibaudet, inversion may often result from the author's concern for variety, ' il s'acharne parfois à changer chaque construction, à intervertir, d'une phrase à l'autre, l'ordre même des mots ',[13] the construction is of much wider importance. It may complement other syntactic devices of style, as in the nominal structures quoted, besides fulfilling an emphatic function in many different contexts, of which the most important perhaps are those of characterization, and in particular of impressionistic description.

(ii) E. AND J. DE GONCOURT, 'GERMINIE LACERTEUX'

It should first be noted that the length of *Germinie Lacerteux* is about 66,000 words, and in the analysis of the

---

[12] V. Brombert, *The Novels of Flaubert, a Study of Themes and Techniques*, Princeton, 1966, p. 72.

[13] *Op. cit.*, p. 237.

inversions the frequency has been adjusted accordingly. Table 9.06 shows that the structure of sentences containing inversion in this novel is the most complex of the texts analysed as regards the proportion of examples with more than one subject, 17%, although table 9.12 shows that there is a higher occurrence of intervening adverbials in Flaubert. The other main features of the analysis are the almost total absence of inversion in conversation, probably an effect of the author's concern for realism, and the high proportion of relative constructions, 67% (table 9.09).

Inversion in the novels of the Goncourt brothers has been examined in part in a work by Loesch [14] who lists various examples. Of these, several types do not occur in the text studied here, namely inversion after a participial phrase, a subordinate clause and after *et*. On the other hand important omissions by Loesch which do occur in *Germinie Lacerteux* include certain relative *invertissants* such as *d'où* and preposition plus *ce que* (Loesch lists only *que*, *où* and *dont*), the comparatives *tel que*, *autant que* and *plus que*, the conjunctions *dès que* and *tout le temps que*, as well as indirect constructions, modal adverbs, and various temporal adverbs, and examples of other syntactic operations. After relatives, adverbial phrases of place are the most common *invertissants* (10% of the examples), a feature noted by Loesch as being important in the descriptive passages : ' So finden sich in den Beschreibungen der Goncourt namentlich die Ortsbestimmungen fast durchweg am Satzkopf '.[15]

The word-order of the Goncourts is also discussed by Priestley [16] who mentions a freer use of inversion as one of their syntactic innovations, citing in particular adverbial *invertissants*, even if the verb is transitive. Comparison with other texts of this period, however, suggests that this is a general tendency not confined to particular authors, and there

---

[14] E. Loesch, *Die impressionistische Syntax der Goncourt*, Nürnberg, 1919.

[15] *Ibid.*, p. 65.

[16] *Reprise constructions in French*.

is little evidence of the nature of the verb, transitive or otherwise, influencing the occurrence of inversion.

Finally the number and range of inversions in *Manette
Salomon* together with their stylistic effect, is examined in
some detail by Ullmann. In this novel inverted order also
occurs frequently, with 300 examples, or two in every three
pages.[17] Just as Ullmann notes that the use of inversion in
Manette Salomon is closer to modern practice than in the
Education sentimentale, the same may be said of *Germinie
Lacerteux* with respect to *Madame Bovary*. The analysis of
Germinie below will also endorse Ullmann's remark that ' the
stylistic effects which the Goncourts derive from inversion are
intense and varied rather than subtle.' [18]

(a) Repetition and accumulation

The fact that the Goncourts' novel has the highest proportions of both relative inversions and of several inverted
subjects is a fairly clear indication that the function of the
construction is primarily one of liaison. Whereas Flaubert used
inversion both to emphasize a descriptive detail and to link the
elements through which it is expanded, inversion in *Germinie
Lacerteux* is closely connected with the device of repetition, the
means by which descriptive impressions are accumulated and
developed.

The functions of inversion in this context will depend on the
type of repetition or accumulation to which it is harnessed. For
instance, the enumeration of impressions may be expressed in
a list of inverted subjects thus :

' Sur son visage pâle des pâleurs que renvoie au teint l'eau
forte mordant le cuivre ... se mêlaient la crânerie, l'énergie,
l'insouciance, l'intelligence, l'impudence, toutes sortes
d'expressions coquines qu'adoucissait chez lui ... un air de
câlinerie féline.' (p. 95)

Here the impressions have been summed up and linked to the
following clause by a further inversion. Alternatively the whole

[17] *Style in the French Novel*, p. 167.
[18] *Ibid.*, p. 169.

inversion structure may be repeated, as in the following expansion of the main verb *savoir* :

> ' Ils ne savent pas ce qu'est la confession, ce qu'est le confesseur pour ces pauvres âmes de pauvres femmes.' (p. 51)

Inversion is also used within repetitive structures, and to conclude them. In the former a relative inversion construction may dispose of an element extraneous to the main impressions, as in the following, where it is the idea of smallness which is primarily developed, as seen from the recurrence of the adjective *petit* :

> ' Elle ne pouvait quitter des yeux ces petits bras sous lesquels sautait le carton de l'école ces petites robes brunes à pois, ces petits pantalons noirs, ces petites jambes dans ces petits bas de laine.' (pp. 191–92)

In the next example it is the whole of the relative's antecedent which is repeated and expanded, and a secondary idea (*ivre/ivresse*) emerges :

> ' Maintenant les rares joies qu'avait Germinie étaient des joies folles, des joies dont elle sortait ivre et avec les caractères physiques de l'ivresse.' (p. 154)

In other instances a chiastic structure lends variety to simple repetition of a single element, as has been noted in various other texts, e.g.

> '... il lui avait semblé que les yeux de sa bonne ne disaient pas ce que disait sa bouche.' (p. 166)

> ' Elle allait où allait le couple, jusqu'au bout.' (p. 239)

Elsewhere the order in a subordinate clause may contrast with that of the main clause, where the antecedent of the one is the repeated subject of the other :

> ' Puis bientôt le charbon que lui vendait le charbonnier d'à côté, du fort charbon de Paris, plein de fumerons, l'enveloppait de son odeur entêtante.' (p. 244)

The emphatic value of an inverted subject at the end of a long sentence may be exploited in impressionistic writing, as the next example shows. Here the concluding subject represents the cause of the enumerated elements which precede it :

> ' A la rue succédait une large route, blanche, crayeuse,

poudreuse ... sillonnée par les ornières, luisantes au bord, que
font le fer des grosses roues et l'écrasement des charrois de
pierres de taille.' (p. 85)

In conclusion, an example from chapter 5 combines many of
the features mentioned above, and demonstrates both the
syntactic complexity of the Goncourts' style and the intricacy
of the device of repetition and accumulation :

> ' Et mollement ... elle laissait jouer et rondir sa taille
> indolente, une taille à tenir dans une jarretière et *que*
> faisaient plus fine encore à l'œil le ressaut des hanches et le
> rebondissement des rondeurs ballonnant la robe, une taille
> impossible, ridicule de minceur...' (p. 60)

(b) *Other impressionistic effects*

As in the examples already quoted, inversion may be used to
facilitate a number of expanded subjects, representing the
developing impressions. In this extract these are balanced by
the two verbs in the inversion construction :

> ' Des portes ouvertes sortait et se répandait sur l'escalier
> l'odeur des cabinets sans air, des familles tassées dans une
> seule chambre, l'exhalaison des industries malsaines, les
> fumées graisseuses et animalisées des cuisines...' (p. 222)

The same construction may be used in a single-clause sentence,
the effectiveness here lying in the two preposed adjectives, with
the next sentence having two subjects and direct order to
balance the inversion :

> ' De cette femme laide s'échappait une âpre et mystérieuse
> séduction. L'ombre et la lumière ... y mettait ce rayonne-
> ment de volupté.' (p. 60)

In a later example the movement of the sentence reflects that
of the subject, with the main clause supported by two relative
clauses, one of which also has inverted order :

> ' Mais sur le cou, sur la poitrine que découvrait la robe
> dégrafée, passaient des mouvements ondulatoires pareils à
> des vagues levées sous la peau et que l'on voyait courir
> jusqu'aux pieds dans un frémissement de jupe.' (p. 127)

Another impression is conveyed by an inverted noun clause,

L

emphasized by final position where the semi-realistic 'jauni par la bile' is balanced by the impressionism of the concluding phrase :

> '... elle se tenait ... comme enterrée dans tout ce noir d'où ne sortaient que son visage jauni par la bile des tons du vieil ivoire, et la flamme chaude de son regard brun.' (p. 139)

In all the above examples there appears a certain symmetry, which is not immediately obvious, such as the coupling of adjectives followed by that of nouns, or the alternation of word-orders; thus the style of the novel may reflect the regular development of its content such as is noted by Ricatte : 'Il y a dans ce roman des symétries voulues ... Une austère régularité, discrète et puissante, gouverne tout le roman.' [19] Such regularity may also be found in inversions such as the following, both with a strongly stressed impressionistic verb, and with similar subjects :

> '... après les trois premières marches, dans la nuit où saignait tout au fond la lumière rouge d'un quinquet.' (p. 208)

> 'Des rues montaient vaguement, où suintait de loin en loin, sur le plâtre blafard des maisons, la lueur d'un réverbère.' (p. 219)

An important aspect of the Goncourts' realism lies in the presentation of the Parisian background. Inversion here has several functions. As is quite common in other authors, it may introduce the subject of the description, e.g.

> 'Quelques toits tout blancs s'espaçaient çà et là ; puis se levait la montée de la butte Montmartre dont le linceul de neige était déchiré par des coulées de terre et des taches sablonneuses.' (p. 276)

It may, however, assume additional importance when the *invertissant* expresses the means by which the inverted subject is perceived, which is particularly effective when the latter contributes to the realism of the decor :

> 'A la lueur de la lumière vacillante apparaissait le sale papier de la chambre, couvert de caricatures...' (p. 224)

[19] R. Ricatte, *La création romanesque chez les Goncourt, 1851–1870*. Paris, 1953, p. 261.

(c) Other functions of inversion : conclusion

Although inversion is more likely to occur in longer sentences than in short ones, it is often found in single-clause sentences in describing the progress of the narrative, e.g.

' Enfin arrivait le 9 Thermidor et la délivrance.' (p. 21)

This is also fairly common where the sentence begins a new paragraph :

' Bientôt se dressa le dernier réverbère pendu à un poteau vert.' (p. 85)

The next example occurs at the beginning of chapter 52, and combines the use of inversion in the context of narrative development with the introduction of sense impressions :

' Au milieu des inquiétudes désespérées que donnait à Mlle de Verandeuil la maladie de sa bonne, se glissait une impression singulière, une certaine peur devant l'être nouveau, inconnu...' (p. 252)

There seems to be only one example in *Germinie Lacerteux* of nominal syntax in conjunction with inversion of the subject, and this is further stressed by its position at the end of a paragraph :

'... elle demeura dans la même pose ... tâtonnant autour d'elle les places où n'avait point encore posé la fièvre de ses mains.' (p. 204)

Elsewhere, however, unusual or abstract subjects may be emphasized in a similar way :

' On reconnaissait là un de ces lieux champêtres où vont se vautrer les dimanches des grands faubourgs, et...' (p. 201)

The above examples tend, however, to be isolated instances of inversion with a particular function. The most striking features of inverted order in *Germinie Lacerteux* are therefore, firstly the frequency with which it occurs, thereby contributing to the literary effect of the work, and secondly its use in the ordered presentation of impressions, and its role in repetition and accumulation, which at times reveals the authors' concern for symmetry of construction and design.

(iii) V. HUGO, 'QUATREVINGT-TREIZE'

The frequency of inversion in *Quatrevingt-treize*, 1·45, is the highest of the five texts, and there is also the greatest number of *invertissants*. This seems to indicate a considerable increase in the use of the construction in Hugo's last novel, since according to Ullmann [20] there are only 250 examples of *inversion facultative* in *Notre Dame de Paris* which compares with 400 found in Balzac's *Splendeurs et misères*. The frequencies for *Quatrevingt-treize* (289 inversions) and *Le père Goriot* (310 inversions) on the other hand differ only by 0·10.

Although the high number of inversions and of different *invertissants* still produces a high ratio of one to the other (table 9.08), the number of different constructions is indicated by table 9.09 where this novel has the lowest proportion of the four types of construction listed. As regards other features of word-order, the analysis does not suggest a sentence structure as complex as that of the two preceding writers. Table 9.12 shows that apart from the order verb-adverb-subject, there is little separation of the main elements, and clauses are rare in this position. Other points arising from the analysis are firstly the number of examples in initial position (table 9.04) and secondly the renewed frequency of *être* (26%) (table 9.10). The examples of inverted order in *Quatrevingt-treize* reveal several interesting aspects of style, besides emphasizing descriptive features and other devices. There emerges an intricate system of oppositions and parallelisms, and the liaison function of inversion is also exploited.

(a) The structure of inversion in ' Quatrevingt-treize '

In the introduction to the Garnier edition of the novel, M. Bedout refers to Hugo's ' style hautain et flamboyant ' and its manifestation in devices such as ' balancements combinés et termes antithétiques '.[21] The validity of Bedout's observations is evident from many of the inversion examples, some of which are stylistically effective, while others are somewhat cumbersome.

---

[20] *Style in the French Novel*, pp. 155 ff.
[21] Paris, 1957, p. xl.

1. The system of oppositions

The three main types of opposition used by Hugo in inversion constructions are those between *invertissant* and subject in a single clause, where the former is an indirect object, between different *invertissants*, and between inversion and non-inversion in consecutive clauses. The first type is based on a contrast between two noun phrases. In the first examples the opposition lies in the qualifiers, the two nouns being repeated :

> ' Plus tard, à la ville tragique succéda la ville cynique.'
> (p. 451)
> ' A la frénésie de mourir succéda la frénésie de vivre...'
> (p. 451)

In the next example both elements of the first noun phrase have an opposition in the second :

> ' Il s'agissait de savoir ... si à un progrès de l'oncle répondrait un recul du neveu.' (p. 534)

These oppositions are combined with enumeration in the following :

> ' Aux danses violentes dans les églises en ruines succédèrent les bals de Ruggeri, de Luquet, de Wenzel, de Mauduit, de la Montansier ; aux graves citoyennes qui faisaient de la charpie succédèrent les sultanes, les sauvages, les nymphes.'
> (p. 452)

The use of repeated structures underlies the second type of opposition, consisting of two *invertissants* with identical syntactic function but with opposite meaning :

> ' Dedans éclatait la mitraille, dehors se dressait la retirade.'
> (p. 518)

In the next example the repetition extends to the form of the dependent clauses :

> ' A l'est apparaissait une blancheur qui était le lever du jour, à l'ouest blêmissait une autre blancheur qui était le coucher de la lune.' (p. 431)

This may be emphasized by the paragraph divisions, with the inverted subjects being linked in a third paragraph :

> ' Au couchant ... se découpaient trois hautes roches, debout comme des pauvres celtiques.

Au levant ... se dressaient huit voiles rangées en ordre et espacées d'une façon redoutable.

Les trois roches étaient un écueil ; les huit voiles étaient une escadre.' (p. 431)

The third important opposition is that of contrasting orders after similar subordinating constructions, e.g.

' C'est là qu'avait été la mèche soufrée allumée par l'Imamus ; c'etait de là que l'incendie était parti.' (p. 529)

2. Parallelisms

Hugo's use of exactly parallel structures has already been exemplified in some of the constructions above. There are, however, two further types of parallelism which involve firstly the verbs in inversion clauses and secondly the *invertissants*. An example of the former also shows an opposition between inverted and direct order, while the parallel lies in the semantic relation between the verbs *finir, se terminer* and *s'arrêter* :

' Finistère, c'était là que finissait la France, que le champ donné à l'homme se terminait et que la marche des générations s'arrêtait.' (p. 480)

There are many instances of repeated inversion structures after the same *invertissants*, the most common of which is the relative *où*, and often with similar subjects :

'... la mêlée est si funeste qu'on ne sait plus où est le juste, où est l'honnête, où est le vrai.' (p. 532)

In the next example, the second subject is a development of the first abstract nominal :

' Au milieu de tout cela s'étalait l'affreuse impudeur humaine ; au milieu de tout cela apparaissaient la forteresse et l'échafaud, la guerre et le supplice...' (p. 547)

3. Thematic liaison

Repetition in *Quatrevingt-treize* is frequently used to link sentences or paragraphs, and again inversion of the subject is exploited in different ways. Thus the subject may be repeated with its function in the sentence either changed or retained, or it may be itself developed or contrasted. Here, for instance, two paragraphs are linked by a repeated nominal which is the subject of both sentences, with inversion ensuring that the two subjects are in immediate contact :

' C'est à cette hauteur que, pour plus de sûreté, avait été placée la porte de fer.

La porte de fer s'ouvrait sur...' (p. 497)

In the next example the order of elements in the noun phrase is reversed, while this remains at least the logical subject of each clause :

' Il arriva au sommet d'un coteau auquel étaient adossés le hameau et la métairie.

Il n'y avait plus ni métairie ni hameau.' (p. 448)

A further example shows how the link may be effected even where the original subject is substantially reduced and has a different grammatical function in the second clause :

' Il arriva à un embranchement de deux chemins où se dressait une vieille croix de pierre. Sur le piédestal de la croix on distinguait...' (pp. 442–43)

Finally the clauses may be linked by association of ideas as in the development of the inverted subject in the first case, or by its antithesis, as in the second :

'... sur lesquels s'ouvraient deux sombres portes carrées. On entrait et on sortait par là.' (p. 466)

' Devant cette mystérieuse complication de bienfaits et de souffances se dresse le Pourquoi ? de l'histoire.

" Parce que ". Cette réponse de celui qui ne sait rien est aussi la réponse de celui qui sait tout.' (p. 472)

4. Other aspects of inversion

In addition to the main syntactic effects associated with inverted order discussed above, several other features emerge from the analysis of *Quatrevingt-treize*. Firstly the inversion clause often contains more than one verb, an extreme example being the following, where there are six :

' Là fourmillaient, se coudoyaient, se provoquaient, se menaçaient, luttaient et vivaient tous ces combattants qui sont aujourd'hui des fantômes.' (p. 467)

Here there is a clear semantic progression from *fourmiller* to *lutter*, before the whole verb phrase is summed up by *vivre*. Secondly there is the device of zeugma, in this example omission of the verb, which may derive its effect from the inversion of the elements in each clause :

> ' Dans la Tourque étaient condensés quinze cents ans, le moyen âge, le vasselage, la glèbe, la féodalité ; dans la guillotine une année, 93.' (p. 546)

Thirdly inversion clauses often occur within enumerations in the novel, where there is otherwise no finite verb, and this frequently occurs when the subjects involve proper names. In such examples the change in structure of the subordinate clause generally adds variety to the list, e.g.

> '... Le Charpentier, qui dirigea l'escadre de Cancale ; Roberjot, qu'attendait le guet-apens de Rastadt ; Prieur de la Marne, qui...' (p. 468)

(b) Inversion of abstract subjects

Throughout the novel various themes may be emphasized, both by their presentation as abstract nominals and by their position in an inverted construction. Themes treated in this way include human emotions, often stressed further by the device of personification, nature and war. The construction may also have a reinforcing effect as in the following example, where a collective term is already stressed by inversion in the preceding clause :

> '... Paris étant le lieu où bat le cœur des peuples. Lá était la grande incandescence plébéienne.' (p. 453)

The abstracts in natural description tend to underline the contrast between transient action and the changelessness of nature. In the first example an anteposed adjective and position at the end of a paragraph add to the effect of inversion terminating a string of adverbial phrases :

> ' La frêle créature ... se sentait en sûreté dans cette nature ... dans cette campagne pure et paisible, dans ces bruits de nids, de sources, de mouches, de feuilles, au-dessus desquels resplendissait l'immense innocence du soleil.' (p. 504)

In the second instance the adjective and substantive structure of the inverted noun phrase parallels that of the antecedent:

    ' On avait autour de soi une tremblante muraille de branches d'où tombait la charmante fraîcheur des feuilles.' (p. 418)

Inversion occurs particularly frequently in Part II of the novel in the description of the *Convention*. In the examples which follow, the short sentences are thrown into relief by the inverted abstract subjects, and by the force of the verb, as well as by the general parallelism of the constructions:

    ' Au-dessous se courbaient l'épouvante, qui peut être noble, et la peur, qui est basse.' (p. 468)

    ' Dans cette cuve où bouillonnait la terreur, le progrès fermentait.' (p. 471)

In the latter the chiastic construction stresses the whole of the metaphor. Finally a double example of personification of two abstract ideas, where the verb and inverted subject constituting the one are separated from the *invertissant* by an adverbial phrase constituting the other:

    ' Ces halliers hypocrites ... étaient comme d'énormes éponges obscures d'où, sous la pression de ce pied gigantesque, la révolution, jaillissait la guerre civile.' (p. 467)

The above examples of inverted order in *Quatrevingt-treize* indicate the structural details of an unusually common construction, and the development and balance of concepts and of rhythmic elements are both striking. As already suggested, certain *invertissants* and structures have clear emphatic or linking functions in common with those of other texts. There are of course also many other examples which reveal the author's sense of the dramatic, as the following, which also concludes a chapter:

    ' Ainsi parlaient ces trois hommes formidables. Querelle de tonnerres.' (p. 461)

Elsewhere inverted order may be associated with a contrast of ideas, the adjoining clauses having direct order. Thus natural detail is opposed to the human action in the following, while at the same time being relevant to it:

    '... impossibilité de voir un homme à dix pas.

L*

> Par instants passait dans le branchage un héron ou une poule d'eau indiquant le voisinage des marais.
> On marchait.' (p. 418)

Nevertheless it seems that Hugo's style as reflected in these examples differs essentially from that of his contemporaries in the way in which word-order supplements and heightens the effect of other devices of style such as repetition, thematic oppositions and abstract nominalizations.

(iv) E. ZOLA, 'GERMINAL'

The analysis of the inversions in *Germinal* suggests several of the essential features of Zola's style. It is not surprising, for instance, to find only three examples in conversation, although there are many more in free indirect style. Unusually, 5% of the total are in a position preceding direct speech (table 9.05). There is also an absence of deletion or deletion and transposition operations, and in 70% of the cases inversion occurs in sentences of only one or two clauses (table 9.07). This simpler sentence structure, together with the fact that 67% have relative or modal adverb *invertissants*, is perhaps indicative of the author's conception of style as expressed in the *Roman expérimental*: ' Un langage n'est qu'une logique, une construction naturelle et scientifique (...) Le grand style est fait de logique et de clarté.' [22] The place of inversion in such a style, and its relation to Zola's technique of observation and analysis is discussed below.

(a) *The relation between inversion and type of discourse in 'Germinal'*

An important innovation in this text is the frequency with which inversion occurs in free indirect speech. The most common *invertissant* here is *peut-être*, and the emergent idea underlying this usage is further brought out if the construction forms a question, thus:

> ' Aussi ... éprouvait-il une inquiétude sur sa mission ...

[22] Paris (Charpentier), 6th ed., 1881, pp. 46–47.

Peut-être aurait-il fallu un avocat, un savant capable de parler et d'agir, sans compromettre les camarades ? ' (p. 218)

Another example uses the emphatic addition and transposition operation :

' N'était-ce pas un cri de famine que roulait le vent de mars, au travers de cette campagne nue ? ' (p. 11)

Free indirect speech in Zola seems almost to attract inversion, as may be seen in the constructions with an adverb of quantity and *c'est ... que*, quoted on p. 299 (B3) above. These inversions also tend to occupy a key position both in the sentence and in the structure of the discourse. The three quantity adverb *invertissants*, besides beginning the sentence, all indicate the change to free indirect style, e.g.

' Dans le cage qui le remontait... Etienne résolut de reprendre sa course affamée, le long des routes. Autant valait-il crever tout de suite que de redescendre au fond de cet enfer...' (p. 63)

On the other hand two of the examples with *peut-être* are used to conclude both the paragraph and the passage in free indirect style, which is then replaced by direct speech :

' C'était une chose décidée, une délégation allair venir, Peut-être, dans quelques minutes, serait-elle là.' (p. 200)

' Comment ne les avait-elle pas vus dans le coron ? Peut-être tout de même en aurait-elle tiré quelque chose.' (p. 252)

Elsewhere inversion also has the function of introducing other narrative styles, and in the following example precedes the opening of free indirect speech :

' Aussi, en bas, l'émotion grandissait-elle. Quoi donc ? est-ce qu'on allait le laisser en route, pendu dans le noir ? ' (p. 60)

A simpler example marks the return to narrative style, although the characteristic imperfect persists :

'... toujours les riches suceraient le sang des pauvres. Aussi ne se pardonnait-il pas la bêtise d'avoir dit autrefois qu'on...' (p. 230)

It seems that the *invertissant aussi*, with its strong co-ordinating function, is particularly suited to this use, which is perhaps parallel to that of the dynamic *et* in such a position, found so often in Flaubert.

The three inversions in direct speech in the part of the novel analysed all follow modal adverbs, one *aussi* and two *peut-être*. The latter examples may have a similar function to those just quoted, since one concludes a speech by Savarine, after which the narrative is resumed, and the other constitutes a single-clause sentence spoken by Etienne, which also concludes a conversation and precedes a further narrative passage. All three constructions, however, are quite simple, with pronoun subjects, and do not endanger the realism of the conversational style, e.g.

'... rasez tout, et quand il ne restera plus rien de ce monde pourri, peut-être en repoussera-t-il un meilleur.' (p. 138)

(b) *Impressionism and personification*

An important aspect of the style of *Germinal* is Zola's technique of presenting impressions without offering an interpretation, a style which Matthews suggests is 'moins descriptif qu'évocateur, (le style) tend moins à nous représenter les choses qu'à nous mettre brusquement face à face elles.' [23] Thus, as already noticed in Flaubert and the Goncourts, Zola uses inversion to convey the order in which impressions are perceived. The construction may be employed in the presentation of objects or people:

' Parfois, en se détachant, luisaient des blocs de houille, des pans et des arêtes, brusquement allumés d'un reflet de cristal.' (p. 41)

' Brusquement, au detour de l'église, parurent les premiers charbonniers qui revenaient de la fosse, le visage noir, les vêtements trempés, croisant les bras et gonflant le dos.' (p. 108)

In the first example the initial impression is conveyed by the verb *luire*, followed by objects in order of perception. In the second, certain physical characteristics of the miners are noted

[23] J. H. Matthews, ' L'impressionnisme chez Zola ', *Le Français Moderne*, xxix (1961), p. 200.

in the clause qualifying the inverted subject. Alternatively, the initial impression may precede the verb :

'Dans la cheminée de fonte, vernie et luisante, brûlait doucement une patée de houille.' (p. 68)

A further device noted by Matthews [24] is that of personification, and this may also be stressed by inversion. As in the examples quoted above, the word-order emphasizes the evocative verb as well as the subject :

'C'était l'usine morte, ce vide et cet abandon des grands chantiers où dort le travail.' (pp. 215–16)

'La salle moite avait cet air alourdi de bien-être, dont s'endorment les coins de bonheur bourgeois.' (p. 92)

In an earlier passage the author introduces a personified subject into a technical description, and it is stressed both by its position and by the delaying presence of an adverb and infinitive :

'Partout ... l'air s'empoisonnait davantage, se chauffait de la fumée des lampes ... gênant sur les yeux comme des toiles d'araignée, et que devait seul balayer l'aérage de la nuit.' (p. 51)

(c) *The technique of observation : conclusion*

Zola's method of observing detail is reflected particularly in his use of terms drawn from the mining industry. These may be emphasized by inversion and often constitute an enumeration at the end of a sentence :

'En haut et en bas de ce plan ... se trouvait un galibot, le freineur en haut, le receveur en bas.' (p. 45)

The setting of the novel and the author's concern for technical detail explains the repetition of certain inversion constructions which become clichés within the book, for instance the frequent co-occurrence of *où* and *glisser* referring to the smooth running of the machinery :

'... les madriers des guides, où glissaient les deux cages.' (p. 27)

[24] *Les deux Zola*, Geneva, 1957, p. 47.

'... de son eau pâle où glissait l'arrière vermillonné des
péniches.' (pp. 71–72)

The frequency of this and similar constructions explains
perhaps the low occurrence of *être*, *avoir* and *faire* (table 9.10),
since the device tends to emphasize the specialized vocabulary
used in description.

Besides technical detail, inverted order may also highlight
incidental observations which, although limited in reference,
often present a more vivid picture to the non-specialist.
Recurrent themes include the appearance of the coal, and
various forms of light and heat which contrast with the cold
darkness of the mine. The contrast between life above ground
and in the mine is made explicit in the following chiasmus :

'... le printemps sentait meilleur et le chauffait davantage,
après ses dix heures de travail dans l'éternel hiver du fond,
au milieu de ces ténèbres humides que jamais ne dissipait
aucun été.' (p. 134)

A further idea emphasized by inversion is that of the poverty
of the miners' surroundings :

' Et ces jardins, ravagés par l'hiver, étalaient la tristesse de
leur terre marneuse, que bossuaient et salissaient les
derniers légumes.' (p. 95)

This setting may also reflect the miserable existence of the
characters of the novel :

' Le vent soufflait toujours, des clartés plus nombreuses
couraient sur les façades basses du coron, d'où montait une
vague trépidation de réveil.' (p. 25)

'... ces éternelles routes noires, sans un arbre, où grouillait
une population affreuse qui la dégoûtait et l'effrayait.'
(p. 194)

In the first example inversion is a means of thematic transition
from the background to the workers. In the second a human
reaction is expressed in a similar transition which is underlined
by the change in position of the subject and also in that of the
qualifying adjectives.

Although inversion is less frequent in Zola than in Hugo or
the Goncourts, it is all the more effective when it occurs in

conjunction with less common verbs and other elements. For example there is throughout the novel the protracted metaphor of the miners' cause as a religion, and this receives particular emphasis from inverted order :

' De tous côtés pleuvaient les adhésions. Jamais religion naissante n'avait fait tant de fidèles.' (p. 239)

A later inversion in final position contains a further metaphor within it :

'... car la sainte et salutaire ignorance devait être le bain où se retremperaient les hommes.' (p. 275)

At the other extreme the employers are also portrayed, ironically, in the language of religion, and here again the idea is echoed by an emphatic and elevated word-order :

' Sa voix avait pris une sorte de peur religieuse, c'était comme s'il eût parlé d'un tabernacle inaccessible, où se cachait le dieu repu et accroupi, auquel ils donnaient tous leur chair, et qu'ils n'avaient jamais vu.' (p. 16)

' Ça remonterait, Dieu n'était pas si solide. Puis à cette croyance religieuse, se mêlait une profonde gratitude pour une valeur, qui, depuis un siècle, nourrissait la famille à ne rien faire.' (p. 78)

Thus it is clear that where inversion is used more sparingly in the novels of the 19th century, the resources of word-order are nonetheless fairly fully exploited in the presentation of the main themes and as a device of style. This text in particular shows increased variety in the lexical items selected for emphasis, in addition to the recurrent themes which are often reflected by similar structures.

(v) G. DE MAUPASSANT, ' BEL-AMI '

Bel-Ami is the text with the lowest frequency of inversion in this period, and it also has the smallest number of *invertissants*, (table 9.08), although the ratio of one to the other is considerably higher than that of Flaubert or Zola, indicating less variety of construction in Maupassant. As in the other novels there are few inversions in direct speech (table 9.03), and many of these are indirect constructions (seven examples out of fifteen). Table 9.04 shows that there is a low proportion of examples in initial position, a result of the small number of mobile *invertissant* constructions, and a correspondingly high proportion in final position. As in Flaubert and the Goncourts, inversion in Maupassant tends to occur in longer sentences (table 9.07), but apart from the 12% of examples with the order verb-adverb-subject, there is little separation of the constituents (table 9.12). The use of *être* in inversion construc-tions is very infrequent (2%), although that of *faire* and *avoir* is more common, as in *Germinie Lacerteux* (table 9.10), possibly indicating the increased importance of the verb in these structures.

The 10% proportion of inversions in comparative construc-tions is high for the period (table 9.09), but the examples are generally of little interest. Ten of the thirteen have the verb *faire* in the inversion clause, in two it is a verb of saying, and in one the first verb is repeated, thus :

' Il marchait plus crânement, le front plus haut, la moustache plus fière, comme doit marcher un gentilhomme.' (p. 189)

An unusual feature of this work is the *invertissant puis*, which occurs four times, on each occasion beginning a paragraph, and always with a verb of movement followed by a personal noun. The subjects thus introduced are then expanded, e.g.

' Puis vinrent les parents, Rose avec le senateur Rissolin.' (p. 359)

' Puis parurent, coup sur coup, Jacques Rival très élégant, et Norbert de Varenne, dont le col d'habit luisait...' (p. 24)

Similarly of the four occurrences of the *invertissant alors*, all in initial position, three begin a paragraph. In addition, three of the examples have the verb *commencer* and one has *passer*, but unlike the inversions after *puis*, the subjects are either collec-tive nouns (cf. example B4, p. 299 above), or abstract :

' Alors commença, dans le journal, une campagne habile et violente contre le ministère qui dirigeait les affaires.' (p. 215)

The form of these temporal constructions suggests that they mark a progression in Maupassant's narrative style.

The *invertissant où* is also used consistently in the narrative to introduce a different type of discourse, namely direct or free indirect speech. In the first example inversion provides a form of emphatic stage direction, while in the second it introduces a notion which explains the tone of the exclamation :

' Madame Walter répliqua d'une voix ferme, d'une voix où vibrait une exaltation secrète "..." ' (p. 322)

' Une colère s'éveillait en lui contre ce morceau de papier, une colère haineuse où se mêlait un étrange sentiment de malaise. C'était stupide cette histoire-là ! ' (p. 150)

(a) *Stylistic variety in Maupassant*

In his study of Maupassant, M. Vial relates the novelist's ' écriture-artiste ' and his different styles, to his use of word-order : ' L'impression produite ne procède pas seulement du jeu des aspects verbaux, mais aussi de l'ordre magique des mots et particulièrement de la place des verbes.' [25]   The examples below of inverted order in Maupassant reveal many affinities with Flaubert and the Goncourts, together with some of the devices noted in Hugo and Zola.

1. Impressionistic description

The technique of description by the accumulation of impressions is used by Maupassant in much the same way as Flaubert, although less systematically. The description of a painting shows a similar use of inversion to indicate visual progression, and as in Flaubert the result often depends on light :

' Le cadre coupait le milieu de la barque où se trouvaient les apôtres à peine éclairés par les rayons obliques d'une lanterne, dont l'un d'eux ... projetait toute la lumière sur Jésus qui s'en venait.' (p. 312)

In the following the syntax reproduces the order of perception of a distant vision :

'... et le jeune homme suivit du regard, par les autres salons, son dos noir où brillaient des perles de jais.' (p. 114)

[25] A. Vial, *Guy de Maupassant et l'art du roman*, Paris, 1954, p. 590.

The importance of light is shown in the next example, where the introduction of the subject is explained in a parenthesis following the verb :

' Puis, tendant le bras vers la poitrine de Georges, où apparaissait comme une lueur, un petit point rouge, il ajouta...' (p. 333)

An important development shown in the impressionistic passages in *Bel-Ami* is the progression which depends on a wider range of senses, in particular smell and hearing. Thus the perceived smells accumulate in the following, until they are explained by the inversion clause which in turn introduces a perceptible noise :

' On sentait dans cette chambre la fièvre, la tisane, l'éther, le goudron, cette odeur innommable et lourde des appartements où respire un poitrinaire.' (p. 165)

Alternatively it may be the noises which accumulate in the order of their perception, and here the inversion clause again provides an explanation, the emphasized subject being expanded by a relative :

' Il entendait dans toute cette vaste maison une rumeur confuse, ce bruissement des grands restaurants fait du bruit des vaisselles ... du bruit des portes un moment ouvertes et qui laissent échapper le son des voix de tous ces étroits salons où sont enfermés des gens qui dînent.' (p. 76)

A similar cause and effect relation is presented in the following, where the inversion clause embedded within the main clause permits the accumulation of noun phrases of similar structure, and thereby delays the subject of the main clause, the physical sensation which is already explained :

'... et il éprouva, en montant l'escalier, dont il éclairait avec des allumettes-bougies les marches sales, où traînaient des bouts de papiers, des bouts de cigarettes, des épluchures de cuisine, une écœrante sensation de dégoût et une hâte de sortir de là...' (p. 34)

2. Devices of repetition and accumulation

Inversions used by Maupassant in the course of repetition

take various forms, as already noted in Hugo. There is for example the repetition and development of the subject, which in turn is connected with the accumulation of impressions :

> ' C'était une chambre de maison garnie, aux meubles communs, où flottait cette odeur odieuse et fade des appartements d'hôtel, odeur émanée des rideaux, des matelas, des murs, des sièges, odeur de toutes les personnes qui...' (p. 330)

Alternatively there may be an expansion of the inverted subjects, with the source of the impression contained in an adverbial phrase following the verb :

> ' La pauvre femme ... émue par les ténèbres où apparaissaient, à la lueur errante de sa bougie, des plantes extravagantes, avec des aspects de monstres, des apparences d'êtres, des difformités bizarres' (p. 349)

There are also inversions which recur in similar contexts, and as in *Germinal*, these are most often relatives. A theme frequently expressed in this way is that of the smell of smoking and tobacco :

> ' Les sièges, les meubles, l'air où flottait l'odeur du tabac, avaient quelque chose de particulier...' (p. 46)

> '... pour ne point demeurer dans cette salle où flottait toujours une odeur âcre de vieilles pipes...' (pp. 207–8)

Other forms of accumulation related to inversion include the enumeration of adjectives qualifying the subject in descriptive passages :

> '... tout le peuple gothique des sommets d'églises que dominait la flèche aiguë de la cathédrale, surprenante aiguille de bronze, laide, étrange et démesurée, la plus haute qui soit au monde.' (p. 201)

The structure itself may be repeated with a common subject, which effectively emphasizes the two verbs :

> '... une demi-douzaine de députés intéressés dans toutes les spéculations que lançait ou que soutenait le directeur.' (p. 119)

Parallel and chiastic structures are much less common in Maupassant than in Hugo, although contrasts between the

orders of subject and verb and of noun and adjective do occur.
In this example the structure of the inverted subject parallels
that of the original form of the repeated antecedent (' de
légers frissons ') :

> ' Il sentait sur sa peau courir de légers frissons, ces frissons
> froids que donnent les immenses bonheurs.' (p. 362)

(b) Verbal emphasis

Although the effect of inversion is most generally to emphasize the subject, it has often been noted in this study that the
verb may similarly receive stress from the construction, and
this confirms Vial's observation quoted above (p. 329). It is
certainly a feature of this text, with a very low occurrence of
être in inversion constructions, that an unexpected verb is
frequently high-lighted as a consequence of inverted order.
The position of the inversion is also relevant, and the following
receives additional emphasis as the conclusion to a paragraph :

> '... la vilaine campagne de Paris où bourgeonnent d'affreux
> chalets bourgeois.' (p. 276)

Where a highly evocative verb is followed by a repeated
subject, both are strongly stressed :

> ' Et, dans le mirage confus où s'égaraient ses espérances,
> espérances de grandeur, de succès, de renommée, de for-
> tune...' (p. 83)

In the following, a prominent verb precedes an expanded
subject :

> '... la promenade circulaire, où rôde la tribu parée des
> filles...' (pp. 14–15)

Verbal emphasis may be used in relation to a particular theme
as in the next examples which are concerned with the imaginative processes of the characters. In the first the verb conveys
the appropriate impression of vagueness and marks the opening
of the recollection :

> ' Sa pensée maintenant revenait en arrière, et devant ses
> yeux éblouis par l'éclatant soleil flottait l'image de Madame
> de Marelle rajustant en face de la glace les petits cheveux
> frisés de ses tempes...' (p. 363)

In the second a similar result is achieved through the delaying
of the subject by a dependent infinitive, the subject also being
stressed by its position at the end of a paragraph :

> ' Il se fatiguait la pensée à imaginer les moindres détails du
> combat, et tout à coup il voyait en face de lui ce petit trou
> noir et profond du canon dont allait sortir une balle. (p. 152)

(c) *Conclusion*

The above examples indicate to some extent the use of
emphatic inversion in *Bel-Ami,* and the extent to which
Maupassant utilises the stylistic devices of his predecessors as
regards word-order, in some cases developing them, and in
others exploiting them less fully. In general the various effects
are obtained sporadically and unsystematically, as for instance
in the single example of an elevated construction in direct
speech, which here characterizes the forceful tones of Rival :

> ' "... sachant la langue et au courant de toutes ces graves
> questions locales auxquelles se heurtent infailliblement les
> nouveaux venus." ' (p. 27)

The frequency of inversion in comparative constructions has
already been discussed, and a further form of comparison
involving inverted order might be mentioned in conclusion.
This is the technique of using a relative inversion clause in
which the verb is in the present tense, thereby achieving a
timeless relevance in the parallel, e.g.

> ' Sa voisine ... portait en elle ce quelque chose de fripé,
> d'artificiel qu'ont, en général, les anciennes actrices...' (p. 49)
> ' On sentait cette odeur particulière des salles de rédaction
> que connaissent tous les journalistes.' (p. 51)

Thus *Bel-Ami,* although having comparatively few inversions, reflects many of the tendencies and uses revealed by the
analysis of the texts of the second half of the 19th century.
The extent to which these may be exploited further will be
shown in the analysis of 20th-century texts in the next two
chapters.

Chapter X

THE TWENTIETH CENTURY (1)

1. SYNTACTIC ANALYSIS OF THE TEXTS
1900–1950

The texts :

A. France, *Les dieux ont soif* [1]

A. Gide, *Les caves du vatican* [2]

M. Proust, *A l'ombre des jeunes filles en fleurs* [3]

A. Malraux, *La condition humaine* [4]

J. Giraudoux, *Combat avec l'ange* [5]

A. Camus, *La peste* [6]

Table 10.01 : Inversion frequencies

FRA/DS	140 : 0·70	
GID/CV	198 : 1·04	
PRO/JF	291 : 1·46	
MAL/CON	283 : 1·42	*(mean* 1·06*)*
GIR/COM	188 : 1·09	
CAM/PES	133 : 0·67	

Table 10.02 : Percentage table to show nature of clause in which inversion occurs

	FRA	*GID*	*PRO*	*MAL*	*GIR*	*CAM*
Main clause	34	29	22	41	25	37
Subordinate clause	64	70	78	58	73	61
Non-subordinating *invertissant* in subordinate clause	2	1	n	1	2	2
	100	100	100	100	100	100
Immobile *invertissant*	62	66	76	57	70	58
Mobile *invertissant*	36	27	17	38	24	34
Other operations	2	7	7	5	6	8
N :	140	198	291	283	188	133

[1] Ed. Brumfitt, London, 1964. (FRA)

[2] In *Romans, récits et soties, œuvres lyriques,* ed. Davet-Thierry, Paris (Pléiade), 1958. (GID)

[3] In *A la recherche du temps perdu I,* Paris (Pléiade), 1954, pp. 431–641. (PRO)

[4] Paris (Gallimard), 1946. (MAL)

[5] Paris (Grasset), 1934 (length, *c.* 77,000 words). (GIR)

[6] In *Théâtre, récits, nouvelles,* ed. Quillot, Paris (Pléiade), 1962, pp. 1217–1472. (CAM)

Table 10.03 : Percentage table to show distribution of inversions according to discourse type

	FRA	GID	PRO	MAL	GIR	CAM
Narrative	86	74	89	75	86	73
Direct speech	11	22	8	19	8	19
Indirect speech	3	1	3	1	3	5
Free indirect speech	—	3	—	5	3	3

Table 10.04 : Percentage table to show position of inversion within the corpus examined

	FRA	GID	PRO	MAL	GIR	CAM
Sentence initial	23	18	17	23	22	25
Paragraph initial	6	6	3	3	2	2
Chapter initial	—	—	—	—	n	1
Speech initial	—	2	—	3	n	1
Total initial	29	26	20	29	25	29
Sentence final	31	33	21	30	29	30
Paragraph final	7	8	n	7	2	7
Chapter final	—	n	—	n	—	—
Speech final	1	2	1	4	1	3
Total final	39	43	22	41	32	40

Table 10.05 : Percentage table to show position of inversion in relation to other types of discourse

	FRA	GID	PRO	MAL	GIR	CAM
Preceding direct speech	4	1	1	7	—	1
Following direct speech	—	1	n	2	—	1
Preceding free indirect	—	—	—	1	—	—
Following free indirect	—	—	—	—	—	—

Table 10.06 : Percentage table to show nature of the inverted noun phrase

	FRA	GID	PRO	MAL	GIR	CAM
Pronoun subject	10	14	15	23	10	15
Substantive subject	89	85	79	69	87	83
Compound inversion	1	1	6	8	3	2
	100	100	100	100	100	100
2 or more subjects	8	6	4	2	7	7
S and dependent (S)	11	8	18	7	14	13

Table 10.07 : The percentage of inversions occurring in sentences of three or more clauses

	FRA	GID	PRO	MAL	GIR	CAM
(S)—3 clauses	27	25	22	17	24	29
4 clauses	14	12	18	11	17	10
5 clauses	5	3	20	5	10	5
6 clauses	1	n	14	3	4	2
7 clauses	—	—	6	1	1	2
7+ clauses	—	—	4	n	—	1
	47	40	84	37	56	49

Table 10.08 : Ratio of inversions to *invertissants*

FRA	140 : 48—2·92
GID	198 : 65—3·05
PRO	291 : 61—4·77
MAL	283 : 65—4·35
GIR	188 : 49—3·84
CAM	133 : 40—3·32
Total	1,233 : 158—7·80 (*mean* 3·70)

Table 10.09 : Percentage table of the most frequently occurring inversions

	FRA	GID	PRO	MAL	GIR	CAM
Relatives	45	46	46	39	51	38
Comparatives	6	6	13	4	5	7
Indirect construction	8	4	8	7	10	10
Modal adverbs	13	13	13	28	13	12

Table 10.10 : Percentage table to show the occurrence of ' être ', ' faire ' and ' avoir '

	FRA	GID	PRO	MAL	GIR	CAM
être	8	7	19	12	21	20
faire	3	1	5	2	3	—
avoir	1	n	4	2	4	3

Table 10.11 : Percentage table showing the distribution of direct speech *invertissants*

	FRA	GID	PRO	MAL	GIR	CAM
Immobile *invertissant*	47	65	84	43	75	44
Mobile *invertissant*	53	26	12	51	19	44
Other operations	—	9	4	6	6	12
N :	15	43	25	53	16	25

Table 10.12 : Percentage table to show the occurrence of adverbials and clauses in inversion constructions

	FRA	*GID*	*PRO*	*MAL*	*GIR*	*CAM*
V(adv)S	16	18	14	11	15	5
(adv)VS	7	7	2	2	2	1
V(S)S	—	—	2	n	n	—
(S)VS	3	2	3	1	2	2

(i) DISTRIBUTION OF THE INVERSIONS

The six texts selected from the first half of the 20th century have an average inversion frequency which, along with that of the first half of the 19th century, is the highest since the 16th century. The frequencies range from $0 \cdot 67$ to $1 \cdot 46$, with France and Camus at one extreme, and Proust and Malraux at the other, and with Gide and Giraudoux around the average of $1 \cdot 06$. A further indication of the extent to which inversion is now re-established in French syntax is the total of 158 different *invertissants* revealed by the analysis (table 10.08), with Gide, Malraux and Proust having the highest individual number of inversions since the 16th-century writers. The average number of *invertissants* per text, fifty-five, is again the highest in the last four centuries of this study.

The large number of examples is the most outstanding feature of inversion in these texts. The details of their distribution indicate in general only slight variations on the previous century, and the trends noted then tend to be confirmed. Thus table 10.02 shows the continuing part played by other syntactic operations, which, for example, account for 8% of the inversions in Camus. The proportion of inversions in subordinate clauses is unusually high in Proust (78%), a figure surpassed by only three other authors in the study, Scarron, La Fayette and Maupassant.

There is a perceptible increase in the occurrence of inversion in direct speech in these texts (table 10.03), which might reflect the formal nature of the style of some of the novels analysed. This is certainly true of Gide, but on the other hand the proportion is low in Proust and Giraudoux (8% in each), and it will also be low in the texts of the 1950s. In these three authors the distribution of the conversational inversions is approximately the same as the overall distribution (table 10.11). There are examples of inversion in free indirect speech in four of the texts, the exceptions being France and Proust, and this device is noticed particularly in Malraux (5%).

As regards position of the inversions, there continue to be more in final position than in initial position (table 10.04), although both are unusually infrequent in Proust, a consequence of the length of the Proustian sentence. Similarly 18% of the Proust examples are followed by a dependent clause (table 10.06), and table 10.7 shows that 84% of his inversions occur in sentences of three or more clauses (cf. Nicolas de Montreux, 89% and Scarron, 86%). The sentences containing inversion are much shorter in the other texts, the proportion of longer sentences ranging from 37% in Malraux to 56% in Giraudoux. Table 10.05 shows that 7% of the inversions in Malraux precede direct speech, the highest proportion in this position since the loss of inversion as an initial *incise* construction.

The slight decrease in the number of constructions with more than one subject in this period (table 10.06) is perhaps indicative of the decline in the techniques of repetition favoured by some of the 19th-century writers. As for the constructions in which inversion occurs, a small increase in the average number of modal adverb *invertissants* corresponds to a decrease in the average number of relatives (table 10.09), although this is again reversed in the texts after 1950. The same table reveals the curiously regular frequency of modal adverb *invertissants* in all the texts except Malraux. There are also a few more comparative and indirect constructions than before.

Finally, table 10.10 shows an increased occurrence of *être* in inversion clauses in Proust, Giraudoux and Camus, although none reaches the 26% frequency of Hugo. The second half of the century will show the frequency again reduced, and France and Gide give some indication of this preference for lexical variety in the verb. All the texts have examples in which a clause separates *invertissant* and verb (table 10.12), and in 2% of the Proust examples it separates verb and subject. The number of adverbs in this position does not reach the 27% frequency of Flaubert, but the order verb-adverb-subject is nevertheless generally common.

(ii) SUPPLEMENTARY TEXTS

In view of the number and diversity of French novels in the 20th-century, four additional works have been examined, representing different styles and preoccupations in the first half of the century. Of these four novels the highest frequency of inversion is found, surprisingly, in Céline's *Voyage au bout de la nuit*,[7] with a frequency of 0·68 for the first 88,000 words, which is similar to that of France and Camus. Next comes Bernanos' *Sous le soleil de Satan*,[8] with a lower frequency of 0·56. Finally two novels with a common philosophy share an unusually low frequency: Sartre's *La nausée*,[9] 0·34, and Simone de Beauvoir's *Le sang des autres*,[10] 0·38. An exceptionally low occurrence of inversion in Sartre's novels is noted by Ullmann,[11] who finds only fourteen examples of 'genuine optional inversion' in *La mort dans l'âme*, most of which appear to be based on rhythmic considerations.

If these four novels are taken into account, the average inversion frequency for this period drops to 0·83. The individual figures suggest, however, and this will be confirmed in the next chapter, that the occurrence of inverted order now depends entirely on the stylistic intentions of the novelist, and inversion as a device of style seems either to be wholly accepted or largely rejected by contemporary authors.

---

[7] *Livre de poche*, 1965, pp. 1–259.

[8] In *Œuvres romanesques*, ed. Béguin, Paris (Pléiade), 1961, pp. 59–308.

[9] Paris (Gallimard), 1938.

[10] 23rd ed. Paris (Gallimard), 1947.

[11] ' Inversion as a Stylistic Device in the Contemporary French Novel ' p. 169.

(iii) EXAMPLES

A. IMMOBILE 'INVERTISSANT'

1. *Zero : GID : 4 ; MAL : 1 ; GIR : 1.*
   ' *Subirent* le même sort toutes les lettres qui se dénonçaient ainsi elles-mêmes par leur origine, orphelinats, maisons de retraites ... ou se trahissaient par l'écriture...' (GIR, p. 125)

2. *Relatives : FRA : 64 inversions, 7 'invertissants' ; GID : 92,9 ; PRO : 136,9 ; MAL : 111,12 ; GIR : 95,9 ; CAM : 51,7*
   ' Tchen le palpait de sa main gauche *à quoi* collaient les vêtements pleins de sang gluant, incapable pourtant de détacher son regard de la fenêtre brisée *par où* pouvait tomber la grenade.' (MAL, p. 116)

3. *Comparatives : FRA : 7,5 ; GID : 12,3 ; PRO : 39,10 ; MAL : 10,3 ; GIR : 9,3 ; CAM : 9,2*
   ' Elles se montraient presque toutes soigneusement coiffées et mises avec *autant de* recherche *que* leur permettait leur malheureux état.' (FRA, p. 153)

4. *Concessives : GID : 3,2 ; PRO : 6,3 ; MAL : 6,1 ; GIR : 1,1 ; CAM : 3,1*
   ' Cependant ... *si* douleureuses *que* fussent ces angoisses, *si* lourd à porter *que* fût ce cœur pourtant vide, on peut bien dire que ces exilés ... furent des privilégiés.' (CAM, p. 1278)

5. *Temporal clause : FRA : 5,4 ; GID : 4,4 ; PRO : 11,7 ; MAL : 4,2 ; GIR : 4,2*
   ' *Au fur et à mesure que* s'effacerait mon ennui que Gilberte eût haussé les épaules, diminuerait aussi le souvenir de son charme, souvenir qui me faisait souhaiter qu'elle revînt vers moi.' (PRO, p. 626)

6. *Causal clause : GID : 1,1 ; MAL : 1,1*
   ' Il eut soin de prendre sa malle avec lui, *parce que* sont suspects les voyageurs sans bagages et qu'il prenait garde de n'attirer point sur lui l'attention '. (GID, p. 833)

7. *Purpose/result clauses : GID : 3,2 ; PRO : 2,1 ; MAL : 1,1 ; GIR : 1,1*
   ' Elle refermait la porte derrière elle, *pour que* ne parvînt à

l'appartement aucun écho du palier...' (GIR, p. 127)

8. *Substantival clause : GID : 2,2 ; MAL : 5,5 ; GIR : 1,1*
   ' Elle *attendit* patiemment, humblement, *que* fussent désertés les abords de la tombe fraîche.' (GID, p. 865)

9. *Hypothetical clause : GID : 2,2 ; PRO : 3,3 ; MAL : 2,2 ; GIR : 1,1*
   ' " Que de souffrances éparses dans cette lumière disparaîtraient, *si* disparaissait la pensée..." ' (MAL, p. 400)

10. *Correlatives : CAM : 1,1*
    ' " Et *autant de fois* qu'une maison recevait de coups, *autant* y avait-il de morts qui en sortaient." ' (p. 1295)

11. *Indirect construction : FRA : 11,5 ; GID : 8,4 ; PRO : 24,9 ; MAL : 21,9 ; GIR : 19,8 ; CAM : 13,4*
    ' Tarrou eut à peine le temps d'entendre son compagnon demander *ce que* pouvaient bien vouloir ces oiseaux-là.' (CAM, p. 1447)

B. MOBILE ' INVERTISSANT '

1. *Attributes : FRA : 2,2 ; GID : 1,1 ; PRO : 1,1 ; GIR : 3,1 ; CAM : 2,1*
   ' " Je me répète qu'il l'est toujours, et que *seules*, jusqu'à présent, m'obligeaient d'impures considérations de carrière..." ' (GID, p. 836)

2. *Adverbs—modal : FRA : 18,7 ; GID : 26,10 ; PRO : 37,8 ; MAL : 80,7 ; GIR : 24,4 ; CAM : 16,5*
   ' *A plus forte raison* en est-il de même dans les relations plus tendres, où l'amour a tant d'éloquence...' (PRO, p. 632)

3. *Adverbs—quantity : PRO : 6,2 ; MAL : 2,2 ; CAM : 2,2*
   ' On était gêné ... de ne pas trouver le salon vide, *tant* y tenaient une place énigmatique et se rapportant à des heures de la vie de la maîtresse de la maison qu'on ne connaissait pas, ces fleurs qui n'avaient pas été préparées pour les visiteurs d'Odette...' (PRO, p. 594)

4. *Adverbs—temporal : FRA : 3,3 ; GID : 7,5 ; PRO : 1,1 ; MAL : 2,2 ; GIR : 2,1 ; CAM : 4,3*

' *Parfois* retentissait un large soufflet, appliqué par la main d'une citoyenne sur la joue d'un insolent...' (FRA, p. 80)

5. *Adverbs—place : FRA : 8,4 ; GID : 4,1 ; MAL : 8,2 ; GIR : 2,2 ; CAM : 2,1*
   ' *Derrière*, couchées sur un bat-flanc ou debout, grouillaient des ombres trop longues : des hommes comme des vers.' (MAL, p. 334)

6. *Adverbs—combination : GID : 1,1 ; PRO : 2,2*
   ' "... il ... se tiendra prêt à nous accueillir vers midi ; *même, sans doute*, pourrons-nous déjeuner avec lui." ' (GID, p. 793)

7. *Adverbial phrase—time : GIR : 3,2*
   ' *Vers cette époque*, survint un événement qui aurait dû rehausser Maléna à ses propres yeux : elle sauva un enfant.' (GIR, p. 242)

8. *Adverbial phrase—place : FRA : 14,8 ; GID : 10,6 ; MAL : 11,6 ; GIR : 4,3 ; CAM : 9,7*
   ' *Et à côté d'elle*, grandissant comme elle, parut l'ombre de deux oreilles pointues.' (MAL, p. 15)

9. *Adverbial phrase—manner : GID : 1,1 ; PRO : 1,1 ; MAL : 1,1*
   ' " Je veux qu'*à ceci* se reconnaisse l'élégance de sa nature, qu'il agisse surtout par jeu et..." ' (GID, p. 837)

10. *Prepositional phrase : FRA : 6,1 ; GID : 3,2 ; MAL : 1,1 ; GIR : 7,3 ; CAM : 10,2*
    ' *De l'appartement* disparut tout ce qui ne convenait plus à Maléna retrouvée.' (GIR, p. 302)

11. *Subordinate clause : PRO : 1,1 ; MAL : 2,1*
    ' *Tandis que l'auto avançait*, s'installait dans l'esprit de Ferral la confession, lue dans quelque bouquin de médecine, d'une femme affolée du désir d'être flagellée...' (MAL, p. 260)

C. OTHER OPERATIONS

1. *Deletion : GID : 2 ; MAL : 3*
   ' Avec son chapeau cronstadt ... on le dirait en tenue de

visite, *n'était* le châle écossais qu'il porte sur l'avant-bras.'
(GID, p. 690)

2. *Deletion and transposition : GID : 5 ; PRO : 17 ; MAL :
   7 ; GIR : 5 ; CAM : 6*
   ' " Cela fait longtemps que j'ai honte, honte à mourir
   d'avoir été, *fût-ce* de loin, *fût-ce* dans la bonne volonté,
   un meurtrier à mon tour.' " (CAM, p. 1423)

3. *Addition and transposition : FRA : 2,2 ; GID : 7,6 ;
   PRO : 4,2 ; MAL : 4,4 ; GIR : 6,5 ; CAM : 5,3*
   ' " *C'est* parce que nos ancêtres ont pensé ainsi *qu'*existent
   ces belles peintures..." ' (MAL, p. 69)

(iv) DETAILS OF THE INVERSIONS

(a) Immobile ' invertissant '

For the first time since the 16th century, every type of
immobile *invertissant* construction is revealed by the analysis
of these six texts, and in addition each construction except the
correlative occurs in at least two of them. The unusual inversions in purpose or result clauses or in a hypothetical clause are
found in all the authors except France and Camus. The six
examples of zero *invertissant*, occurring in these authors are
interesting in that the construction is not necessarily confined
to verbs of movement, although there are examples with
précéder, entrer and *venir* in Gide, and *suivre* in Malraux. The
construction in Giraudoux is quoted above (p. 340), where the
subject of the less usual *subir* is followed by a dependent clause
containing an enumeration, and the remaining example is in
Gide :

' La veilleuse s'éteignit, mais s'allumèrent aussitôt deux
appliques pariétales, plus désobligeantes que le lustre du
milieu. ' (p. 828)

This inversion, on the analogy of verbs of motion, conveys the
idea of immediacy, besides disposing of a lengthy subject and
forming part of a chiasmus.

In the 20th century inversion after a temporal conjunction
becomes more common than in a concessive clause, and lends
itself to various stylistic effects. In these texts there is a

greater variety in *invertissants* than hitherto, with thirteen
different ones in twenty-eight examples, and they are also
followed by a greater range of verbs. The example from Proust
(quoted p. 340 above) is notable both for the *invertissant*,
which occurs only in this author in the present analysis, and for
the fact that the subordinate clause itself is an *invertissant*.[12]
The other example with *au fur et à mesure que* has the verb *se
corrompre*. All the texts except Camus have constructions
with *quand* followed by *venir*, and several have instances of
tant que and *durer*, the structures which constituted the
majority of examples in preceding periods. The greatest
variety is found in Proust, where there are collocations such as
aussitôt que with *retourner* or *survenir*, *cependant que* and
décliner, and *depuis que* and *s'évanouir*. Interesting examples
also occur in other authors, such as the following in *Les dieux
ont soif*, where the temporal clause *invertissant* is unusually
close to the beginning of a paragraph :

'Evariste, pendant que se préparait la mort du Juste, dormit
du sommeil des disciples au jardin des Oliviers.' (FRA,
p. 333)

The unusual and somewhat anomalous construction of
inversion in a causal clause is found twice in this analysis.
The Gide example (p. 340 above) contrasts with the clause
having direct order which follows, and has something of the
legal flavour inherent in absolute inversions with similar verbs
although the enumeration usual in such contexts never comes.
The second example is in Malraux :

'Et puisque n'existaient ni son passé qu'il venait d'inventer,
ni le geste élémentaire et supposé si proche sur quoi se
fondait son rapport avec cette femme, rien n'existait.'
(MAL, p. 295)

The inversion begins a complex sentence structure which
includes a further inversion, and it is balanced by the occurrence of the same verb, in direct position, at the end of the
sentence. With reference to this same example, Le Bidois

[12] Also quoted by R. Le Bidois, *L'inversion du sujet dans la prose contemporaine*, pp. 398–99.

maintains that ' l'inversion est due surtout au développement des sujets ',[13] although the same cannot be said of the Gide inversion. It may also be noted that the majority of causal inversions quoted by Le Bidois have the auxiliary verb *être*, which may again indicate some relation to the absolute inversion construction.

Three of the seven examples of inversion in purpose or result clauses express purpose, one of which, in Gide, occurs in direct speech. This example is also interesting as unlike all but one of the other examples, the verb does not express an idea of arrival :

> ' "... le nom du destinataire ... est laissé en blanc, de manière que le puisse toucher n'importe quel porteur." ' (GID, p. 806)

The *invertissants* found in the texts are *pour que* (2), *de manière que* (2), *de sorte que* (1) and *sans que* (3). Le Bidois attributes the frequency of the latter to its function of negation, which thus attracts the element it is negating, the verb.[14] Although this may be the case in theory, the two Proust examples in this analysis may well be explained by other means, the first being a question of rhythm and euphony, and the second a consequence of a dependent clause following the subject, all of which is in parenthesis :

> ' Le 1er janvier sonna toutes ses heures sans qu'arrivât cette lettre de Gilberte.' (PRO, p. 609)

> ' Et, au milieu de la gymnastique que je faisais, sans qu'en fût à peine augmenté l'essoufflement que me donnaient l'exercice musculaire et l'ardeur du jeu, je répandis ... mon plaisir auquel...' (PRO, p 494)

The three hypothetical clause *invertissants* are *si, comme si*, and *à moins que*, all of which are found in Proust, and one or two of them in the other three texts. *Si* occurs in a reinforced form more commonly than in isolation, so there are three examples of *comme si*, and one where *si* is strengthened by an adverb :

---

[13] *Ibid.*, p. 314.
[14] *Ibid.*, p. 320.

M

' " Et que je risquerais la mienne (vie) agilement, si seulement s'offrait quelque belle prouesse ... à oser ! " ' (GID,
p. 823)

One of the two occurrences of *à moins que* is also followed by an
adverbial. Thus the dissonant co-occurrence of *si* and a verb is
avoided in all but two instances, and even here the verb
phrase is sufficiently long to dispel at least some of the artificia-
lity mentioned by Le Bidois [15] (see example A9, p. 341 above).
These examples also disprove the assertion by Wartburg and
Zumthor that inversion after the hypothetical *si* does not
exist.[16]

Inversion in a substantival clause (*proposition complétive*)
has been noted previously in this study only in Rabelais, but
is not uncommon in several modern writers, in particular in
this analysis Malraux and Robbe-Grillet. The verb which most
frequently has inverted order in its object clause is *attendre*,
examples being found in Gide, Giraudoux and Malraux. In
addition, Gide has a construction with *sembler* :

' Il lui semblait que n'avait pas le droit d'échapper ainsi
Julius '. (GID, p. 841)

The examples in Malraux also follow this pattern of inversion
after a transitive verb expressing a mental attitude, i.e.
supposer, importer, savoir, souhaiter and *être bon que*, e.g.

' " ... qu'il me paraît défendable de souhaiter que ne disparaisse pas d'Asie la seule organisation puissante qui..."
(MAL, p. 380)

These may be compared with similar verbs in the Rabelais
examples, such as *penser, être bon, vouloir* and *regretter*.

(b) Mobile ' invertissant ' and other operations

The analysis of these texts likewise reveals all the major
mobile *invertissant* construction types, the exceptions being
the archaic direct object, infinitival, participial phrase and
negative particle *invertissants*. These constructions are

---

[15] *Ibid.*, p. 321.
[16] W. von Wartburg and P. Zumthor, *Précis de syntaxe du français
contemporain*, Berne, 1947, p. 331.

generally less interesting, since they all occur sporadically in earlier works, although a few of the *invertissants* are unusual. While every variety of adverbial *invertissant* occurs, several are infrequent, in particular adverbial phrases of time and manner, although the number of adverbs, especially those of time and place, increases. The subordinate clauses followed by inversion are all temporal. The examples from Malraux and Proust (see p. 342 above) are complicated structures where inversion may facilitate comprehension. In the remaining inversion from Malraux however, the construction is undoubtedly emphatic:

'Puis, pendant que les clameurs retombées s'étouffaient lourdement sous l'indestructible silence, monta un cri de chien qui hurle à la mort, coupé net: un homme égorgé.' (MAL, p. 109)

Of the inversions resulting from a deletion operation, the two Gide examples are hypothetical, whereas those from Malraux show the loss of an impersonal pronoun, all three having the verb *rester*. Two of these occur in parallel sentence positions, thus:

'Restait la Grâce, c'est-à-dire l'amour illimité...

Restait aussi la charité;' (MAL, p. 77)

Finally, as regards the addition and transposition operation, which has a higher frequency in the 20th century, it will be noted that in the example quoted on p. 343 (above), the *invertissant* contained within *c'est ... que*, is a causal subordinate clause, the only instance of such a structure in the whole study.

2. STYLISTIC ANALYSIS OF THE TEXTS 1900–1950

(i) A. FRANCE, 'LES DIEUX ONT SOIF'

The above analysis of the types of inversion found in the six texts suggests that the style of *Les dieux ont soif* is more traditional in this respect than that of the others, with the exception perhaps of Camus, since he and France both share a low inversion frequency. The types of immobile *invertissant* which characterize the extension of inverted order in the 20th century do not occur at all in the France text, that is zero *invertissant*, together with inversion in concessive, causal, purpose and hypothetical clauses. Certain adverbial *invertissants* are not found either, and there is no example of inversion after a subordinate clause. Table 10.02 also shows the low frequency of other operations, 2% of the total, and this consists of addition and transposition examples only.

Although the inversion constructions used by France are very similar to those of authors in previous centuries, differences are revealed by the particular *invertissants*. With a total of forty-eight *invertissants*, and 2·92 inversions to each (table 10.08), there are more *invertissants* in relation to the number of inversions than in any 19th-century text analysed above. This extension of inverted order in traditional constructions is seen in temporal clauses and in structures where the *invertissant* is an adverb of time or place. Thus there are examples of inversion after *quand*, *lorsque*, *tant que* and *pendant que*. Among the adverbial *invertissants* are occurrences of *à gauche* and *à droite*. Besides a high frequency of inversion after adverbial clauses of place, the two examples of addition and transposition contain this structure, e.g.

' C'est dans cette nef que, deux fois la semaine, de cinq heures du soir à onze heures, se tenaient les assemblées publiques.' (p. 37)

Other features revealed by the tables include a proportion of examples preceding direct speech (table 10.05), shorter sentences containing inversion (table 10.07) and few inversions with a pronoun subject or compound structure (table 10.06). Tables 10.06 and 10.12 show that the sentence structure of *Les dieux ont soif* is as complex as that of the other texts, if not more so, with 11% of the inverted subjects having a dependent clause, and 16% with an adverb between verb and subject.

(a) Inversion and direct speech

The 4% of the inversion constructions which introduce a passage of direct speech (table 10.05) emphasize the change in discourse in several ways. In the first example the sentence following inversion expands the inverted subject :

' Cependant, autour de lui, de moment en moment, grandis-
sait la clamour sinistre :

— Marat est mort : les aristocrates l'ont tué ! ' (p. 100)

This whole structure has considerable emphatic value : the
separation of *cependant* and the verb by two adverbial phrases
heightens the tension and this is continued by the inversion of
the noun phrase. In two other examples an inversion construction is related to a later *incise* structure. In the first case the
inverted subject is also the first speaker in the conversation
thus introduced, and in the second it is the listener :

' A peine Élodie eut-elle tourné les yeux sur lui :

— Venez, Evariste ! fit-elle vivement.' (p. 77)

'... Gamelin ... bondit dans la chambre bleue où chaque nuit
l'attendait Élodie.

— Tu es vengée, lui dit-il.' (p. 178)

Inversion within conversation is infrequent in *Les dieux ont
soif* (11% of the examples) (table 10.03), but sometimes occurs
to emphasize themes which are important to the speakers.
Thus certain revolutionary ideals are highlighted in the speech
of Gamelin :

' " J'ai conçu et exécuté le nouveau jeu de cartes révolutionnaire dans lequel aux rois, aux dames, aux valets sont
substituées les Libertés, les Egalités, les Fraternités ; les
as, entourés de faisceaux, s'appellent les Lois..." ' (p. 60)

In this example inversion stresses both the revolutionary
slogan and the deeper significance of the parallelism between
invertissants and subjects. Elsewhere an adverb in initial
position and consequently an *invertissant* adds dramatic value
to a speech :

' " J'ai embrassé cet enfant : peut-être ferai-je guillotiner sa
mère." ' (p. 226)

The speech of clerics also contains inversion, with four notable
examples by Longuemare in dialogue with Brotteaux. The
naïve, yet pompous style of the priest is emphasized, perhaps
with a little irony, by the following which concludes a paragraph and his speech :

' " Ah ! monsieur, que cette soupe aux châtaignes est

parfumée ! Elle me rappelle la table couronnée d'enfants où
souriait ma mère." ' (p. 157)

The ironic use of inversion is more evident in the next example
by Brotteaux in conversation with his former mistress :

' " Vous ne pouvez concevoir, chère amie, l'empire que garde
le clergé sur la multitude des ânes ... Je voulais dire ' des
âmes ' ; la langue m'a fourché." ' (p. 133)

The examples quoted above indicate that the inversions
found in conversation in this novel are mostly unexceptional,
and while lending emphasis to certain ideas do not themselves
create an impression of unnatural speech.

(b) Inversion and narrative technique

Allusions to Antiquity and traces of a Classical style are
found less in this novel than in some of the other works of
Anatole France. Nonetheless such references do occur and may
be stressed by inversion, as in the following simile, where the
subject receives additional emphasis from its position at the
end of the sentence :

' Henry était jeune et beau : Achille n'unissait pas tant de
grâce à tant de vigueur, quand il revêtit les armes que lui
présentait Ulysse.' (p. 134)

In a further example inversion, with an adverbial between verb
and subject, contributes to suspense, and permits the introduction of a Classical reference developing the inverted subject :

'... il leur fallait traverser un groupe de citoyens en carmagnole que haranguait, du haut de la galerie, un jeune militaire
beau comme l'Amour de Praxitèle sous son casque de peau
de panthère.' (p. 77)

Inversion occurs in descriptions in the novel, whether of
crowds or individuals, and often reinforces the pictorial
vividness of the background. In the following example of a
single-clause sentence with inverted order, the construction
emphasizes the mood of a barely discernible crowd :

' Sur la place toute noire s'agite une foule incertaine,
inquiète...' (p. 232)

In another passage the crowd is examined more closely, with again a climactic effect achieved by the position of two adverbials between verb and subject :

' Dans ces corridors, pleins d'ombres sanglantes, passaient chaque jour, sans une plainte, vingt, trente, cinquante condamnés, vieillards, femmes, adolescents...' (p. 199)

The same delaying technique is found in the description of individuals, and here the intervening adverbial has political significance, as well as indicating a visual impression :

' Ce matin-là, devant un bureau, au pied de la chaire, se tenait, en bonnet rouge et carmagnole, le menuisier de la place de Thionville, le citoyen Dupont aîné...' (p. 37)

In the following, two inversions permit an ordered progression to a new object of description, with an interposed adverbial providing an incidental simile :

' La cour était fermée ... par des étables devant lesquelles s'élevait, comme un tertre glorieux, un tas de fumier, que, à cette heure, retournait de sa fourche une fille plus large que haute, les cheveux couleur de paille.' (p. 124)

There is a similar sentence pattern later in the novel, where two inversions emphasize the same idea, freedom, at the beginning and end of a descriptive passage :

' Sur une cour, où s'élevait un arbre de la Liberté ... la chapelle ... présentait son pignon nu, percé d'un œil-de-bœuf et d'une porte cintrée, que surmontait le drapeau aux couleurs nationales, coiffé du bonnet de la Liberté. Les Jacobins...' (p. 149)

Inversions in short sentences in descriptive passages may contribute to an elevated style. In the next examples the word-order underlines the ironic impression produced by the long, rather high-flown, noun phrases :

' A sa douleur filiale se mêlaient une sollicitude patriotique et une piété populaire qui le déchiraient.' (p. 100)

' Dans le club de Robespierre régnait la prudence administrative de la gravité bourgeoise.' (p. 149)

Inversion may be one feature in the expansion of a simple structure : additional variety in the following lies in the

development of the second nominal before the first, and in the
omission of the second verb :

> ' Fédéralisme, indivisibilité : dans l'unité et l'indivisibilité
> était le salut : dans le fédéralisme, la damnation.' (p. 151)

(c) Other features of sentence structure

Although this novel has a higher frequency of more than
one inverted subject than do the other texts (table 10.06),
there are few cases where the subject comprises more than two
nominals. In one of these five noun phrases are inverted :

> ' Jean Blaise ... échangeait ... des propos facétieux où
> passaient sans ordre ni mesure Verboquet le Généreux,
> Catherine Cuissot qui colportait, les demoiselles Chaudron,
> le sorcier Calichet et les figures plus récentes de Cadet
> Rousselle et de madame Angot.' (p. 120)

This enumeration also echoes the adverbial ' sans ordre ni
mesure ' separating verb and subject. In a further example
three inverted subjects, one with a dependent clause, balance
the accumulation of postposed epithets in the preceding
clause :

> ' les hôtels ... n'offraient plus que des façades irrégulières,
> pauvres, sales, percées de fenêtres inégales, étroites, in-
> nombrables, qu'égayaient des pots de fleurs, des cages
> d'oiseaux et des linges qui séchaient.' (p. 41)

Elsewhere the nominals may be emphasized by their final
position, and in the example below, this is reinforced by a
chiasmus, with inverted and non-inverted order after the
relative que :

> ' (une peinture) d'après une composition de Boucher, que le
> père de Jean Blaise avait fait poser en 1770 et qu'effaçaient
> depuis lors le soleil et la pluie.' (p. 52)

There are also instances of inversion of a collective noun which
is expanded by an enumeration :

> ' Là, logeait une multitude d'artisans, bijoutiers, ciseleurs,
> horlogers, opticiens, imprimeurs, lingères ... et quelques
> vieux hommes de loi qui ...' (p. 41)

Subject nominals with a preposed qualifying adjective are

stressed in various ways by inversion. Thus the inversion clause may conclude a paragraph, while reintroducing in passing the subject of the preceding passage :

'... et il résolut d'aller dès le lendemain lui offrir ce que refusait le pusillanime Caillou.' (p. 143)

In the following the construction is more complicated ; inversion stresses the subject of the subordinate clause, which qualifies the pronoun object, while forming an effective semantic contrast with the main clause :

' Ceux que n'avait pas chassés le terrible décret, quelques gouttes d'eau les dispersent.' (p. 233)

Repetitive constructions feature in several of the inversions. In the first of the following examples the verb-adverbial structure is repeated in front of a common subject, and in the second it is the verb-subject structure which is repeated after a single *invertissant* :

' Là se tenait sans pompe et s'excerçait par la parole le plus grand des pouvoirs de l'Etat.' (p. 150)

' Sur leur poitrine ... se croisait le fichu blanc où se recourbait la bavette du tablier bleu.' (p. 137)

It may be noted that structural repetitions seem to be more frequent in Anatole France than reiteration of lexical items as seen in other authors. Finally, one of the examples in which one or more clauses are interposed between *invertissant* and verb is outstanding for its length, as will be observed frequently in Proust :

' Gamelin déplora qu'à l'apogée de la peinture française, si tardive, puisqu'elle ne datait que de Lesueur, de Claude et de Poussin et correspondait à la décadence des écoles italienne et flamande, eût succédé un si rapide et profond déclin.' (p. 118)

The role of inversion in *Les dieux ont soif* is, as suggested above, primarily one of liaison, although it may occasionally stress important themes in speech. Inversion rarely occurs in the major stylistic devices of Anatole France ; it is, for instance, hardly ever used in ironic passages. Thus France is not one of the innovators of the 20th century in his use of word-

M*

order, despite an increased variety in *invertissants*. Instead inversion is part of the carefully-worked structure of an elevated style, with the constructions having little individual stylistic significance.

(ii) A. GIDE, 'LES CAVES DU VATICAN'

The 198 inversions found in *Les caves du vatican* represent a frequency of 1·04, which is similar to that of the Giraudoux novel, and although high, it is by no means as high as that of Malraux and Proust.   With the exception of *Les faux-monnayeurs*, an analysis of the fictional works of Gide reveals on average a much lower occurrence of inversion.[17]   There are ninety-two examples in *L'Immoraliste*, sixty-five in *La porte étroite*, thirty-two in *La symphonie pastorale*, and forty-three in *Thésée*. Ullmann notes approximately 170 occurrences of optional inversion in *Les faux-monnayeurs*,[18] which, being a longer novel, would still produce a lower frequency than that of the *Caves*.

The analysis of the *Caves* yields examples of each type of immobile *invertissant*. Mobile *invertissants* not found in the *Caves* are adverbs of quantity, adverbial phrases of time, and subordinate clauses, although the first two have been found in *L'Immoraliste* and *La porte étroite* respectively.   The outstanding feature of this novel is the proportion of inversions in direct speech, 22% (table 10.03), the highest for the texts of this period and for all the texts in this study since 1850. The high proportion of inversions in final position, 43%, may also be noted (table 10.04).   On the other hand there are fewer examples with several subjects or a dependent clause, and of compound inversion, and only 40% of the total occur in sentences of three or more clauses (table 10.07). Table 10.12 shows that the occurrence of adverbials between elements in

---

[17] The details relating to other works of Gide are taken from a dissertation on inversion which I submitted to the University College of North Wales in 1968 as part of the Diploma in Linguistics.

[18] ' Inversion as a Stylistic Device in the Contemporary French Novel '. p. 169.

inversion constructions is highest in Gide. The importance of this novel for the study of inverted order is also indicated by the number of different *invertissants* which occur (table 10.08). As in the *Condition humaine* there is a total of 65, but with a much lower proportion of inversions to *invertissants* in Gide than in Malraux.

(a) *Characterization by inverted order in speech*

Although the inversions which occur in direct speech in this novel have a particular function in so far as the main characters are concerned, the high frequency of the construction implies, as suggested by Ullmann for *Les faux-monnayeurs* that ' the author did not wish to imitate conversational usage.' [19] The improbability of some of the dialogue is indicated by several of the inversions used by minor characters. In the first of the examples which follow the speaker is a seven-year old girl, and the second unlikely speech is made in the midst of a crisis :

' "... c'est celle de Notre-Dame de Lourdes, que m'a donnée la tante Fleurissoire." ' (p. 693)

' " Tout ce que j'ai compris, c'est que ses deux petits enfants sont dans cette chambre au second, où bientôt vont atteindre les flammes." ' (p. 724)

Most of the conversational examples are found in the speech of three main characters, Julius de Baraglioul (16), Lafcadio (9) and Protos (7), together with four by Amédée Fleurissoire and one by Anthime Armand-Dubois. Inverted order in the spoken language of the two bourgeois, Julius and Anthime, has a parodying effect and is one linguistic facet of what Hytier terms Gide's ' irony ' :

' Gide a répandu abondamment l'ironie sur ses personnages qui vivent dans le conformisme bourgeois, Julius le catholique, et Anthime le francmaçon.' [20]

Inversion in the speech of Protos and Lafcadio, on the other hand, represents a style which is adopted according to the guise of the speaker or the identity of the person addressed.

[19] *Ibid.*, p. 171.
[20] J. Hytier, *André Gide*, Alger, 1938, p. 132.

Julius, the intellectual with aspirations to the Académie Française, is one of Gide's cultured characters, in whose speech inversion, as suggested by Ullmann,[21] is not entirely out of place, especially when discussing abstract subjects. Seven of the sixteen examples occur in the context of religion, e.g.

' "... on peut être parfait chrétien sans pourtant faire fi des légitimes avantages que nous offre le rang où Dieu a trouvé sage de nous placer." ' (p. 862)

Inversions are found in his speech regardless of the person addressed and are typical of the pretentious nature of the character himself. The extremely literary example already quoted in part occurs in a conversation with Lafcadio, and another, where there is a pun on the inverted subject, in a dialogue with Anthime :

' "... je me répète ... que seules, jusqu'à présent, m'obligeaient d'impures considérations de carrière, de public et de juges ingrats dont le poète espère en vain récompense." ' (p. 836)

' "... et sans doute cette apparente inconséquence cache-t-elle une séquence plus subtile et cachée." ' (p. 813)

The style of Amédée is somewhat similar, and it is interesting to note that the two least usual of the inversions he uses occur in conversation firstly with Julius and secondly with a supposed cleric :

' " Mais à quoi voulez-vous que je prenne intérêt tant que durera mon inquiétude ? " ' (p. 796)

' "... c'est solitaire que s'enfonce l'obscur sentier que je suis, que je dois suivre." ' (p. 818)

The remaining examples have the *invertissants que* and *comme*.

The role of inversion as an indication of bourgeois conformity, and thus contributing to a specific stylistic register, is shown most strikingly in the speech of the two characters who are not themselves bourgeois. All the examples of inversion spoken by Lafcadio occur in his conversations with Julius and in no other context, e.g.

' "... je ne discerne pas encore nettement les raisons que peut

[21] *Loc. cit.*

avoir Monsieur... (il regarda la carte), que peut avoir de s'intéresser particulièrement à moi, le comte Julius de Baraglioul." ' (p. 719)

As for the underworld character Protos, each time inversion is found in his speech he is masquerading either as a priest or, on one occasion, as a university professor. The consequent contrast between the conversational style of the criminal himself and that of his assumed characters, bears out Hytier's statement :

' Ce Protos est d'ailleurs un conformiste à sa manière : il sait qu'on ne sort d'une société que pour entrer dans une autre qui a ses lois.' [22]

Inversion here is a linguistic device to be adopted along with physical disguise, as already seen in the character of Vautrin, this time in the parodied representation of the clergy, as well as in that of the bourgeois. The following examples show Protos speaking in three different disguises and situations, the first as the Abbé Salus talking to Julius' sister, the second as the Abbé Cave to Anthime, and the third as the professor in conversation with Lafcadio :

' "... la Loge a installé ... je ne sais quel suppôt du Quirinal ... devant lequel enfin, ô honte ! au jubilé s'est incliné la tout entière chrétienté." ' (p. 751)

' "... le nom du destinataire par prudence est laissé en blanc, de manière que le puisse toucher n'importe quel porteur." ' (p. 806)

' "... je n'ai pas la permission, ce qui s'appelle la permission de m'enivrer, fût-ce un jour par hasard." ' (p. 853)

(b) *Inversion as a vehicle for irony*

While inversion in conversation is a means of characterization and parody, the examples in the narrative are equally exploited for their ironic effects. Such irony may be directed at various institutions, at the characters or at the narrative itself. In two instances where Free-Masonry receives ironic mention, inversion is used with emphatic and delaying effect :

[22] *Ibid.*, p. 132.

'... malgré les faux frais où l'entraînerait sans doute la
malignité de la Loge.' (p. 774)

'... derrière qui jusqu'alors s'était dissimulée la Loge.'
(p. 750)

Elsewhere the subject is the Roman Catholic Church and its
members. The following example constitutes an ironic
reference to the commercial aspect of religious art, with
inversion again having a delaying effect and emphasizing the
subject :

' La Madone ... n'est pas une de ces statues modernes comme
en fabrique de nos jours, avec le carton-roman plastique de
Blafaphas, la maison d'art Fleurissoire-Lévichon.' (p. 699)

In an example of double inversion the opposition effected by
a prepositional phrase *invertissant* stresses the tension between
Catholic and liberal institutions :

' Au premier enthousiasme des feuilles orthodoxes ré-
pondaient à présent les huées des organes libéraux ; à
l'important article dans l'*Osservatore* ... faisait pendant la
diatribe du *Tempo Felice*...' (p. 705)

Elsewhere the devotion of the convert suffers ironic treatment
and the key element is stressed by inversion :

' Sans bruit, Véronique poussait la porte, puis glissait
furtivement, les yeux au sol, comme passe un convers
devant les *graffiti* obscènes.' (pp. 681–82)

' (Anthime) acceptait les coups de ce visage serain qu'ap-
prête l'âme vraiment dévote.' (p. 705)

As regards the characters in the novel, inversion frequently
emphasizes their ironic presentation. Irony resulting from the
opposition between appearance and reality is underlined by
inversion in the portrayal of Protos in his first disguise :

'... il fallait pour mener à bien cette quête ... une audace, une
habileté, un tact, une éloquence, une connaissance des êtres
et des faits, une santé que seuls pouvaient se piquer d'avoir
quelques gaillards tels que Protos...' (p. 749)

The aspirations of Julius are revealed in the narrative with
ironic overtones, as well as through the dialogue :

'... il se trouva tout porté vers l'Académie : déjà semblaient

l'y destiner sa belle allure, la grave onction de son regard et
la pâleur pensive de son front.' (p. 690)

A similar procedure may be noted at the beginning of the
Caves, where the description of the Baraglioul family is
accompanied by a number of inversions, some suggestive of a
historical document, and others ironic in the emphasis on a
certain vocabulary :

> ' En 1828, il reçut de Charles X la couronne de comte —
> couronne que devait porter si noblement un peu plus tard
> Juste-Agénor ... dans les ambassades où brillait son intelli-
> gence subtile et triomphait sa diplomatie.' (p. 689)

Finally Gide frequently directs his irony at his own narrative,
and often uses inversion within an interrogative construction.
Thus he follows the movements of Amédée :

> ' Que ne s'attarde-t-il sur la terrasse qu'inonde une occiden-
> tale lueur ? ' (p. 698)

Later the author interrupts the description of Amédée's
vision, thus :

> ' Arrête, ô ma plume imprudente ! où palpite déjà l'aile d'une
> âme qui se délivre, qu'importe l'agitation malhabile d'un
> corps paralysé qui guérit ? ' (p. 702)

In another example the character of Amédée is questioned :

> ' Si grande que fût la naïveté d'Amédée, pouvait-il vraiment
> supposer que son ami partageait jusqu'à ce dernier point son
> bonheur ? ' (p. 763)

and elsewhere the language of description suggests an ironic
interpretation of Amédée's thoughts :

> ' Le soleil cependant s'était couché ; déjà s'atténuaient les
> reflets derniers de sa gloire, que Fleurissoire ému contem-
> plait.' (p. 827)

(c) Recurring inversion structures : conclusion

Two structures involving inverted order recur regularly
throughout the *Caves*, namely chiastic constructions and
inversions where there are several predicates. The form of the
chiasmus is generally that of two relative clauses having direct
and inverted order, often with different types of subjects, thus :

' Un carnet relié en cuir de Russie se trouvait là ; que prit Julius et qu'il ouvrit.' (p. 716)

There may however be two substantival subjects, e.g.

' Lafcadio, que n'effrayait pas le vin sec et que la naïveté de l'autre amusait, fit déboucher un second Montebello.' (p. 852)

An unusual example, has the same verb in each clause, with inversion causing them to be juxtaposed, which has the effect of prolonging the meaning of the verb, and further delaying the subject :

'... il fait souvenir le savant de certain soir tranquille et d'or au bord du Nil, où, comme cette prière enfantine s'élève, s'élevait une fumée bleue, toute droite vers un ciel tout pur.' (p. 700)

There are many instances where the inversion construction includes several verbs. The verbs may have similar or contrasting meanings, both types being stressed by inversion :

' Le brouillard léger du matin et cette profuse lumière où s'évaporait et s'irréalisait chaque objet favorisaient encore son vertige.' (p. 809)

' Il ne comprenait plus où commençait, où s'arrêtait son rêve, ni si maintenant il veillait, ni s'il avait rêvé...' (p. 702)

Similarly one *invertissant* may have two dependent clauses, as in the following, which effectively juxtaposes real and metaphorical movement :

' un médiocre rêve où s'agitaient à ses côtés ses parents et se dressaient toutes les conventions saugrenues de leur monde...' (p. 873)

The parallel is closer in an earlier example, where the structures are syntactically identical and semantically very similar :

' Grâce à quoi régnait entre eux une manière de concorde, planait sur eux une sorte de demi-félicité...' (p. 681)

The inversion constructions in *Les caves du vatican* not only represent considerable syntactic innovations, as shown by the extended use of less orthodox structures, but also important developments in style. Thus inversion is used regularly to achieve certain effects of characterization, both of persons and of milieux, and to emphasize various attitudes on the part of the author and his characters, in particular those of irony and parody. The examples in which inversion is employed for syntactic variety by means of opposition and chiasmus are generally less frequent than in previous authors, although equally effective, and they are perhaps more closely linked with the structure of the novel than hitherto.

(iii) M. PROUST, 'A L'OMBRE DES JEUNES FILLES EN FLEURS'

The inversion frequency for the Proust extract is the highest of the texts of this period, 1·46, but it is closely followed by Malraux (1·42) and in the contemporary period by Butor (1·36). The number of optional inversions found by Ullmann in the first part of *Du côté de chez Swann*, 275,[23] suggests a similar distribution in the first volumes of *A la recherche du temps perdu*. The total of *invertissants*, sixty-one, is surpassed by both Gide and Malraux (table 10.08), resulting in a higher ratio of inversions to *invertissants* in Proust, 4.77.

Several outstanding features emerge from the syntactic analysis above, in particular the low occurrence of mobile *invertissants* 17% (table 10.02). Such a proportion is elsewhere generally found only in texts with few inversions (cf. Prévost, 13%, and later Sarraute, 10%), but also with the exception of Maupassant (17%), and more significantly Butor (19%). Other key points in the Proust examples which will find a parallel in Butor are the number of inversions in sentences of three or more clauses, 84%, (table 10.07) (87% in Butor), and with a dependent clause, 18% (table 10.06) (21%).

Certain types of inversion occur in vast numbers in Proust. The section studied here contains sixty-nine examples of the relative *invertissant que* and twenty-four of the comparative *comme*, albeit with a greater variety of verbs than in previous texts. On the other hand there are no examples of zero *invertissant*, of inversion in causal and final clauses, and few adverbial *invertissants*. Le Bidois in his comprehensive study also

[23] *Style in the French Novel*, p. 173.

quotes few examples of absolute inversion from the entire novel, one with *rester* and one each with *suivre* and *venir*.[24] He notes only five examples of causal clauses, so the absence of the construction here is not surprising. He does, however, quote many examples of inversion in substantival clauses occurring elsewhere in Proust.[25] More remarkable is the absence of all time and place adverbial *invertissants* except for one temporal adverb, particularly since Le Bidois notes that inversion after a place adverbial may occur as often as six times on a page.[26] Inversion after time adverbials seems, however, to be infrequent—Le Bidois has found eighteen in the fifteen volumes of *A la recherche* which may be compared with seven in *Les caves du vatican* and four in *La peste*. The examples below are intended to show firstly how the structure of inversion is expanded by Proust to become an integral part of his syntax, and secondly its stylistic use in characterization, both through conversation and the narrative.

(a) *Proust's exploitation of inverted order*

The important extension of the use of inversion is reflected in the frequency of the construction, the number of hitherto unusual *invertissants* and, most notably, in lengthy sentence structures. These syntactic features have in turn various stylistic functions, with, for instance, accumulations of inversions forming parallelisms and intricate structures producing delaying effects.

In passages where inversions accumulate, there is generally a multiplicity of stylistic functions, as the author combines effects which in other writers tend to occur individually. In this example three inversions have both individual and combined effects of style :

‘ Alors je connus cet appartement d'où dépassait jusque dans l'escalier le parfum dont se servait Madame Swann, mais qu'embaumait bien plus encore le charme particulier et

---

[24] *L'inversion du sujet*, pp. 25 ff.

[25] *Ibid.*, pp. 288–90.

[26] *Ibid.*, p. 149.

douloureux qui émanait de la vie de Gilberte.' (p. 503)
In the first relative clause with its delayed subject the syntax
underlines the idea of wafting perfume, with the second inversion continuing to retard, as well as emphasize, the identity of
its user. The stressed verb of the next clause refers back, in its
literal meaning, to *le parfum*, and looks forward figuratively to
the introduction, again delayed by inversion and a dependent
clause, of Gilberte. In addition the whole sentence presents the
opposition between Odette and her daughter, with both names
in parallel key positions.

Parallel structures where inversion occurs are much more
fully developed than in previous writers, e.g.

' Qu'on retire du plateau où est la fierté une petite quantité de
volonté qu'on a eu la faiblesse de laisser s'user avec l'âge,
qu'on ajoute dans le plateau où est le chagrin une souffrance
physique acquise et à qui on a permis de s'aggraver...'
(p. 586)

In each structure beginning with the *invertissant où* there is the
same antecedent and verb, followed by contrasting abstract
subjects and abstract objects of the opposing main verbs
retirer and *ajouter*, after which come relative clauses with the
same subject, *on*, and direct order. In the next example the
general syntactic structure is the same in each part, but with a
contrast between simple and compound inversion and with the
relative inversion occurring slightly later in the second half:

' Or, peut-être simplement Swann savait-il que la générosité
n'est souvent que l'aspect intérieur que prennent nos sentiments égoïstes ... Peut-être avait-il reconnu dans la sympathie que je lui exprimais un simple effet ... de mon amour
pour Gilberte, par lequel ... seraient ... dirigés mes actes.'
(pp. 491–92)

Finally an example where word-order is paralleled and verb
forms contrasted throughout:

' Mais savais-je seulement ... que c'était du thé que je
buvais ? L'eussé-je su que j'en eusse pris tout de même,
car ... cela ne m'eût pas rendu le souvenir du passé et la
prévision de l'avenir.' (p. 507)

Inversion structures which occur in the course of particularly long sentences are frequently expanded and distorted, with much greater separation of the components than has been seen hitherto. Thus in the example quoted in part already, a relative inversion is interrupted in the same way as the main clause :

'Peut-être avait-il reconnu dans la sympathie que je lui exprimais un simple effet — et une confirmation enthousiaste — de mon amour pour Gilberte, par lequel — et non par ma vénération secondaire pour lui — seraient fatalement dans la suite dirigés mes actes.' (pp. 491–92)

A subordinate clause may also include a further inverted subordinate clause in parenthesis, and in the following the structural break emphasizes a parallel between *l'artiste* and Vinteuil :

'Aussi faut-il que l'artiste — et c'est ce qu'avait fait Vinteuil — s'il veut que son œuvre puisse suivre sa route, la lance...' (p. 532)

Where there is the progressive accumulation of parentheses, inversion may highlight one of them :

'Mais Odette était seulement à côté de lui alors (non en lui comme le motif de Vinteuil), ne voyant donc point — Odette eût-elle été mille fois plus compréhensive — ce qui, pour nul de nous (...) ne peut s'extérioriser.' (p. 534)

Here the repetition of the name along with the compound inversion of the hypothetical construction increases the emphasis.

The most striking expansion, however, is that of compound inversion constructions. A structure in which the subject is necessarily repeated permits considerable manipulation of its constituents without any great loss of clarity, and the constructions become increasingly complex. Firstly compound inversion occurs when the original subject is particularly long, having both complements and a dependent clause, e.g.

'Encore la distribution des qualités et des défauts dont il hérite se fait-elle si étrangement que...' (p. 565)

Alternatively noun subject and verb may be separated by a

parenthetical construction containing two or more clauses:

' Peut-être ces jeunes gens — on en verra qui étaient dans ce cas — n'avaient-ils pas connu Bergotte.' (p. 555)

Elsewhere the initial development of the subject is so intricate that the original structure is repeated before the inversion, which even then is modified:

' Peut-être cette classe sociale particulière qui comptait alors des femmes comme lady Israëls, mêlée à celles de l'aristocratie, et Madame Swann, qui ... peut-être cette classe, du moins avec le même caractère et le même charme, n'existe-t-elle plus.' (p. 639)

Finally both adverbials and clauses may occur between *invertissant* and noun subject, which in turn has a dependent clause preceding the main inversion structure:

' Mais peut-être en moi — et ces deux explications ne s'excluent pas, car un seul sentiment est quelquefois fait de contraires — l'espérance que j'avais de recevoir enfin une lettre avait-elle rapproché de moi l'image de Gilberte...' (p. 609)

As already mentioned, there are relatively few inversions in final position in this work, by virtue of the unusually long sentences. Thus where inversion does conclude a sentence, whether long or short, the construction has a marked emphatic effect, e.g.

' Il y avait pourtant seize personnes, parmi lesquelles j'ignorai absolument que se trouvât Bergotte.' (p. 547)

The delaying function of inverted order is also clearly seen in this position, and in the next two examples this is reinforced by the adjective *inattendu*:

' (ces ministres) bénéficiaient enfin du prestige qui s'attache à un nom aristocratique et de l'intérêt qu'éveille comme un coup de théâtre un choix inattendu.' (pp. 434–35)

'... nous l'avons lue, dévorée, dans l'angoisse affreuse dont nous étreignait un malheur inattendu.' (pp. 627–28)

This delaying device is more effective in other positions when there are many more elements interspersed, e.g.

'... quand j'entrais dans la sombre antichambre où planait

perpétuellement, plus formidable et plus désirée que jadis à
Versailles l'apparition du Roi, la possibilité de les ren-
contrer...' (pp. 503–4)

In addition this construction may underline one of the important themes of Proust's work. In the next example inversion
stresses the sound provoking Marcel's feelings and memory,
and in the second the construction delays the expression of the
experience to which the elusive phrase of Vinteuil sonata is
compared :

' j'éprouvais ... une nostalgie que vint aggraver le son du cor,
comme on l'entend la nuit de la Mi-Carême...' (p. 488)

' (la Sonate) était aussi loin de ma perception claire qu'un
nom qu'on cherche à se rappeler et à la place duquel on ne
trouve que du néant, un néant d'où une heure plus tard, sans
qu'on y pense, s'élanceront d'elles-mêmes, en un seul bond,
les syllabes d'abord vainement sollicitées.' (p. 530)

(b) *The language of Proust's characters*

The linguistic portrayal of characters in Proust is achieved in
two ways, firstly through their own conversation and secondly
through the author's comments on their speech. Similarly
inversion has a dual role, both characterizing the speech of an
individual and emphasizing the author's remarks.

1. Inversion in conversation

In this part of the novel inversion occurs most frequently in
the speech of M. de Norpois (ten examples). There are three
examples each in the conversations of Swann, Odette and
Madame Bontemps, and single examples from various other
characters. Seven inversions introduce and emphasize
fashionable references which are in keeping with the character
of the speaker. Thus English terms or expressions are frequently quoted by Odette and inverted order stresses the
affected explanation :

' "... vous qui êtres le grand favori, le grand crack, comme
disent les Anglais." ' (p. 537)

The incongruity of other quotations may be highlighted by

inversion as in the following : the emphatic subject, if not the expression itself, seems out of place alongside the subjunctive in Swann's speech ;

> ' " Pour les gens nerveux, il faudrait toujours qu'ils aimassent, comme disent les gens du people, ' au-dessous d'eux ' afin que..." ' (p. 563)

The gulf between the social classes is thus widened by contrasting syntax. In other instances the quotation introduced by inversion may be somewhat ridiculous, as in the following by Madame Cottard :

> '... c'est le grand art. Comme dirait mon mari, c'est le *nec plus ultra*." ' (p. 604)

Inversion in direct speech does not emphasize unusually striking themes, since, as stated by Le Bidois, Proust uses conversation to show his characters not in moments of crisis, but ' dans leurs périodes de calme, au cours de leur vie normale et quotidienne.' [27]

In this context inverted order both indicates the linguistic register of the bourgeois speakers and stresses the limited scope of their conversation. For instance deletion and transposition adds an elevated note to an unexceptional form of expression and content :

> ' " L'ailleurs nos contemporaines veulent absolument du nouveau, n'en fût-il plus au monde." ' (p. 607) (Mme Bontemps)

A major topic of conversation in Proust's society is other members of it, and in each of the examples below the subject is stressed by inverted order, the first spoken by M. de Norpois and the others by Mme Bontemps :

> "... mais comme un livre ennuyeux, ce qu'au moins ne sont pas les siens, tel est ce Bergotte." ' (p. 474)

> ' "... j'aimerais savoir comment vous jugez le chapeau qu'avait Mme Trombert." ' (p. 604)

> ' "... vous a-t-on dit que l'hôtel particulier que vient d'acheter Mme Verdurin sera éclairé à l'électricité ? " ' (p. 607)

[27] R. Le Bidois, ' Le langage parlé des personnages de Proust ', *Le Français Moderne*, vii (1939), pp. 197–218.

2. The attitude of the author

The author's comments on the language of his characters may accompany both direct and indirect speech. In the following example inversion stresses a conversational idiosyncrasy:

> ' "... Gilberte saurait ... que j'y avais, comme n'avait cessé de le répéter Madame Cottard, ' fait d'emblée, de prime abord, la conquête de Madame Verdurin." ' (pp. 607–8)

Elsewhere this emphasis may be not so much on the actual words as on the way in which they are pronounced. Thus inverted order underlines Marcel's interpretation of Swann's words:

> '... car il répondit à Gilberte : " Tu es une bonne fille " de ce ton attendri par l'inquiétude que nous inspire pour l'avenir la tendresse trop passionnée d'un être destiné à nous survivre.' (p. 567)

In the next example Gilberte's laughter is emphasized by final position, and inversion also has a linking function, introducing the underlying idea in the subsequent sentence :

> ' Alors je sentis ce qu'il y avait de douloureux pour moi à ne pouvoir atteindre cet autre plan ... de sa pensée, que décrivait son rire. Ce rire avait l'air de signifier : ...' (p. 584)

In the following, similar ideas are stressed, with inversion introducing the comparison :

> '... elle éclata de rire. Souvent son rire en désaccord avec ses paroles semblait, comme fait la musique, décrire dans un autre plan une surface invisible.' (p. 490)

Thus *A la recherche du temps perdu* marks a turning point in the use of word-order in the modern novel. Proust's contribution is outstanding as concerns both the syntactic and stylistic development of inverted order. In the Proustian sentence structures are intricately interwoven and the possibilities of word-order exploited to the full, a feature underlying the whole of his style. Because of this close relation between syntax, style and content, inversions in Proust are less easy to classify according to particular stylistic effects than in other authors and only a few of these could be discussed here. On the other hand the emphatic value of inversion is widely felt, as in the examples characterizing the conversations of a certain social milieu and the author's attitude towards them.

(iv) A. MALRAUX, 'LA CONDITION HUMAINE'

With only slightly fewer examples of inversion than Proust, the frequency of the construction in Malraux, 1·42, is surprisingly high, and the *Condition humaine* also shares with Gide the highest number of *invertissants* in the texts analysed for this period (table 10.08). The word-order favoured by Malraux is, however, less complex than that of the other two novelists. Table 10.07 shows that only 37% of the inversions occur in longer sentences, the lowest proportion of this period and similarly table 10.12 reveals less separation of the major constituents than in the other authors studied, with the exception of Camus. There are also very few examples of inversion of several subjects, or of subjects with a dependent clause (table 10.06). An unusually high proportion of inversions occur in a main clause, 41% (table 10.02), and the text may be compared with Zola and Chateaubriand in this respect. Consequently there are more examples of constructions with a pronoun subject and of compound inversion (table 10.06). Table 10.09 shows that there are twice as many inversions after modal adverbs than in the other texts, although these are shared between only seven *invertissants* (see p. 341 above). On the other hand the proportion of relative constructions is low, 39%, but with more *invertissants* than in the other texts. Other notable features are the 5% which occur in free indirect speech (table 10.03) and the fact that 7% precede direct speech (table 10.05). There are examples of all the less usual inversion constructions in the *Condition humaine*, including inversion in hypothetical and causal clauses and after a preceding subordinate, but no cases of inverted order after an attributive adjective, and few adverbial *invertissants* other than adverbs of place and manner.

Since the essential difference between Malraux and Proust in their use of inverted order lies in the simplicity of construction in the former, complex structures have a much greater stylistic effect, and are generally reserved for particular contexts, such as elevated speech or letters. Inversion is also used to mark a change in style of speech, to facilitate and emphasize the introduction of exotic names and details, and to a lesser extent in impressionistic description.

(a) *Inversion and narrative form*

As indicated above, inverted order is unusually frequent in Malraux before a passage of direct speech, but its function is not so much one of introducing conversation as of marking a change in the form of narration. Thus inverted order also underlines the transition to and from indirect and free indirect styles, besides occurring within interrogative and exclamatory structures in direct speech and elsewhere. In the following, for instance, the inversion construction emphasizes the end of a narrative passage, and the subject effects a link with the conversation which is provoked by a particular sound:

' Himmelrich montra du pouce ... la direction d'où était venu le cri de l'enfant...' (p. 246)

Alternatively a passage of free indirect speech may be concluded by inversion with the change to direct speech, and the juxtaposition of the two forms is particularly useful in the following, where the idea formulated in the first is made explicit in the second:

' Il était probable que les tanks ne pourraient quitter le front ; mais s'ils atteignaient la ville, il serait impossible de les arrêter tous par des fosses, dans ces quartiers où se croisaient tant de ruelles.

— Les tanks ne quitteront absolument pas le front, dit-il.' (p. 48)

Modal adverb *invertissants* are often found in interrogative structures by virtue of the nuance of doubt which is present to a greater or lesser degree. This is common in conversation, e.g.

' " S'ils sont vainqueurs, dit l'un, peut-être serons-nous payés ce mois-ci ? (...)

— Mais s'ils sont battus, peut-être dira-t-on que nous avons
trahi ? ' (p. 110)

but also, as noted already in Zola, in free indirect speech :

' Peut-être était-ce sa voix, son calme, son amitié même qui
agissait ? ' (p. 247)

There is also an instance of a relative inversion concluding an
exclamation, thereby reinforcing this structure and adding
emphasis to the subject :

'... assemblée de vaincus où des multitudes reconnaîtraient
leurs martyrs, légende sanglante dont se font les légendes
dorées ! ' (p. 362)

A number of examples of compound inversion occur in free
indirect speech in this text, a construction which seems particularly suited to the presentation of thought processes, e.g.

' " Là était la seule certitude. Peut-être la Révolution eût-
elle pu être conduite autrement ; mais c'était trop tard.'
(p. 176)

In a more complex structure a single *invertissant* is followed by
two clauses, one with compound and the other with simple
inversion, the two separated by the development of the train
of thought :

' Sans doute, au plus profond, Gisors était-il espoir comme il
était angoisse, espoir de rien, attente, et, fallait-il que son
amour fût écrasé pour qu'il découvrît cela.' (p. 373)

Although inversions in free indirect speech are generally in
short sentences, the form is used in chapter VII to report
Ferral's line of thought during a ministerial meeting, and this
is characterized by long sentences together with an accumulation of inversions :

' Peut-être le grand individualisme ne pouvait-il se déve-
lopper ... que ... (...) Ce n'était pas à la fin du XVIIIe siècle,
parmi les révolutionnaires ivres de vertu, que se promenaient
les grands individualistes, mais à la Renaissance...' (p. 385)

(b) *The stylistic uses of inversion in Malraux*

1. Inversion and the Oriental setting

In many cases inversion is occasioned by the form of noun

phrases containing Chinese names, and consequently these
occur in an emphatic position, e.g.

'" Ils n'accepteraient pas plus les Soviets que ne les accepte
Chang-Kaï-Shek." ' (p. 165)

In the following the stylistic effect is increased by the evocative
verb in the inversion clause :

'Les émigrés de tous pays dont regorgeait Shanghaï
avaient montré à Gisors combien...' (p. 73)

Similarly inversion stresses various aspects of local colour :

'... au fond d'une arche énorme surmontait une pagode
rongée de lierre déjà noir.' (p. 161)

'... les jarres phosphorescentes alignées comme celles
d'Ali-Baba, et où dormaient, invisibles, les illustres cyprins
chinois.' (p. 49)

In the next example the speaker's accent receives emphasis :

'" Peut-être méprise-t-ong beaucoup celui qu'on tue." '
(p. 73)

The social and political background of the novel is also stressed
in this way :

'Peu à peu apparurent : deux établissements de crédit
(foncier et agricole) ; quatre sociétés de culture : hévéas,
cultures tropicales ... — Au centre, la Société de travaux
publics...' (p. 105)

2. Impressionistic description

The inversions Malraux uses in descriptions evoking a series
of impressions differ from those of previous writers in that the
impression represented by the inverted subject is generally not
developed. Since the sentences are also usually short, the effect
of a concluding inversion is often somewhat abrupt, while its
emphatic value is increased, e.g.

'Dans la ville endormie, la délégation veillait de toutes ses
fenêtres illuminées, que traversaient des bustes noirs. Ils
marchèrent, leurs deux ombres semblables devant eux.'
(p. 175)

In the following the lack of development is clearly indicated ;

'A quelques mètres un amas de débris rouges, une surface

de verre pilé où brillait un dernier reflet de lumière, des ...
déjà il ne distinguait plus rien : ' (p. 279)

The majority of impressions stressed by inversion are visual
and they are particularly striking where the verb and subject
represent an unusual collocation, e.g.

' Derrière, couchées sur un bat-flanc ou debout, grouillaient
des ombres trop longues : des hommes, comme des vers.'
(p. 334)

The subject in the following is developed in detail :

' Dans cette brume sale brillaient sur les panses des lampes-
tempête des effets de lumière, points d'interrogation
renversés et parallèles.' (p. 220)

In the few examples of aural impressions in emphatic position,
unlike those of visual description, the subjects are expanded in
the subsequent phrase or clause. In the next example the
explanation follows immediately, in opposition to the inverted
subject, in paragraph final position :

' Au-dessus de l'ébranlement sourd des pas et du tic-tac de
toutes les horloges de la boutique, s'établit un grondement de
lourde ferraille: l'artillerie de l'armée révolutionnaire.' (p.156)

3. Emphasis

Malraux' use of inversion as an emphatic device is particularly noticeable when the inverted subject is an abstract noun,
generally concluding a sentence, e.g.

'... révélés ... par cette lumière que rien ne faisait vaciller et
d'où semblait émaner une sordide éternité.' (p. 28)

Such emphasis may also be extended to the verb phrase,
especially in the course of personification :

' Sous son sacrifice à la révolution grouillait un monde de
profondeurs auprès de quoi...' (p. 12)
'... derrière cette nuit dense et basse sous quoi guettait la
ville déserte, pleine d'espoir et de haine.' (p. 67)

Emphasis may also be placed on the verb where an inversion
forms part of a repetitive structure. Thus in the next example
the hypothetical inversion stresses the first of three occurrences
of *posséder* :

' Mais, n'eût-il de sa vie possédé une seule femme, il avait
posédé, il posséderait à travers cette Chinoise ... la seule chose
dont il fut avide : lui-même.' (p. 276)

Elsewhere the repeated element may be stressed by a
chiasmus :

' Le sourire lui donnait la vie à la fois intense et abandonnée
que donne le plaisir.' (p. 140)

The less common inversion constructions are also used to
emphasize a repeated verb with contrasting subjects. Thus in
the hypothetical construction quoted on p. 341 *disparaître*
is highlighted in an unusual chiasmus, and in the causal clause
quoted on p. 344 *exister* is similarly stressed, with the repeated
forms separated by a further inversion.

4. Complex structures

The overall simplicity of construction in this text has
already been mentioned, and sentences of five or six clauses
contrast sharply with the rest of the narrative. Where the
subject is inverted in long sentences it is not uncommon for
this to be accompanied by a further inversion in a later clause,
e.g.

'... ce n'était pas, comme le croyaient alors les subtils de
Pékin, qu'il s'amusât à jouer par procuration des vies dont
le séparait son âge.' (p. 81)

In the next example the second inversion in a six-clause
sentence concludes a chapter :

'... comme si cette contemplation épouvantée eût été la seule
voix que pût entendre la mort, comme si cette souffrance
d'être homme dont il s'imprégnait jusqu'au fond du cœur
eût été la seule oraison que pût entendre le corps de son fils
tué.' (p. 373)

Thus inverted order lends variety and emphasis to a sentence
which is already outstanding because of its length as well as its
pathos.

Several inversions in a longer sentence are also found in a
certain style of public speaking, as in the following extract from
Ferral's speech at the Ministry of Finance :

' "... il me paraît défendable de souhaiter que ne disparaisse
pas d'Asie la seule organisation puissante qui y représente
notre pays — dût-elle sortir des mains qui l'ont fondée." '
(p. 380)

The second inversion with the imperfect subjunctive occurs at
the conclusion of the speech. A less formal style is used in
personal letters, but in the following, written by Valérie to
Ferral, the second inversion marks a change to a disconnected
style, indicated by the accumulation of short clauses :

' "... mais peut-être mourrez-vous sans vous être aperçu
qu'une femme est aussi un être humain. J'ai toujours
rencontré (peut-être ne rencontrai-je jamais que ceux-là
mais tant pis...) des hommes qui..." ' (p. 258)

The syntactic analysis of *La condition humaine* reveals an
extremely frequent use of inverted word-order in a style which
is predominantly simple, even to the point of terseness. This is
indicated both by the high proportion of mobile *invertissant*
constructions and the infrequency of longer sentences with
inversion. The stylistic effects obtained depend more than
usual on the length of the sentence in which inversion is found,
those in shorter structures being used for emphasis or impressionistic effects and for indicating a change in narrative style,
in the alternation between the author's observations and the
characters' thoughts, while those in longer sentences have a
contrastive effect and may stress repetitive devices or a certain
style of speech or writing.

(v) J. GIRAUDOUX, 'COMBAT AVEC L'ANGE'

The inversion frequency for *Combat avec l'ange* with 188
examples is 1·09, which is higher than that of *Les caves du
vatican*. It seems likely that, considering the relative length of
the work, there is a similar frequency in *Suzanne et le pacifique*,
where Ullmann has found around 150 examples,[28] and this
suggests that inverted order is a device favoured by the
author. Despite the higher frequency, this text does not have
a large number of *invertissants* (table 10.08), and the proportion

[28] ' Inversion as a stylistic device ', p. 169.

of inversions to *invertissants* is above average. 51% of the examples are in relative clause constructions (table 10.09), the highest proportion in the texts of this period, although surpassed by all except Robbe-Grillet in the contemporary works analysed. The number of constructions with *être*, 21%, is also the highest (table 10.10). Table 10.04 shows that a fairly low proportion of the inversions occur in final position, 32%, but as already noted in Proust, this is less surprising in view of the longer sentences in which inversion is found (table 10.07). Although the propostion of 56% of the examples in sentences of three or more clauses is the second highest in the table, the sentence structure of Giraudoux is by no means as complex as that of Proust, as is also shown in table 10.12; although the order verb-adverb-subject occurs in 15% of the examples, there is little further separation of the constituents by clauses or adverbials.

As with Gide and Proust, inversion in Giraudoux occurs predominantly in subordinate clause constructions (table 10.02). All types of immobile *invertissant* are found with the exception of causal constructions, although the less common structures, such as inversion in hypothetical or final clauses, occur only sporadically. There are four examples of inversion in temporal clauses; while in two cases *quand* is followed by *venir* or *arriver*, the remaining two examples with *dès que* show greater variety :

'... l'humanité n'est pas caste à se priver du plaisir, dès que s'offre l'occasion, de montrer son visage rouge.' (p. 125)

'... dans quelques jours, dès qu'aurait sonné ce tocsin de Notre-Dame, qui ne sonne que pour l'incendie ... je ne serais plus qu'un soldat...' (pp. 256-57)

Mobile *invertissants* are fairly infrequent and unexceptional, all the modal adverb examples, for instance, occurring with *ainsi, encore, du moins* or *peut-être*. The proportion of other syntactic operations is also relatively low. An *invertissant* of unusual frequency in this text is the attributive *que* which is discussed below, along with various other features of Giraudoux' syntax.

(a) *The attributive ' que ' ' invertissant '*

The high proportion of inversions having the verb *être* is due in part to the unusual frequency of the attributive *que invertissant*. Although only isolated examples of this are found in other works, there are twelve occurrences in *Combat avec l'ange*, and these are used to various stylistic effects. Since attributive constructions equate two concepts they are particularly useful in the expression of metaphor, besides having the emphatic properties of other inversion structures.

The construction is thus an effective means of achieving a metaphorical relation between two abstract nouns, e.g.

' Maléna ... se laissa aller à ce suicide qu'était pour elle le sommeil.' (p. 298)

Other less predictable metaphors include :

' Cette petite civilisation qu'était ma vie...' (p. 14)

'... cette minuscule lueur qu'est encore sa pensée...' (p. 109)

'... cette lutte pour saisir le present qu'est la jalousie ' (pp. 168–69)

Elsewhere an attributive inversion may emphasize a repeated element rather than a metaphorical one, e.g.

'... un recours à ce petit déversoir au sublime qu'est le sublime ennui...' (p. 78)

In a further example an idea rather than a single word is repeated and stressed :

' On les voyait se parler sans avoir recours à cette traduction informe qu'est la parole ! ' (p. 315)

Finally a number of inverted subjects may contain a repeated item, as in this passage where the adjective *vrai* contrasts with the preceding notion of disguise, with inverted order suggesting progressive revelation :

'... un carnaval où la population s'était simplement déguisée en population heureuse, avec ces moyens de fortune qu'étaient les vrais fronts, les vraies bouches, les vrais yeux...' (p. 294)

(b) *Repetitive structures*

The device of repetition which seems to be particularly favoured by Giraudoux, assumes added complexity with

N

inverted order. Some structures are relatively simple, since there is little concern for lexical variety as in the following, where both antecedent and subject are repeated and undergo similar expansions :

> '... il n'avait qu'un repos, la minute de repos absolu que lui donnait son ascenseur, le sordide et obscur ascenseur...' (p. 181)

Alternatively *invertissant* and verb may be repeated with contrasting subjects :

> ' Ce que disait sa parole n'était pas si différent de ce que disait son corps.' (p. 21)

In the next example a repeated verb is balanced by repetition of part of the inverted subject, again with each element elaborated on its second occurrence :

> ' (le petit doigt) qui remuait comme continuent à remuer ces pattes d'insecte, d'insecte frappé à mort et cloué par l'épingle sur son bouchon.' (p. 299)

The more complicated structures involve an additional semantic opposition. In the following, inversion permits a parallel development with repeated verb and contrasting subjects :

> ' Elle fit durer le début de notre liaison exactement ce que dure une fin de liaison.' (p. 37)

The opposition *vrai-faux* occurs several times in conjunction with inversion as well as an element of repetition, e.g.

> '... si sur moi était apparue ... un peu de vraie douceur, de fausse douceur...' (p. 14)

> ' Une fausse tête, qui ne pèse pas ce que pèse une vraie...' (p. 130)

The addition of *c'est ... que* permits the emphatic repetition of an *invertissant*, and in the example below, this is followed by contrasting subjects :

> ' C'était bien du chant de crapaud, de cette voyelle entre toutes les voyelles que me venait cette angoisse et en même temps cette douceur.' (p. 267)

In a final example, inversion results in contrasting lexical structures using repeated elements :

' En créant le pauvre, je créais un éblouissement de pauvreté. Il reste éblouissement pour moi. Pour le pauvre il est ce qu'est un éblouissement qui dure, un hébètement.' (p. 223) The progression *pauvre-éblouissement-pauvreté* of the opening sentence is followed by *éblouissement-pauvre-éblouissement* with inversion permitting the development of the final item by *durer*, which balances the earlier verb *rester*.

(*c*) ' *Préciosité* '

The tendency towards *préciosité* in the language of Giraudoux at times underlies the inversion structures. In the following, for instance, the inversion seems gratuitous and the sentence unbalanced by the length of the adverb separating verb and subject :

' L'averse ruissela. Tout ce qu'aimait particulièrement Dieu devint luisant, les feuilles, les chevaux, les eaux.' (p. 227) The next examples constitute somewhat sentimental comparisons with almost identical constructions, the *invertissant ainsi* coupled with an *incise* construction, the inverted subject having a dependent relative in each case :

' Ainsi devait être, pensait Maléna, la soirée où la femme va annoncer au mari qu'elle porte un enfant.' (p. 114)
' Ainsi, m'avait dit un ami, s'enfuit le chien qui adore son maître et qui se sent devenir enragé.' (p. 9)
In the following an unreal effect is heightened by the double subject and complement :

'... ces flacons de talc dont tiraient fraîcheur et calme toutes les articulations et jointures de Maléna.' (p. 139)

(*d*) *Conclusion*

The high occurrence of inversion in Giraudoux and his fairly complex sentence structure adds little to the stylistic contributions of Gide and Proust in this period. Through inverted order certain lexical patterns are more readily established, and the enumeration of nominals is facilitated as well as their repetition, e.g.

'... elle voyait l'occasion de garder pour elle le désespoir de la

séparation, de l'absence, l'angoisse que donnent les gares, les facteurs, les défilés, peut-être le veuvage.' (p. 256)
As in other authors the constructions are frequently used to emphasize key themes in the novel, such as that of happiness, with which the second chapter opens :
' Ici se pose la question du bonheur.
J'indique ce qu'est le bonheur pour ceux qui ne le connaissent pas.' (p. 30)
Occasionally traces of the author's *préciosité* are underlined by, or even consist of, inversion of the subject.

(vi) A. CAMUS, ' LA PESTE '

The fewest inversions and *invertissants* in the texts of this period are found in *La peste*, although the 37% occurrence of inversion in main clauses, which is second only to Malraux (table 10.02), does indicate some variety in *invertissant* if not in construction type. *La peste* has the highest proportion of inversions resulting from further syntactic operations, some of which are found in conversation, and also one of the highest frequencies in direct speech (table 10.03).

Although the novel has the lowest proportion of relative inversions, 38% (table 10.09), with the exception of the one correlative structure inverted order occurs only in the commonest syntactic constructions. Thus there are no examples of zero *invertissant* or of inversion in temporal clauses, the only text of the six where this is so, or in any less usual subordinating constructions. Furthermore 20% of the examples have the verb *être* (table 10.10), and table 10.12 shows that the constructions in Camus are simpler than those of the other texts in that the occurrence of intervening adverbs and clauses is relatively infrequent. An average number of examples have several subjects or a dependent clause (table 10.06), and 49% occur in sentences of three or more clauses.

In many respects, such as frequency, type of inversion and sentence length, the analysis of Camus is remarkably similar to that of Stendhal (see chapter VIII). In *La peste* Camus, like Stendhal, uses inversion for the sake of clarity and emphasis in a documentary, and at times journalistic style. It is the use of inversion in this context, along with conversational usage, which is examined below.

The function of inversion in ' La peste '

The subject matter of Camus' *chronique* imposes a simple, straightforward form of expression, with elements of a journalistic style, both in the narrative and in the documentary extracts from the *carnets* of the observer Tarrou. The speech of this character, himself a journalist, also contains some of the characteristics of his written style. Inverted order forms part of this style when it is employed for clarity, for emphasis and also for a more elevated effect in the journalist's commentary. At other points in the narrative inversion has a contrastive effect in opposing normality and crisis.

(a) Journalistic usage and the style of Tarrou

Inversion which occurs in the interests of clarity and emphasis in explicitly journalistic passages is paralleled by similar constructions within the narrative. The first example below of the relative *invertissant que* occurs in a newspaper extract, with the elaborate subject stressed by its position in the interrogative structure :

' " Nos édiles ne sont-ils avisés du danger que pouvaient présenter les cadavres putréfiés de ces rongeurs ? " ' (p. 1237)

The second is a paraphrase of a similar extract, in the narrative, with some underlying irony :

' A les lire (les journaux), ce qui caractérisait la situation, c'etait " l'example émouvant de calme et de sang-froid " que donnait la population. Mais dans une ville refermée sur elle-même ... personne ne se trompait sur " l'exemple " donné par la communauté '. (pp. 1411–12)

A similar order of ideas in the two sentences here is obtained by different syntactic means, with *population* and *communauté* both occupying key positions. Similarly the *invertissant tel* is used in both contexts, firstly in Tarrou's diary and secondly with reference to the diary itself :

'Le professeur B ... répond "Non". Cent vingt-quatre morts, tel est le bilan de la quatre-vingt-quatorzième journée de peste.' (p. 1314)

'"En temps de peste, défense de cracher sur les chats," telle était la conclusion des carnets.' (p. 1311)

Inversion, particularly after *comme*, may be used to introduce journalistic comment or opinion :

'L'opinion publique, c'est sacré ... Et puis, comme disait un confrère : "C'est impossible, tout le monde sait qu'elle a disparu de l'Occident ! " ' (p. 1432)

Alternatively it may introduce a postscript :

'Ainsi parlaient les chroniqueurs, et ce n'était pas leur métier d'en dire plus.' (p. 1402)

Modal adverbs with inversion also occur frequently throughout the narrative to link events in a documentary style :

'Il la trouva couchée dans leur chambre, comme il lui avait demandé de la faire. Ainsi se préparait-elle à la fatigue du déplacement. Elle souriait.' (p. 1221)

Inversion as a feature of a fairly literary journalistic style is exemplified in both the writing and speech of Tarrou. Less usual modal adverb *invertissants* occur in the following, where the second is a spoken example :

'Fréquemment éclatent des scènes dues à la seule mauvaise humeur qui devient chronique.' (p. 1315)

'"Tout au plus m'a-t-il fourni une occasion. Quand j'ai eu dix-sept ans ..." ' (p. 1419)

Similarly hypothetical constructions with the imperfect subjunctive are found. In the first of the following examples, taken from the *carnets*, the restrictive clause is in emphatic position. In the second, part of a long speech to Rieux, a certain pathos is achieved by repetition of both the inversion structure and the word *honte* :

'Et ... on s'aperçoit que personne n'est capable réellement de penser à personne, fût-ce dans le pire des malheurs.' (p. 1414)

'"Cela fait longtemps que j'ai honte, honte à mourir d'avoir été, fût-ce de loin, fût-ce dans la bonne volonté, un meurtrier à mon tour." ' (p. 1423)

(b) The documentary narrative and the main themes of the novel

The most common function of inverted order in *La peste* is one of syntactic clarity. Thus relative inversions in particular are frequently used in parentheses or to dispose of long subject nominals :

> ' Des êtres que liaient l'intelligence, le cœur et la chair, en furent réduits à chercher les signes de cette communication ancienne dans les majuscules d'une dépêche de dix mots.' (p. 1272)

Inversion in this example permits the clear and emphatic exposition of the recurring theme of separation. Alternatively inversion may place a vital subject in a strong sentence final position. This is noted throughout in the author's treatment of the plague, whether rumoured, emergent or rife :

> '... tendant à bout de bras les feuilles où éclate le mot " Peste " '. (p. 1314)

> ' Il lui dit au revoir à la porte de la maison où l'attendait un malade suspect.' (p. 1338)

> ' Paneloux n'avait pas quitté les hôpitaux et les lieux où se rencontrait la peste.' (p. 1397)

There is an early example in which inversion stresses the personification of the spreading disease :

> ' C'était là une des façons qu'avait la maladie de détourner l'attention et de brouiller les cartes.' (p. 1277)

In an essentially factual narrative, inversion occasionally emphasizes other abstract ideas, as in the following constructions which occur on the same page :

> ' Alors commençait l'abstraction et la difficulté en effet, car...'

> ' Alors commençaient les luttes, les larmes, la persuasion, l'abstraction en somme.' (p. 1289)

Adverbial phrases of place and prepositional phrases are types of *invertissant* frequently used to express an opposition between normality and the state of plague. For instance the following descriptive passage introduces a meeting to plan Tarrou's escape, which belies the normality of the setting :

> ' Dans le ciel progressaient de petits nuages blancs et ronds

que, tout à l'heure, la montée de la chaleur avalerait d'un
coup.' (p. 1340)

Similarly everyday routine in the next description is stressed by
inverted order and contrasts with the elevated style and
weighty content of a sermon which precedes it :

'De la rue montaient des bruits de voix, des glissements de
véhicules, tout le langage d'une ville qui s'éveille.' (p. 1297)

The same constructions, however, also emphasize a state of
turmoil, e.g.

'De tous les côtés, montaient des gémissements sourds ou
aigus qui ne faisaient qu'une plainte monotone.' (p. 1386)

The next example highlights a barely concealed reference to
the German occupation :

'De loin en loin, claquaient les coups de feu des équipes
spéciales chargées, par une récente ordonnance, de tuer les
chiens et les chats qui auraient pu communiquer des puces.'
(p. 1309)

(c) Direct speech

The majority of examples which are found in conversation in
La peste have either an indirect speech *invertissant* or the
modal adverb *peut-être*. The style of the priest Paneloux,
however, is an exception, besides revealing a notable increase
in frequency of inversion. In the sermon already mentioned,
there are six examples of inverted order in barely two pages,
of which three *invertissants* are adverbs, the others being
comme, c'est ... que and the indirect *ce que*. Inversion is undoubtedly fitting in this solemn context, where all the examples
are either Biblical or learned, e.g.

' " Vous savez maintenant ce qu'est le péché, comme l'ont su
Cain et ses fils, ceux d'avant le déluge, ceux de Sodome et de
Gomorrhe, Pharaon et Job et aussi tous les maudits." '
(p. 1296)

In his account of an incident in the *Légende dorée*, the priest
uses rhetorical devices of repetition and contrasting word-order
in the correlative construction already quoted (p. 341 above).
As the sermon reaches its climax, the inversion after *c'est* ...

que has an impressive delaying effect, with the multi-syllabic subject introducing a long subordinate clause :

' " C'est ici, mes frères, que se manifeste enfin la miséricorde divine qui a mis en toute chose le bien et le mal, la colère et la pitié, la peste et le salut." ' (p. 1297)

At no other point in the novel does inverted order occur so frequently or with such effect. Thus it seems that since the construction is rarely found where the context does not demand clarity or emphasis, its use is otherwise reserved for certain elevated styles, either of aspiring journalism or of religious solemnity. With regard to emphatic usage, the frequent co-occurrence of inversion and references to the plague, its effect and surroundings, cannot be overlooked.

Chapter XI

THE TWENTIETH CENTURY (2)

1. SYNTACTIC ANALYSIS OF THE TEXTS
1950–1960

The texts :

H. Bazin, *Lève-toi et marche* [1]
A. Robbe-Grillet, *Le voyeur* [2]
M. Butor, *L'emploi du temps* [3]
N. Sarraute, *Le planétarium* [4]

Table 11.01 : Inversion frequencies

BAZ/LEV	126 : 0·69
RG/VOY	181 : 1·17
BUT/EMP	271 : 1·36 (*mean* 0·92)
SAR/PLA	77 : 0·44

Table 11.02 : Percentage table to show nature of clause in which inversion occurs

	BAZ	*RG*	*BUT*	*SAR*
Main clause	32	43	19	10
Subordinate clause	67	57	77	90
Non-subordinating *invertissant* in subordinate clause	1	n	4	—
	100	100	100	100
Immobile *invertissant*	67	56	77	85
Mobile *invertissant*	29	40	18	10
Other operations	4	4	5	5
N :	126	181	271	77

[1] Paris (Grasset), 1952 (*c.* 80,000 words). (BAZ)
[2] Paris (Editions de minuit), (*c.* 68,000 words). (RG)
[3] Paris (Editions de minuit), 1957. (BUT)
[4] Paris (Gallimard), 1959 (*c.* 77,000 words). (SAR)

Table 11.03 : Percentage table to show distribution of inversions according to discourse type

	BAZ	RG	BUT	SAR
Narrative	94	90	94	78
Direct speech	5	n	5	12
Indirect speech	1	3	1	—
Free indirect speech	—	7	—	10

Table 11.04 : Percentage table to show position of the inversion within the corpus examined

	BAZ	RG	BUT	SAR
Sentence initial	25	33	3	3
Paragraph initial	5	7	7	—
Chapter initial	1	—	—	—
Speech initial	1	—	1	—
Total initial	32	40	11	3
Sentence final	30	25	5	34
Paragraph final	10	13	12	3
Chapter final	—	—	—	—
Speech final	—	—	n	—
Total final	40	38	17	37

Table 11.05 : Percentage table to show position of inversion in relation to other types of discourse

	BAZ	RG	BUT	SAR
Preceding direct speech	10	3	1	6
Following direct speech	3	2	—	1

Table 11.06 : Percentage table to show nature of the inverted noun phrase

	BAZ	RG	BUT	SAR
Pronoun subject	15	10	7	4
Substantive subject	83	87	93	96
Compound inversion	2	3	—	—
	100	100	100	100
2 or more subjects	6	7	8	10
S and dependent (S)	12	10	21	6

Table 11.07 : The percentage of inversions occurring in
sentences of three or more clauses

	BAZ	RG	BUT	SAR
(S)—3 clauses	21	18	18	12
4 clauses	11	7	23	21
5 clauses	2	1	22	12
6 clauses	3	2	13	13
7 clauses	—	—	7	5
7+ clauses	1	n	4	1
	38	28	87	64

Table 11.08 : The ratio of inversions to *invertissants*

BAZ	126 : 49—2·57
RG	181 : 63—2·87
BUT	271 : 59—4·60
SAR	77 : 28—2·75
Total	655 : 115—5·70 (*mean* 3·20)

Table 11.09 : Percentage table of the most frequently occurring
inversions

	BAZ	RG	BUT	SAR
Relatives	54	40	63	64
Comparatives	3	3	4	8
Indirect construction	3	7	3	8
Modal adverbs	16	12	6	5

Table 11.10 : Percentage table to show the occurrence of
' être ', ' faire ' and ' avoir '

	BAZ	RG	BUT	SAR
être	6	7	8	6
faire	2	3	1	8
avoir	—	—	2	5

Table 11.11 : Percentage table showing the distribution of
direct speech *invertissants*

	BAZ	RG	BUT	SAR
Immobile *invertissant*	83	100	57	89
Mobile *invertissant*	17	—	36	11
Other operations	—	—	7	—
N :	6	1	14	9

Table 11.12 : Percentage table to show the occurrence of
adverbials and clauses in inversion constructions

	BAZ	RG	BUT	SAR
V(adv)S	5	18	20	29
(adv)VS	2	3	4	3
V(S)S	—	1	1	3
(S)VS	—	1	4	3

(i) DISTRIBUTION OF THE INVERSIONS

The average frequency of inversion in the four contemporary
texts, 0·92, falls between two extremes, 1·36 in Butor and 0·44
in Sarraute. Although there is a slight decrease in the average
frequency, after 1·06 in the previous period, the evolution of
inversion as a stylistic device seems complete, since the extent
of its occurrence now appears to represent personal choice.
The average number of *invertissants* per text is also lower, fifty
as compared with fifty-five in the pre-1950 period, but this is
still higher than at any stage since the 16th century. The lower
total of *invertissants*, 115 as against 158, (table 11.08), is
perhaps a result of the fewer number of texts analysed, and
thus less informative.

Table 11.02 shows a decreased frequency of other operations,
an average of 4·5% per text, as opposed to 6% in the previous
period, but these are nonetheless a firmly established feature
of inversion. A high proportion of examples occur in subordinate clauses in Butor, and as in Proust this characterizes a text
with a complex sentence structure and thus considerable
subordination. There are, moreover, ten examples of the
subordination of a mobile *invertissant*, or 4% of the total, in
L'emploi du temps. Few examples of inversion are found in
direct speech (table 11.03), despite a notable frequency of the
construction in free indirect speech in Robbe-Grillet and
Sarraute.

As before, inversions tend to occupy final rather than initial
position in the sentence, except in Robbe-Grillet, (table 11.04),
although there are few examples of either in Butor, a further
consequence of longer sentences as in Proust. The proportion
of inversions in sentences of three or more clauses in Butor is,

at 87%, the highest in all the texts examined except de Montreux (89%), the favoured sentence length for inversion being four or five clauses (table 11.07). Inversion sentences in the remaining authors, however, tend to be shorter, and the proportion of longer sentences in Robbe-Grillet, 28%, is by contrast the lowest in all the texts studied.

Table 11.05 shows unusual frequencies of inversion preceding direct speech in Bazin and in Sarraute. Occurrence of compound inversion is low (table 11.06), and its total absence from both Butor and Sarraute is unusual, particularly in view of the frequency of inversion in the former. As indicated in the previous chapter, a renewed frequency of relative *invertissants* is accompanied by a decrease in modal adverbs (table 11.09). It is striking that two texts with a relatively high number of modal adverb *invertissants*, Bazin and Robbe-Grillet, have fewer relative inversions than Butor and Sarraute, where the reverse is true, and this indicates a relation between the two types of construction which has become increasingly evident in the course of this study.

It is clear from table 11.10 that the frequency of *être* in inversion structures continues to decrease, with the average of 7% per text representing half that of the previous period. Finally the details of word-order resumed in table 11.12 are interesting for the features shared by three of the novelists, the exception being Bazin. Thus the order verb-adverb-subject is found in a substantial number of examples in Robbe-Grillet, Butor and Sarraute, and in addition these texts all have examples of clauses placed between *invertissants* and verb, or between verb and subject, suggesting a more complex order in the *nouveau roman* which contrasts sharply with that of a more traditional writer.

(ii) EXAMPLES

A. IMMOBILE 'INVERTISSANT'

1. *Zero* : *BAZ* : *2* ; *RG* : *2* ; *BUT* : *6*
   ' *Avait* également *disparu*, dans la poche de sa canadienne, la fine cordelette ramassée le matin même.' (RG, p. 163)

2. *Relatives* : *BAZ* : 68 inversions, 11 '*invertissants*' ;
   RG : 73,7 ; *BUT* : 172,11 ; *SAR* : 49,5
   ' Elle ouvre de grands yeux *où* mousse et pétille une
   joyeuse excitation ...' (SAR, p. 157)

3. *Comparatives* : *BAZ* : 4,2 ; *RG* : 6,3 ; *BUT* : 12,4 ;
   SAR : 6,3
   ' Elle était de proportions mêmes, plus petite que la
   normale *autant que* permettaient d'en juger ses mutila-
   tions.' (RG, p. 71)

4. *Concessives* : *BAZ* : 1,1 ; *RG* : 3,1 ; *BUT* : 1,1
   ' *Quelle que* fût la raison de son absence, Pascal pouvait
   écrire.' (BAZ, p. 173)

5. *Temporal clause* : *BAZ* : 5,3 ; *RG* : 1,1 ; *BUT* : 2,2 ;
   SAR : 4,3
   ' C'est entré en lui et cela grossit en lui — le contentement
   d'être ici ..., *pendant que* battent contre la coque étanche du
   vaisseau précieux les eaux toujours grossissantes de la
   convoitise, de la curiosité, cela le remplit...' (SAR, p. 198)

6. *Result clause* : *BUT* : 3,2
   ' et (cette immense collection de romans policiers) suffit à
   leur lecture *de telle sorte qu'*il ne s'y trouve que fort peu de
   textes récents, et *que* n'y figure point le Meurtre de
   Bleston ' (BUT, p. 89)

7. *Substantival clause* : *RG* : 4,3 ; *BUT* : 1,1
   ' Il plongea de nouveau la main dans la poche intérieure de sa
   veste et en retira le portefeuille, pour *vérifier que* s'y trouvait
   encore le fragment de journal découpé la veille...' (RG, p. 75)

8. *Correlatives* : *BUT* : 2,1
   ' *Plus* se prolongeait mon visage autour de ses traits, *plus*
   j'observais ses attitudes au cours de ce déjeuner à la
   lumière de la lampe, et *plus* devenait contraignante cette
   impression que...' (p. 167)

9. *Indirect construction* : *BAZ* : 4,4 ; *RG* : 12,8 ; *BUT* :
   9,6 ; *SAR* : 6,6
   ' Elle sait *de quoi* est faite cette transfusion silencieuse qui
   s'opère au-dessus d'elle tandis qu'elle gît entre eux.'
   (SAR, p. 51)

B. MOBILE 'INVERTISSANT'

1. *Attributes : RG : 7,2 ; BUT : 2,1 ; SAR : 1,1*
' *Seuls* émergeaient franchement de l'obscurité le coin d'une table massive et quelques décimètres de plancher mal joint.' (RG, p. 134)

2. *Adverbs—modal : BAZ : 20,8 ; RG : 21,8 ; BUT : 15,7 ; SAR : 2,1*
' *Tout naturellement* se mêlent à mes phrases de ce soir certains fragments du texte ancien que je viens de lire.' (BUT, p. 280)

3. *Adverbs—quantity : BAZ : 2,2 ; RG : 1,1*
' Et ses paupières s'alourdissaient tandis que *peu à peu* fléchissait cette rage de l'apôtre-maison qui...' (BAZ, p. 268)

4. *Adverbs—temporal : BAZ : 3,3 ; RG : 2,2 ; BUT : 2,2 ; SAR : 1,1*
'... il se lève ... " Ah, il faut que je parte. Il est temps..." et *puis* vient l'explosion, mais très légère ... à peine quelques égratignures...' (SAR, p. 264)

5. *Adverbs—place : BAZ : 3,3 ; RG : 10,8 ; BUT : 3,2*
' *Au delà* s'alignaient les maisons et leurs boutiques...' (RG, p. 164)

6. *Adverbs—combination : RG : 1,1*
' *Peut-être même* avait-elle essayé de descendre jusqu'à l'eau par un éperon escarpé...' (RG, p. 175)

7. *Adverbial phrase—time : BAZ : 3,1*
' *Le matin même* était arrivée une lettre d'un certain André Carmélie, ancien élève de...' (BAZ, p. 62)

8. *Adverbial phrase—place : BAZ : 5,5 ; RG : 29,12 ; BUT : 25,9 ; SAR : 2,2*
' Lorsque, rentré ici, le samedi 8 décembre, tandis que *sur cette fenêtre* s'appesantissent la pluie et la nuit, s'accrochaient un instant les gouttes avant de couler..., j'ai examiné ce petit ouvrage...' (BUT, p. 153)

9. *Adverbial phrase—manner : BAZ : 1,1*
' *Au courrier de midi* me parvenait une lettre dont je reconnus aussitôt l'écriture fine...' (BAZ, p. 182)

10. *Prepositional phrase : RG : 2,1 ; BUT : 1,1 ; SAR : 2,1*

'... et *du visage entier* — comment peut-on s'y méprendre ?
Qui oserait protester ? — rayonne une secrète et rare
beauté.' (SAR, p. 95)

11. *Subordinate clause : BUT : 1,1*

' (*tandis que nous admirions ces antres de marbre*, j'ai appris
par l'" Evening News " du lendemain, brûlait dans le 9e
arrondissement un hangar)...' (BUT, p. 241)

C. OTHER OPERATIONS

1. *Deletion : BAZ : 2 ; RG : 2*

' *Manque* aussi la fourche, que j'aimerais lui prêter.'
(BAZ, p. 70)

2. *Deletion and transposition : BAZ : 1 ; RG : 1 ; BUT : 5*

'... donnant l'adresse de Matthews and Sons que je savais
par cœur pour l'avoir tant de fois écrite sur des enveloppes,
ne serait-ce que pour régler mon arrivée ici.' (BUT, p. 17)

3. *Addition and transposition : BAZ : 2,2 ; RG : 4,2 ; BUT : 9,6 ; SAR : 4,4*

' Les verres de cette série étaient dépourvus de pied ;...
C'est dans l'un d'eux — incolore — *que* venait de boire le
voyageur.' (RG, p. 123)

(iii) DETAILS OF THE INVERSIONS

(a) Immobile ' invertissant '

Unlike the texts studied in the previous period, several
immobile *invertissant* constructions are not found in the present
material, namely inversion in hypothetical and causal clauses.
Constructions of particular interest include those with zero
invertissant and the result, final and temporal clauses, examples of the last occurring in all four works, and seemingly
well-established as an inversion construction.   The lexical
variety already mentioned also contributes to the apparent
novelty of many of the examples.

The two cases of zero *invertissant* in Bazin are unexceptional,
each having the verb *suivre* and a dependent clause following

the subject. In Robbe-Grillet, however, in addition to the construction with *disparaître* quoted above (p. 390), there is an instance of a passive verb followed by a list of five subjects :

'Sont alignés sur une même oblique : la grande main, la tête blonde, la lampe à pétrole, le bord de la première assiette (du côté droit), le montant gauche de la fenêtre' (p. 226)

The examples in Butor all have the verb *intervenir* and occur in a few pages in chapter IV in complex repetition structures ; on nearly every occasion this construction begins a paragraph, e.g.

'intervenaient aussi les images lugubres de ces sarcophages blancs ou gris, décorés de portraits grossiers...

    intervenait l'image de la maquette en plâtre peint...' (p. 244)

In spite of the frequency of temporal clause *invertissants* there is only one example with a common verb, which is in Sarraute, and here the *invertissant* itself is uncommon :

'Billets déchirés cent fois avant que ne vienne enfin ce ton libre.' (p. 290)

In addition to six constructions with *quand* in the four texts, there are two examples with *avant que* (Butor and Sarraute), one with *pendant que* (Sarraute), and one with *jusqu'à ce que :*

'(cette masse) semblait fondre sur la chaise, jusqu'à ce qu'intervienne ce sursaut des épaules...' (BAZ, p. 26)

The unfamiliarity of such temporal conjunctions is suggested by the fact that Le Bidois finds no examples of *avant que* in *A la recherche du temps perdu* only two with *jusqu'à ce que*, and four with *pendant que*, as against some fifty occurrences of inversion after *quand*.[5]

The examples of inversion in result clauses are all in Butor, the *invertissants* being *sans que, de telle sorte que* and *afin que*. In the example already quoted (p. 391 above) the inversion occurs in the second of two clauses dependent on a single conjunction. It may be noted that this construction in direct speech also concludes a paragraph. These inversions all occur in long sentences, and the remaining two also have a dependent

[5] *Op. cit.*, p. 302.

clause or lengthy complement. Substantival clause inversions are found particularly in Robbe-Grillet, along with one example in Butor. The verbs introducing inversion in *Le voyeur* are *attendre que, être sûr que* and *vérifier que*. In addition the Butor example uses *éviter que* in a much longer sentence than those in Robbe-Grillet, where there are never more than three clauses in the inversion sentence.

(b) Mobile ' invertissant ' and other operations

Table 11.02 showing the distribution of the inversions indicates a relatively low frequency of mobile *invertissant* constructions, with the exception of Robbe-Grillet where the frequency is 40%. Except for one inversion after a subordinate clause in Butor (quoted p. 393 above), there are no unusual constructions in this category, and the number of inversions after an adverbial is generally low. An exception to this is the frequency of inversion after an adverbial phrase of place in the two authors who use inverted order most often, Butor and Robbe-Grillet, as well as a high incidence of inversion following adverbs of place in the latter.

Included in the attributive constructions are four examples of the *invertissant seul* in Robbe-Grillet, all with different verbs. Two constructions have *être* and a past participle, and the others use *émerger* (quoted p. 392 above) and *choquer* :

' Seule choquait, sur la façade, cette grande distance qui...'
(p. 192)

There are few unusual modal adverb *invertissants*, other than *naturellement* in Butor and two instances of *probablement* in Robbe-Grillet, one of which has compound inversion :

' Probablement le garagiste venait-il de graisser l'articulation du frein, dont...' (p. 82)

The same is true of other adverbial *invertissants*, with the analysis showing much greater lexical variety, but few very unusual examples. It may, however, be noted that there are instances of inversion after *immédiatement* in Robbe-Grillet, *ailleurs* in Bazin, and *de nouveau* in Butor. Also the following addition and transposition structure occurs twice in Butor :

'C'est maintenant que commence la véritable recherche.'
(pp. 37 and 38)

Finally the ten examples of inversion after an adverb of place in Robbe-Grillet are notable both for the range of *invertissants* and for the fact that, unusually, the verb *être* does not occur in any of them, e.g.

'En deçà, se répète la succession des devantures.' (p. 77)

'Par terre s'empilaient encore des paniers et des caisses.' (p. 70)

(iv) SUPPLEMENTARY TEXT

In view of the bias towards the *nouveau roman* in the choice of contemporary texts, a further novel has been analysed in order to compare the inversion frequencies. This was Gracq's *Le rivage des Syrtes*,[6] the analysis of which revealed 192 inversions in the first 88,000 words, a frequency of 0·96. Had this been included in the main study, the average for inversion in this period would nevertheless have remained the same.

2. STYLISTIC ANALYSIS OF THE TEXTS

(i) H. BAZIN: 'LÈVE-TOI ET MARCHE'

The inversion frequency in *Lève-toi et marche*, 0·69, is a low one for the 20th century. It is similar to that of Camus writing a few years earlier (0·67), but with more *invertissants* in the Bazin novel, resulting in a very low ratio of inversions to *invertissants* (table 11.08). The proportion of mobile *invertissant* constructions, 29%, is fairly high for the period, with the 4% occurrence of other operations being roughly the same for each text (table 11.02). With only 5% of the examples occurring in direct speech (table 11.03), this novel reflects a general trend in the works analysed, and the proportion of inversions in initial and final positions is again about average (table 11.04). On the other hand table 11.05 shows that 10% of the inversions precede direct speech, the highest proportion in the works examined in this study, with a further

[6] Paris (Corti), 1951.

3% of the examples following conversation. The sentences in which inversion is found are generally short, only 38% having three or more clauses, of which 21% are three-clause sentences (table 11.07). Similarly there is little separation of the constituents in the inversion clause (table 11.12), with no examples of an interposed clause, and only 7% with separation by adverbials. 70% of the inversions follow relative pronouns or modal adverbs (table 11.09), and in each case the number of different *invertissants* is the highest of the four texts chosen in this period. The analysis of Bazin reveals another general tendency in the infrequency of the verb *être* in inversion structures, 6% (table 11.10).

There are no examples of inversion in a final or result clause in this text, or after an attribute. It is the only novel of the four in which all types of adverbial *invertissant* are found, but there is no example of an inversion after a prepositional phrase. The two deletion constructions use the verbs *manquer* (quoted p. 393 above) and *rester*. The examples which follow illustrate Bazin's use of inverted order in association with a major theme in the novel, and the inversions which occur within, or in relation to, direct speech, are also examined.

(a) *Inversion and the theme of sickness*

All but the final chapters of *Lève-toi et marche* take the form of a first person narrative by a victim of progressive paralysis, and it is not surprising, therefore, to find a preoccupation with illness and deformity reflected in constructions with emphatic word-order. Approximately 12% of the inversions have subjects of this type, and a further 8% reveal the narrator's tendency to stress, somewhat unflatteringly, the physical characteristics of the healthy people around her.

There are five examples in which the inverted subject constitutes a medical term, e.g.

‘ Après l'épaule, mon coude s'était mis à enfler, tandis que s'éternisait le panaris indolore qui me rongeait le médius.’ (p. 172)

In the following the verbs are also strongly stressed, and they

represent something of an obsession on the part of the narrator :
'On peut accepter la mort lente : celle du savant que con-
sume la radiodermite, celle du médecin des lépreux que finit
par dévorer le bacille de Hansen.' (p. 172)

Inversion occurs with more general terms to indicate various
characteristics of the sick, and in the next examples both
adjective and subject position are used effectively. The first
construction occurs in the early part of the book, and the anteposed adjective in the concluding inversion underlines, together with the emphatic verb, the apparent paradox :

'... et je suis de ces infirmes qu'afflige une terrible santé.'
(p. 38)

The second example is from the concluding narrative in which
the girl's death is described. Here the important idea contained in the postponed adjective is placed in a strong sentence
final position by virtue of inverted order :

'Ce fut tout ce que put s'imposer sa lucidité défaillante.'
(p. 273)

The narrator's ironic attitude towards her own deformities is
reflected to some extent in the syntax. In the example below,
the victim is almost light-hearted, as is suggested by the short
sentences :

'Mais elles (mes jambes) n'ont pas pu m'obéir. A peine
ont-elles esquissé une molle grenouillade. Certes les bras
vont sauver la situation.' (p. 17)

Inversion in initial position may also be used for emphatic
effect, particularly since it is less common :

'Ici, se place la pire période de ta vie : celle de l'enlisement.'
(p. 204)

As already suggested, the presentation of other characters in
the novel lays frequent emphasis on physical description, and
there are a number of inversion constructions, often in final
position, where the stressed subject is such a detail :

'Elle ... m'offre un dernier sourire, d'une qualité nouvelle, un
sourire sur qui pèsent ses immenses paupières.' (p. 202)

These observations are not infrequently tinged with malice, e.g.

'Mais avec cette fille nul besoin d'émincer le morceau, que

globe tout rond sa bouche ouverte. Elle a ce grand appetit
des pécheresses pour les mérites d'autrui.' (p. 109)
' Mathilde ... tourne vers lui un menton inquiet où tremblent
de gélatineuses bajoues.' (p. 186)
The tendency to alight on a physical detail in the course of the
narrative or description may be emphasized either by an initial
inversion or by an unusual *invertissant* :
> ' Mauvais signe, quand remuent les oreilles du fauve. Celles
> de Nouy bougent.' (p. 103)
> '... cette masse ... semblait fondre sur la chaise, jusqu'à ce
> qu'intervienne ce sursaut des épaules qui, toutes les cinq
> minutes, la redressait...' (p. 26)

(*b*) *Conversation and inverted order*

The small number of inversions in direct speech in this novel,
six in all, is explained by the colloquial nature of the conversations. The *invertissants* which do occur are *que* and *où* (two examples of each), along with one indirect construction and *du
moins*. Nevertheless these constructions do not necessarily have
simple verbs or subjects, only one example having the verb *être*.
A striking feature is the occurrence of inversion alongside
various colloquialisms, as in the following remark by a doctor :
> ' " Fais l'imbécile, ma cocotte, et nous verrons ce qu'il
> adviendra du joli boulot qu'ont réussi mes confrères du
> côté de ta neuvième dorsale." ' (p. 60)
Popular expressions may be emphasized, somewhat incongruously, by inversion of the subject :
> ' " D'ailleurs, tu sais, tant qu'il sera dans son cabinet que
> fréquentent tous les combinards du neuvième, Nouy destera
> ce qu'il est." ' (p. 146)
> ' " La police prétend qu'il se trouvait jeudi ... dans un café
> de la Bourse où avait lieu un ' arrivage de jonc suisse ',
> comme ils disent." ' (p. 212)
The high proportion of inversions preceding direct speech, on
the other hand, has already been noted. These constructions
do more than mark a change in narrative style, as has been seen
in previous works analysed. The majority of the examples

describe the speaker, often his physical appearance as well as his attitude or voice, and only rarely does an *incise* construction follow the speech :

'N'importe qui, chargé de la retrouver sans le connaître, irait droit au lit du pasteur que dénoncent son port de tête et la sobriété de ses gestes.
— Vous, Constance ! ' (p. 191)

'... et presque aussitôt parvint à mon oreille un murmure, un souffle, un chuchotement :
— Si encore tu savais jouer aux échecs...' (p. 134)

The inverted subject in the following combines three aspects of the speaker :

' Elle s'excuse avec des phrases banales que transfigurent sa voix chantante, son port de tête enfantin et le battement précipité de ses grands cils.' (p. 106)

The emphatic description of the speaker in the next example has additional significance, since boredom is often attributed to Constance by other people, whereas she herself finds it only in those round her :

' Ses lunettes de fil de fer (...) lui creusent la racine du nez, où viennent se replier les rides du grand ennui.' (p. 158)

Inversion in this position may also introduce a detail describing the listener, e.g.

' Elle souffle, près de l'oreille de Mademoiselle Calieun, là où s'attache la violette : ' (p. 218)

Finally an example in which the stressed nominal is also related to the subject of the conversation :

' " Pourquoi ? Il est vrai que cela m'arrive. Le fer à repasser..." Je lui montre mes doigts où persiste une trace brunâtre.' (p. 136)

The analysis of inversion in *Lève-toi et marche* reveals some variation in the traditional use of word-order, but not the complexity or experimental nature of the syntax of the *nouveaux romanciers*. Thus while inversion is extremely rare in conversations in the novel, its occurrence elsewhere is linked with that of an important theme. The wide range of verbs which figure in inversion constructions and the infrequency of *être* seem to indicate an increase in the emphatic function of the structure as a whole, which is illustrated by the following example of opposition between verbs and subjects in successive inversions :

> '... le petit ton sérieux des gens qui croient ... me cribler de ces mots techniques qu'évitent les véritables professionnels, mais sur lesquels se jettent les débutants pour créer autour d'eux un halo verbal.' (pp. 143–44)

Inversions of this type appear to become more common in the contemporary novel than the many routine constructions noted in earlier works.

(ii) A. ROBBE-GRILLET, 'LE VOYEUR'

Of the *nouveaux romanciers* studied here, both Robbe-Grillet and Butor make considerable use of inverted word-order. In addition to a high frequency of inversion, 1·17, *Le Voyeur* is one of the texts in the modern period with the most *invertissants*, sixty-three (table 11.08), to be compared with the total of sixty-five in Gide and Malraux, while having a lower ratio of inversions to *invertissants* than either. The proportion of mobile *invertissant* constructions, 40%, is the highest of the 20th-century texts analysed (table 11.02), and this also contributes to the high proportion of inversions in initial position (table 11.04). There is only one example of inversion in direct speech, an indirect construction, but, by contrast, twelve examples in free indirect style, eight of which have a mobile *invertissant*. The inversions in this novel occur primarily in one- or two-clause sentences, with only 28% found in sentences of three or more clauses (table 11.07), of which more than half comprise only three clauses. Table 11.09 shows that only 52% of the inversions are accounted for by relative or modal adverb *invertissants*, and the proportion of 62% of examples which are found in the four most common constructions is the lowest for the 20th-century texts. Finally table 11.12 reveals that the order verb-adverb-subject is found in 18% of the examples, but that other forms of separation of the major constituents occur only sporadically.

All types of immobile *invertissant* constructions are found in this text, except for result clauses. There is also a wide variety of mobile *invertissants*, in particular place adverbials, but no adverbial phrases of time or manner preceding inversion. From the examples discussed below it will be seen that for certain experimental writers like Robbe-Grillet, a relatively free word-order is an integral part of the novelist's technique. Thus the order of the sentence may reflect perception of reality through the objects described, and also contribute to the movement of the prose, to which this author attaches so much importance.[7]

Descriptions in the ' nouveau roman '

The importance of description is seen in Robbe-Grillet's account of its function in the *nouveau roman :*

' Elle (la description) ne parle plus que d'objets insignifiants, ou qu'elle s'attache à rendre tels. (...). Elle paraît naître d'un menu fragment sans importance ... à partir duquel elle invente des lignes, des plans, une architecture.' [8]

It is therefore not surprising to find not only a sizeable proportion of the inversions in *Le voyeur* occurring after place adverbials, but also the exploitation of this device with a view to an explicit creative function.

Much of the description of objects in *Le voyeur* is characterized by the use of geometrical terms which are thrown into relief in various ways by the sentence structure. The *invertissants* found in this formal description are predominantly place adverbials, along with some relatives and occasional instances of other structures. In these examples the geometrical figure is contained in the inverted subject :

' Au-dessus venait une sorte de cage cylindrique à barreaux verticaux, abritant un signal lumineux placé au centre.' (p. 255)

' Sur son socle carré s'élève une tige cylindrique à cannelures,

---

[7] ' Le mouvement de l'écriture ... est plus important que celui des passions et des crimes ', *Pour un nouveau roman*, Ed. de Minuit, 1963, p. 32.

[8] *Ibid.*, pp. 126–27.

supportant le réservoir — demi-sphère à convexité dirigée vers le bas'. (p. 226)

'... sur les autres étagères, se déployaient d'autres séries rectangulaires variant par la taille et la forme des éléments...' (p. 123)

It will be noted that despite the precision of adjectives such as *cylindrique* and *rectangulaire*, the nouns which they qualify are fairly indeterminate, so that the idea of a certain shape is stressed both by its position in the sentence and by its contrast to the other elements. Elsewhere the shape may be expressed in a verb; inverted order in this case permits both emphasis of the verb and expansion of the subject. The verb *s'aligner* occurs in two inversions after place adverbials, and these examples may be compared with a similar usage of *aligner* in the zero *invertissant* structure quoted on p. 394 (above):

' Devant lui, le long du quai, s'alignaient les façades qui le remenaient vers l'entrée de la digue.' (p. 52)

' Au delà s'alignaient les maisons et leurs boutiques : la quincaillerie au coin de la place, la boucherie, le café...' (p. 164)

Constructions such as the above may assume the additional function of indicating the relation between the objects described and human perception, a relation essential to the author's conception of reality.[9] Thus in the next example, the order of elements follows the order in which they are perceived, with the object emerging out of the progression of light, size, shape and colour:

' Juste au-dessous brillait un petit objet rectangulaire de couleur bleue — qui devait être un paquet de cigarettes.' (p. 68)

In the following the author returns to the geometrical shape after the object has been defined :

'... à l'endroit où prenait naissance, presque perpendiculairement, la longue digue aux lignes parallèles qui fuyaient en

---

[9] ' Les objets de nos romans n'ont jamais de présence en dehors des perceptions humaines, réelles ou imaginaires ', *Pour un nouveau roman*, pp. 116–17.

faisceau vers le fanal où elles semblaient converger.' (p. 73)
A similar use of the verb *fuir* in a clause dependent on the
inverted subject is seen in the next example, and in both cases
seems to indicate the destructive aspect of Robbe-Grillet's
descriptions,[10] the ' déception inhérente ' : [11]

'Devant lui s'élève la paroi extérieure de la digue, fuyant
verticale et rectiligne vers le fanal.' (p. 240)

Thus through mobility of elements in the sentence, the syntactic structure may be seen to mirror the creative and destructive
processes of the description of objects.

Inversion is not only important for the process of perceiving
various objects. Its emphatic value is seen in a new light in the
following structures in which emphasis falls on a subject whose
presence is barely perceived or only surmised. The first two
examples stress the confusion of objects by their position at
the end of a sentence and paragraph respectively :

'Ensemble ils auraient exploré ... les régions rarement
découvertes que peuplent des formes à la vraisemblance
équivoque.' (p. 32)

'... le phare surgit soudain devant lui, très haut dans le ciel,
au milieu de la masse des constructions annexes où se
mêlaient murs et tourelles.' (p. 220)

The inverted position of the subjects listed in the next example
underlines the fluid nature of the comparison :

'Dans la demi-conscience du réveil, l'image claire ... de la
fenêtre ... se met à faire le tour de la pièce, d'un mouvement
uniforme ... dont la lenteur est comme celle d'un fleuve,
passant ainsi aux places successives que doivent occuper la
chaise au pied du lit, l'armoire, la seconde armoire, la table
de toilette, les deux chaises rangées côte à côte.' (p. 232)

Elsewhere it is the movement of both the objects described
and of the prose itself which is suggested by a change in word-
order, e.g.

[10] ' (La description) faisait voir les choses et voilà qu'elle semble maintenant
les détruire, comme si son acharnement à en discourir ne visait qu'à en
brouiller les lignes, à les rendre incompréhensibles, à les faire disparaître
totalement ', *ibid.*, p. 127.

[11] *Loc. cit.*

' De tous côtés s'étendait maintenant la série des ondulations successives, couvertes d'une végétation rase et roussâtre d'où rien n'émergeait plus...' (p. 203)

Successive inversions may be used to oppose solid objects and fluid elements, without loss of movement :

' Elle regardait toujours dans la même direction, là où se trouvait tout à l'heure la mer, mais où se dressait maintenant la paroi verticale de la jetée — toute proche.' (p. 23)

There are a number of passages in which two or more inversions are juxtaposed, and it is notable that they tend to combine the devices associated with inverted order already mentioned, e.g.

' Après une chute presque verticale venait une paroi irrégulière, où saillaient par endroits des becs aigus, des replats, des arêtes. Tout en bas sortaient de l'écume, entre ces blocs plus imposants, un groupe de rochers coniques...' (p. 204)

Here the shapes emphasized in the various subjects contrast with the vague, watery elements from which they emerge, while the movement of this process is reflected in the choice of verbs and sentence structure. In the next example a clause containing a further inversion separating *invertissant* and verb has the effect of delaying and emphasizing still more the concrete subject which concludes a paragraph :

' Contre le fond gris du ciel, où ne subsistaient que de rares et fugitives places bleues voilées de gaze, se dressait le phare tout proche.' (p. 105)

Finally inversion may be used to stress certain details, often unexpected and insignificant, from which a description is built up. Thus there are two descriptions of marine life where details accumulate after the inverted subject :

' A côté, sur une claie, brillait un poisson solitaire, raide et bleu, fusiforme, long comme un poignard et bariolé de vaguelettes.' (p. 70)

' Entre cette extrémité et les herbes rases bordant la route, était écrasé le cadavre d'une petite grenouille, cuisses ouvertes, bras en croix, formant sur la poussière une tache à peine plus grise.' (p. 91)

In describing certain objects the author frequently selects a minor detail for emphasis, to which the major item is subordinate, e.g.

> 'Sur la coiffeuse, au milieu des pots et des flacons, légèrement incliné en arrière, se trouvait le cadre en métal chromé contenant la photographie.' (p. 172)

In the next example the reverse procedure produces the same effect :

> 'Devant lui se dressait un nouveau personnage, apparu contre le chambranle de la porte intérieure située près du tiroir-caisse. Mathias lui adressa un vague salut.' (p. 57)

No sooner is the subject introduced, somewhat impersonally, than he is subordinated to the surrounding objects presented in the complement. Alternatively an adverbial between verb and subject may effectively detract from the importance of the latter :

> 'Sur le mur, au-dessus de la plus haute rangée d'apéritifs, était fixée par quatre punaises la pancarte jaune.' (p. 222)

The majority of inversions in *Le voyeur* occur in contexts similar to those indicated above. There are a number of mobile *invertissant* constructions which are emphatic and contrast with longer structures. These may constitute part of a single-sentence paragraph as in the following free indirect construction :

> 'De toute façon il aurait mieux valu s'en aller, puisque tel était son plan.' (p. 162)

In the next example the line of free indirect speech represents the observer's thoughts in the course of conversation :

> ' " A marée haute on manœuvre facilement."
>
> Peut-être ne plaisantait-il pas.
>
> "Je n'étais pas forcé de partir," dit le voyageur.' (p. 163)

These examples, however, bear little relation to the thematic structure of the work. Although most of the inversions are unremarkable in themselves, the mobility of syntactic elements is an important, if not immediately striking feature in the experimental technique of the novel, and one which is exploited to the full by Butor.

(iii) M. BUTOR, 'L'EMPLOI DU TEMPS'

Several outstanding features of Butor's syntax have already been mentioned in the previous chapter in a comparison with that of Proust. Apart from the very high frequency of inversion and complex sentence structure in *L'emploi du temps*, it may be noted that the work contains examples of every type of immobile *invertissant* construction, although there are by contrast comparatively few adverbial *invertissants*, with no instances of adverbial phrases of time or manner figuring in inversion constructions. An unusual fact which emerges from the syntactic analysis is that the proportion of inversions found in paragraph initial or final positions, 7% and 12% respectively, is higher than that of the corresponding sentence positions (table 11.04), and it will be seen below that this feature is related to the form of the novel. Butor's writings on the novel also suggest his awareness of the stylistic potential of sentence length, which is thoroughly explored in this work :

> ' Il faudra appeler à son secours toutes les ressources de la langue (...) ... les petites phrases vont se rassembler en grandes phrases, quand il le faudra, ce qui permettra d'utiliser à plein, comme certains grands auteurs d'autrefois, le magnifique éventail de formes que nous proposent nos conjugaisons.' [12]

The importance of inverted order in relation to the units of the sentence and paragraph is discussed below, with particular reference to inversions in key positions and those related to the device of repetition.

(a) *The position of inversion in the paragraph*

Although the overall proportion of inversions in key position in this novel is low (table 11.04), there are a large number of examples at the beginning or end of a paragraph. The use of an emphatic device such as inverted order is not unexpected in this position, since Butor exploits paragraphing to indicate a

---

[12] *Essais sur le roman*, Paris, 1969, p. 123.

certain progression, both in the narrative and on the printed
page :

> ' Le blanc, la juxtaposition pure et simple de deux para-
> graphes décrivant deux événements éloignés dans le temps
> apparut alors comme la forme du récit la plus rapide pos-
> sible, une vitesse qui efface tout.' [13]

There are examples of inversion in both initial and final
positions in the paragraph, in which this dual function of paragraphing is fully apparent. It will be noted that in each of the
cases quoted, the paragraphs are linked by the punctuation,
the use of a comma in place of a full stop drawing the reader's
attention to the spacing and its significance. Thus in this
example of relative inversion, the blank on the page is indicative of passing time, with the notion stressed by inversion :

> '... donnant son véritable rôle à cette figure de femme ...,
> Ethra, dans la course de laquelle passent les années,
>
> me faisant remarquer, lui, James Jenkins...' (pp. 212–13)

In the following, the same technique underlines the idea of
isolation :

> ' cette Ann dont ... je ne puis pas écrire le nom sans jalousie ...
> sans se sentiment de gel et d'isolement que doivent éprouver
> les fantômes,
>
> cette Ann qui ne sait pas encore que...' (p. 265)

The instances of inversion in final position quoted above both
form part of a string of paragraphs in which the device is
repeated. This repetitive element is strongly stressed where an
inversion opens each paragraph, as in the examples of *intervenir* with zero *invertissant* quoted on p. 394 (above). In the
same chapter the enumeration technique is emphasized further
by the use of the same adverbials after each occurrence of the
verb, e.g.

> ' intervenaient dans cette représentation non seulement les
> images qui défilaient devant mes yeux, mais...' (p. 241)
> ' intervenaient dans cette représentation de Rome, non

[13] *Ibid.*, p. 117.

seulement l'Athènes conquise, non seulement Pétra, Baalbeck et Timgad, mais aussi cette ville de Bleston...' (p. 244)
The paragraph structure emphasized by recurring inversion here stresses the intrusive thoughts of the author as he watches a film show, with the spacing indicating a time lapse between their occurrence. A similar use of inversion has been noticed by Spitzer in *La Modification*,[14] in a device which he terms ' la phrase rituelle ', where the structure ' passe la gare de...' is repeated at the beginning of paragraphs to introduce an action within the framework of the main action.

A less typical example of inversion in closely related paragraphs is the following, where the idea implicit in the inverted subject concluding one paragraph is expanded at the beginning of the second with, perhaps, a break to represent a pause in the chain of thought :

  ' ' cette Ann qui ... ne se doute pas encore ... de ce malheur que sont pour moi ses fiançailles,

    cette Ann aimante ... que ...' (p. 265)

The majority of inversions in key positions, however, occur in a conventional form of paragraphing, but to similar effect, most of them being in final position. Thus in the next examples there is a progression in time, or in time and space, between the inverted subject concluding one paragraph and the first element of the next :

  '... leur humus fourré de charognes et de minerais qu'écrasaient les pas des reptiles, toute la nuit.

    Puis la gelante aube allégeante a apaisé la houle...' (p. 256)
' A l'horizon plat, de chaque côté, se dressaient de hautes cheminées inactives.

    Pendant deux kilomètres j'ai marché sans que s'interrompe la succession des '' ermitages '' réguliers...' (p. 33)
Other effects achieved by this structure include physical and emotional separation, the latter concluding a section within a chapter :

  '... se sont rejoints cette Ann et ce James comme il y a un mois s'étaient rejoints Lucien et Rose.

<hr />

[14] L. Spitzer, *Etudes de style*, Paris, 1970, p. 507.

O

Toute une figure s'est achevée dans cette exclusion de moi-même ' (p. 258)

'... dans une sorte de rêve très tenu, s'est mise à murmurer la voix de Rose, parlant si agréablement français ... s'est mise à murmurer la voix de Rose, commençant déjà à m'égarer loin de vous ' (pp. 250–51)

There is also an example of double inversion, in the second of which a protracted metaphor is terminated and the literal subject resumed :

'... comme les raies en quoi se décompose l'éclat d'un corps incandescent sur l'écran noir d'un spectroscope..., comme les harmoniques en quoi se décompose le timbre d'un son. Elles subsistent encore ce soir, ces bandes de souvenir...' (p. 292)

In conclusion there should be mentioned two instances of repeated inversion constructions in key positions. In the pair which conclude their respective paragraphs the same event is referred to first in future time and then in the present. In each case the concluding inversion represents the change from a descriptive to an introspective passage, together with a suggestion of monotony inherent in the repetition :

' Je reviens du Théâtre des Nouvelles où j'ai vu un film sur les grands lacs canadiens, où passera lundi prochain, comme toutes les quatre semaines, un programme composé uniquement de dessins animés.' (p. 185)

' Au sortir de chez Matthews and Sons je suis allé au Théâtre des Nouvelles où passait, comme toutes les quatre semaines, un spectacle entièrement composé de dessins animés.' (p. 193)

An inversion which opens a section in chapter I is repeated a few paragraphs later, with the repetition re-emphasizing an idea already stressed by the *invertissant*. Again there is a hint of monotony with the recurrence of the conjunction *car* :

' C'est maintenant que commence la véritable recherche ; car tous les événements que j'ai enregistrés jusqu'ici...' (p. 37)

' C'est maintenant que commence la véritable recherche, car

je ne me contenterai pas de cette abréviation vague...'
(p. 38)

Thus the occurrence of inversion in key positions in the paragraph underlines certain aspects of Butor's technique, in particular narrative progression, often within a repetition, which may also be represented by inverted order itself.

(b) Forms of repetition

In several of the examples quoted above, an inversion structure is repeated at regular intervals, with each new development of a certain theme. It also happens that a theme which is taken up at various points in the novel is characterized by the recurrence of certain lexical and syntactic structures. Thus references to a peculiarly unattractive ring are underlined by similar inversions in chapters I, III and V :

'... j'avais remarqué sa bague, un anneau d'or dont le chaton est une bulle de verre dans laquelle est enfermée une mouche en parfait état de conservation...' (p. 56)

'... sur ce chaton de verre à l'intérieur duquel ce n'était certes pas par l'effet d'une coïncidence qu'était enfermée une mouche...' (p. 154)

'... sa mère agitant en signe d'au revoir sa main droite où brillait le chaton de verre enfermant la mouche.' (p. 286)

Another theme which seems to attract relative inversions is the description of railway bridges. In all but the first example there is a progression from details of the immediate surroundings to the railway and distant places :

'... le pont épais, haut de deux étages ... sur lequel passait un train, le pont semblable à ceux que j'ai vus après...' (p. 16)

'... sous un réverbère qui venait de s'allumer de l'autre côté près du grand pont de chemin de fer, sur lequel hurlaient de longs trains partant vers l'Ecosse...' (p. 140)

'... traversant les quartiers miséreux que possède l'Université ... à l'orient des ponts de chemins de fer sur lesquels venait de passer le train qui emportait Lucien.' (p. 194)

Finally a repeated theme may receive parallel treatment in

a chiasmus. In each example below the inversion clause
expresses the same idea :
'les soirées s'allongent, comme se raccourcissaient les
après-midi de novembre, chaque jour mordant un peu
plus...' (p. 103)
'les soirées durent encore jusqu'à neuf heures, mais les voici
qui diminuent comme diminuaient les après-midi en
décembre, quant...' (p. 159)
Butor's predilection for long sentences results in some
complex repetitions. The structure of all or part of a paragraph
may centre on the repetition of subject or verb in a key
sentence, or of the whole construction. Inversion is employed
in these cases for both clarity and emphasis, as in this example
of a repeated subject
'... je n'ai pas pu vous parler, à l'"Oriental Bamboo" qu'à
mon insu avaient atteint les mauvaises flammes, ces flammes
qui sont parties de mes mains, qui ont couru...' (p. 242)
Alternatively an idea expressed in the inverted subject may be
repeated in a related or derived form :
'... les briques d'où il me semblait que me parvenait comme
un bruissement, comme il me semblait que j'entendais bruire
des roues et des pas dans les rues voisines, comme il me
semblait que...' (p. 257)
Repetition of an inverted verb may be used both to expand
an idea, where the two forms occur close together,
'... par lesquels m'atteignaient, nous atteignaient, Bleston,
une légende très antique ..., une légende dont...' (p. 295)
or as a unifying feature in the paragraph, e.g.
'... jusqu'au moment où m'est parvenu, au travers de toutes
ces paroles prisonnières, de ce concert de coups, de cuivres
et de plaintes, gelé dans cette fenêtre, m'est parvenu le
raclement d'une voiture de police...' (p. 197)
In the next example the recurring *réapparaître* is stressed by
inversion, with the construction thus underlining the meaning :
'... où, sur le cran ..., réapparaissait l'azur de la Crète,
réapparaissaient derrière les pierres et les peintures, celles du
palais de Minos, réapparaissaient toutes les images que j'y

avais vues le lundi 16 juin ... toutes les images ... qui...'
(p. 224)

An accumulation of repeated elements is seen in the following,
expanding a hypothetical clause, before its explanation :

' et si je reste sur ma chaise, devant cette feuille, devant cette
table, devant cette fenêtre où fondait la neige, où collaient
les brouillards de janvier, où vient de trembler un très
lointain éclair violacé, c'est que...' (p. 223)

In this example the third element of one repetition (' devant
cette fenêtre ') introduces a further three elements of parallel
structure. A final example shows how the *invertissant* may be
expanded and followed by a repeated verb and noun structure,
thus uniting the elements and underlining the idea of *rejoindre* :

'... puisqu'en dehors de moi, malgré moi mais par moi ... se
sont rejoints cette Ann qui m'avait aimé ... cette Ann que
je m'efforçais de rejoindre ..., se sont rejoints cette Ann et ce
James dont ...' (p. 258)

(c) *The emphatic function of inverted order*

As in *Le voyeur*, the descriptive passages of *L'emploi du
temps* are characterized both by an attention to detail and a
concern for forms and shapes, and the emphatic function of
inversion is exploited in each case. In the first examples
below, the word-order permits both emphasis on the verb and
the development of the inverted subject :

'... entre ces façades funèbres sur lesquelles s'alignent de
guingois, telles celles de craie sur les tableaux noirs des
écoles élémentaires...' (p. 24)

'... et les cailloux où se discernent encore parfois une arête
vive, un fragment de courbe classique, un reste de palmette,
une découpure d'acanthe usée, parmi les cailloux qui...'
(p. 122)

The impersonal character of the town of Bleston is echoed by a
formal use of language, in which a certain geometrical pattern
is found, with frequent inversions, e.g.

' Au point où se rencontrent les deux grands côtés, je suis

passé sous l'architrave que soutiennent quatre colonnes doriques trapues...' (pp. 16–17)

'... horizontalement sur le plan : Sea Street, que prolonge Mountains Street qui traverse la Slee sur New Bridge, à peu près verticalement : ' (p. 44)

The separation of elements in an inversion clause may underline a thematic separation. Thus in the following an interposed clause indicates passing time, and the adverb placed between *invertissant* and verb further delays the inverted subject, to suggest a long process of development :

'... mais c'est au cours de ces semaines routinières, quand j'ai peu à peu senti sa lymphe passer dans mon sang.., que sourdement s'est développée cette haine passionnée à son égard...' (p. 38)

In the next example, the main elements are separated by first an adverbial and then an adverbial with dependent clause, stressing the time lapse between entries in the journal :

' et dans le seul intervalle laissé intact, entre les fragments d'avril et de janvier, va s'intercaler, conformément à l'ordre complexe qui s'est peu à peu imposé à moi dans ce récit .., la deuxième semaine de mars.' (p. 293)

The examples quoted above reveal the extent to which certain technical innovations by Butor in the novel form correspond to a particular use of word-order. Thus in a work where the paragraph becomes a unit of considerable importance, the function of inversion in key positions and in repetitions is greatly extended. In choosing to present the novel in the form of a diary, Butor is able to achieve a juxtaposition of the time described and the time of writing, and particular syntactic constructions may be related to incidents mentioned at various points of time in the novel. The author's awareness of the reality of the pages of the journal, as opposed to that of his characters, is also stressed by inversion, e.g.

' (capable) de me faire entendre de vous, Ann, à qui s'adressent toutes ces phrases, île vers qui tendent toutes ces lignes comme des vagues, puisque ce texte ... est devenu maintenant comme une lettre...' (p. 245)

'... au travers de toutes ces craquelures que sont mes phrases...' (p. 276)
' cette blancheur que je dénonce, semblable au silence du dormeur que lézarde après coup le souvenir de ses rêves.' (p. 277)

Thus the traditional functions of inversion, such as those of liaison and emphasis, are expanded to the extent that the constructions link not sentences but paragraphs, and that important themes stressed by inversion are repeated at intervals of a hundred or more pages, corresponding to the time scale of the novel.

(iv) N. SARRAUTE, 'LE PLANÉTARIUM'

Despite the very low frequency of inversion in *Le planétarium* the analysis reveals a number of features which the novel shares with the other three works and even exploits to the extreme. For instance, in 29% of the examples an adverbial separates the verb and inverted subject, the highest proportion in the entire study, and 6% of the inversions include an intervening clause in the structure (table 11.12). There is also the highest frequency of inversion in direct and free indirect speech of the four works analysed (table 11.03), and in common with Bazin, Sarraute occasionally uses inversion to introduce conversation (table 11.05).

As a consequence of the almost exclusive occurrence of inversion in subordinate clauses, 90% of the examples (table 11.02), there are few initial inversions, but an average proportion in final position (table 11.04), as well as a high proportion of relative inversions, 64% (table 11.09). Apart from four examples of temporal clause *invertissants*, there are few unusual structures in this text, the four commonest constructions accounting for 83% of the inversions (table 11.09). There are no examples of zero *invertissant* or of inversion in a concessive clause, few adverbials, and the only other operation producing inverted order is the addition of *c'est ... que*. Finally it may be noted that this text has the highest incidence of common verbs of the four analysed (table 11.10). It will be seen

below how the occurrence of inversion is related to the form of
the novel, and the extent to which fairly complex syntactic
structures are employed.

(a) *Inversion and the form of the novel*

Like Butor, Sarraute uses a form in which the important
unit is the paragraph, and occasionally an inversion may be
directly linked to this :

' Elle entend le déclic léger que fait la clef dans la serrure...
L'arrachement, l'affreuse séparation va se consommer.'
(p. 80)

Here as in *L'emploi du temps*, an inverted subject precedes a
gap on the printed page which corresponds to a notion expressed in the following paragraph. However, whereas Butor's
paragraphs were frequently linked by a single sentence and
repetition of structures within it, the striking feature of the
Planétarium is the use of incomplete sentences, where *points
de suspension* indicate a continuing line of thought and a new
paragraph represents a change in time or thought patterns.
The influence of this method of presentation upon the syntax
of the novel is reflected in the number of inverted subjects
which precede the dots in various contexts.

A change in narrative style may be conveyed in this way,
and it is clearly not by chance that the majority of inversions
in or preceding direct speech, or in free indirect style, should
conclude interrupted sentences. The inversions which introduce conversation, as in Bazin, generally refer to a characteristic of the speaker or his voice, e.g.

' Voix claire et bien posée. Regard où glisse, pudique, une
lueur de piété filiale, de tranquille fierté ... " Mon père..." '
(p. 147)

In this example, as in the following, the deliberate break
between the sentences underlines the idea of gradual intrusion
contained in both verbs and subjects :

' Elle perçoit dans sa propre voix une amertume enfantine où
perce pourtant une pointe d'hesitation, presque d'espoir ...
" Des poignées comme celles-ci..." ' (pp. 15–16)

The same nuance is found in the following instance using the same verb, where the pause reinforces the idea of hesitancy, since the interpretation and the evidence for it are not then immediately juxtaposed :

' cet air de ne pas vouloir toucher à ces choses-là, de ne pas vouloir se commettre, où perce à peine une pointe très fine de blâme, de dégoût ... " C'est fragile, vous savez, les vieilles gens " ' (p. 133)

Such a device is particularly effective in conveying the hesitant and disconnected nature of ordinary speech, while inversion of the subject nevertheless permits a clean break by emphasizing the final element :

' " Je crois que je préfère celle-ci, la vue est plus belle ... on en rit encore dans la famille, trésor que se transmettent les héritiers ... Mais pourquoi en rire ? " ' (p. 223)

Most of the conversational inversions in *Le planétarium* occur in indirect constructions, which lend themselves equally well to this device, e.g.

' " Ce que je pense plutôt, c'est qu'Alain ... Vous savez ce que signifie le symbole de l'appartement ... Alain est un orphelin." ' (p. 239)

' " Ah ! elle est bonne, celle-là, c'est excellent ... Voila où ménent les bergères ... Elles mènent loin..." ' (p. 84)

The latter extract indicates the repetitive nature of speech, while the change in word-order avoids monotony. Free indirect style also provides examples of this type :

' Son père n'a pu s'y tromper un seul instant : c'était donc cela que signifiait cet air hagard, tout à coup, hébété ... Pensez donc...' (p. 151)

Here the inverted subject concludes the free indirect construction and the idea is resumed in a direct form of thought presentation. Reproductions of thought processes which use present tenses throughout also employ inversions in key positions as the idea develops :

' Cette peur qu'il sent grandir maintenant, c'est celle, il la reconnaît, qu'ont semée, fait germer en lui de vieux romans policiers ... cette scène...' (pp. 270–71)

In the following, the inversion precedes a change from a declarative to an interrogative structure :

' ... plantes de serre, luxe que s'offrent les hommes arrivés ... est-ce que vous pouvez vous plaindre de quelque chose, ta mère et toi ? ' (p. 124)

Elsewhere the sentence may be suspended in the course of an enumeration which is facilitated by inversion, e.g.

' Il sent posé sur son visage, appuyant sur ses yeux, pénétrant en lui son regard d'où ruisselle le regret la nostalgie ... Ils ont été surpris, encerclés, les étrangers...' (p. 162)

The discontinuity here suggests some hesitancy in interpreting another person's emotions and delays their explanation and also illustrates what Sartre has called Sarraute's ' style trébuchant, tâtonnant '.[15]   In the following, a much longer structure precedes the indirect thoughts of the characters concerned, introduced by *dire que*, which will to some extent justify the reactions listed in the inverted subject :

' une même vague les a traversés où se mêlaient un peu de gêne, de la pudeur, de la pitié, un peu de mépris, de l'étonnement, et une grande quantité de satisfaction ... dire que...' (p. 161)

Repetitions and expansions similar to those already quoted from Butor may be interspersed with, or relieved by, disconnected structures :

' une voix cassée, hésitante ... la voix craintive des vieilles solitaires, la voix méfiante, hostile des vieilles rentières avares, que guettent dans les escaliers silencieux les assassins sournois, faux camelots venant leur proposer des brosses, des machines à laver, faux inspecteurs venant faire le relevé de leurs compteurs à gaz ... une voix (...) ' (pp. 170–71)

In the above the third occurrence of *voix* with its various epithets is expanded into a new inverted structure in which there is first of all an accumulation of associated terms— *guetter, silencieux* and *sournois*, and then the repetition of *faux*, before the initial idea is resumed. However, such constructions

---

[15] Preface to N. Sarraute, *Portrait d'un inconnu*, Paris, 1956, p. 14.

are perhaps most effective when the inverted subject represents the climax of a certain train of thought, and the structural break emphasizes more clearly the subsequent change of idea, or return to consciousness :

> ' ces cubes hideux, sans vie, où dans le désespoir glacé, sépulcral, qui filtre des éclairages indirects, des tubes de néon, flottent de sinistres objets de cabinets de dentiste, de salles d'opération ... Elle se redresse, elle...' (p. 18)

(b) *Sentence structure*

In a novel whose main theme is essentially the portrayal of human thought, a fairly flexible word-order is important, since it permits the expansion of any element in an emphatic position. Although the number of inversions is not high in *Le planétarium*, this aspect of word-order is often exploited. For instance, the verb phrase may be expanded or repeated to indicate a complete action prior to the introduction of the subject :

> ' Elle s'était sentie soudain exposée ... frissonnant sous ce regard d'où coulait sur elle et la recouvrait une rancune froide, un mépris d'homme choyé...' (p. 200)

Similarly, parallel inverted structures may be used with the verb further developed in the second part, and emphasized by its repetition :

> ' cette vaine satisfaction que donne la gloire, de cette joie frelatée, mesquine que pourrait lui donner la victoire, la revanche sur ses ennemis...' (p. 197)

An adverbial clause which separates verb and subject may complete the description of an action before the introduction of the actor, e.g.

> ' cette plume que sait planter sur un chapeau d'un geste rapide, désinvolte, audacieux une modiste de génie...' (p. 193)

In the following, a metaphorical process is summed up in a later clause, which receives additional emphasis by the intervention of the inverted subject :

' De son chapeau sortent en cascades des flots de rubans, des
objets de toutes sortes, cela coule, lui échappe...' (p. 105)
In a further example, an interposed clause describes the main
actions :

'... un petit rond attendrissant, naïf comme celui que font
quand elles s'ouvrent et se tendent ainsi en avant les
bouches des enfants, elle...' (p. 111)

Inversion is also used at times in the formation of both
parallel and chiastic constructions. In the example of a
repeated inversion structure below, the antecedent is expanded
progressively, and inversion permits the comparison between
two emphatic subjects :

' sur ce ton doux, par-delà le blâme, qu'ont les prêtres, sur ce
ton qui marque les distances, que prennent les médecins, cet
air de ne pas vouloir...' (p. 133)

In the following, the juxtaposition of two orders results in a
parallel construction, with the opposition *déjouer-jouer* combined with that of *cruel* and *facétieux :*

' c'est le seul moyen de déjouer ce tour cruel que lui a joué un
sort facétieux...' (p. 204)

Somewhat different is the chiasmus below, where the contrasting subjects are separated by elements creating a further
opposition :

' une vieille vanité fatiguée qu'un attouchement trop appuyé
laisse insensible, mais qu'excite parfois délicieusement le
contact le plus léger, mais si inattendu, mais si délicat...'
(p. 290)

In conclusion it may be noted that as in *L'emploi du temps*,
word-order in *Le planétarium* is closely linked to the author's
experiments with the form of the novel. In both works the
traditional functions of inversion continue to be exploited,
although the loose thematic structure of Sarraute's novel
makes it impossible to associate a certain device of style with
any one recurring theme. The use of inverted order for
emphasis and clarity is, however, developed by these two
writers in ways similar to those already noticed in novelists
such as Proust, through considerable expansion and repetition

of the constituents. It has furthermore been seen that whereas the emphatic properties of inversion are important in Butor from the point of view of linking paragraphs, in Sarraute it is the relation of sentences within the paragraph which depends to perhaps a still greater extent on this device.

CHAPTER XII

CONCLUSION

1. THE SYNTACTIC ANALYSIS

(a) THE INFORMATION CONTAINED IN THE TABLES

(i) *Frequency of inversion*

The forty-four texts analysed in the previous chapters have yielded a total of 9,031 inversions and 433 different *invertissants*. The estimated number of inversions allowing for adjustment to ten texts whose length was less than 88,000 words is 9,442. The average frequency of inversion per page of *c.* 440 words in the texts of each period is as follows:

16th century (1) 2·64		19th century (1) 1·08
(2) 1·50		(2) 0·89
17th century (1) 0·74		20th century (1) 1·06
(2) 0·80		(2) 0·92
18th century (1) 0·52		
(2) 0·68		

and the changing frequency over the 500-year period may be summarised thus:

Average frequency for 16th-century texts : 2·07
,,   ,,   ,, 17th- and 18th ,, : 0·69
,,   ,,   ,, 19th- and 20th ,, : 1·00

from which it may be concluded that inversion of the subject in modern literary French is likely to occur at an average rate of one per page, whereas in the 16th century the frequency was just over two per page. In the 17th and 18th centuries this rate fell to 0·69, and at one point, in the texts for the period 1700–1750, inversion was found to occur only once in every two pages.

(ii) *Structural features*

This division of the material into three major periods may be maintained with respect to certain other features revealed by the analysis of the inversions. Thus the simplification of the constructions with inverted order which accompanies the decrease in their frequency in the 17th and 18th centuries is shown by a comparison of the average proportion of examples in each period having (1) a pronoun subject, (2) the verbs *être, faire* or *avoir*, (3) the more common type of *invertissant* :

(1) *Proportion of pronoun subjects*
    1500–1600 : 20%, 19%
    1600–1800 : 37%, 22%, 33%, 40%
    1800–1960 : 16%, 12%, 18%, 10%
(2) ' *être* ', ' *faire* ', ' *avoir* '
    1500–1600 : 28%, 29%
    1600–1800 : 38%, 39%, 38%, 37%
    1800–1960 : 26%, 21%, 19%, 12%
(3) *Relatives, comparatives, indirect constructions and modal adverbs*
    1500–1600 : 39%, 65%
    1600–1800 : 78%, 89%, 89%, 84%
    1800–1960 : 74%, 72%, 74%, 74%

It is evident that the texts analysed in the period 1600–1800 not only have a much lower frequency of inversion, but the examples which do occur have on average markedly higher proportions of pronoun subjects, common verbs and more usual constructions than do those in the texts of the other periods. In addition the examples in the 18th-century texts have a lower than average proportion of inversions with several subjects and followed by dependent clauses, although the 17th-century texts have more in common with earlier works in this respect. The further complication of clauses and adverbials separating the major constituents in a sentence containing inversion only becomes really noticeable in texts after 1800. Before that date such structures represent on average well below 10% of the examples in each case, as compared with about 20% in the later periods. The proportion of inversions found in sentences of three or more clauses is highest in the texts of the period 1550–1700, with average occurrences of 76%, 73% and 64%. In all the other periods the mean lies between 46% and 57%. This contrast may be indicative to some extent of the tendency noted particularly in the 17th-century texts to use inversion to lend variety and balance to longer sentences.

(iii) *Direct speech*

In the texts up to 1650, inversions in direct speech represent on average more than 30% of the total, with an unusually high frequency in the works of the first half of the 17th century, a further indication of the concern for elegance, or, in the case of Sorel, of the parody of elegant style. In the later periods, however, the number decreases fairly steadily, and the use of inverted order in conversation becomes comparatively rare after 1850. *Les caves du vatican* is the only text with more than 20% of the examples found in conversation, and in the contemporary period Sarraute alone has a proportion above 10%.

In most cases the distribution of the inversions in conversation tends to be similar to that in the text as a whole, although the proportion of immobile *invertissant* constructions is generally lower in direct speech.

It has also been seen that inversion occurs in free indirect speech in works where this technique is characteristic of the author. Thus in novels by Flaubert, Zola and Malraux, inverted order is used to a limited extent to emphasize this style, besides occurring sporadically in this context in other writers.

(iv) *Position of the inversions*

In nearly all the texts studied, more than half the inversions occupy a key position in the sentence, the tendency after 1700 being for more to occur finally than initially. The use of inversion to conclude a paragraph becomes more marked in the 19th- and 20th-century texts, and the same is true, although to a much lesser extent, of inversions terminating a passage in direct speech.

The 16th-century texts revealed a certain relation between inversions in the narrative and the introduction of passages in direct speech, with the narrative often being resumed with an initial inversion. Although this tendency rapidly dies out, it has been noted that certain authors of the last two centuries may use inversion to stress a change of narrative style in this way.

(v) *Form and distribution of inversions*

The distribution of inversions according to main or subordinate clause or mobile or immobile *invertissant* is somewhat uneven throughout the five centuries. It emerges quite clearly that in the 16th century, as in the Old French period, inversion was much more common in a main clause than in a subordinate one, whereas in the 20th century the reverse is true. While the immobile *invertissant* constructions generally outnumber the mobile *invertissants* by about two to one in the 19th and 20th centuries, the distribution varies with each text in the 17th and 18th centuries. Inversion resulting from syntactic operations other than transposition occurs regularly in each text from 1700, representing an average of around 6% of the examples.

The four major constructions involving inversion occur in every text studied, that is relative, comparative, indirect construction and modal adverb *invertissants*. The following types of *invertissant* are also very common, and the novels in which they are not found are randomly distributed over the ten periods :

> concessive clause (36 texts)
> adverbial phrase of place (36)
> addition and transposition (35)
> deletion and transposition (35)
> temporal adverbs (33)
> attributives (33)

(*b*) THE 'INVERTISSANTS'

Certain types of construction containing inversion, and many individual *invertissants* are found only in the earliest texts studied, before falling into disuse. The most important construction in this respect is inversion following a co-ordinating conjunction, found commonly in the 16th century but dying out in the course of the 17th, the final trace of it in these texts occurring in Furetière. Inversion in this category occurs with *et* and *si* in both the 16th and 17th centuries, but there are only two examples with *mais*, in Rabelais and Helisenne de Crenne. *Or* is used rather more often in both halves of the 16th century. It has been seen that the emphatic function of this liaison inversion may then be assumed by modal adverb *invertissants* which undergo a corresponding increase in frequency. Another type of *invertissant* which even in 1500 might be considered archaic, is the negative particle, examples of which are found only in the first four 16th-century works. Inversion after a direct object, infinitival and participial phrase is customary in the 16th century only, although direct object and present participle *invertissants* are also found at the beginning of the 17th.

Individual *invertissants* may disappear because the lexical item or collocation itself becomes archaic, not because of any stabilization of word-order. These include the relatives *quel*, *dont* (for *d'où*), and *icelluy* preceded by a proposition, all of which occur in the 16th-century works only. The same is true of the comparatives *si*, *tant* and *plus* followed by *comme* rather than *que*, and of adverbial phrases of place using archaic prepositions such as *jouxte* and *joignant de*. The texts of the ten periods reveal fifty-two different modal adverb *invertissants*, of which thirty-four are found in texts up to 1650 only. Equally, thirty-three of the fifty-five different temporal adverb *invertissants* occur in 16th-century texts only, as do eighteen of the twenty-seven adverbs of quantity. Inversion after a subordinate clause is a 16th-century construction which is revived in texts dating from the end of the 18th century, although the works which have been analysed here suggest that this is only so when the preceding clause is a temporal one, the instances of inversion after a causal clause or indirect structure occurring solely in the first half of the 16th century.

An interesting result of the analysis is the revival in the

19th and 20th centuries of constructions which had apparently died out by the 17th century, such as the subordinate clause *invertissant* discussed above. These include inversion after a temporal conjunction, an example with *depuis que* being found as early as Laclos. It is striking that after 1800 the range of these *invertissants* seems to be wider than before, when examples had been limited to *quand, lorsque* and *tant que*. The 19th- and 20th-century novels studied reveal *invertissants* such as *cependant que, avant que, à mesure que* and *maintenant que*, while there are no instances in these texts of *après que, alors que* and *comme*, as found by Le Bidois in Proust and other writers (*L'inversion du sujet*, pp. 304 ff.).

A similar pattern is noticed in the case of inversion in causal, purpose result, hypothetical and substantival clauses. The 16th-century texts provide examples of the *invertissant comme* in a causal construction, whereas in the first half of the 20th century inversion occurs after both *parce que* and *puisque*, and Le Bidois also notes examples of *c'est que* and *ce n'est pas que* in Gide and Saint-Exupéry among others (*ibid.*, p. 135). Also in the 16th century the *invertissant en sorte que* is found in purpose and result constructions, while in the 20th century inversion is found after *afin que, pour que, sans que* and *de manière que*. Inversion in a hypothetical clause occurs with *si* in both 16th- and 20th-century texts, with *en cas que* and *selon que* only in the former, and with *comme si* and *à moins que* only in the latter. Finally, inversion in a substantival clause is found in the first instance only in Rabelais, and later in a number of 20th-century writers, but with the exception of the construction *être bon que* the introductory verbs used by the modern authors are different from those in Rabelais.

While inversion after adverbs of time and quantity is found regularly throughout the periods studied, these categories also show certain *invertissants* re-emerging, and increased variety in the modern period. Among the adverbs of quantity, for instance, the *invertissants plus* and *peu* are found in texts up to 1650 and from 1900, together with the forms *au plus, tout au plus* and *peu à peu* in the 20th century. This may also be noted in correlative constructions where the immobilized *invertissant* is an adverb of quantity. Such inversions are to be found in a number of the 16th- and 17th-century texts, but later return in only isolated instances in the works by Stendhal, Camus and Butor, using the same three *invertissants* as in the earlier works, *tant*, *autant* and *plus*. Similarly the temporal adverbs *déjà*, *tout à coup*, *à présent* and *de nouveau* occur in the first half of the 16th century, and again after 1850, when new *invertissants* also emerge such as *parfois*, *enfin*, *brusquement*, *immédiatement* and *fréquemment*. This tendency is even more pronounced in the case of adverbs of place, where fourteen of the twenty-eight different *invertissants* in the texts analysed occur after 1850.

Thus while certain *invertissants* become archaic in the first 150 years of the period studied, others re-emerge in the 19th and 20th centuries to be more fully exploited, alongside many new *invertissants* which accompany the higher frequency of inversion. Various *invertissants* disappear temporarily in the 17th and 18th centuries when inverted order is less common, and tends to be confined to certain structures and clichés. Such constructions include zero *invertissant* and a number of adverbs of time, manner and place, which may now be considered quite unexceptional, such as *tant*, *alors*, *puis* and *en vain*. The *invertissants* found in texts belonging to every period studied are therefore surprisingly few, and apart from most relatives and indirect constructions, they include only the comparative *comme*, the attributive adjective *tel*, and the modals *ainsi*, *aussi*, *encore* and *à peine*.

(*c*) THE USEFULNESS OF THE SYNTACTIC ANALYSIS

The material presented in the form of percentage tables at the beginning of each chapter is of some linguistic interest prior to the examination of individual examples in their context. Firstly, the frequency tables provide a formal outline of the history of inversion as reflected in major French novels from 1500 to the end of the 1950s, and in addition permit comparative studies to be made within each period. Secondly, the analysis enables us to trace the development of different inversion structures and the changing syntactic contexts in which they occur. Finally, details of the *invertissants* may be compared with those provided by previous studies of word-order in the Old French and Middle French periods, a notable feature being the early disappearance of many forms common in the 14th century listed by Price and others (see chapter I).

Further information arising out of this research which might have been presented in a similar form includes details of the nature of the verb, such as voice, transitivity and tense, the position of any adjectives contained in the inverted noun phrase, and the presence of other elements in the sentence such as a dependent infinitive, direct object or subject complement.[1] Since these items are not, however, strictly relevant to the occurrence of inversion, and no general tendencies are immediately discernible, they have been omitted from the study, except with regard to particular examples in which features such as a preposed adjective may contribute to the stylistic interest of the inverted construction. A small sample from the texts analysed might therefore serve to show how far the variation in inversion frequency is mirrored by changing frequencies in other aspects of word-order, and whether any parallel developments can be distinguished.

The syntactic information is presented in a way which is sufficiently formal to allow it to be subjected, if necessary, to statistical significance tests. For instance, a chi-squared test was used to test the stylistic value of inversion in final position in Madame Bovary.[2] The results showed that the distribution

---

[1] See, for example, Y. Galet, *L'évolution de l'ordre des mots dans la phrase française de 1600 à 1700*, Paris, 1971, which is devoted to the position of personal pronouns dependent on an infinitive, in sentences of the type ' tu me veux détourner '. Statistics are provided from texts ranging from Old French to the present day, which might profitably be related to the history of inversion, and a feature of comparable stylistic interest is the concluding section on archaic usage in 19th- and 20th-century literature.

[2] The χ^2 test is a statistical technique used to demonstrate whether an observed distribution differs significantly from the expected distribution. The χ^2 value for sentences of three clauses was $6 \cdot 5$ ($p < 0 \cdot 01$), and for those of four clauses, $16 \cdot 2$ ($p < 0 \cdot 001$).

of inversion constructions in Flaubert's sentences is significantly different from what might be expected, and that in sentences of three and four clauses, inversion in final position has considerable stylistic value if this is estimated in terms of probability.[3]

The material provided by the syntactic study could also be of use in discourse analysis. For example, the relations might be studied between an inverted subject and other items in a context larger than the clause or sentence. It would be interesting to know, for instance, if an inverted subject has a different grammatical function or form in neighbouring clauses such as its reoccurrence in pronominal form, and if the structure is repeated in similar or different situations, with results such as those already noted in the study of the style of Butor.

2. THE STYLISTIC ANALYSIS

The analysis of the stylistic role of inversion in the texts has revealed a great variety of effects to which the device has contributed, some of them common to novels of an apparently diverse nature, belonging to different periods.

The stylistic uses of inversion may be classified according to their value in the context of each novel, ranging from the functional inversions which are an integral part of the language of nearly all the works studied, to the highly idiosyncratic constructions and effects employed by only a few novelists. The emphatic properties of inversion are exploited to stress an idea of special importance in particular texts, or as part of the narrative technique. In certain cases this has been seen to lead to the formation of clichés within a novel or novels with similar themes, and also to the parody of the style these clichés characterize.

Inversion may thus be an integral part of the style of an author, whether it is, for example, classical, pastoral or documentary, as well as a factor in a variety of techniques such as

---

[3] Cf. Enkvist's formula : ' The style of a text is the aggregate of the contextual probabilities of its linguistic items ', ' On defining style, an essay in applied linguistics ', in *Linguistics and Style*, ed. J. Spencer, London, 1964, p. 28.

archaism, irony or impressionistic description. Inverted order can also be used to reflect the content it conveys, the sequence of ideas or objects perceived, and in a wider context it is often seen to illustrate the personal style of a character in speech or writing, or to stress such elements as the presence or intervention of an omniscient narrator.

(i) INVERSIONS WITH LITTLE EXPRESSIVE VALUE

The inversions frequently referred to as functional, because their occurrence is closely related to the linguistic features of the immediate context, are to be found in every work studied, and they constitute the majority of examples in those texts where inversion has otherwise little to contribute to the style as a whole. In such instances inverted order has a syntactic role rather than a stylistic one, the word-order being determined by either the phonological structure of the elements, their length, or the presence of dependent clauses or subject couplements. Thus inversion is used to avoid non-euphonious juxtapositions, to avert a *cadence mineure*, where the nature of the verb is an important consideration, and to prevent the separation of relatives and antecedents, thereby contributing to a harmonious, balanced and coherent sentence structure. The length of the *invertissant*, as well as of the subject, may also be of relevance, since it seems that inversion is more likely to occur after a short element such as *tel* or *là* than after a long one, a conclusion also drawn by Price from his study of Froissart.[4] Inversion under these circumstances, then, has little value as far as individual style is concerned, although it may nevertheless be relevant to expressive values, depending on the semantic context.

In addition to the influence on word-order of the linguistic structure of the main elements, inversion may result from considerations of clarity and liaison. Here, too, its importance is functional or syntactic, although the predominance of such constructions may be characteristic of a certain narrative style, as seen in the case of des Essarts. It has been noted on several

---

[4] ' Aspects de l'ordre des mots dans les " Chroniques de Froissart " '.

occasions that inverted order frequently leads to greater clarity than would have been achieved by direct order. This may involve the use of inversion to maintain structural relations between elements, to facilitate subordination, or to preserve the order of ideas. An extension of this is the linking function of inversion across different forms of discourse where, for instance, the final idea in the speech of one characters is repeated as an *invertissant* to open the speech of another (see also des Essarts, p. 57).

The remaining inversions where expressiveness is not normally a key factor are those where the choice lies not between two syntactic orders, but between two constructions, one of which generally necessitates inversion. Such routine examples include indirect structures, concessive clauses, attributives and the deletion and transposition operation (as an alternative to a hypothetical clause), although in all but the last case, instances of direct order have occasionally been found. However, while inversion is virtually obligatory in such constructions, this does not preclude the writer from exploiting them for reasons of style, mainly to emphasize important ideas, such as the use of *tel* underlining moral purpose in Fénelon.

(ii) THE USE OF INVERSION TO EMPHASIZE NARRATIVE FORM AND TECHNIQUE

Certain relations between narrative form and inversion have been noticed firstly in the characterization of different types of narration by the variation in frequency of inverted order, and secondly in the use of inversion to mark transitions between the narrative and speech. The first relation was seen particularly in 16th- and 17th-century works, where the contrasting forms, framework narrative, *contes* or *nouvelles*, and discussion between the characters, were paralleled by different frequencies of inversion, the last traces of this being found in the opposition between the narrative and *récits* in the *Princesse de Clèves*. This technique is fully developed in Yver, where the changing frequencies in certain of the *nouvelles* reflect both the style of the speaker and the literary genre, while a similar approach had already been adopted by Helisenne de Crenne, with the contrasting frequencies in the main parts of the *Angoisses douloureuses* again corresponding to changes in genre. Distinctions drawn between the epistolary styles of the characters in Laclos and Rousseau may be seen as a continuation of this technique, particularly in the latter, where both writer and recipient may be identified by the frequency of inversion.

The use of the device to mark transitions between narrative and speech has already been mentioned with regard to the syntactic analysis. The construction is particularly effective in the passage from narrative to free indirect style, where the structural division is less marked than in the case of direct or indirect speech, as was shown in particular in *Germinal*.

Certain aspects of narrative technique may be emphasized in a similar way, and here the value of inversion is increased in that there is no corresponding alteration in genre or a formal change in the type of discourse. Thus in Scarron, Furetière and Diderot, inverted order often stresses the opposition between the self-conscious narrator and the actions of his characters, or, in the case of Furetière, the style of other novelists. In the *Paysan parvenu* it is the thoughts and reactions of the personal narrator which are thus emphasized. Inversion, particularly in key position, also underlines less striking changes, such as the transition from a digressive passage to the main narrative found in Stendhal (see p. 282).

Finally, the importance of inversion in this respect is reflected in the work of the modern experimental writers, where it has been seen that the emphatic properties of inversion are combined with effects achieved by typographical devices, as in Butor and Sarraute.

(iii) INVERSIONS EMPHASIZING A PARTICULAR LITERARY STYLE

Connected with the use of inversion to highlight aspects of narrative technique is its exploitation as a means of emphasizing the style favoured by specific authors. Examples in which inversion stresses aspects of major stylistic importance range from those illustrating the burlesque style of Scarron to the lyrical outpourings of Rousseau and Madame de Staël, from the pastoral novels of de Montreux and d'Urfé to the documentary techniques of Furetière, Stendhal and Camus. The author's preoccupations are frequently reflected by the clichés which evolve from many of these styles, such as the recurring structure *où* and *se reposer* in de Montreux, and *où* followed by *brûler* and other verbs connected with heat and light in Zola. Where such inversions are used to the extent that they are felt to characterize a particular style, they are reproduced for satirical purposes by other writers, as shown, for instance, in the studies of Sorel and Voltaire.

(iv) INVERSION ASSOCIATED WITH OTHER DEVICES OF STYLE

In the usage of an author inversion may be one of several means of emphasis or it may become a predominating stylistic feature, and the same is true of its use in particular devices such as irony, personification and nominalization, to mention but a few. Clearly in the case of techniques such as the latter, inversion is an external factor, albeit an important one, in examples such as those in which a nominalization or a personified subject receives further stress from its postposition.

In other instances, however, the stylistic device itself is constituted by inversion, and not merely emphasized by it. This is so, for instance, in certain archaizing effects in des Essarts and du Fail, and later in Vigny and Hugo. The occurrence of inversion in direct speech is important in this respect, with the device helping to characterize the speakers through their language, whether to convey an impression of elegance, as in the 17th century and in certain 18th-century works, or to parody elevated styles of conversation, as seen, for example, in Proust and Gide. Conversely, the lack of inversions is at times equally significant, particularly cases such as the representation of the *langue bourgeoise* in Scarron, and the realism of the conversation found in the contemporary writers studied.

(v) THE RELATION BETWEEN FORM AND CONTENT

The role of word-order in the French novel is not confined to the linguistic functions already noted, or to the expression or emphasis of certain literary devices. Some of the most important examples of inversion which have been quoted are those where the form of the sentence echoes the content it conveys, to the extent that key thematic structures may be reflected in the language. This has been noticed in quite a number of the novels studied which use repetitive and accumulative structures, parallelisms and oppositions. Thus in the latter, a chiastic construction often presents contrasting ideas which are underlined by the different orders, a device which has been exploited particularly in Hugo's *Quatrevingt-treize*.

In other writers inversion is employed to achieve a delaying effect, which corresponds to the presentation of ideas. Thus in novelists such as Flaubert in particular, and also in the Goncourts and Zola, the process of perception and the order of impressions are reflected in the syntax, and such structures are often additionally effective by virtue of the presence of intervening adverbials and clauses. A striking combination of form and content was also noted in Balzac, where the delaying effects provided by inversion, together with the increased stress on the verb, were exploited to suggest the deceptive nature of the character of Vautrin. Word-order here was employed not for purposes of revelation, but for reasons of dissimulation.

This technique may also be discerned in authors whose characters use inversion in speech under clearly defined circumstances. Thus Gide's Protos adopts a certain word-order along with his various disguises, while the use of inversion by men and women in Duclos' novels was seen to depend on the social situation.

The stylistic analysis of the material provided by a detailed syntactic study of the texts has thus pinpointed many different contexts in which inversion is to be found in the French novel, and a variety of uses, some more idiosyncratic than others, to which it may be put. Aspects of form and content have combined to reveal characteristic tendencies of the style of many authors, and from this have emerged certain features common to writers of different periods, as well as some highly individual and specialized ones. The conclusion drawn is that while the basic functions of inversion, namely liaison and emphasis, are employed by nearly every novelist studied, the construction may be exploited to varying degrees by certain authors for vastly different purposes and effects.

3. THE UBIQUITY OF INVERSION IN MODERN FRENCH

The syntactic and stylistic analyses described above will, it is hoped, help to indicate how conservative have been the estimates of grammarians and theorists from the 16th century onwards regarding the use of inverted order in French. Furthermore it seems clear that studies attempting an exhaustive list of structures in which inversion may occur, particularly in modern French, cannot hope to do justice to the variety of such usage. It should also be evident that inversion in the contemporary language is not necessarily confined to an elevated style of speech or writing, since the more common forms of the device occur in virtually any context. It may be that inversions which are found to a surprising extent in writers using a familiar style are the product of a search on the part of the apparently unlettered narrator for literary flavour. Among the inversions found in novels which have not been analysed in full in this book is the following instance of zero *invertissant* in Céline's *Voyage au bout de la nuit* :

‘ *Vous demeurent* seulement précieux les menus chagrins, celui de...’ (p. 453)

and even more unexpected are relative inversions in Charrière's *Papillon* :

‘ Louis Dega était bien tranquille à la tête de son bar de Marseille, *où* se réunissait chaque nuit la fleur du milieu du midi, et *où*, comme un rendez-vous international, se rencontraient les grands vicieux voyageurs du monde.’ [5]

[5] H. Charrière, *Papillon*, Paris (Laffont), 1970, p. 26.

Yet inversion is not only common in literary works or in novels written in a *récit parlé* style as above. It is frequently to be heard in everyday speech of both a colloquial and a more elevated nature. Two examples spoken by a radio announcer on Europe I in January, 1969, illustrate this. The following occurred in a summary of Stravinsky's *Firebird* :

' Soudain apparaissent trois jeunes filles.'

Although the announcement was undoubtedly prepared, its style was a familiar one. The second inversion, however, seemed wholly spontaneous :

' Ecoutez ça dans une version chantée qu'interprète Madame —.'

Since such constructions are to be heard in the speech of virtually any Frenchman, it seems that the relative inversion here is simply an alternative to the use of a participial adjective (' interprété par ') in a sentence containing the same order of ideas. This lends additional support to Harmer's observation that,

' Inversion appears ... to be so instinctive in French in the relative clause that it is to be found in the humble dictionary definition, the writer of which can hardly be supposed to have been preoccupied with style ..., and in the spoken language of the educated, when the verbal form is monosyllabic, despite the general avoidance in speech of an inverted word order ... and in cases where pure considerations of balance and stress are obviously not involved '.[6]

Unusual types of inversion are to be noted with ever-increasing frequency in newspapers and non-fictional writing and are relatively common in academic prose. The following instance of an attributive adjective *invertissant* from *L'Aurore* in May, 1961, is quoted by Sauvageot [7] to exemplify the rapidity in transmission achieved by this construction :

' Dramatiques ont été les événements qui ont déterminé le général de Gaulle à faire jouer ... l'article 16...'

A similar example with an additional inversion occurs in a

[6] L. C. Harmer, *The French Language Today*, London, 1954, pp. 70–71.

[7] A. Sauvageot, *Français écrit, français parlé*, Paris, 1962, p. 37.

volume of Damourette and Pichon, and illustrates the logical and emphatic properties of the device :

' Particulièrement intéressants sont les exemples dans lesquels est considérée comme une substance unique et continue la succession de plusieurs individus vivants...' [8]

Finally, a desire for euphony and a balanced structure, common to both fictional and non-fictional writers, is revealed in this causal construction :

' Turoldus en ce vers 4002 signe son œuvre en disant que le poème s'arrête là *parce que s'arrête* l'histoire qu'il rapporte ' [9]

It must, then, surely be concluded that the evolution of inversion as a key feature of French syntax and an important device of style lends little support to the idea of a language of legendary clarity, which owes much to a traditionally fixed and logical word-order. Instead the modern idiom has freed itself from the false constraints imposed by innumerable grammarians, as is often to be seen from the examples of inversion unwittingly provided by the latter themselves. The most perceptive judgement on French word-order must indeed be that passed by G. and R. Le Bidois in their *Syntaxe du français moderne* : [10]

' Rien n'est plus relatif que ce terme d'inversion (...) Y a-t-il en français un ordre des mots qui soit assez fréquent pour qu'on puisse l'appeler l'ordre normal de la phrase ? '

[8] J. Damourette & E. Pichon, *Des mots à la pensée VI*, Paris, 1911–40, p. 423.

[9] M. Delbouille, *Sur la genèse de la ' Chanson de Roland '*, Brussels, 1954, p. 93.

[10] Paris, 1967, t. II, p. 5.

BIBLIOGRAPHY

(*a*) *List of Novels Studied* (in chronological order) [1]

Sixteenth Century (1)

F. RABELAIS, *Gargantua et Pantagruel*, in *Œuvres complètes I*, ed. Jourda (Garnier), 1962.

HELISENNE DE CRENNE, *Les angoisses douloureuses qui procedent d'amours* (Langlier), 1543.

H. DES ESSARTS, *Le premier livre d'Amadis de Gaule* (Hachette), 1918.

MARGUERITE DE NAVARRE, *L'Héptaméron*, ed. François (Garnier), 1960.

Sixteenth Century (2)

J. YVER, *Le printemps d'Iver*, Tierce edition (Jean Ruelle), 1572.

B. POISSENOT, *L'Esté* (Claude Micard), 1583.

N. DE MONTREUX, *Le premier livre des bergeries de Juliette* (Gilles Beys), 1585.

N. DU FAIL, *Contes et discours d'Eutrapel*, in *Propos rustiques, Baliverneries, Contes et discours d'Eutrapel*, ed. Guichard (C. Gosselin), 1842.

Seventeenth Century (1)

H. D'URFÉ, *L'Astrée*, ed. Vaganay, Strasbourg (Bibl. Romanica), 1925.

C. SOREL, *Histoire comique de Francion*, in *Romanciers du XVIIe siècle*, ed. Adam (Bibl. de la Pléiade), 1958.

M. LE ROY DE GOMBERVILLE, *La première partie de Polexandre*, dernière édition (Courbé), 1641.

M. DE SCUDÉRY, *Artamène ou Le grand Cyrus*, 2nd ed. (Courbé), 1650.

Seventeenth Century (2)

P. SCARRON, *Le romant comique*, in *Romanciers du XVIIe siècle*.

[1] All works in this section are published in Paris unless otherwise stated.

A. FURETIÈRE, *Le roman bourgeois*, in *Romanciers du XVIIe siècle.*

MME DE LA FAYETTE, *La princesse de Clèves*, in *Romanciers du XVIIe siècle.*

F. DE FÉNELON, *Les aventures de Télémaque*, ed. Rousseaux (Cité des Livres), 1930.

Eighteenth Century (1)

A.-R. LESAGE, *Histoire de Gil Blas de Santillane*, ed. Bardon (Garnier), 1955.

ABBÉ PRÉVOST, *Histoire du Chevalier des Grieux et de Manon Lescaut*, ed. Deloffre-Picard (Garnier), 1965.

P. DE MARIVAUX, *Le paysan parvenu*, ed. Deloffre (Garnier), 1959.

C.-P. DUCLOS, *Histoire de Mme de Luz* in *Œuvres* (Didier), 1855.

—— *Les confessions du conte de xxx* in *Romanciers du XVIIIe siècle*, ed. Etiemble (Bibl. de la Pléiade), 1965.

—— *Acajou et Firphile*, in *Œuvres.*

Eighteenth Century (2)

F. DE VOLTAIRE, *Romans et contes*, ed. Bénac (Garnier), 1949.

J.-J. ROUSSEAU, *Julie ou la Nouvelle Héloïse*, ed. Pomeau (Garnier), 1960.

D. DIDEROT, *Jacques le fataliste*, in *Œuvres romanesques*, ed. Bénac (Garnier), 1951.

C. DE LACLOS, *Les liaisons dangereuses*, ed. Le Hir (Garnier), 1959.

Nineteenth Century (1)

F.-R. DE CHATEAUBRIAND, *Atala, René, Les Natchez* in *Œuvres complètes*, ed. Sainte-Beuve (Garnier), 1929.

MME DE STAEL, *Corinne ou l'Italie* (Charpentier), 1841.

A. DE VIGNY, *Cinq-Mars ou une conjuration sous Louis XIII*, in *Œuvres complètes II*, ed. Baldensperger (Gallimard), 1948.

STENDHAL, *Le rouge et le noir*, ed. Martineau (Garnier), 1957.

H. DE BALZAC, *Le Père Goriot*, ed. Castex (Garnier), 1960.

Nineteenth Century (2)

G. FLAUBERT, *Madame Bovary*, in *Œuvres I*, ed. Thibaudet-Dumesnil (Bibl. de la Pléiade), 1951.

E. and J. DE GONCOURT, *Germinie Lacerteux* (Flammarion), 1921.

V. HUGO, *Quatrevingt-treize*, in *Romans III* (Ed. du Seuil), 1963.

E. ZOLA, *Germinal*, Fasquelle (*Livre de poche*), 1968.

G. DE MAUPASSANT, *Bel-Ami*, ed. Delaisement (Garnier), 1959.

Twentieth Century (1)

A. FRANCE, *Les dieux ont soif*, ed. Brumfitt, London (Oxford University Press), 1964.

A. GIDE, *Les caves du Vatican*, in *Romans, récits et soties, œuvres lyriques*, ed. Davet-Thierry (Bibl. de la Pléiade), 1958.

M. PROUST, *A l'ombre des jeunes filles en fleurs I*, in *A la recherche du temps perdu, I* ed. Clarac-Ferré (Bibl. de la Pléiade), 1954.

A. MALRAUX, *La condition humaine* (Gallimard), 1946.

J. GIRAUDOUX, *Combat avec l'ange* (Grasset), 1934.

A. CAMUS, *La peste*, in *Théâtre, récits, nouvelles*, ed. Quillot (Bibl. de la Pléiade), 1962.

Twentieth Century (2)

H. BAZIN, *Lève-toi et marche* (Grasset), 1952.

A. ROBBE-GRILLET, *Le voyeur* (Ed. de Minuit), 1955.

M. BUTOR, *L'emploi du temps* (Ed. de Minuit), 1957.

N. SARRAUTE, *Le planétarium* (Gallimard), 1959.

Additional twentieth-century texts

G. BERNANOS, *Sous le soleil de Satan*, in *Œuvres romanesques*, ed. Béguin (Bibl. de la Pléiade), 1961.

L.-F. CÉLINE, *Voyage au bout de la nuit*, Gallimard (*Livre de poche*), 1965.

J.-P. SARTRE, *La nausée* (Gallimard), 1938.

S. DE BEAUVOIR, *Le sang des autres* (Gallimard), 23rd ed., 1947.

J. GRACQ, *Le rivage des Syrtes* (Corti), 1951.

P

(b) Linguistic, stylistic and literary references

Amadís de Gaula in *Libros de Caballerias españoles*, ed. Buendia, Madrid, 1954.

G. ANTOINE, *La coordination en français*, Paris, 1958.

F. BAR, *Le genre burlesque en France au XVIIe siècle — étude de style*, Paris, 1960.

M. BARDÈCHE, *Stendhal romancier*, Paris, 1947.

L. BERGH, ' Quelques réflexions sur l'inversion apres la conjonction *et* en ancien et en moyen français ', in *Mélanges ... Michaëlsson*, Göteborg, 1952, pp. 43–55.

J. D. BIARD, *The style of La Fontaine's Fables*, Oxford, 1966.

A. BLINKENBERG, *L'ordre des mots en français moderne*, 2nd ed., Copenhagen, 1958.

L. BLOOMFIELD, *Language*, New York, 1933, and London, 1935.

H. BOCHET, *L'Astrée — ses origines, son importance dans la formation de la littérature classique*, reprinted Geneva, 1967.

W. BOOTH, ' The Self-conscious Narrator in Comic Fiction ', *Publications of the Modern Language Association of America*, lxvii (1952), pp. 163–85.

V. BROMBERT, *The Novels of Flaubert, a Study of Themes and Techniques*, Princeton, 1966.

M. BUTOR, *Essais sur le roman*, Paris, 1969.

C. CAMPROUX, ' Télescopage morpho-syntaxique ? ' *Le Français Moderne*, xxxv (1967), pp. 161–83.

H. CHARRIÈRE, *Papillon*, Paris, 1970.

L. CHIFLET, *Essay d'une parfaicte grammaire de la langue françoise*, Paris, 1668.

N. CHOMSKY, *Aspects of the Theory of Syntax*, Cambridge, Mass., 1965.

H. CLOUZOT, ' Le Printemps d'Yver ', *Revue du XVIe siècle*, xviii (1931), pp. 104–29.

H. COULET, *Le roman jusqu'à la Révolution I*, Paris, 1967.

M. CRESSOT, *Le style et ses techniques*, 6th ed., Paris, 1969.

—— *La phrase et le vocabulaire de J.-K. Huysmans*, Geneva, 1938.

J. DAMOURETTE — E. PICHON, *Des mots à la pensée VI*, Paris, 1911–40.

C. DÉDÉYAN, *Lesage et ' Gil Blas '*, Paris, 1965.

—— *Madame de Lafayette*, Paris, 1955.

M. DELBOUILLE, *Sur la genèse de la ' Chanson de Roland '*, Brussels, 1954.

F. DELOFFRE, *Une préciosité nouvelle, Marivaux et le Marivaudage*, 2nd ed., Paris, 1967.

P. DESPORTES, *Œuvres profanes*, ed. V. E. Graham, Geneva, 1958–63.

D. DIDEROT, *Lettre sur les sourds et muets*, ed. P. H. Meyer, Geneva, 1965.

N. ENKVIST, ' On Defining Style, an Essay in Applied Linguistics ', in *Linguistics and Style*, ed. J. Spencer, London, 1964.

R. C. FLOWERS, *Voltaire's Stylistic Transformation of Rabelaisian Satirical Devices*, Washington, 1951.

L. FOULET, ' Comment ont évolué les formes de l'interrogation ', *Romania*, xlvii (1921), pp. 243–348.

—— ' Etudes de syntaxe française ', *Romania*, xlv (1919), pp. 220–49.

—— ' L'influence de l'ancienne langue sur la langue moderne ', *Romania*, lii (1926), pp. 147–56.

—— *Petite syntaxe de l'ancien français*, 3rd ed., Paris, 1965.

E. FROMAIGEAT, ' Les formes de l'interrogation en français moderne ', *Vox Romanica*, iii (1938), pp. 1–47.

Y. GALET, *L'évolution de l'ordre des mots dans la phrase française de 1600 à 1700*, Paris, 1971.

G. GALLICHET, *Essai de grammaire psychologique du français moderne*, 2nd ed., Paris., 1950.

J. GARNIER, *Institutio gallicae linguae in usum iuventutis germanicae*, Geneva, 1558.

J.-M. GAUTIER, *Le style des ' Memoires d'outre-tombe ' de Chateaubriand*, Geneva, 1959.

C. P. GIRAULT-DUVIVIER, *Grammaire des grammaires ou analyse raisonnée des meilleurs traités*, 13th ed., Paris, 1848.

G. GOEBEL, *Zur Erzähltechnik in den ' Histoires comiques ' des 17. Jahrhunderts*, Berlin, 1965.

G. GOUGENHEIM, *Système grammatical de la langue française*, Paris, 1938.

J. H. Greenberg, *Universals in language*, Cambridge, Mass., 1963.

G. Hainsworth, *Les 'Novelas exemplares' de Cervantes en France au XVIIe siècle*, Paris, 1933.

L. C. Harmer, *The French Language today*, London, 1954.

L. Hjelmslev, 'Role structural de l'ordre des mots' in *Grammaire et psychologie* (numéro spécial du *Journal de psychologie*), Paris, 1950, pp. 51–60.

E. Huguet, *Etude sur la syntaxe de Rabelais, comparée à celle des autres prosateurs de 1450 à 1550*, Paris, 1894.

J. Huizinga, *The Waning of the Middle Ages*, trans. Hopman, London, 1968.

J. Hytier, *André Gide*, Alger, 1938.

P. Jourda, *Marguerite d'Angoulême*, Paris, 1930.

—— 'Un précurseur de M. Barrès : Bénigne Poissenot et les Assassins', *Revue du XVIe siècle*, x (1923), pp. 207–13.

R. W. Langacker, 'French Interrogatives : A Transformational description', *Language*, xli (1965), pp. 587–600.

G. Lanson, *L'art de la prose*, 9th ed., Paris, 1911.

R. Lapesa, *Historia de la lengua española*, 7th ed., Madrid, 1968.

G. and R. Le Bidois, *Syntaxe du français moderne*, 2nd ed., Paris, 1967.

R. Le Bidois, 'L'inversion absolue du substantif sujet', *Le Français Moderne*, ix (1941), pp. 111–28.

—— *L'inversion du sujet dans la prose contemporaine (1900–1950) étudiée plus spécialement dans l'œuvre de Marcel Proust*, Paris, 1952.

—— 'Le langage parlé des personnages de Proust', *Le Français Moderne*, vii (1939), pp. 197–218.

—— 'Variations stylistiques sur l'ordre des mots', *Le Monde*, 20 novembre 1968.

L. Le Bourgo, *Duclos, sa vie et ses ouvrages*, Bordeaux, 1902.

E. Lerch, *Historische französische Syntax III*, Leipzig, 1934.

B. Lewinsky, *L'ordre des mots dans 'Bérinus'*, Göteborg, 1949.

E. Loesch, *Die impressionistische Syntax der Goncourt*, Nürnberg, 1919.

P. LOHR, *Le Printemps d'Yver und die Quelle zu Fair 'Em '*, Diss ... München, Berlin, 1912.

J. LYONS, *An Introduction to Theoretical Linguistics*, Cambridge, 1968.

J. MATTHEWS, *Les deux Zola*, Geneva, 1957.

—— ' L'impressionnisme chez Zola ', *Le Français Moderne*, xxix (1961), pp. 199–205.

C. MAUPAS, *Grammaire et syntaxe françoise*, 3rd ed. Rouen, 1632.

G. MAYER, *La qualification affective dans les romans d'H. de Balzac*, Paris, 1940.

P. MEISTER, *Charles Duclos*, Geneva, 1956.

E. MÉRIMÉE, *A History of Spanish Literature*, New York, 1930.

P. MORILLOT, *Scarron, étude biographique et littéraire*, Paris, 1888.

D. MORNET, *La Nouvelle Héloïse de J.-J. Rousseau, étude et analyse*, Paris, 1950.

H. MULLER, ' The Beginnings of French Fixed Word-Order ', *Modern Language Notes*, lvii (1942), pp. 546–52.

H. NISSEN, *L'ordre des mots dans la Chronique de Jean d'Outremeuse*, Uppsala, 1943.

M. NÖJGAARD, ' L'objet direct et l'ordre des mots en français moderne ', *Le Français Moderne*, xxxvi (1968), pp. 1–18 and 81–97.

R. OHMANN, ' Generative Grammars and the Concept of Literary Style ', *Word*, xx (1964), pp. 423–39.

—— ' Literature as Sentences ' reprinted in *Contemporary Essays on Style*, ed. Love-Payne, Illinois, 1969, pp. 149–57.

A. OUDIN, *Grammaire françoise rapportée au langage du temps*, 2nd ed. Paris, 1690.

M. PAPIĆ, *L'expression et la place du sujet dans les Essais de Montaigne*, Paris, 1970.

E. PHILIPOT, *Essai sur le style et la langue de Noel du Fail*, Paris, 1914.

G. PRICE, ' Aspects de l'ordre des mots dans les " Chroniques " de Froissart ', *Zeitschrift für romanische Philologie*, lxxvii (1961), pp. 15–48.

L. PRIESTLEY, ' Reprise Constructions in French ', *Archivum Linguisticum*, vii (1955), pp. 1–28.

P. RAMUS, *Gramere*, 2nd ed. Paris, 1572.

G. REYNIER, *Le roman réaliste au XVIIe siècle*, Paris, 1914.

—— *Le roman sentimental avant ' l'Astrée '*, Paris, 1908.

R. RICATTE, *La création romanesque chez les Goncourt, 1851–1870*, Paris, 1953.

P. RICKARD, ' The Word-Order Object-Verb-Subject in Medieval French ', *Transactions of the Philological Society*, 1962, pp. 1–39.

—— *La langue française au XVIe siècle*, Cambridge, 1968.

M. RIFFATERRE, *Le style des ' Pléiades ' de Gobineau*, Geneva-Paris, 1957.

A. DE RIVAROL, *De l'universalité de la langue française*, ed. M. Hervier, Paris, 1929.

A. ROBBE-GRILLET, *Pour un nouveau roman*, Paris, 1963.

R. H. ROBINS, *General Linguistics : An Introductory Survey*, London, 1964.

P. RONSARD, *Franciade, Œuvres complètes XVI*, ed. P. Laumonier, Paris, 1950.

S. ROSENBERG, *Modern French ' ce ' : the neuter pronoun in adjectival predication*, The Hague-Paris, 1970.

J. ROUSSET, *Forme et signification (Essais sur les structures littéraires de Corneille à Claudel)*, Paris, 1964.

P. SAGE, *Le préclassicisme*, Paris, 1962.

O. SAHLMANN, *Das Leben und die Werke des Noel du Fail*, Leipzig, 1909.

C. SAINTE-BEUVE, *Tableau historique et critique de la poésie française au XVIe siècle*, Paris, 1843.

N. SARRAUTE, *Portrait d'un inconnu*, preface by J.-P. Sartre, Paris, 1956.

A. SAUVAGEOT, *Français écrit, français parlé*, Paris, 1962.

R. A. SAYCE, *Style in French Prose. A method in analysis*, Oxford, 1958.

J. SGARD, *Prévost romancier*, Paris, 1968.

J. SMIÉTANSKI, *Le réalisme dans Jacques le Fataliste*, Paris, 1965.

L. Spitzer, *Etudes de style*, trans. Kaufholz-Coulon-Foucault, Paris, 1970.

R. Sturel, ' La prose poétique au XVIe siècle ' in *Mélanges* ... *Lanson*, Paris, 1922, pp. 47–60.

A. Thibaudet, *Gustave Flaubert*, 2nd ed., Paris, 1935.

J. Thorne, ' Generative Grammars and Stylistic Analysis ' in *New Horizons in Linguistics*, ed. J. Lyons, London, 1970, pp. 185–97.

——' Stylistics and Generative Grammars', *Journal of Linguistics, i* (1965), pp. 49–59.

S. Ullmann, ' Inversion as a Stylistic Device in the Contemporary French Novel ', *Modern Language Review*, xlvii (1952), pp. 165–80.

——' L'inversion du sujet dans la prose romantique ', *Le Français Moderne*, xxiii (1955), pp. 23–38.

——*Style in the French Novel*, 2nd ed., Oxford, 1964.

——' Valeurs stylistiques de l'inversion dans " l'Education Sentimentale " ', *Le Français Moderne*, xx (1952), pp. 175–88.

L. Versini, *Laclos et la tradition*, Paris, 1968.

A. Vial, *Guy de Maupassant et l'art du roman*, Paris, 1954.

P. Wadsworth, *The Novels of Gomberville—a critical study of ' Polexandre' and ' Cythérée '*, Yale, 1942.

R.-L. Wagner, Review of Lewinsky, *Zeitschrift für romanische Philologie*, lxvi (1950), pp. 373–76.

R.-L. Wagner-F. Baulier, ' Contribution à l'étude de l'inversion du sujet après la conjonction *et* ', *Le Français Moderne*, xxiv (1956), pp. 249–57.

W. von Wartburg-P. Zumthor, *Précis de syntaxe du français contemporain*, 2nd ed., Berne, 1958.

I. Watt, *The Rise of the Novel*, London, 1968.

I. Wespy, ' Die historische Entwicklung der Inversion des Subjekts im Französischen und der Gebrauch derselben bei Lafontaine ', *Zeitschrift für neufranzösische Sprache und Literatur*, vi (1884), pp. 150–209.

E. Zola, *Le roman expérimental*. 6th ed., Paris, 1881.

INDEX OF FRENCH AUTHORS

GENERAL INDEX